MILLENNIAL VIOLENCE

CASS SERIES ON POLITICAL VIOLENCE

ISSN 1365-0580

Series Editors – DAVID C. RAPOPORT, University of California, Los Angeles
PAUL WILKINSON, University of St Andrews, Scotland

MILLENNIAL VIOLENCE

Past, Present and Future

Edited by

JEFFREY KAPLAN

FRANK CASS
LONDON • PORTLAND, OR

First published in 2002 in Great Britain by
FRANK CASS PUBLISHERS
Crown House, 47 Chase Side,
Southgate, London N14 5BP

and in the United States by
FRANK CASS PUBLISHERS
c/o ISBS
5824 N.E. Hassalo Street
Portland, Oregon 97213-3644

Website: www.frankcass.com

British Library Cataloguing in Publication Data

Millennial Violence : past, present and future. – (Cass
series on political violence ; no.13)
1. Terrorism – Religious aspects 2. Violence – Religious
aspects 3. Political violence 4. Millennialism
I. Kaplan, Jeffrey, 1954–
303.6'25

ISBN 0 7146 5294 6
ISBN 0 7146 8259 4
ISSN 1365-0580

Library of Congress Cataloging-in-Publication Data

Millennial violence : past, present, and future / edited by Jeffrey Kaplan.
    p. cm. – (Cass series on political violence, ISSN 1365-0580; 13)
'First appeared as ... a special issue of Terrorism and political
violence, Vol.14, No.1 (Spring, 2002)' – Verso t.p.
Includes bibliographical references and index.
    ISBN 0-7146-5294-6 (hardback) – ISBN 0-7146-8259-4 (pbk.)
    1. Violence–Religious aspects. 2. Two thousand, A.D.
3. Millennialism. I. Kaplan, Jeffrey, 1954– II. Terrorism and political
violence. III. Series.
    BL65.V55 M55 2002
    363.3'2 – dc21

This group of studies first appeared as 'Millennial Violence: Past, Present and
Future', a special issue of *Terrorism and Political Violence*,
Vol.14, No.1 (Spring, 2002), published by Frank Cass and Co. Ltd.

Printed in Great Britain by
Antony Rowe Ltd., Chippenham, Wiltshire

Contents

Foreword

DAVID C. RAPOPORT

The editors of the *Cass Series on Political Violence* are delighted to welcome this volume to our collection. It carefully examines three government-authorized reports on an issue that has always interested students of terrorism; the problem of anticipating surprise attacks. This is the first time the issue has been addressed in our series.

One does not need much imagination to realize that predicting the time and place of rebel terrorist attacks is extremely difficult and important. Because the disparity of the forces involved is so unequal, surprise is essential to terrorists, who know that they must make every effort to keep that surprise from being compromised. The simple fact is that without surprise there would be virtually no rebel terrorism, as we understand that activity.

There are many ways to gather information for the task; too many and too complicated to discuss in a Foreword. But I will mention three briefly to provide context. Traditionally, reliable informants within an underground group provide the most useful information. But employing informants is a notoriously risky enterprise, partly because authorities are tempted to use them as 'double agents' to induce or provoke the infiltrated group to act in ways which make it peculiarly vulnerable to police surprises. The history of terrorism makes it quite clear that the 'double agent' and terrorist activity have been inseparable, a relationship that has always raised very serious moral and legal questions.

In fact, the scandals associated with the use of double agents by American intelligence in Central America has been a major factor in the American government's conspicuous reluctance to use them to track Islamic groups. To a large extent, informants were replaced by electronic surveillance, combined with 'ordinary' police observation of suspicious circumstance and actions. But these two methods produce both too much information and misinformation. Beyond that, they require time to paint a clear picture and disasters may occur in the interval. In May of this year the problems besetting US intelligence prior to September 11 which came from this intelligence-gathering form became strikingly clear. Now the intelligence failures are serious political issues and will continue to be so for a long time to come.

A third way to procure information is to confer with those who have studied groups the government deems suspicious. This seems particularly plausible for groups driven by an esoteric religious ideology, which often seems like nonsense to those unfamiliar with it. In the 1993 siege of the Branch Davidian compound at Waco, Texas, for example, the ability of the authorities to conduct their negotiations was frustrated by their belief that the meaningless 'Bible babble' of the Branch Davidians was designed to delay and manipulate negotiations. This special view of the other's language, many thought, helped cause the terrible tragedy that ensued.

The criticism Waco generated finally convinced the FBI to make a major effort to see what it could learn from its critics, many of whom spent a good portion of their academic lives studying such groups. In the next important American incident with a religious group, that of the Montana Freemen, this cooperation seemed to pay off because the crisis ended peacefully – as Jeffrey Kaplan's concise introduction aptly describes.

In the summer of 1999, which now seems such a long time ago, Jeffrey Kaplan and I participated in an academic conference in Stockholm that focused on how one might anticipate attacks by religious terrorist groups. I was particularly interested by allusions to the reports produced by elements associated with the American, Swedish, Israeli and Canadian governments. Their common inspiration was the anxiety that there might be significant explosions of Christian millenarian violence in the year 2000 because some groups thought that the Second Coming and/or the Apocalypse were imminent. We were told that the reports leaned heavily on academic sources, though the sources were used in very different ways. Intrigued by the descriptions, we wondered how useful those reports would be to law enforcement officials, the public and scholars.

I asked Kaplan to organize a study of the reports for the journal *Terrorism and Political Violence*. The contents would first of all include the texts themselves, for they were significant documents and would remain interesting to scholars for some time afterwards. He would then have academic authorities analyze and compare reports, and a crucial object would be to see how the reports' conclusions compared with the events of the year.

When I explained the project to our publishing firm Frank Cass, Stewart Cass immediately and enthusiastically agreed and gave funds to subsidize a translation of the extensive Israeli report. Although the Israelis, Americans and Canadians released their reports, the Swedes, unfortunately for our purposes, were more cautious and thought it wiser to keep theirs confidential.

The volume Kaplan organized has some unusual features. It is the first study of three separate, but virtually simultaneous, national government reports on the same issue. Each report has a significant academic imprint, though the imprint is manifested in very different ways. With respect to the American case, academics who participated in the process leading up to the studies, though not in the actual constructions, describe their impressions of the final product. Although there were references to first millennium experiences and to Aum Shinrikyô, a non-Christian millenarian group that used nerve gas, the references were not discussed. To supply additional necessary context, Kaplan persuaded recognized authorities to discuss Aum Shinrikyô (Ian Reader) and agitation at the end of the first millennium in medieval Europe (Richard Landes and E. Randolph Daniel).

The impetus for the reports was the belief that the date had enormous religious significance for millenarian groups. But it was also noted that the violent attacks expected would be intensified by the probability that the Y2K computer problem would produce a general chaos on 1 January 2000.

Calamities precipitated millenarian eruptions (Michael Barkun's classic *Disaster and the Millennium* suggests) more often than any other circumstance. But if disaster was such a crucial ingredient in explaining historical events, were the reports justified in stressing the importance of the date by itself now? All the contributors to the volume except one think that the reports, especially the American one, misrepresented the crucial significance of the calendar, and Eugene Gallagher's impressive essay redefines the way we ought to think about dates and other precipitating circumstances.

Releasing the American report (*Project Meggido*) created some interesting unexpected effects, because the media ran with the story. The public grew uneasy and bin Laden's al-Qaeda (which operated on a different calendar) unexpectedly seized 'our' millennial moment for its purposes. Attempts to cross the Canadian border were made and aborted. A planned attack on the Los Angeles airport was frustrated. The police were on high alert, and the fact may have contributed to their effectiveness, even though they were looking for other would-be assailants! Would that we were so blessed in the future always.

This volume necessarily focuses on Christian experiences, but cannot avoid discussing some Jewish questions because all Christian millenarian visions imagine a critical role for the Jews as potential victims, collaborators, and as the guardians of sacred places. Other religious traditions are beyond the volume's purview, but nonetheless the problem of significant dates generating violence is important elsewhere.

Islam is a case in point. One Islamic tradition, particularly strong among Shiites, is that the Mahdi will emerge at the beginning of a new Islamic century. In 1979, during the first minutes of the fourteenth century according to the Islamic calendar, an attack was made on the Grand Mosque in Mecca, and the ensuing struggle produced over 10,000 casualties. It happened during the annual *Hajj*, when millions of pilgrims flood Saudi Arabia, a number swollen that year by the anticipation of the new century. The experience suggests that even when the date is critical, we still have to address the questions of place and effect. Other examples illustrate the point too. 1979 was also the year of the Iranian Revolution; and while one cannot argue the Revolution was 'caused' by the fact that a new century was beginning, it seems reasonable to think that the date strengthened the religious elements involved. There are many other examples in the history of Islam. The Mahdi-inspired uprising in the Sudan against the Egyptians in 1881, also at the beginning of a new Islamic century, is familiar to the Western world because the legendary British general, 'Chinese' Gordon, was killed when Khartoum fell.

The importance of dates is not confined to religious traditions. The Waco tragedy in Texas occurred on 19 April, as did the Oklahoma City bombing two years later because the commissioners of the second act wanted it understood as a reprisal for the first. Dates important to potential *victims* also generate attacks. Traditionally, Passover has often been dangerous for Jews living in the Diaspora, and Israelis have learned to be especially alert at that time against possible Palestinian efforts.[1]

Kaplan's general introduction focuses on why Christian groups did not respond in the ways anticipated. All readers will find his arguments and those throughout the volume instructive and provocative. They provide an excellent jumping off point to continue other systematic studies comparing different religious traditions and the relationship between sacred and secular experiences.

NOTE

1. A few days before the Oklahoma City Bombing a student in my class wanted an explanation for a newspaper story that described the Israelis as locking up all dogs during the Passover period in the Hebron area. I said that if you were a Jew you would expect attacks then, and that the troops who would be circulating in the area during the evening anticipating attacks did not want their movements advertised by barking dogs. To make the point clearer I added that 19 April was approaching, a time when 'all Americans should keep their eyes on Texas'.

Acknowledgements

The immediate origin of *Millennial Violence: Past, Present and Future* may be traced to discussions with Professor David C. Rapoport which took place at an idyllic post-workshop dinner by a lake on the outskirts of Stockholm in the summer of 1999. The workshop was one of several that year, held throughout the Western world (and in Israel as well) which were sponsored by various academic institutions, governments and intelligence agencies. All were concerned with the possibility – then thought of as real and threatening – of millennial violence undertaken by Christian sectarian groups, apocalyptic new religious movements, or deranged individuals which might be occasioned by the millennial New Year which would occur on 1 January 2000. Jerusalem and the United States were thought to be potential epicenters of this violence, although many European states were concerned as well.

David C. Rapoport's idea for this volume in the *Cass Series on Political Violence*, which would analyse the origins and credibility of these concerns and, in particular, consider what lessons might be learned from the non-events of the Year 2000, appears today in the post-11 September world more important than ever. Thus, I am grateful to Professor Rapoport for his support and guidance throughout this project. Special thanks too are owed to Professor Ehud Sprinzak for providing the Israeli report reprinted in this issue, and for his ideas and suggestions for this volume which were proffered in subsequent visits to Stockholm, as well as to Dr. Heléne Lööw of Stockholm University for assistance in the genesis of the project.

It goes without saying that much appreciation is owed to the individual contributors to this volume for their time and care in preparing and meticulously revising their papers for this publication. In this regard, I am particularly indebted to Benjamin Beit-Hallahmi for stepping in at a very late date and providing not only a fine paper, but much appreciated assistance in the preparation of the introductory essay for this issue. Similarly, the assistance of Dick Anthony was invaluable both for his much needed feedback and for providing a number of articles and references on the topic of 'brainwashing' in cultic groups, which helped greatly to inform the discussion of this topic in the Introduction.

As this collection will form the basis of a panel at the 2002 American Academy of Religion meetings in Toronto, much is owed to Catherine Wessinger, Eugene Gallagher (also a contributor to this volume) and Mike Ashcraft for their support in writing the proposal and supporting paperwork to make this discussion possible.

And finally, many thanks are due to Graham Hart of Frank Cass & Co. for his forbearance in accepting a manuscript that was considerably larger than expected, and for his assistance throughout the editorial process.

JEFFREY KAPLAN
University of Wisconsin Oshkosh

1

Introduction

JEFFREY KAPLAN

Although many dire scenarios of deranged millenarians, unhinged by the coming of the second millennium of the Christian calendar, were offered by governments and pundits alike, little of note did take place at the New Year of the year 2000. Ominously in light of what was to come on 11 September 2001, the only serious plot to commit terrorist violence was reportedly undertaken by operatives of al-Qaeda, when a group led by Ahmad Rassam and including Mokhtar Haouari, Abdelmajid Dahoumane, and Abdel Ghani Meskini (who later exchanged his testimony against his comrades for leniency) were arrested when trying to enter the United States or were extradited to the USA subsequent to the initial arrests. Their putative target appears to have been Los Angeles International Airport, which would be crowded with holiday travelers.[1] With the advantage of hindsight, it is significant that the threat of real terrorist violence came not from Western millenarians, but from an Islamist movement which emerges from a culture whose lunar calendar did not reflect the turn of the chronological millennium and whose attraction to taking action on the New Year seems to have been occasioned by the opportunity of expected crowds at airports and public events and, apparently, the widespread press speculation that millennial violence was imminent.[2] The full import of these arrests was unknown at the time, and before 11 September set new paradigms for our understanding of terrorism, the threat of millennial violence was considered to be both real and serious by many governments, and by more than a few scholars. The context of the times is thus important, for it is imperative to understand the bases of these fears before a realistic attempt can be made to analyze the reactions of states or the state of scholarship on the topic of millenarian violence. What follows, then, will seek to delineate some of the key contextual issues underlying this anthology from both a global political perspective and from the perspective of the academic study of religious violence. This will be followed by an introduction to the contents of this anthology.

The Context: Scholars and Law Enforcement

It would be fair to say that before the events at Waco, Texas, in 1993, the topic of religious violence as an epiphenomenon, and millenarian violence as a specific form of religious violence, was the province of a handful of academics from a variety of disciplines.[3] The problem was not yet on the radar of states, and security agencies evinced little interest. This disconnect between scholars knowledgeable in religion and law enforcement authorities on the one hand, and the perception of the FBI agents on scene in Waco that David Koresh's pronouncements were nothing more than 'Bible babble' intended to prolong the siege on the other, led in no small measure to the disaster which followed.

As the Waco siege dragged on, religious studies scholars clamored to have their voices heard. Several, most notably James Tabor and Phillip Arnold, injected themselves into the situation, approaching the FBI directly and appealing indirectly via media interviews to David Koresh and the Branch Davidians.[4] The Davidians proved amenable to this scholarly mediation, but the FBI did not and, save that it was through Tabor that David Koresh's interpretation of the Seven Seals of Revelation became available to the public, nothing came of the effort.[5]

In the aftermath of the events at Waco, however, law enforcement did begin to reach out to scholars – and some scholars pursued law enforcement with increased ardor – resulting in slowly evolving but fundamental changes in both camps. The first concrete steps were taken by the Justice Department which oversees the FBI and the Department of the Treasury, which consulted two senior academics: scholars of religion Nancy Ammerman and Lawrence Sullivan, who gave extensive critiques of the mistakes made at Waco.[6]

That these contacts with the scholarly community were made by agencies other than the FBI directly is significant, for as post-J. Edgar Hoover directors have discovered to their cost, the FBI has a notoriously closed and very conservative institutional culture which, even as the organization faced a number of severe embarrassments in the 1990s, showed few signs of substantial reform. This highly conservative institutional culture has not only proved resistant to establishing communications with sources of knowledge outside of the Bureau, but has hampered communications with other federal security or local police agencies as well.[7] So it was in the beginning with the effort to open the organization to the input, and the insights, of students of religion who insisted that, in the last analysis, religion must be taken seriously in negotiations with volatile religious groups.[8] It was not an easy sell to the FBI, nor was it an entirely satisfactory situation among scholars – particularly those concerned with the study of new religious movements who felt that their experience and specialized knowledge would lend important insights to law enforcement which would perhaps be of greater operational value than that of a scholar focused on Protestant Christianity (Ammerman) or a comparativist scholar (Sullivan).

The FBI was clearly reluctant to widen the circle of advisors, and although the reasons for this reluctance are speculative at best, again, context may offer some insights into the considerations then at play. Much of that reluctance may have had to do with the increasingly outspoken criticism of the FBI by religious studies scholars – particularly those concerned with the study of new religious movements. This criticism reached a crescendo in the bloody aftermath of Waco, and in many ways, it is yet to abate. Much of the literature of the time – often no more than op-ed pieces printed in local newspapers, emit far more heat than light and are notable today primarily for the (hopefully) momentary triumph of emotion over analysis.[9] For some in the field, that anger is seemingly yet to abate.[10] The angry defense of the Branch Davidians by many (if not most) in the community of new religious movement scholars, combined with the attempt by James Tabor and Phillip Arnold to intervene as the crisis was yet ongoing, could not have endeared new religious movement scholars to the FBI.

Thus, in the wake of Waco with pressure from the Justice Department to include religious scholars among its circle of advisors, the FBI did establish contacts in the academy. Among NRM scholars, Catherine Wessinger, Phillip Arnold, and, at a later stage, Jean Rosenfeld came to be most closely identified with the effort.[11] These early contacts were tentative, but nonetheless contact had been made, allowing the effort to establish a more formal relationship between the FBI and religious studies scholars to continue.

The advisory relationship between the FBI and religious studies scholars would be tested in 1996 with the standoff at the compound of the so-called Justice Freemen in Montana, which began on 13 March and was resolved on 13 June. The Freemen mixed various Christian Patriot ideas (reified in the press as the 'militia movement') with strong elements of Identity Christianity and came up with a belief system that demonized the federal government and attempted to replace the existing legal and economic system with an idiosyncratic mixture of their own. But what to the Freemen was free expression of religious liberty to the federal government was bank fraud and to their neighbors was the paper terrorism of baseless liens on personal property which soon was supplemented by very real threats of violence. The FBI, reportedly with great reluctance, belatedly decided at that point to intervene.[12]

Before Waco, the FBI had a record of almost unblemished success in surrounding dissident compounds and inducing even the most heavily armed groups to surrender, often without a shot being fired. Nowhere was this better exemplified than at the rural Arkansas redoubt of the Covenant, Sword and Arm of the Lord, a Christian Identity enclave well known in the radical right for its rather vast arsenal of weapons and its stated vow of never surrendering to ZOG (Zionist Occupation Government) regardless of the cost or the prevailing balance of forces. In April 1985, in an operation conducted along the same lines as Waco, a force of some 300 FBI agents surrounded CSA and, after a few days, the group surrendered.[13] Stung by the avalanche of criticism following the deaths at Waco, the Bureau was far more reluctant to become involved in the Montana situation.

In the end of course, there were few choices and the FBI did become involved in apprehending the Freemen. This time, however, great caution was exercised in an operation marked by remarkable restraint on all sides. Scholars were consulted this time, with Michael Barkun taking the lead and religious studies scholars Catherine Wessinger, Phillip Arnold and Jean Rosenfeld taking part as well.[14] How much influence their advice had in the successful outcome is, however, hard to determine precisely. As noted above, the FBI's Critical Incident Response Group (CIRG) found working with Barkun more amenable than with the religious studies scholars, and in actuality the FBI tended to rely on his advice rather than that of the religious studies scholars, as, according to Catherine Wessinger, they appeared more comfortable relating to a political scientist.[15]

Whatever the impact of the advice rendered by religious scholars at Montana, the outcome of the standoff was satisfactory – if glacially slow – in that there was no loss of life on either side and the arrests which the FBI were charged with making were carried out. The neighbors of the Freemen were relieved of a constant source of irritation if not fear, and the press was generally supportive.

In this regard, it should be noted that the scholars involved in advising the FBI solicited considerable input from a wide variety of colleagues, and, for the most part, this assistance was forthcoming. Members of the New Religious Movements group of the American Academy of Religion in particular were consulted, and a number came forward to render assistance.[16] Others, myself included, declined to become involved.[17]

Following the Montana incident, relations deepened between the FBI and the religious studies scholars – particularly those involved with the New Religious Movements group. In 1998, American Academy of Religion representatives met with the FBI in Washington, and a number of scholars – including several contributors to this issue – have accepted invitations to meet with the FBI or to address the FBI Academy at Quantico, Virginia. The FBI has attended every AAR meeting since 1998, both sitting in on public forums and meeting privately with groups of scholars.[18] At the AAR meeting in Nashville in 2000, scholars were invited to attend a simulated hostage negotiation, and again, approximately 35 scholars accepted the invitation. For the near future, it appears that a law enforcement presence is going to be a permanent feature of AAR meetings.

The Strange History of the Brainwashing Controversy among NRM Scholars[19]

Given this extensive contact, the *Megiddo Report* could not but be influenced by this interchange, nor could it avoid being drawn into the controversies of the field. Of those, none is more divisive than the cult/brainwashing theory, which has roiled the world of new religious movement scholarship for the last 30 years. In the 1970s, following the sudden proliferation of new religious movements in America – many of them influenced by Asian religious traditions – and the sensational trial of Patricia Hearst in 1975 in which the defense unsuccessfully evoked a 'brainwashing' defense to charges that she had joined the Symbionese Liberation Army in a bank robbery and other crimes – the view that members of the so-called cults were victims of diminished mental capacity, or more popularly, brainwashing, was prevalent in the press and in the wider culture as well. The theory was based to a great extent on studies of Korean War prisoners by Robert Lifton and others.[20] However, this claim has been much disputed and has been rejected in *amicus* briefs by professional associations, i.e. SSSR, ASA, APA, and by several courts in brainwashing legal cases.[21] Yet upon this rock, public if not necessarily academic careers were built, opportunities for lucrative legal consultancies and opportunities to serve as highly remunerated expert witnesses were opened, and organizations were founded which together formed the disparate anti-cult movement in North America and in Europe.[22]

The argument, which increasingly became identified with Margaret Singer and psychiatrist Louis West,[23] went well beyond the confines of academia, and became the centerpiece of attempts to legally remove adult converts from new religions by establishing 'conservatorships' for them by concerned relatives, or by resorting to 'coercive deprogramming' – a euphemism for kidnapping and intensive psychological pressure on the victim to recant his or her religious convictions.[24] Singer and West's position on the so-called brainwashing controversy – although never embraced by a significant number of academics in the fields of social psychology and the psychology of religion[25] – was influential through the 1980s, but by the end of the decade had been disavowed in a draft report of the American Psychological Association. Brainwashing was in any case by then much out of favor with academics concerned with the study of new religious movements. The controversy found its way into the courts in a case related to the Church of Scientology[26] where, based on the findings of the APA report and the testimony of Dick Anthony among others, Singer was not allowed to testify on the basis that her views lacked scientific merit. Anthony recalls of this history:

> I don't remember any new religious movement scholars other than myself testifying, the case never went to trial, the action was all in pretrial motions and supporting documents, e.g. a motion to exclude Singer's and Ofshe's testimony as ideological rather than scientific ... based upon the argument in my 1990 article

published in *In Gods We Trust* ... in an earlier case I and the lawyer in that case had turned it into a motion in *limine* re. Singer and Ofshe's proposed testimony in that case, and in the Fishman case the prosecutor with my help used the same motion and plugged in the new facts with very little change otherwise. I supported the brief with a **56** page declaration expanding the argument in relation to this case and attached the APA and ASA *amicus* briefs to it, which had been submitted elsewhere, and also attached the Dimpac report as well as my 1990 article debunking Singer and Ofshe's brainwashing theory and testimony. My declaration interpreted those attached documents in a certain way and the court endorsed my reasoning in the decision excluding Singer and Ofshe's testimony.

My declaration and the brief were supported and endorsed in a declaration by the well-known Harvard clinical psychologist Perry London, who was not an NRM scholar. The primary point of his declaration from the standpoint of the prosecution was to add his prestige in backing up the argument in the motion in *limine* and in my declaration. However, he also added the results of an internet psychological literature search he had done showing that the brainwashing, coercive persuasion, and thought reform concepts were not generally accepted within mainstream psychological research and theory. He sent me an initial draft of his declaration and I returned it to him with suggested changes. He had been recruited to submit it not because he knew anything in particular on NRMs or had ever done research or published on them, but rather because he had previously published on Korean War alleged brainwashing. Singer and Ofshe responded to these documents with declarations, and I responded to their arguments in two additional declarations.[27]

A flurry of civil litigation later, the brainwashing thesis appeared, academically if not yet legally, 'dead on arrival'.[28]

But as with most things in the social sciences, no idea is ever truly dead; it simply changes form and appears as a revision of an already revisionist idea. Thus, several important academic students of new religious movements in the 1990s began to re-examine the brainwashing theory, and argued that there were, indeed, some elements of truth to it. Most influential in this regard is Benjamin Zablocki, whose work suggests that, while the Singerian idea of predatory cult leaders lurking in the shadows and fully able to exert a Svengali-like influence on the unwary is nonsensical, there is nonetheless a significant degree of pressure amounting to coercive psychological control exerted on those members who would attempt to leave.[29] Of course, Zablocki's ideas were hardly expected to be received with acclaim by the current mainstream of new religious movement scholarship, and criticism from all sides has not been lacking.[30] Nor has Margaret Singer disappeared from the scene. She continues to publish, albeit as irregularly as she did in the early 1980s.[31] It would be fair to say that the brainwashing controversy remains bitterly acrimonious, and despite the positive step taken with the courageous publication of a collection by Zablocki and sociologist of Religion Thomas Robbins which gives equal space to all sides of the 'cult wars' on the brainwashing and other contentious issues in the field,[32] little middle ground is currently to be found.

It was therefore something of a surprise to the community of new religious movement scholars when the public version of the *Megiddo Report* appeared, for the report cited Margaret Singer's conception of 'cultic relationships' in its definition of apocalyptic cults.[33] The use of Margaret Singer's work to describe 'cults', for most new religious movement scholars, harked back to an earlier day and a stage of the cult wars which had seemed long over. Indeed, the public version of the *Megiddo Report* appeared to be an unusual bricolage of ideas taken from a variety of sources. None of these sources, with the sole exception of Michael Barkun's work on Christian Identity, was taken from the work of any of the scholars who had been involved with CIRG at the time of the Freemen standoff or beyond.[34] More unusual still was the selection of apocalyptic groups covered in the *Megiddo Report*. These included a grab bag of groups drawn from Christian Identity and other sectors of the radical right, the Christian Patriot subculture here called the militia movement, and, for reasons unknown, the Black Hebrew Israelites – an African-American sect that has been residing amidst some controversy, but no violence, in Israel for some time.[35] Significantly, the last chapter dealt with the 'Significance of Jerusalem' for millennial groups.

It is not however my purpose here to analyze the text of the *Megiddo Report*.[36] Articles by Michael Barkun, Eugene Gallagher and Benjamin Beit-Hallahmi do precisely this in greater depth than could be attempted here. Rather, this is to note that, as an early product of the newly won cooperation between law enforcement and scholars of religion, the document appears to suggest that religious studies scholars exerted little if any influence on the FBI's perceptions of potentially violent millennial groups. And those perceptions had a significant real world impact.

The *Megiddo Report* Goes Public

In the winter of 1999, a number of articles began to appear in the press throughout the United States reporting an FBI warning of possible millennial violence. *US News and World Report* first broke the story in September 1999. It was at this time that news of the existence of the *Project Megiddo* report became public knowledge, and in November the FBI announced that it would release the report to the general public.[37] Before the public debut of the *Megiddo Report*, it was the subject of classified briefings with local law enforcement officials across the United States. In the end, the publicly available *Megiddo Report* was a somewhat redacted copy of the secret report.[38]

While it is easy to say, in retrospect, that the fears of millennial violence underscored by the *Megiddo Report* were vastly overblown, in the context of the times, this was not immediately obvious. The *Megiddo Report* warned of the effect not only of the turn of the calendar to a new millennium, but of the impact of the much feared Y2K computer glitch on millennial communities already in a state of excitement about the coming of the new millennium.[39] As Eugene Gallagher notes sagely in this issue: 'the calendar doesn't drive millennial thought; millennial thought drives the calendar.'[40] However, this wisdom was not applicable to the Y2K problem, which at the time seemed to be very much driven by the calendar. And there was a small but highly public group of academics who did argue for the existence of a trans-national community of millenarians who were sufficiently excited by the prospect of the End of Days occurring on or near midnight, 31 December 1999, to lend further credibility to the FBI's warnings.[41]

Naturally enough, these headlines spurred a good deal of media interest, and so it was that in Attorney General Janet Reno's weekly news conference of 4 November 1999, many of the questions concerned the *Project Megiddo* report which had yet to be released to the public. The brief exchange between Reno and journalists, well illustrates the uncertainty and suspicion which characterized both sides of the exchange:

> Q: But based – if I could follow this for just one other question. When you read these reports, it seems all very dire.
>
> And of course, that's what they are focusing on, of course. But when you read them, is there a sense that you get from your briefings that something like this is inevitable or very remote? Or how would you characterize the warnings?
>
> RENO: I think the warnings are just common-sense warnings: 'Let's take appropriate reasonable care.'
>
> Q. The FBI has said repeatedly, including in the Project Megiddo report, that they have little if any evidence that extremists groups – militias, Christian identity groups – are planning any malicious activity around Y2K. In fact, they do say what you just said, that it is more of a general warning, 'Be on the lookout.'
>
> Do you think putting out reports like Project Megiddo, which has sort of an interesting name in and of itself, does that cause unnecessary worry or maybe even paranoia?
>
> RENO: I don't think it should cause worry. I think we are in a time when we have got to take reasonable precautions. When we have information, we should make sure that it is available in a reasonable way, in a prudent manner. In this world, with the weapons we have, with people's ability to move quickly, it just requires that we all figure out how we live together with strong feelings on the part of many, but without the violence that can tear us apart.[42]

So great was the media receptivity to the menace of crazed, heavily armed millenarians that the FBI itself tried to rein in what had the makings of a rumor panic. Thus on 20 October 1999, the FBI's Press Office issued a statement which attempted, with little success, to bring some sense of proportion to the discussion. Noting that the FBI had for several years been trying to reach out to the members of citizen militias, and that the majority of these weekend warriors were law abiding and peaceful (if a bit touchy on questions of Second Amendment rights), the Bureau sought to create the image of an agency which was on guard; cautious but not overly concerned. The release was artfully crafted, and well worth reproducing in full below:

For Immediate Release
FBI National Press Office October 20, 1999 Washington, DC

The FBI today issued the following statement to clarify the 'USA Today' story titled 'FBI: Militias a threat at millennium:'

For several years, the FBI has had a program of reaching out to militias and their members to explain the FBI's role in investigating violations of law and to stress open lines of communication with militia groups. This was done also to assure the militias that there was no intent to deny anyone their constitutional rights nor was there a targeting of any militia groups who were otherwise engaged in legitimate, protected activity. The FBI realizes that the majority of militia members engage in and support law abiding activities. However, the FBI will investigate illegal activities coming within the purview of its investigative responsibilities. In fact, the FBI is fully cognizant of the fact that some militias have taken positive steps towards ridding themselves of violent extremist elements. It is these violent extremist elements that could be violating laws which could subject them to investigations by the FBI. Often, these extreme members will splinter from more established groups and engage in violence autonomously. These elements are often very small cells or lone actors. The contact with militia members has proven effective, in that the more mainstream militia groups have been helpful in identifying the more extremist elements of the militia who may resort to acts of violence.

'Project Megiddo' is the culmination of an FBI research initiative which analyzed the potential for extremist criminal activity in the U.S. by individuals or domestic groups who attach special significance to the year 2000. In an effort to educate investigators and officials in the law enforcement community about potential violence associated with or motivated by the arrival of the year 2000, the FBI conducted extensive research into the various ideologies and concepts which serve to motivate groups or individuals with violent agendas. Many extremists place

significance on the next millennium, and may present challenges to
law enforcement authorities. The significance is based primarily
upon apocalyptic religious beliefs or political beliefs concerning the
New World Order conspiracy theory. The report is intended to
provide a clear, measured, and responsible picture of potential
extremism motivated by the next millennium, and to increase
awareness among law enforcement officials of the unique challenges
that may be presented by extremists motivated by millennial
agendas.

The study is being distributed to appropriate law enforcement
personnel from around the country and provides an overview of
various extremist ideologies, specifically those which advocate or
call for violent action beginning in the year 2000. Such ideologies
motivate violent white supremacists who seek to initiate a race
war; apocalyptic cults which anticipate a violent Armageddon;
radical elements of private citizen militias who fear that the United
Nations will initiate an armed takeover of the United States and
subsequently establish a One World Government; and other
groups or individuals which promote violent millennial agendas.
The report also discusses how extremists interpret biblical and/or
other religious scriptures to justify their agendas, and how certain
extremist elements point to the so-called Y2K computer crisis as
an indicator of imminent social chaos and unrest.

In addition to addressing key millennial concepts and the
ideological or religious motivations behind millennial extremism,
Project Megiddo outlines a number of issues of which law
enforcement officers should be cognizant, including indicators of
potential violence, possible preparations for violence, and a
general discussion of possible targets of millennial extremists.
Law enforcement officials are encouraged to further educate
themselves on the various issues discussed in the project.[43]

With the FBI's warnings of millennial mayhem on the horizon,
journalists naturally enough combed their virtual rolodexes and
searched the web for experts to interview. The thrust of the stories had
been set by the FBI's press releases and backgrounder sessions, making
it a very difficult task for any academic authority to modify, much less

change, the import of the stories. In effect, the media line was very much in sync with the popular image of millenarian believers as dangerously unstable, inherently violent, and as the clock ticked down to midnight, 31 December, increasingly irrational. In the end, most scholars interviewed in the national press simply took the middle road, saying in effect that violence was certainly possible, but not inevitable.[44]

As local papers picked up and ran with the national wire service stories, there was a search for local experts to interview to discuss the impact of the anticipated millennial madness on the state and local level. University professors, watchdog organizations and 'long-time observers' stepped up to the microphones and the story grew in the retelling. In 'mediaese', the story now had legs and was running free.

Among American academics, there was no shortage of scholars interested in the millennium. Indeed, historians of every imaginable sub-discipline, theologians and ethicists, folklorists and political scientists, sociologists and psychologists, anthropologists and many, many more had been discussing putting together some sort of a project, program or institute or something (anything) to study the subject of the change of the millennium. Many attempts were made, some successful, some not, as academics grappled with the logistics (and often, with each other) of defining and obtaining funding for millennium-related projects. Out of this creative ferment came one of the more successful such endeavors, the Center for Millennial Studies (CMS) centered at Boston University.

The CMS was very much the product of the vision of rhetorician Stephen O'Leary from the University of Southern California and medievalist Richard Landes from Boston University, with important contributions from a number of other scholars. The Center features annual conferences, a web site packed with interesting documents, a newsletter, and perhaps most important, it reflects the relentless energy and intensive focus on all things millennial of its director, Richard Landes. More to the point, the Center became a recognizable source of quotable expertise on the millennium, first in America, and later abroad, with Israel constituting a particularly receptive audience. And comments were not lacking, nor were interviews or appearances on television and radio shows of a variety of formats.

From its inception, the CMS was a different kind of scholarly animal. For one thing, it was unabashedly slick, or in the words of one amazed journalist, it had definite 'marketing savvy'.[45] The Center aimed to bridge the worlds of scholarship and the popular press, and in general, this goal was accomplished, albeit not without some considerable glitches. Even more than most scholars, those associated with CMS, in particular Richard Landes and Stephen O'Leary, went to great lengths to be accessible to the media. And while the Center, from director to associated scholars, did indeed provide an accessible source of scholarly insight to the press and public, there was simply no way to effectively counter the 'millennial madness' story.[46]

Few scholars who have interacted with the mass media are without their horror stories of firmly established preconceptions and storylines written well in advance of any real research by the interviewer. And if the FBI's own press release could not slow the media train, what hope did scholarly observers have of effectively countering the narrative of crazed millenarians at the turn of the millennium?

The problem in fact would appear to be two-fold. On the one hand, no scholar could in good conscience state that nothing would happen on the New Year save that the millenarians, like the rest of us, would probably awake with a good hangover and a vague sense of disappointment, if not surprise, that the sun had come up and life after 1 January 2000 would go on pretty much as it had before. There was always the chance that an individual or small group would in fact seize on the millennium as an opportunity to strike a 'blow against the empire' when everyone was watching and any act of violence would be guaranteed maximum global publicity. Indeed, the very intensity of the media spotlight and the ubiquity of public speculation that acts of violence would occur could well have had the ironic effect of catalyzing the very events that people most feared. On the other hand, all too often the media heard what it wanted (or expected) to hear, and the cautionary aside that violence was possible would be the soundbite of the moment, with the view that violence was really not what most millennialists had in mind relegated to cutting room floor. For knowledgeable scholars, it was in many ways a no win situation.

For these same scholars however, there were in 1999 a dizzying number of events, meetings, conferences and workshops held in North America, Europe and Israel. Some were academic, and some, as noted earlier, were sponsored by states or intelligence agencies. The noise surrounding the *Megiddo Report* also appears to have spurred the creation of other reports on millennial violence. One of the best, the publicly available Canadian Security Intelligence Service's 'Doomsday Religious Movements' is included in this issue. Some European police or intelligence services wrote similar reports estimating the threat of millennial violence on a continent-wide and national basis,[47] but these have not been released as of yet, and as Leena Malkki notes in her essay on Finland's notably blasé attitude toward the threat of millennial violence, this was by no means an interest of every European state.[48]

Notably different is the Israeli report, also included in this issue. The product of four noted Israeli scholars chaired by Ehud Sprinzak and including Ya'akov Ariel, Uri Ne'eman, and Amnon Ramon, and dated September 1999, the report provides a scholarly and remarkably complete discussion of the groups and individuals who might present a risk of violence or suicidal action in Israel on the New Year.[49] It includes as well a remarkably frank discussion of potential sources of information (including several scholars included in this issue) and methods of dealing with potential problems. In the event, less of note took place in Israel than in the US, but as a product of the very real concerns reflected in the report, an American apocalyptic sect, the Concerned Christians, were deported from the country before the New Year.[50]

This then was the context in which the *Megiddo Report* and those of other states and security services were released, and through which the ongoing (if tenuous) relationship between law enforcement and the community of religious scholars continues to unfold. But the questions remain: were the fears of millennial violence at the coming of the Year 2000 justified, and, particularly in the light of 11 September, what have we learned? It is precisely these questions that this Special Issue set out to answer.

In the section of papers specifically tasked with analyzing the *Megiddo Report*, the Canadian Security Service report, and the Israeli report, Michael Barkun, Eugene V. Gallagher and Benjamin Beit-Hallahmi approach the issues from very different perspectives. In 'Project Megiddo, the FBI, and the Academic Community', Michael Barkun recounts from an insider's perspective the interactions between scholars of religion and law enforcement in the post-Waco period that were the earliest roots of the *Megiddo Report*. 'Questioning the Frame: The Canadian, Israeli and US Reports', by Eugene V. Gallagher provides analysis of the texts of the three reports which focuses on three common threads: 'On three particular topics the reports are especially revealing: the focus on the year 2000, the connections between millennialism and violence, and the treatment of Jerusalem as a central focus of biblical millennialism.'[51] Rounding out the section is a paper by an Israeli scholar, Benjamin Beit-Hallahmi, whose paper, 'Ten

Comments on Watching Closely the Gaps Between Beliefs and
Actions', ranges widely over the texts of the three reports, the
contentious issues in the field of new religious movements scholarship,
and the unique aspects of the Israeli situation.

The next section presents three very different papers which seek to
examine wider issues related to the year 2000 and millennial violence.
Leading off is Ian Reader, whose work on Aum Shinrikyô is well
known. His paper, 'Spectres and Shadows: Aum Shinrikyô and the Road
to Megiddo', examines the lessons that the Aum Shinrikyô case has –
and does not have – for Western societies fearful of a repetition of
Aum's resort to weapons of mass destruction. A very different kind of
reality check is offered by a Finnish scholar, Leena Malkki, in her
'Apocalypse – Not in Finland: Millenarianism and Expectations on the
Eve of the Year 2000'. To scholars from the United States, and even
more to those from the adrenalin-driven state of Israel, Finland often
appears to be, to quote a song from the Talking Heads, 'A place where
nothing ever happens'. Yet Finland is more the norm than the exception
in Europe, where to many millennial fears and religiously motivated
violence appears to be 'an American disease', as Malkki's paper
suggests. Finally, the triumvirate of Dick Anthony, Thomas Robbins,
and Steven Barrie-Anthony offer a more theoretically driven
contribution: 'Cult and Anticult Totalism: Reciprocal Escalation and
Violence'. Dick Anthony and Thomas Robbins have contributed a
remarkable body of literature to the study of new religious movements
and to the question of cult-related violence in the United States, while
Anthony, as suggested earlier in this Introduction, played a key role in
debunking Margaret Singer's brainwashing theories. 'Cult and Anticult
Totalism: Reciprocal Escalation and Violence' extends their theoretical
work, offering a model that builds on Robert Lifton's work on totalism
to suggest a model of religious violence:

> Religio-ideological totalism entails an absolutistic division of
> humanity into dualistic categories such as saved/damned,
> human/subhuman, godly/demonic, etc. Totalistic 'cults' are not
> necessarily violent, but the psychology of totalism does feature an
> impulse to validate an absolutistic worldview by *confronting*
> demonized exemplars of evil as contrast symbols. Such
> confrontations can become violent under certain circumstances,
> which may include totalistic persecution by the anticult movement.

As Robert Lifton has noted, 'Totalism begets Totalism', and anticult confrontations of totalistic movements may themselves take a totalistic and hence persecutory form.[52]

The final section of this issue seeks to provide some depth and, again, historical context to the issue emerging from the millennial fears of the year 2000 with two contrasting views of the turn of the first millennium – the year 1000. Were there concerns in medieval Europe that the turn of the calendar would herald the End of Days and the imminent return of Christ? In 'What Happens when Jesus Doesn't Come: Jewish and Christian Relations in Apocalyptic Time', Richard Landes suggests that, at least at some levels of medieval society, this was the case and that, as a result, the Jews in particular were made to pay the price:

> This widespread, public belief in the approaching 'End of Days' reached a first climax at the approach of AD 1000 and then, after that passed, perhaps more intensely, at the millennium of the Passion in 1033.[53]

Arguing for a more cautious reading of the sources, E. Randolph Daniel's 'Medieval Apocalypticism, Millennialism and Violence' takes the opposite viewpoint, and both articles provide the reader with a fascinating introduction to medieval apocalypticism, drawing in the process parallels with the present day.

Together, these eight articles and three primary source documents are offered both as a contribution to the study of millennial violence and, it is hoped, as a source through which lessons relevant to the perception of the events of 11 September – and the reaction of states to those events – may be drawn.

NOTES

1. 'Bomb Plot Suspect Sought By United States, Canada Is Detained in Algeria' *The Washington Post* (8 Dec. 2000), p.A44; 'Algerian Guilty In Plot to Bomb Landmarks in US', *The Washington Post* (9 March 2001), p.A03; 'Training Camp Links Millennium, Embassy Bombers', CNN.Com (5 July 2001).
2. That al-Queda leaders were avid readers of the Western press, and were not averse to following the lead of irresponsible Western journalism – itself based on a seemingly endless supply of instant 'terrorism experts' – is evidenced by the hard drive of a computer recovered from the al-Queda leadership in Afghanistan. It attributes their chemical weapons program to persistent press reports that such weapons were within the

realm of possibility for terrorist groups: 'despite their extreme danger, we only became aware of them when the enemy drew our attention to them by repeatedly expressing concern that they can be produced simply'. Alan Cullison and Andrew Higgins, 'Files Found: A Computer in Kabul Yields a Chilling Array Of al-Qaeda Memos – Talk of "Hitting Americans" And Making Nerve Gas; Spats Over Salaries, Rent – A Guide to "The Company"', *The Wall Street Journal* (31 Dec. 2001), p.A1.

3. The Ur text of millenarian violence is of course, that of the historian Norman Cohn, *Pursuit Of The Millennium: Revolutionary Millenarians And Mystical Anarchists Of The Middle Ages* (New York: Oxford University Press, 1957, 1970). The topic was taken up in a collection by Sylvia L. Thrupp (ed.), *Millennial Dreams In Action: Studies in Revolutionary Religious Movements* (New York: Schocken, 1970). By then, discussion of millenarian violence was becoming increasingly the province of anthropologists and applied to pre-modern societies. The political scientist Michael Barkun, also a contributor to this volume, was much influenced by Cohn's work and in a visionary set of publications demonstrated the relevance of Cohn's theories to the contemporary United States. See for example Michael Barkun, *Disaster and the Millennium* (New Haven, CT: Yale University Press, 1974). Another political scientist, David Rapoport, contributed several seminal articles on the topic, and through his editorship of *Terrorism and Political Violence* the topic was brought to a wider audience of academics and policy makers. See David Rapoport, 'Fear and Trembling: Terrorism in Three Religious Traditions', *American Political Science Review* 78 (Sept. 1984); 'Messianic Sanctions for Terror', *Comparative Politics* 20 (1988). *Terrorism and Political Violence* devoted a special issue to the topic of religious violence edited by Mark Jurgensmeyer with 'Violence and the Sacred in the Modern World', *Terrorism and Political Violence* 3/3 (Autumn 1991), although few of the articles in the collection dealt with specifically millenarian forms of violence. The journal indeed published my own first academic article on millenarian violence with Jeffrey Kaplan, 'The Context of American Millennarian Revolutionary Theology: The Case of the "Identity Christian" Church of Israel', *Terrorism and Political Violence* 5/1 (Spring 1993), and in 1995 published a special issue, edited by Michael Barkun, 'Millennialism and Violence', *Terrorism and Political Violence* 7/3 (Autumn 1995), reissued in book form as Michael Barkun (ed.), *Millennialism and Violence* (London: Frank Cass & Co., 1996). That the field of terrorism studies continued to resist the inclusion of religiously motivated violence as an analytical paradigm, no better evidence can be offered than Alex Schmid and Albert Longman, *Political Terrorism: A New Guide to Actors, Authors, Concepts, Data Bases, Theories and Literature* (New York: Transaction, 1988), which, a decade after the Iranian Revolution, continued to group motivational categories of terrorist violence as subsets of Political, Criminal or Pathological terrorism.

4. James D. Tabor, 'Religious Discourse and Failed Negotiations', in Stuart A. Wright (ed.), *Armageddon in Waco* (Chicago: University of Chicago Press, 1995), p.273. Tabor recounts these events in greater depth in James D. Tabor and Eugene V. Gallagher. *Why Waco?: Cults and the Battle for Religious Freedom in America* (Berkeley, CA: University of California Press, 1995).

5. James D. Tabor and Eugene V. Gallagher. *Why Waco?*

6. For an account, see Michael Barkun, '*Project Megiddo*, the FBI, and the Academic Community', in this issue. See also Nancy T. Ammerman, 'Waco, Federal Law Enforcement, and Scholars of Religion', in Stuart A. Wright (ed.), *Armageddon in Waco* (note 4), pp.282–96. Michael Barkun, a political scientist, became involved in working with the FBI subsequent to the events at Waco as well, although at a somewhat later stage than Ammerman and Sullivan.

7. 'FBI Agents Ill-Equipped to Predict Terror Acts', *The Washington Post* (24 Sept. 2001), p.A01. Mark Riebling, *Wedge: The Secret War Between the FBI and CIA* (New York: A. A. Knopf, 1994); John T. Elliff, *The Reform of FBI Intelligence Operations* (Princeton, NJ: Princeton University Press, 1979).

8. Nancy T. Ammerman, 'Waco, Federal Law Enforcement, and Scholars of Religion'

(note 6); Eugene V. Gallagher, '"Theology is Life and Death": David Koresh on Violence, Persecution and the Millennium', in Catherine Wessinger (ed.), *Millennium, Persecution and Violence: Historical Cases* (Syracuse, NY: Syracuse University Press, 2000), pp.82–100.

9. For a taste of the times, see James R. Lewis, *From the Ashes: Making Sense of Waco* (Lanham, MD: Rowman & Littlefield, 1994).

10. One such example may be the unusual article by new religious movement scholar Stuart Wright taking the FBI to task for its failure to follow the steps outlined in 'complex hostage barricade situations' as written in a manual distributed to law enforcement agencies: Michael J. McMains and Wayman C. Mullins, *Crisis Negotiations: Managing Critical Incidents and Hostage Situations in Law Enforcement and Corrections* (Cincinnati, OH: Anderson, 1996). That Prof. Wright lacks both training and experience in law enforcement, combined with previous criticism of the FBI which implied (correctly) that whatever the Bureau faced at Waco, it could not be justly called a hostage situation in the conventional sense, makes this rather fundamentalist approach to the McMains and Mullins text appear to be somewhat anomalous. See Stuart A. Wright, 'Anatomy of a Government Massacre: Abuses of Hostage-Barricade Protocols During the Waco Standoff', *Terrorism and Political Violence* 11/2 (Summer 1999), pp.39–68. Wright either reacts to, or anticipates, pre-publication criticism of his paper, finding all such criticism 'untenable'. See in the same issue criticisms of Wright's thesis by Eugene Gallagher (a scholar of religion), Jayne Seminare Docherty (a scholar of conflict resolution) and Kerry Noble (a member of the Christian Identity Covenant, Sword and Arm of the Lord compound who had experienced a similar FBI operation from the other end of the gun), as well as Wright's response to these criticisms, pp.74–92. (Noble parenthetically has since left Identity and renounced his former racist beliefs.) Undaunted, Prof. Wright extended his critique to the legal profession and the practice of trial law in Stuart A. Wright, 'Justice Denied: The Waco Civil Trial', *Nova Religio* 5/1 (Oct. 2001), pp.143–51. A personal communication from James Lewis to Benjamin Beit-Hallahami dated 1998 and noted in Beit-Hallahami's contribution to this volume, confirms the prevalence of anger by scholars in the NRM field toward the FBI over Waco. In referring to the ill-fated 1995 journey undertaken by James R. Lewis, J. Gordon Melton and a chemist, Barry Fisher, to Japan at the behest of Aum Shinrikyo which is discussed in Beit-Hallahami's article in this volume, Lewis states: 'This was only a few years after Waco, and scholars like Gordon [Melton] and myself were still upset about the way in which a relatively innocent group had been massacred by government stupidity. We were thus in the mood to entertain the idea that the Aum Shinrikyo people might actually be innocent.' See Benjamin Beit-Hallahami, 'Ten Comments on Watching Closely the Gaps Between Beliefs and Actions', this issue. For a more enlightening view of the Waco negotiations, Jayne Seminare Docherty, *Learning Lessons from Waco: When the Parties Bring Their Gods to the Negotiation Table* (Syracuse, NY: Syracuse University Press, 2000); and Docherty 'Why Waco has not Gone Away: Critical Incidents and Cultural Trauma', *Nova Religio* 5/1 (Oct. 2001), pp.186–202.

11. Catherine Wessinger suggests that from the perspective of the FBI, their advice, based on unofficial feedback, was probably irrelevant as it was doubtful that the FBI listened to what they had to say. Email to author, 21 Jan. 2002.

12. James Brooke, 'Armed Group in Montana Has Sown Hate and Fear', *The New York Times* (31 March 1996); 'Freeman Depended on Government Subsidies', *The New York Times* (30 April 1996). David Johnston, 'In Montana, FBI Tries a Kinder, Gentler Approach', *The New York Times* (30 March 1996). For a good overview, see Catherine Wessinger, *How the Millennium Comes Violently: From Jonestown to Heaven's Gate* (New York: Seven Bridges, 2000), ch. 6.

13. For an insider account, see Kerry Noble, *Tabernacle of Hate* (Prescott, Ontario: Voyageur Publishing, 1998). On CSA, see Jeffrey Kaplan, *Encyclopedia of White Power: A Sourcebook on the Radical Right* (Walnut Creek, CA: AltaMira, 2000),

pp.71–8. It should be noted that one difference was telling: the FBI handled the CSA operation itself. At Waco, the Bureau was forced to step into the mess created by the incompetence of the Bureau of Alcohol, Tobacco and Firearms (BATF). For an insider's story of this chaotic agency, see James Moore, *Very Special Agents* (Urbana and Chicago, IL: University of Illinois Press, 2001).

14. Catherine Wessinger, 'Religious Studies Scholars, FBI Agents, and the Freemen Standoff', *Nova Religio* 3/1 (Oct. 1999), p.37. Jean Rosenfeld, 'The Justus Freemen Standoff: The Importance of the Analysis of Religion in Avoiding Violent Outcomes', in Catherine Wessinger ed., *Millennium, Persecution and Violence* (note 8), pp.323–44.

15. Catherine Wessinger, 'Religious Studies Scholars, FBI Agents, and the Freemen Standoff', p.37. Off the record, several scholars involved in attempting to advise the FBI have suggested there was a gender dimension involved as well. That this may have been a factor was confirmed in a private communication to the author by a European security official who was in contact with the FBI's Critical Incident Response Group (CIRG) several years later. There may have been, on the part of the agents involved, some irritation at the number of faxes – to them and to others in the chain of command including attorney General Janet Reno – which were being sent by some of the NRM scholars involved. For better or worse, the nuisance factor (or more charitably, persistence) should not be overlooked when considering the relationship between the FBI and religious scholars.

16. For published accounts, see for example the 'Nova Religio Symposium: Scholars of New Religions and Law Enforcement Officials', *Nova Religio* 3/1 (Oct. 1999): Jane Seminare Docherty, 'Bridging the Gap Between Scholars of Religion and Law Enforcement Negotiators', pp.8–26; Eugene V. Gallagher, 'Negotiating Salvation', pp.27–35; Catherine Wessinger, 'Religious Studies Scholars, FBI Agents, and the Freemen Standoff', pp.36–44; Lonnie D. Kliever, 'Meeting God in Garland: A Model of Religious Tolerance', pp.45–53; and Stephen O'Leary, 'Law Enforcement and New Religious Movements', pp.54–59.

17. In my own case, I was contacted by three of the scholars involved with the FBI, but felt that cooperation with the FBI was incompatible with doing fieldwork among volatile religious communities, including radical right wing and other millennialist groups. Moreover, my reading of the history of the interactions between intelligence agencies and scholars was not sanguine. I therefore had no contact with the FBI itself. On this history, see for example, Irving L. Horowitz, *The Rise and Fall of Project Camelot* (Boston: MIT Press, 1967); or Robin W. Winks, *Cloak and Gown: Scholars in the Secret War, 1939–1961* (New Haven, CT and London: Yale University Press, 1996). Indeed, an unavoidable cost of the deepening relationship between some new religious movement scholars and the FBI is a disruption of former collegial relations. Where once a request for information was assumed to be between colleagues and that the information exchanged would be utilized for strictly academic purposes – i.e., published with full attribution and in the expected year or more of lead time normative in academic publishing – it became around the time of the Freemen siege an open question of whether information given in confidence would be passed on to law enforcement. This opened up myriad ethical dilemmas for fieldwork scholars which remain unresolved.

18. Jane Seminare Docherty, 'Bridging the Gap Between Scholars of Religion and Law Enforcement Negotiators', p.8 (note 16); Catherine Wessinger, 'Religious Studies Scholars, FBI Agents, and the Freemen Standoff', p.42.

19. For their extensive and helpful critiques of earlier drafts of this section, I am much indebted to Benjamin Beit-Hallahami and Dick Anthony.

20. Robert Jay Lifton, *Thought Reform and the Psychology of Totalism* (New York: W. W. Norton & Co, 1961, 1989).

21. Email to author from Dick Anthony, 30 January 2002. This formulation rather too much simplifies this history – a history which is immensely complex and, for the most part, beyond the scope of this 'Introduction'. For extensive discussion of this history from a psychological and legal perspective, see Dick Anthony, 'Religious Movements and

Brainwashing Litigation', in Thomas Robbins and Dick Anthony, *In Gods We Trust: New Patterns of Religious Pluralism in America* (New Brunswick, NJ: Transaction Books, 1990), pp.295–343; Dick Anthony and Thomas Robbins, 'Negligence, Coercion and the Protection of Religious Belief', *Journal of Church and State* 37 (Summer 1995), pp.509–36; and, for a European dimension which brings in the relevant history of the CIA brainwashing experiments, Dick Anthony, 'Pseudoscience and Minority Religions: An Evaluation of the Brainwashing Theories of Jean-Marie Abgrall', *Social Justice Research* 12/4 (1999), pp.421–56. The latter article suggests the importance of the Euro–American connection in the dissemination of anti-cult materials and ideas. Finally, for a summary and concise statement of what Anthony refers to as the three phases of brainwashing theory, see Dick Anthony, 'Tactical Ambiguity and Brainwashing Formulations: Science or Psuedo Science', in Benjamin Zablocki and Thomas Robbins, *Misunderstanding Cults: Searching for Objectivity in a Controversial Field* (Toronto: University of Toronto Press, 2001), pp.215–317.

22. For a good, brief synopsis of this history, see J. Gordon Melton, 'The Modern Anti-Cult Movement in Historical Perspective', in Jeffrey Kaplan and Heléne Lööw (eds.), *The Cultic Milieu: Oppositional Subcultures in an Age of Globalization* (Walnut Creek, CA: Alta Mira Press, 2001). For the diverse literature of the anti-cult movement, see for example, James A. Rudin and Marcia R. Rudin, *Prison or Paradise?: The New Religious Cults* (Philadelphia: Fortress Press, 1980); David G. Bromley, *The New Vigilantes: Deprogrammers, Anti-Cultists and the New Religions* (Beverly Hills, CA: Sage Publications, 1980); Anson D. Shupe, Jr., David G. Bromley and Donna L. Oliver, *The Anti Cult Movement in America: A Bibliography and Historical Survey* (New York: Garland Publishing, 1984); or Ronald Enroth, *Youth Brainwashing, and the Extremist Cults* (Grand Rapids, MI: Zondervan, 1977). For a broader interpretation of the subject which includes watchdog movements of every description, see Jeffrey Kaplan, *Radical Religion in America* (Syracuse, NY: Syracuse University Press, 1997), ch. 5.

23. In this regard, Dick Anthony writes:

> While [West's] testimony in the Hearst trial had some impact, thereafter he didn't testify with one or two exceptions. [Richard] Ofshe was much more the co-creator of the brainwashing argument than West, he and [Margaret] Singer co-authored two seminal articles, and usually testified together in the same cases applying the argument from those articles in a legal context, Ofshe as a sociologist testifying on the nature of the cultic-brainwashing organization and Singer as a clinical psychologist testifying on the brainwashed character of individuals in the organization.

(Email from Dick Anthony, 30 Jan. 2002).

24. In deprogramming too there is an Ur text: Ted Patrick, and Tom Dulack, *Let Our Children Go!* (New York: E. P. Dutton, 1976).

25. Social psychology deals with attitude change and persuasion. The psychology of religion deals with conversion. Email from Benjamin Beit-Hallahami, 22 Jan. 2002. See Robert B. Caldini, *Influence: Science and Practice* (Glenville, IL: Scott Foresman, 1985).

26. The reference here is to the Fishman case. All of the relevant data and documents are available at www-2.cs.cmu.edu/~dst/Fishman/ClamBed.html.

27. Email from Dick Anthony, 30 Jan. 2002.

28. J. Gordon Melton, 'The Modern Anti-Cult Movement in Historical Perspective' (note 22); Dick Anthony and Thomas Robbins, 'Law, Social Science and the "Brainwashing" Exception to the First Amendment', *Behavioral Sciences and the Law* 10 (1992), pp.5–29. See also 'Religious Movements and "Brainwashing" Litigation: Evaluating Key Testimony', in Thomas Robbins and Dick Anthony, *In Gods We Trust: New Patterns of Religious Pluralism in America* (New Brunswick, NJ: Transaction Books, 1990); Dick Anthony and Thomas Robbins, 'Negligence, Coercion, and the Protection of Religious Belief', *Journal of Church and State* 37 (Summer 1995).

29. For Zablocki's controversial theories, and for his history of the brainwashing concept and how it came to be, in his terms, 'blacklisted' by the academic experts most responsible for the demise of Singer and West as credible sources of knowledge on new religious movements, see Benjamin Zablocki, 'The Blacklisting of a Concept: The Strange History of the Brainwashing Conjecture in the History of the Sociology of Religion', *Nova Religio* 1/1 (Oct. 1997), pp.96–121; 'Exit Cost Analysis: A New Approach to the Scientific Study of Brainwashing', *Nova Religio* 1/2 (April 1998), pp.216–49. This material is reprised and refined in Zablocki, 'Toward a Demystified and Disinterested Scientific History of Brainwashing', in Benjamin Zablocki and Thomas Robbins, *Misunderstanding Cults* (note 21), pp.159–214. Agreeing in part with Zablocki is Stephen Kent, a Canadian sociologist of Religion. See Stephen A. Kent, 'Brainwashing Programs in the Family/Children of God and Scientology', in Benjamin Zablocki and Thomas Robbins, *Misunderstanding Cults* (note 21), pp.349–78. Dick Anthony, for his part, disagrees with this view. He states:

> I think that you've [Kaplan] overstated the difference between Singer and Ofshe's theory on the one hand and Zablocki's on the other, I view the original CIA theory, (first generation brainwashing theory) Singer and Ofshe's brainwashing theory (second generation brainwashing theory) and various versions of third generation brainwashing theory, e.g. Abgrall's, Paul Martin's, Stephen Kent's, Zablocki's as all essentially the same theory, i.e. manipulated altered states leads to suggestibility leads to involuntary commitments to brainwashing organizations. I think this view of it will eventually be the conventional wisdom and for the most part is now. Zablocki and I have in the last two years had a complex debate on the NRM listserv wherein I develop this view at additional length beyond my chapter, with Zablocki attempting to defend the novelty of his position and its separation from Singer's. Of the 50 or so NRM scholars on the list, virtually no-one agrees that his position differs significantly from Singer's, as Zablocki acknowledges.

(Email from Dick Anthony, 30 Jan. 2002.)
It would be fair to say however, that it is in the nature of listserv dialogs that only a few of the most highly motivated scholars take the time and effort to post their opinions – most remain silent lurkers or, despairing of the Internet as a mode of reasoned debate, choose not to belong to listserv groups at all.

30. See for example, David G. Bromley, 'Listing (in Black and White) on Sociological Thought Reform', *Nova Religio* 1/2 (April 1998), pp.250–66; 'A Tale of Two Theories: Brainwashing and Conversion as Competing Political Narratives', in Benjamin Zablocki and Thomas Robbins, *Misunderstanding Cults* (see note 21), pp.318–48; Dick Anthony, 'Tactical Ambiguity and Brainwashing Formulations: Science or Pseudo-Science', *Misunderstanding Cults*, pp.215–317.

31. Margaret Singer and Richard Ofshe, 'Thought Reform Programs and the production of Psychiatric Casualties', *Psychiatric Annals* 20 (1990), pp.188–93; Michael D. Langone, with a preface by Margaret Thaler Singer, *Recovery From Cults: Help for Victims of Psychological and Spiritual Abuse* (New York: Norton, 1993); Margaret Thaler Singer and Lalich Janja, *Cults in Our Midst* (San Francisco: Jossey-Bass, 1995).

32. Benjamin Zablocki and Thomas Robbins, *Misunderstanding Cults* (see note 21). Those issues involve primarily research ethics and are contested as acrimoniously as the brainwashing issue. For a taste of these controversies, see Benjamin Beit-Hallahmi, 'Ten Comments on Watching Closely the Gaps Between Beliefs and Actions', this issue. A published symposium airing these issues edited by Timothy Miller was published in *Nova Religio* 2/1 (Oct. 1998), pp.8–54. The contributions were: Massimo Introvigne, 'Blacklisting or Greenlisting? A European Perspective on the New Cult Wars'; Thomas Robbins, 'Objectivity, Advocacy and Animosity'; James T. Richardson, 'The Accidental Expert'; and Stephen A. Kent and Theressa Krebs, 'Academic Compromise in the Social Scientific Study of Alternative Religion'.

33. Federal Bureau of Investigation, *Project Megiddo*, available in HTML format from the

Cesnur website (www.cesnur.org/testi/FBI_004.htm) and in PDF from , 26, n.36–38. The work cited is Margaret Thaler Singer and Lalich Janja, *Cults in Our Midst*. In reality, the word 'surprise' might be mild. 'Dismay' would probably be more appropriate.

34. This is not to say that the authors of the *Megiddo Report* were aware of Prof. Barkun's association with the Bureau at the time the report was written. Whether they were aware of this fact or not is unknown. Email to author from Michael Barkun, 23 Jan. 2002.

35. The *Megiddo Report* cites only the Southern Poverty Law Center's *Intelligence Report* and press accounts as sources for the Black Hebrew Israelites section. Neither source is particularly noted for dispassionate or objective analysis. For a more penetrating view, see A. Paul Hare (ed.), *The Hebrew Israelite Community* (Blue Ridge Summit, PA: University Press of America, 2000).

36. Those 'special few' who might be interested in my own analysis of the text of *Project Megiddo* and who are fluent in Hebrew may consult: Jeffrey Kaplan, 'A Funny Thing Happened on the Way to Armageddon: A Preliminary Consideration of Millennialism, Violence and Disengagement in America', *State and Society* (University of Haifa), forthcoming.

37. Mike Brunker, 'FBI to Police: Be Wary of Millennium Mayhem Militias and Cults Spark Fears of Violence', *MSNBC.COM* (20 Oct. 1999).

38. A request was made to the FBI for permission to publish the unedited version of the report for this issue. What followed was apparently a long and difficult internal argument, but in the end, the insular institutional culture of the Bureau won out and permission was denied. However, off the record and from non-Bureau sources, it was asserted (with considerable reliability) that the difference between the public and secret version of the *Megiddo Report* was virtually nil. Very little was deleted from the public version, and what was deleted seems to have been based on the same sort of public and press sources that characterize the public document, making the decision not to release the full document appear to be all the more the product of the FBI's culture of secrecy rather than from concern for revealing sources or methods.

39. See in particular the 'Executive Summary' of the *Megiddo Report* (p.5), and the coverage of the militia movement and the American radical right who were seen as particularly susceptible to Y2K-driven paranoia. See also, 'FBI Says Fringe Groups may be Plotting Violence', *The Washington Post* (1 Nov. 1999); or Michael J. Sniffen, 'FBI Warns of Millennium Attacks', *The Associated Press* (21 Oct. 1999), which were typical of these press articles.

40. Eugene V. Gallagher, 'Questioning the Frame: The Canadian, Israeli and US Reports', this issue.

41. See for example the transcript of the NPR program *Fresh Air*, in which Terry Gross interviews Richard Landes, a contributor to this issue, and an academic who was well ahead of the millennial curve in warning of possible violence at the millennium. The transcript is available at the interestingly irreverent site *The Skeptic Tank*, in which a number of primary source documents and scholarly articles are archived for download. The title of the file is: 'Millennial Studies: Lunatics Waiting for the End Again'. See www.skeptictank.org/

42. 'Weekly Media Briefing With Attorney General Janet Reno', US Department Of Justice, Washington, DC, Thursday 4 Nov. 1999.

43. Document available at: www.lib.umich.edu/libhome/Documents.center/text/megiddo. txt.

44. Recalling the time, Stephen O'Leary, a veteran of numerous press interviews, put it this way: I would take the 'best case scenario and the worst case scenario and split the difference'. Conversation with Stephen O'Leary, 26 May 2000.

45. Shiela Gibson, 'Something to Crow About', *Skeptic* 7/3 (1999), pp.20–23.

46. In fact, the panic had the desirable side effect of providing popular attention – and sources of funding – to researchers, making it somewhat counter-productive to disagree too strongly with the journalistic consensus that the threat of millenarian violence was very real.

47. I attempted, for example, to obtain the Swedish report for this issue, but after more than a year, the request remained mired in the impenetrable recesses of the Swedish bureaucracy. One source familiar with the report however, said it was basically the same as the *Megiddo Report*, save that it drew greatly from my *Radical Religion in America*, although for no better reason than that I had spent much time in Sweden and the book was thus handy.
48. Leena Malkki, 'Apocalypse – Not in Finland. Millenarianism and Expectations on the Eve of the Year 2000', this issue.
49. Ehud Sprinzak, Ya'akov Ariel, Uri Ne'eman and Amnon Ramon, 'Events at the End of the Millennium: Possible Implications for the Public Order in Jerusalem', this issue.
50. 'Millennial Madness, Jerusalem Jitters', *US News and World Report* (18 Jan. 1999), pp.32–4.
51. Eugene V. Gallagher, 'Questioning the Frame: The Canadian, Israeli, and US Reports', this issue.
52. Dick Anthony, Thomas Robbins and Steven Barrie-Anthony 'Cult and Anticult Totalism: Reciprocal Escalation and Violence', this issue.
53. Richard Landes, 'What Happens when Jesus Doesn't Come: Jewish and Christian Relations in Apocalyptic Time', this issue.

MILLENNIUM-RELATED SECURITY REPORTS

Project Megiddo[1]

FBI (United States)

Table of Contents:

For over four thousand years, MEGIDDO, a hill in northern Israel, has been the site of many battles. Ancient cities were established there to serve as a fortress on the plain of Jezreel to guard a mountain pass. As Megiddo was built and rebuilt, one city upon the other, a mound or hill was formed. The Hebrew word 'Armageddon' means 'hill of Megiddo.' In English, the word has come to represent battle itself. The last book in the New Testament of the Bible designates Armageddon as the assembly point in the apocalyptic setting of God's final and conclusive battle against evil. The name 'Megiddo' is an apt title for a project that analyzes those who believe the year 2000 will usher in the end of the world and who are willing to perpetrate acts of violence to bring that end about.

I. EXECUTIVE SUMMARY

The year 2000 is being discussed and debated at all levels of society. Most of the discussions regarding this issue revolve around the topic of technology and our society's overwhelming dependence on the multitude of computers and computer chips which make our world run smoothly. However, the upcoming millennium also holds important implications beyond the issue of computer technology. Many extremist individuals and groups place some significance on the next millennium, and as such it will present challenges to law enforcement at many levels. The significance is based primarily upon either religious beliefs relating to the Apocalypse or political beliefs relating to the New World Order (NWO) conspiracy theory. The challenge is how well law enforcement will prepare and respond.

The following report, entitled 'Project Megiddo', is intended to analyze the potential for extremist criminal activity in the United States by individuals or domestic extremist groups who profess an apocalyptic view of the millennium or attach special significance to the year 2000. The purpose behind this assessment is to provide law enforcement agencies with a clear picture of potential extremism motivated by the next millennium. The report does not contain information on domestic terrorist groups whose actions are not influenced by the year 2000.

There are numerous difficulties involved in providing a thorough analysis of domestic security threats catalyzed by the new millennium. Quite simply, the very nature of the current domestic terrorism threat places severe limitations on effective intelligence gathering and evaluation. Ideological and philosophical belief systems which attach importance, and possibly violence, to the millennium have been well-articulated. From a law enforcement perspective, the problem therefore is not a lack of understanding of motivating ideologies: The fundamental problem is that the traditional focal point for counterterrorism analysis – the terrorist group – is not always well-defined or relevant in the current environment.

The general trend in domestic extremism is the terrorist's disavowal of traditional, hierarchical, and structured terrorist organizations. Even well-established militias, which tend to organize along military lines with central control, are characterized by factionalism and disunity. While several 'professional' terrorist groups still exist and present a continued threat to domestic security, the overwhelming majority of extremist groups in the United States have adopted a fragmented, leaderless structure where individuals or small groups act with autonomy. Clearly, the worst act of domestic terrorism in United States history was perpetrated by merely two individuals: Timothy McVeigh and Terry Nichols. In many cases, extremists of this sort are extremely difficult to identify until after an incident has occurred. Thus, analysis of domestic extremism in which the group serves as the focal point of evaluation has obvious limitations.

The Project Megiddo intelligence initiative has identified very few indications of specific threats to domestic security. Given the present nature of domestic extremism, this is to be expected. However, this is a function of the limitations of the group-oriented model of counterterrorism analysis and should not be taken necessarily as reflective of a minor or trivial domestic threat. Without question, this initiative has revealed indicators of potential violent activity on the part of extremists in this country. Militias, adherents of racist belief systems such as Christian Identity and Odinism, and other radical domestic extremists are clearly focusing on the millennium as a time of action. Certain individuals from these various perspectives are acquiring weapons, storing food and clothing, raising funds through fraudulent means, procuring safe houses, preparing compounds, surveying potential targets, and recruiting new converts. These and other indicators are not taking place in a vacuum, nor are they random or arbitrary. In the final analysis, while making specific predictions is extremely difficult, acts of violence in commemoration of the millennium are just as likely to occur as not. In the absence of intelligence that the more established and organized terrorist groups are planning millennial violence as an organizational strategy, violence is most likely to be perpetrated by radical fringe members of established groups. For example, while Aryan Nations leader Richard Butler publicly frowns on proactive violence, adherents of his religion or individual members of his organization may commit acts of violence autonomously.

Potential cult-related violence presents additional challenges to law enforcement. The potential for violence on behalf of members of biblically-driven cults is determined almost exclusively by the whims of the cult leader. Therefore, effective intelligence and analysis of such cults requires an extensive understanding of the cult leader. Cult members generally act to serve and please the cult leader rather than accomplish an ideological objective. Almost universally, cult leaders are viewed as messianic in the eyes of their followers. Also, the cult leader's prophecies, preachings, orders, and objectives are subject to indiscriminate change. Thus, while analysis of publicly stated goals and objectives of cults may provide hints about their behavior and intentions, it is just as likely to be uninformed or, at worst, misleading. Much more valuable is a thorough examination of the cult leader, his position of power over his followers, and an awareness of the responding behavior and activity of the cult. Sudden changes in activity – for example, less time spent on 'Bible study' and more time spent on 'physical training' – indicate that the cult may be preparing for some type of action.

The millennium holds special significance for many, and as this pivotal point in time approaches, the impetus for the initiation of violence becomes more acute. Several religiously motivated groups envision a quick, fiery ending in an apocalyptic battle. Others may initiate a sustained campaign of terrorism in the United States to prevent the NWO. Armed with the urgency of the millennium as a motivating factor, new clandestine groups may conceivably form to engage in violence toward the US Government or its citizens.

Most importantly, this analysis clearly shows that perceptions matter. The perceptions of the leaders and followers of extremist organizations will contribute much toward the ultimate course of action they choose. For example, in-depth analysis of Y2K compliancy on the part of various key sectors that rely on computers has determined that, despite a generally positive outlook for overall compliance, there will be problem industries and minor difficulties and inconveniences.[2] If they occur, these inconveniences are likely to cause varying responses by the extreme fringes. Members of various militia groups, for example, have identified potentially massive power failures as an indication of a United

Nations-directed NWO takeover. While experts have indicated that only minor brownouts will occur, various militias are likely to perceive such minor brownouts as indicative of a larger conspiracy.[3]

The Senate Special Committee on the Year 2000 Technology Problem has stated that some state and local governments could be unprepared, including the inability to provide benefits payments.[4] [3] This could have a significant impact in major urban areas, resulting in the possibility for civil unrest. Violent white supremacists are likely to view such unrest as an affirmation of a racist, hate-filled world view. Likewise, militia members who predict the implementation of martial law in response to a Y2K computer failure would become all the more fearful.

II. INTRODUCTION

Are we already living on the precipice of the Apocalypse – the chaotic final period of warfare between the forces of good and evil signaling the second coming of Christ, as forecast in the New Testament's Book of Revelation? Or, will life on earth continue for another 1,000 years, allowing humans to eliminate disease and solve the mysteries of the aging process so they can live as long as Methuselah, colonize space, commune with extraterrestrials, unravel the secrets of teleportation, and usher in a golden age of peace and productivity?[5]

At first glance, some of the predictions compiled in Prophecies for the New Millennium that claim to foretell how the millennium will affect the United States seem benign. In fact, those predictions capture some of the countless ways that domestic terrorists view how the millennium will affect the world. The threat posed by extremists as a result of perceived events associated with the Year 2000 (Y2K) is very real.

Numerous religious extremists claim that a race war will soon begin, and have taken steps to become martyrs in their predicted battle between good and evil. Three recent incidents committed by suspects who adhere to ideologies that emphasize millennial related violence illustrate those beliefs: Buford O. Furrow, Jr., the man charged in the August 1999 shootings at a Los Angeles area Jewish day care center, told authorities 'its time for America to wake and kill the Jews'; Ben Smith, who committed suicide after shooting at minorities in Indiana and Illinois, killing two and injuring ten, over the July 4, 1999 weekend, was found to have literature in his home that indicated the year 2000 would be the start of the killing of minorities; and John William King, the man convicted in the dragging death of James Byrd, Jr., a black man in Jasper, Texas, believed that his actions would help to initiate a race war. Each of these men believed in the imminence of a racial holy war.

Meanwhile, for members of the militia movement the new millennium has a political overtone rather than a religious one. It is their belief that the United Nations has created a secret plan, known as the New World Order (NWO), to conquer the world beginning in 2000. The NWO will be set in motion by the Y2K computer crisis.

Religious motivation and the NWO conspiracy theory are the two driving forces behind the potential for millennial violence. As the end of the millennium draws near, biblical prophecy and political philosophy may merge into acts of violence by the more extreme members of domestic terrorist groups that are motivated, in part, by religion. The volatile mix of apocalyptic religions and NWO conspiracy theories may produce violent acts aimed at precipitating the end of the world as prophesied in the Bible.

When and how Christ's second coming will occur is a critical point in the ideology of those motivated by extremist religious beliefs about the millennium. There is no consensus within Christianity regarding the specific date that the Apocalypse will occur. However, within many right-wing religious groups there is a uniform belief that the Apocalypse is approaching. Some of these same groups also point to a variety of non-religious indicators such as gun control, the Y2K computer problem, the NWO, the banking system, and a host of other 'signs' that the Apocalypse is near. Almost uniformly, the belief among right-wing religious extremists is that the federal government is an arm of Satan. Therefore, the millennium will bring about a battle between Christian martyrs and the government. At the core of this volatile mix is the belief of apocalyptic religions and cults that the battle against Satan, as prophesied in the Book of Revelation, will begin in 2000.

An example of the confrontational nature and belief system of religiously motivated suspects illustrates the unique challenges that law enforcement faces when dealing with a fatalist/martyr philosophy. It also illustrates the domino effect that may occur after such a confrontation. Gordon Kahl, an adherent to the anti-government/racist Christian Identity religion, escaped after a 1983 shootout with police that left two Deputy US Marshals dead. He was later killed during a subsequent shootout with the FBI and others that also left a county sheriff dead. In response to the killing of Kahl, Bob Mathews, a believer in the racist Odinist ideology, founded The Order. After The Order committed numerous crimes, its members were eventually tracked down. Mathews escaped after engaging in a gun battle and later wrote, 'Why are so many men so eager to destroy their own kind for the benefit of the Jews and the mongrels? I see three FBI agents hiding behind some trees ... I could have easily killed them ... They look like good racial stock yet all their talents are given to a government which is openly trying to mongrelize the very race these agents are part of ... I have been a good soldier, a fearless warrior. I will die with honor and join my brothers in [heaven].' Exemplifying his beliefs as a martyr, Mathews later burned to death in an armed standoff with the FBI.

In light of the enormous amount of millennial rhetoric, the FBI sought to analyze a number of variables that have the potential to spark violent acts perpetrated by domestic terrorists. Religious beliefs, the Y2K computer problem, and gun control laws all have the potential to become catalysts for such terrorism. The following elements are essential to understanding the phenomenon of domestic terrorism related to the millennium:

When Does the New Millennium Begin?

As the nation and the world prepare to celebrate the arrival of the new millennium, a debate has arisen as to the correct date for its beginning. Although the true starting point of the next millennium is January 1, 2001, as established by the US Naval Observatory in Washington, DC, our nation's official time keeper, many will celebrate January 1, 2000, as the start of the millennium. The majority of domestic terrorists, like the general public, place a greater significance on January 1, 2000.

Blueprint for Action: The Turner Diaries

Many right-wing extremists are inspired by *The Turner Diaries*, a book written by William Pierce (under the pseudonym Andrew Macdonald), the leader of the white supremacist group National Alliance. The book details a violent overthrow of the federal government by white supremacists and also describes a brutal race war that is to take place simultaneously. To date, several groups or individuals have been inspired by this book:

- At the time of his arrest, Timothy McVeigh, the man responsible for the Oklahoma City bombing, had a copy of *The Turner Diaries* in his possession. McVeigh's action against the Murrah Federal Building was strikingly similar to an event described in the book where the fictional terrorist group blows up FBI Headquarters.

- The Order, an early 1980s terrorist cell involved in murder, robberies, and counterfeiting, was motivated by the book's scenarios for a race war. The group murdered Alan Berg, a Jewish talk show host, and engaged in other acts of violence in order to hasten the race war described in the book. The Order's efforts later inspired another group, The New Order, which planned to commit similar crimes in an effort to start a race war that would lead to a violent revolution.[6]

- Most recently, *The Turner Diaries* provided inspiration to John William King, the man convicted for dragging a black man to his death in Jasper, Texas. As King shackled James Byrd's legs to the back of his truck he was reported to say, 'We're going to start the Turner Diaries early.'[7]

During the year 2000 and beyond, *The Turner Diaries* will be an inspiration for right-wing terrorist groups to act because it outlines both a revolutionary takeover of the government and a race war. These elements of the book appeal to a majority of right-wing extremists because it is their belief that one or both events will coincide with Y2K.

Interpretations of the Bible

Religiously based domestic terrorists use the New Testament's Book of Revelation – the prophecy of the endtime – for the foundation of their belief in the Apocalypse. Religious extremists interpret the symbolism portrayed in the Book of Revelation and mold it to predict that the endtime is now and that the Apocalypse is near. To understand many religious extremists, it is crucial to know the origin of the Book of Revelation and the meanings of its words, numbers and characters.

The Book of Revelation was written by a man named 'John' who was exiled by the Roman government to a penal colony – the island of Patmos – because of his beliefs in Christ.[8] While on the island, he experienced a series of visions, described in the Book of Revelation. The writing in the Book of Revelation is addressed to churches who were at the time experiencing or were threatened by persecution from Rome because they were not following the government. For this reason, some believe the Book of Revelation was written in code language, much of which was taken from other parts of the Bible.

One interpretation describing the essence of the message contained in Revelation is that God will overcome Christianity's enemies (Roman Government/Satan) and that the persecuted communities should persevere.[9] For right-wing groups who believe they are being persecuted by the satanic government of the United States, the Book of Revelation's message fits perfectly into their world view. This world view, in combination with a literal interpretation of the Book of Revelation, is reflected in extremist ideology, violent acts, and literature. For this reason, it is imperative to know the meaning of some of the 'code words' frequently used:

- Four (4) signifies the world.

- Six (6) signifies imperfection.

- Seven (7) is the totality of perfection or fullness and completeness.

- Twelve (12) represents the twelve tribes of Israel or the 12 apostles.

- One-thousand (1000) signifies immensity.

- The color white symbolizes power and can also represent victory, joy and resurrection.

- The color red symbolizes a bloody war.

- The color black symbolizes famine.

- A rider on a pale green horse is a symbol of Death itself.

- 'Babylon' is the satanic Roman Government, now used to describe the US government.[10] [9]

Black Hebrew Israelites, a black supremacist group, typify the use of numerology from the Book of Revelation. They believe group members will comprise the 144,000 people who are saved by God in the second coming that is outlined in Revelation (7: 1–17). In the Book of Revelation, John is shown a vision of 144,000 martyrs who have survived and did not submit to Satan. This number is derived from the assertion that the twelve tribes of Israel consisted of 12,000 people each.

Groups not only use the Bible to interpret the endtimes, but use it to justify their ideology. Phineas Priests, an amorphous group of Christian Identity adherents, base their entire ideology on Chapter 25 of the Book of Numbers. The passage depicts a scene where Phineas kills an Israelite who was having relations with a Midianite woman and God then granted Phineas and all of his descendants a pledge of everlasting priesthood. Modern day followers of the Phineas Priest ideology believe themselves to be the linear descendants of Phineas and this passage gives them biblical justification to punish those who transgress God's laws. Therefore, the group is ardently opposed to race mixing and strongly believes in racial separation. The number 25 is often used as a symbol of the group.

Apocalyptic Religious Beliefs

To understand the mind set of why religious extremists would actively seek to engage in violent confrontations with law enforcement, the most common extremist ideologies must be understood. Under these ideologies, many extremists view themselves as religious martyrs who have a duty to initiate or take part in the coming battles against Satan. Domestic terrorist groups who place religious significance on the millennium believe the federal government will act as an arm of Satan in the final battle. By extension, the FBI is viewed as acting on Satan's behalf.

The philosophy behind targeting the federal government or entities perceived to be associated with it is succinctly described by Kerry Noble, a former right-wing extremist. He says the right-wing 'envision[s] a dark and gloomy endtime scenario, where some Antichrist makes war against Christians.'[11] The House of Yahweh, a Texas based religious group whose leaders are former members of the tax protesting Posse Comitatus, is typical: Hawkins (the leader) has interpreted biblical scripture that the Israeli Peace Accord signed on October 13, 1993, has started a 7-year period of tribulation which will end on October 14, 2000, with the return of the Yeshua (the Messiah).[12] He also has interpreted that the FBI will be the downfall of the House of Yahweh and that the Waco Branch Davidian raids in 1993 were a warning to the House of Yahweh from the federal government, which he terms 'the beast.'[13] Similarly, Richard Butler, leader of the white supremacist group Aryan Nations, said the following when asked what might have motivated the day care shooting by Buford O. Furrow, Jr., one of his group's followers: 'There's a war against the white race. There's a war of extermination against the white male.'[14]

The New World Order Conspiracy Theory and the Year 2000 Computer Bug

Unlike religiously based terrorists, militia anxiety and paranoia specifically relating to the year 2000 are based mainly on a political ideology. Some militia members read significance into 2000 as it relates to their conception of the NWO conspiracy.[15] The NWO conspiracy theory holds that the United Nations (UN) will lead a military coup against the nations of the world to form a socialist or One World Government. UN troops, consisting mostly of foreign armies, will commence a military takeover of America. The UN will mainly use foreign troops on American soil because foreigners will have fewer reservations about killing American citizens. US armed forces will not attempt to stop this invasion by UN troops and, in fact, the US military may be 'deputized' as a branch of the UN armed forces. The American military contingent overseas will also play a large part in this elaborate conspiracy theory, as they will be used to help conquer the rest of the world. The rationale for this part of the theory is that American soldiers will also have less qualms about killing foreigners, as opposed to killing their own citizens.

Under this hypothetical NWO/One World Government, the following events are to take place: 1) private property rights and private gun ownership will be abolished; 2) all national, state and local elections will become meaningless, since they will be controlled by the UN; 3) the US Constitution will be supplanted by the UN charter; 4) only approved churches and other places of worship will be permitted to operate and will become appendages of the One World Religion, which will be the only legitimate doctrine of religious beliefs and ethical values; 5) home schooling will be outlawed and all school curriculum will need to be approved by the United Nations Educational, Scientific and Cultural Organization (UNESCO); and 6) American military bases and other federal facilities will be used as concentration camps by the UN to confine those patriots, including the militias, who defy the NWO. Other groups beside the UN that are often mentioned as being part of the NWO conspiracy theory are Jews, Communists, the Council on Foreign Relations, the Bilderbergers and the Trilateral Commission. Law enforcement officials will probably notice different versions of this theory, depending upon the source.

The NWO conspiracy theory is particularly relevant to the millennium because the year 2000 is considered to be a triggering device for the NWO due to the element of computer breakdown. Many computers around the world are based on a numerical system in which the year is only registered by the last two digits. A number of militia members accept the theory that on January 1, 2000, many computers will misinterpret this date as January 1, 1900, and malfunction and/or shut down completely. They further believe that these major computer malfunctions will cause widespread chaos at all levels of society – economic, social and political. This chaos will theoretically create a situation in which American civilization will collapse, which will then produce an environment that the UN will exploit to forcibly take over the United States. Therefore, these militia members (as well as other groups) believe that the year 2000 will be the catalyst for the NWO.

According to James Wickstrom, former leader of the defunct Posse Comitatus and 'Minister' of the True Church of Israel, anyone who holds any powerful political influence knows that the Y2K crisis may be the final fuse that will lead to the NWO that 'David Rockefeller and the rest of his satanic jew seedline desire to usher in upon the earth.'[16] He claims that Jews have conspired to create the Y2K problem and that the prospect of impending computer failure is very real. Similarly, *The New American*, an organ of the ultraconservative John Birch Society, speculates that the Y2K bug could be America's Reichstag fire, a reference to the 1933 arson attack on Germany's Parliament building that was used by Hitler as an excuse to enact police state laws. Similar to this train of thought, Norm Olson, leader of the Northern Michigan Regional Militia, believes constitutional rights probably will be suspended before the real crisis hits. He states: 'It will be the worst time for humanity since the Noahic flood.'[17]

However, there are some extremists who do not attach any major significance to the Y2K problem. In his article, 'The Millennium Bug and "Mainstreaming" the News', William Pierce of the National Alliance tells his followers not to worry, or at least, not to worry very much about the Y2K issue. Pierce predicts that the main event that will occur on New Year's Day 2000 is that crazed millennialists will go 'berserk when the Second Coming fails to occur.' Also, 'a few right-wing nuts may launch a premature attack on the government, figuring that without its computers the government won't be able to fight back.' Pierce claims that the lights will remain on, and that airplanes will not fall from the sky. He says that he is able to make such a prediction with some degree of confidence because, 'contrary to what some cranks would have you believe, the computer professionals and the government have been working on the Y2K problem for some time.'[18]

Gun Control Laws

The passage of the Brady Bill and assault weapons ban in 1994 were interpreted by those in the militia movement and among the right-wing as the first steps towards disarming citizens in preparation for the UN-led NWO takeover. Some are convinced that the registration of gun owners is in preparation for a confiscation of firearms and eventually the arrest of the gun owners themselves. An article by Larry Pratt, Executive Director for Gun Owners of America, interprets a 1995 UN study of small arms, done reportedly in cooperation with US police, customs and military services, as part of the UN's plan to take over the US. Pratt goes on to say that the 'UN is increasingly assuming the jurisdictional authority of a federal world government with the US as just one of scores of member states. And gun control – meaning civilian disarmament – is high up on the agenda of the UN.'[19] Speculation like this only serves to fuel the already existing paranoia of militia and patriot groups.

The right-wing believes that many of the restrictions being placed on the ownership of firearms today mirror events in *The Turner Diaries*. In his book, Pierce writes about the United States government banning the private possession of firearms and staging gun raids in an effort to arrest gun owners. The book discusses the government/police use of black men, assigned as 'special deputies' to carry out the gun raids. Many members of the right-wing movement view the book as prophetic, believing that it is only a matter of time before these events occur in real life.

In the aftermath of the school shootings in Littleton, Colorado, President Clinton, Congress, and Attorney General Reno acted swiftly to propose new laws aimed at restricting the sales of guns to juveniles and to close loopholes in existing laws. In May 1999, the Senate passed a bill to ban the importation of high capacity ammunition magazines and require background checks for guns sold at gun shows. In light of the enormous importance and prominent role that extremist groups place on the Second Amendment, it is probable that recent government actions aimed at controlling guns are perceived to be compelling signs of the UN-led NWO takeover.

III. CHRISTIAN IDENTITY

Christian Identity is an ideology which asserts that the white Aryan race is God's chosen race and that whites comprise the ten lost tribes of Israel.[20] There is no single document that expresses this belief system. Adherents refer to the Bible to justify their racist ideals. Interpreting the Book of Genesis, Christian Identity followers assert that Adam was preceded by other, lesser races, identified as 'the beasts of the field' (Gen. 1: 25). Eve was seduced by the snake (Satan) and gave birth to two seed lines: Cain, the direct descendent of Satan and Eve, and Abel, who was of good Aryan stock through Adam. Cain then became the progenitor of the Jews in his subsequent matings with the non-Adamic races. Christian Identity adherents believe the Jews are predisposed to carry on a conspiracy against the Adamic seed line and today have achieved almost complete control of the earth.[21] This is referred to as the two-seedline doctrine, which provides Christian Identity followers with a biblical justification for hatred.

The roots of the Christian Identity movement can be traced back to British-Israelism, the conviction that the British are the lineal descendants of the 'ten lost tribes' of Israel. It is a belief that existed for some time before it became a movement in the second half of the 19th century. The writings of John Wilson helped to extend the idea of British-Israelism to Anglo-Israelism, which included other Teutonic peoples – mostly northern European peoples from Germany, Italy, France and Switzerland. British-Israelism was brought to America in the early part of the 1920s, where it remained decentralized until the 1930s. At that time, the movement underwent the final transformation to become what we know as Christian Identity, at which time its ties to the original English movement were cut and it became distinctly American.

Wesley Swift is considered the single most significant figure in the early years of the Christian Identity movement in the United States. He popularized it in the right-wing by 'combining British-Israelism, a demonic anti-Semitism, and political extremism.'[22] He founded his own church in California in the mid 1940s where he could preach this ideology. In addition, he had a daily radio broadcast in California during the 1950s and 60s, through which he was able to proclaim his ideology to a large audience. With Swift's efforts, the message of his church spread, leading to the creation of similar churches throughout the country. In 1957, the name of his church was changed to The Church of Jesus Christ Christian, which is used today by Aryan Nations (AN) churches.

One of Swift's associates, William Potter Gale, was far more militant than Swift and brought a new element to Christian Identity churches. He became a leading figure in the anti-tax and paramilitary movements of the 1970s and 80s. There are numerous Christian Identity churches that preach similar messages and some espouse more violent rhetoric than others, but all hold fast to the belief that Aryans are God's chosen race.

Christian Identity also believes in the inevitability of the end of the world and the Second Coming of Christ. It is believed that these events are part of a cleansing process that is needed before Christ's kingdom can be established on earth. During this time, Jews and their allies will attempt to destroy the white race using any means available. The result will be a violent and bloody struggle – a war, in effect – between God's forces, the white race, and the forces of evil, the Jews and nonwhites. Significantly, many adherents believe that this will be tied into the coming of the new millennium.

The view of what Armageddon will be varies among Christian Identity believers. Some contend there will be a race war in which millions will die; others believe that the United Nations, backed by Jewish representatives of the anti-Christ, will take over the country and promote a New World Order. One Christian Identity interpretation is that white Christians have been chosen to watch for signs of the impending war in order to warn others. They are to then physically struggle with the forces of evil against sin and other violations of God's law (i.e., race-mixing and internationalism); many will perish, and some of God's chosen will be forced to wear the Mark of the Beast to participate in business and commerce. After the final battle is ended and God's kingdom is established on earth, only then will the Aryan people be recognized as the one and true Israel.

Christian Identity adherents believe that God will use his chosen race as his weapons to battle the forces of evil. Christian Identity followers believe they are among those chosen by God to wage this battle during Armageddon and they will be the last line of defense for the white race and Christian America. To prepare for these events, they engage in survivalist and paramilitary training, storing foodstuffs and supplies, and caching weapons and ammunition. They often reside on compounds located in remote areas.

As the millennium approaches, various right-wing groups pose a threat to American society. The radical right encompasses a vast number and variety of groups, such as survivalists, militias, the Ku Klux Klan, neo-Nazis, Christian Identity churches, the AN and skinheads. These groups are not mutually exclusive and within the subculture individuals easily migrate from one group to another. This intermixing of organizations makes it difficult to discern a singular religious ideology or belief system that encompasses the right-wing.

Nevertheless, Christian Identity is the most unifying theology for a number of these diverse groups and one widely adhered to by white supremacists. It is a belief system that provides its members with a religious basis for racism and an ideology that condones violence against non-Aryans. This doctrine allows believers to fuse religion with hate, conspiracy theories, and apocalyptic fear of the future. Christian Identity-inspired millennialism has a distinctly racist tinge in the belief that Armageddon will be a race war of Aryans against Jews and nonwhites. The potential difficulty society may face due to the Y2K computer glitch is considered by a number of Christian Identity adherents to be the perfect event upon which to instigate a race war.

There are a number of issues concerning the Christian Identity belief system that create problems when determining the threat level of groups. First, Christian Identity does not have a national organizational structure. Rather, it is a grouping of churches throughout the country which follows its basic ideology. Some of these churches can be as small as a dozen people, and some as large as the AN church, which claims membership in the thousands. In addition, some groups take the belief to a higher extreme and believe violence is the means to achieve their goal. This lack of structure creates a greater potential for violent actions by lone offenders and/or leaderless cells. It is important to note that only a small percentage of Christian Identity adherents believe that the new millennium will bring about a race war. However, those that do have a high propensity for violence.

Secondly, there are many factions of the right-wing, from Christian Identity to militias, all of which are intermingled in ideology and members. In some cases it is easy for a person to be a member of more than one group or to move from one to another. Often, if a member of one group believes the group is lax in its convictions, he or she will gravitate to a group that is more radical.

The third concern is the increased level of cooperation between the different groups. This trend can be seen throughout the right-wing. Christian Identity followers are pairing up with militias to receive paramilitary training and have also joined with members of the Ku Klux Klan and other right-wing groups. This cohesiveness creates an environment in which ideology can easily spread and branch out. However, it makes the job of law enforcement much more difficult as there are no distinctive borders between groups or ideology.

Lastly, the formation of splinter groups or state chapters from larger organizations presents an increased level of threat due to the likelihood that the leader has diminished control over the members and actions of the smaller groups. The AN is a large group that adheres to the Christian Identity belief system. The group espouses hatred toward Jews, the federal government, blacks and other minorities. The ultimate goal of the AN is to forcibly take five northwestern states – Oregon, Idaho, Wyoming, Washington and Montana – from the United States government in order to establish an Aryan homeland. It consists of a headquarters in Hayden Lake, Idaho, and a number of state chapters, which often act as their own entities. While the leader may not support or encourage acts of violence, it is easy for small cells of members or splinter groups to take part in violent acts without the knowledge of the leader. The individuals are associated with the group as a whole and carry the name of the group, but may perpetrate acts on their own.

These factors make a threat assessment concerning millennial violence difficult to determine. There is a moderate possibility of small factions of right-wing groups, whether they be members of the same group, or members of different groups, acting in an overtly violent manner in order to initiate the Apocalypse.

Several problems associated with the assessment for violence can be seen when looking at the structure and actions of the AN. The AN has been headquartered at Hayden Lake since the late 1970s and remains a focal point for the group's activities. Its annual World Congress attracts a number of different factions from the right-wing, including members and leaders of various right-wing groups. The World Congress is often viewed as a sort of round table to discuss right-wing issues. These meetings have led to an increased level of contact between AN members and members and leaders of other groups. This degree of networking within the right-wing may further the AN's base of support and help advance its cause.

One of the greatest threats posed by the right-wing in terms of millennial violence is the formation of a conglomeration of individuals that will work together to commit criminal acts. This has happened with some frequency in the past. Bob Mathews formed a subgroup of the AN, called The Order, which committed a number of violent crimes, including murder. Their mission was to bring about a race war and there are several groups that currently exist which hold these same beliefs. Dennis McGiffen, who also had ties to the AN, formed a cell called The New Order, based on Mathews' group. The members were arrested before they could follow through on their plans to try to start a race war. Chevie Kehoe, who was convicted of three homicides, conspiracy and interstate transportation of stolen property, also spent some time at the AN compound. Most recently, Buford O. Furrow, Jr., the man accused of the August 10, 1999, shooting at the Jewish Community Center in Los Angeles, California, also spent some time at the AN compound working as a security guard.

A relatively new tenet gaining popularity among Christian Identity believers justifies the use of violence if it is perpetrated in order to punish violators of God's law, as found in the Bible and interpreted by Christian Identity ministers and adherents. This includes killing interracial couples, abortionists, prostitutes and homosexuals, burning pornography stores, and robbing banks and perpetrating frauds to undermine the 'usury system.' Christian Identity adherents engaging in such behavior are referred to as Phineas Priests or members of the Phineas Priesthood. This is a very appealing concept to Christian Identity's extremist members who believe they are being persecuted by the Jewish-controlled US government and society and/or are eagerly preparing for Armageddon. Among adherents today, the Phineas Priesthood is viewed as a call to action or a badge of honor.

IV. WHITE SUPREMACY

There are a number of white supremacy groups that do not necessarily adhere to Christian Identity or other religious doctrines. White supremacy groups such as the National Alliance, the American Nazi Party and the National Socialist White People's Party are largely politically, rather than religiously, motivated.

The National Alliance is probably best known for its leader, William Pierce, who is one of the most recognized names in the radical right. Pierce wrote *The Turner Diaries* and *Hunter* and hosts a weekly radio program, American Dissident Voices. Via these outlets, Pierce is able to provide his followers with an ideological and practical framework for committing violent acts. The rhetoric of these groups largely shadows that of Adolf Hitler's in content and political ideology. In 1997, Pierce stated that:

> Ultimately we must separate ourselves from the Blacks and other non-whites and keep ourselves separate, no matter what it takes to accomplish this. We must do this not because we hate Blacks, but because we cannot survive if we remain mixed with them. And we cannot survive if we permit the Jews and the traitors among us to remain among us and to repeat their treachery. Eventually we must hunt them down and get rid of them.[23]

The end goal of National Socialist and Christian Identity devotees is the same: an all white nation. However, Christian Identity followers appear to be more of a threat concerning the millennium because of their religious beliefs.

There are also white supremacist groups which adhere to the general supremacist ideology, but are not political or religious in nature. For example, the Ku Klux Klan (KKK) proposes racial segregation that is not generally based on religious ideals. The KKK is one of the most recognized white supremacist groups in the United States. Its history is expansive and its actions of cross burnings and rhetoric of hate are well known. There is currently not a singular KKK group with a hierarchical structure, but many different KKK groups with a common ideology.

The KKK, as a whole, does not pose a significant threat with regard to the millennium. That is not to say that a member of the KKK will not act on his own or in concert with members of another group. Law enforcement has been very successful in infiltrating a number of these groups, thereby keeping abreast of their plans for action. The KKK also draws the attention of many watchdog groups, and the Southern Poverty Law Center produces a quarterly publication entitled

'Klanwatch.' It would be difficult for any of the known KKK groups to participate in millennial violence without law enforcement knowing.

Again, there is a great deal of movement that is possible throughout the right-wing, regardless of prior beliefs. If a member of a Christian Identity faction does not feel that his current group is taking enough violent action, it is possible for that member to move on to other ideologies or organizations such as Odinism, the World Church of the Creator (WCOTC) or the National Socialist movement. Because of this movement, it is also likely that communication exists between various factions of the right-wing, from religious groups to skinheads. Their end goals are similar.

The WCOTC presents a recent example of violence perpetrated by a white supremacist in order to bring about a race war. The major creed upon which Ben Klassen founded the religion is that one's race is his religion. Aside from this central belief, its ideology is similar to many Christian Identity groups in the conviction that there is a Jewish conspiracy in control of the federal government, international banking, and the media. They also dictate that RAHOWA, a racial holy war, is destined to ensue to rid the world of Jews and 'mud races.' In the early 1990s, there was a dramatic increase in membership due to the growing belief in the Apocalypse and that RAHOWA was imminent.

In 1996, Matt Hale, who has come upon recent fame by being denied a license to practice law in Illinois, was appointed the new leader of the Church of the Creator. Hale made a number of changes to the group, including changing the name of the organization to the World Church of the Creator, giving it the feel of a widespread movement.

As publicly reported, there is information to indicate that the WCOTC has violent plans for the millennium. Officials who searched Benjamin Smith's apartment, the man who went on a racially motivated killing spree over the 4th of July weekend, found a loose-leaf binder of handwritings. These writings described a holy war among the races and included a reference to the new millennium. Passages included plans of how white supremacists would shoot at non-whites from motor vehicles after the dawning of the new millennium.[24] While the group's rhetoric does include the belief in a race war and the creation of an all white bastion within the United States, other than Smith's writings, there is no indication that it is linked to the millennium.

In addition, there have been recent incidents that have demonstrated the willingness of members to take part in violent action. WCOTC members in Southern Florida are thought to be tied to several racially motivated beatings. Within the last year, four Florida members were convicted for the pistol-whipping and robbery of a Jewish video store owner. They were supposedly trying to raise money for 'the revolution.'[25]

Finally, Odinism is another white supremacist ideology that lends itself to violence and has the potential to inspire its followers to violence in connection to the millennium. What makes found on the website for the militia group United States Theatre Command (USTC).[26] The USTC website prominently features the NWO theory as it portrays both Camp Grayling in Michigan and Fort Dix in New Jersey as detention centers to be used to house prisoners in an upcoming war. Specifically in reference to a photograph of Camp Grayling, the USTC website states: 'Note that the barbed wire is configured to keep people in, not out, and also note in the middle of the guard towers, a platform for the mounting of a machine gun.' Specifically in reference to a photograph of Fort Dix, the USTC website states: 'Actual photos of an "Enemy Prisoner of War" camp in the United States of America! (Fort Dix, New Jersey to be exact!) Is there going to be a war here? Many more are suspected to be scattered throughout the United States.'

What makes Odinists dangerous is the fact that many believe in the necessity of becoming martyrs for their cause. For example, Bob Mathews, the leader of The Order, died in a fiery confrontation with law enforcement. Also, William King relished the fact that he would receive the death penalty for his act of dragging James Byrd, Jr. to his death. Odinism has little to do with Christian Identity but there is one key similarity: Odinism provides dualism – as does Christian Identity – with regard to the universe being made up of worlds of light (white people) and worlds of dark (non-white people). The most fundamental difference between the two ideologies is that Odinists do not believe in Jesus Christ. However, there are enough similarities between the myths and legends of Odinism and the beliefs of Christian Identity to make a smooth transition from Christian Identity to Odinism for those racist individuals whose penchant for violence is not being satisfied.

V. MILITIAS

The majority of growth within the militia movement occurred during the 1990s. There is not a simple definition of how a group qualifies as a militia. However, the following general criteria can be used as a guideline: (1) a militia is a domestic organization with two or more members; (2) the organization must possess and use firearms; and (3) the organization must conduct or encourage paramilitary training. Other terms used to describe militias are Patriots and Minutemen.

Most militias engage in a variety of anti-government rhetoric. This discourse can range from the protesting of government policies to the advocating of violence and/or the overthrow of the federal government. However, the majority of militia groups are non-violent and only a small segment of the militias actually commit acts of violence to advance their political goals and beliefs. A number of militia leaders, such as Lynn Van Huizen of the Michigan Militia Corps – Wolverines, have gone to some effort to actively rid their ranks of radical members who are inclined to carry out acts of violence and/or terrorism.[27] Officials at the FBI Academy classify militia groups within four categories, ranging from moderate groups who do not engage in criminal activity to radical cells which commit violent acts of terrorism.[28] It should be clearly stated that the FBI only focuses on *radical elements* of the militia movement capable and willing to commit violence against government, law enforcement, civilian, military and international targets. In addition, any such investigation of these radical militia units must be conducted within strict legal parameters.

Militia anxiety and paranoia specifically relating to the year 2000 are based mainly on a political ideology, as opposed to religious beliefs. Many militia members believe that the year 2000 will lead to political and personal repression enforced by the United Nations and countenanced by a compliant US government. This belief is commonly known as the New World Order (NWO) conspiracy theory (see Chapter I, Introduction). Other issues which have served as motivating factors for the militia movement include gun control, the incidents at Ruby Ridge (1992) and Waco (1993), the Montana Freemen Standoff (1996) and the restriction of land use by federal agencies.

One component of the NWO conspiracy theory – that of the use of American military bases by the UN – is worth exploring in further detail. Law enforcement officers, as well as military personnel, should be aware that the nation's armed forces have been the subject of a great deal of rumor and paranoia circulating among many militia groups. One can find numerous references in militia literature to military bases to be used as concentration camps in the NWO and visiting foreign military personnel conspiring to attack Americans. One example of this can be [this section was deleted from the public version of the document by the FBI].

Law enforcement personnel should be aware of the fact that the majority of militias are reactive, as opposed to proactive. Reactive militia groups are generally not a threat to law enforcement or the public. These militias may indeed believe that some type of NWO scenario may be imminent in the year 2000, but they are more inclined to sit back and wait for it to happen. They will stockpile their guns and ammunition and food, and wait for the government to curtail their liberties and take away their guns. When the expected NWO tragedy does not take place, these reactive militias will simply continue their current activities, most of which are relatively harmless. They will not overreact to minor disruptions of electricity, water and other public services.

However, there is a small percentage of the militia movement which may be more proactive and commit acts of domestic terrorism. As stated earlier, the main focus of the militias connected to the Y2K/millennium revolves around the NWO conspiracy theory. While the NWO is a paranoid theory, there may be some real technological problems arising from the year 2000. Among these are malfunctioning computers, which control so many facets of our everyday lives. Any such computer malfunctions may adversely affect power stations and other critical infrastructure. If such breakdowns do occur, these may be interpreted as a sign by some of the militias that electricity is being shut off on purpose in order to create an environment of confusion. In the paranoid rationalizations of these militia groups, this atmosphere of confusion can only be a prelude to the dreaded NWO/One World Government. These groups may then follow through on their premeditated plans of action.

VI. BLACK HEBREW ISRAELITES

As the millennium approaches, radical fringe members of the Black Hebrew Israelite (BHI) movement may pose a challenge for law enforcement. As with the adherents of most apocalyptic philosophies, certain segments of the BHI movement have the potential to engage in violence at the turn of the century. This movement has been associated with extreme acts of violence in the recent past, and current intelligence from a variety of sources indicates that extreme factions of BHI groups are preparing for a race war to close the millennium.

Violent BHI followers can generally be described as proponents of an extreme form of black supremacy. Drawing upon the teachings of earlier BHI adherents, such groups hold that blacks represent God's true 'chosen people', while condemning whites as incarnate manifestations of evil. As God's 'authentic' Jews, BHI adherents believe that mainstream Jews are actually imposters. Such beliefs bear a striking resemblance to the Christian Identity theology practiced by many white supremacists. In fact, Tom Metzger, renowned white supremacist, once remarked, 'They're the black counterpart of us.'[29] Like their Christian Identity counterparts, militant BHI followers tend to see themselves as divinely endowed by God with superior status. As a result, some followers of this belief system hold that violence, including murder, is justifiable in the eyes of God, provided that it helps to rid the world of evil. Violent BHI groups are of particular concern as the millennium approaches because they believe in the inevitability of a race war between blacks and whites.

The extreme elements of the BHI movement are prone to engage in violent activity. As seen in previous convictions of BHI followers, adherents of this philosophy have a proven history of violence, and several indications point toward a continuation of this trend. Some BHI followers have been observed in public donning primarily black clothing, with emblems and/or patches bearing the 'Star of David' symbol. Some BHI members practice paramilitary operations and wear web belts and shoulder holsters. Some adherents have extensive criminal records for a variety of violations, including weapons charges, assault, drug trafficking, and fraud.

In law enforcement circles, BHI groups are typically associated with violence and criminal activity, largely as a result of the movement's popularization by Yahweh Ben Yahweh, formerly known as Hulon Mitchell, Jr., and the Miami-based Nation of Yahweh (NOY). In reality, the origins of the BHI movement are non-violent. While the BHI belief system may have roots in the United States as far back as the Civil War era, the movement became more recognized as a result of the teachings of an individual known as Ben Ami Ben Israel, a.k.a. Ben Carter, from the south side of Chicago. Ben Israel claims to have had a vision at the age of 27, hearing 'a voice tell me that the time had come for Africans in America, the descendants of the Biblical Israelites, to return to the land of our forefathers.'[30] Ben Israel persuaded a group of African-Americans to accompany him to Israel in 1967, teaching that African-Americans descended from the biblical tribe of Judah and, therefore, that Israel is the land of their birthright. Ben Israel and his followers initially settled in Liberia for the purposes of cleansing themselves of bad habits. In 1969, a small group of BHI followers left Liberia for Israel, with Ben Israel and the remaining original migrants arriving in Israel the following year. Public source estimates of the BHI community in Israel number between 1500 and 3000.[31] Despite promoting non-violence, members of Ben Israel's movement have shown a willingness to engage in criminal activity. For example, in 1986, Ben Israel and his top aide, Prince Asiel Ben Israel, were convicted of trafficking stolen passports and securities and forging checks and savings bonds.[32]

BHI in Israel are generally peaceful, if somewhat controversial. The FBI has no information to indicate that Ben Israel's BHI community in Israel is planning any activity – terrorist, criminal, or otherwise – inspired by the coming millennium. Ben Israel's claims to legitimate Judaism have at times caused consternation to the Israeli government. BHI adherents in Israel have apparently espoused anti-Semitic remarks, labeling Israeli Jews as 'imposters.'[33] Neither the Israeli government nor the Orthodox rabbinate recognize the legitimacy of BHI claims to Judaism. According to Jewish law, an individual can be recognized as Jewish if he/she was born to a Jewish mother or if the individual agrees to convert to Judaism.[34] At present, BHI in Israel have legal status as temporary residents, which gives them the right to work and live in Israel, but not to vote. They are not considered to be Israeli citizens. While BHI claims to Judaism are disregarded by Israeli officials and religious leaders, the BHI community is tolerated and appears to be peaceful.[35]

While the BHI community in Israel is peaceful, BHI adherents in the United States became associated with violence thanks to the rise of the NOY, which reached the height of its popularity in the 1980s. The NOY was founded in 1979 and led by Yahweh Ben Yahweh. Ben Yahweh's followers viewed him as the Messiah, and therefore demonstrated unrequited and unquestioned obedience. Members of the organization engaged in numerous acts of violence in the 1980s, including several homicides, following direct orders from Ben Yahweh. Seventeen NOY members were indicted by a federal grand jury in Miami in 1990–91 on charges of RICO, conspiracy, and various racketeering acts. Various members were convicted on RICO conspiracy charges and remain imprisoned.

While the overwhelming majority of BHI followers are unlikely to engage in violence, there are elements of this movement with both the motivation and the capability to engage in millennial violence. Some radical BHI adherents are clearly motivated by the conviction that the approach of the year 2000 brings society ever closer to a violent confrontation between blacks and whites. While the rhetoric professed by various BHI groups is fiery and threatening, there are no indications of explicitly identified targets for violence, beyond a general condemnation and demonization of whites and 'imposter' Jews. Militant BHI groups tend to distrust the United States government; however, there are no specific indications of imminent violence toward the government.

VII. APOCALYPTIC CULTS

For apocalyptic cults, especially biblically based ones, the millennium is viewed as the time that will signal a major transformation for the world. Many apocalyptic cults share the belief that the battle against Satan, as prophesied in the Book of Revelation, will begin in the years surrounding the millennium and that the federal government is an arm of Satan. Therefore, the millennium will bring about a battle between cult members – religious martyrs – and the government.

In the broadest meaning, cults are composed of individuals who demonstrate 'great devotion to a person, idea, object or movement.'[36] However, using that definition, many domestic terrorist groups could be characterized as cults, including Christian Identity churches, Black Hebrew Israelites, and some militias. For law enforcement purposes, a narrower interpretation of groups that qualify as cults is needed. A more useful definition of cults incorporates the term 'cultic relationships' to describe the interactions within a cult.[37]

Specifically, a cultic relationship refers to 'one in which a person intentionally induces others to become totally or nearly totally dependent on him or her for almost all major life decisions, and inculcates in these followers a belief that he or she has some special talent, gift, or knowledge.'[38] This definition of cults provides important distinctions that are vital for analyzing a cult's predilection towards violence.

The origin of the cult, the role of its leader, and its uniqueness provide a framework for understanding what distinguishes cults from other domestic terrorist groups that otherwise share many similar characteristics. These distinctions are: (1) cult leaders are self-appointed, persuasive persons who claim to have a special mission in life or have special knowledge; (2) a cult's ideas and dogma claim to be innovative and exclusive; and (3) cult leaders focus their members' love, devotion and allegiance on themselves.[39] These characteristics culminate in a group structure that is frequently highly authoritarian in structure. Such a structure is a sharp contrast to the rapidly emerging trend among domestic terrorist groups towards a leaderless, non-authoritarian structure.

While predicting violence is extremely difficult and imprecise, there are certain characteristics that make some cults more prone to violence. Law enforcement officials should be aware of the following factors:

Sequestered Groups: Members of sequestered groups lose access to the outside world and information preventing critical evaluation of the ideas being espoused by the leader.

Leader's History: The fantasies, dreams, plans, and ideas of the leader are most likely to become the beliefs of the followers because of the totalitarian and authoritarian nature of cults.

Psychopaths: Control of a group by charismatic psychopaths or those with narcissistic character disorders.

Changes in the Leader: Changes in a leader's personality caused by traumatic events such as death of a spouse or sickness.

Language of the Ideology: Groups that are violent use language in their ideology that contains the seeds of violence.

Implied Directive for Violence: Most frequently, a leader's speeches, rhetoric, and language does not explicitly call for violence, rather it is most often only implied.

Length of Time: The longer the leader's behavior has gone unchecked against outside authority, the less vulnerable the leader feels.

Who is in the Inner Circle: Cults with violent tendencies often recruit people who are either familiar with weapons or who have military backgrounds to serve as enforcers.

Apocalyptic cults see their mission in two general ways: They either want to accelerate the end of time or take action to ensure that they survive the millennium. For example, Aum Shinrikyo wanted to take action to hasten the end of the world, while compounds in general are built to survive the endtime safely. An analysis of millennial cults by the FBI's Behavioral Science Unit describes how rhetoric changes depending on whether the leader's ideology envisions the group as playing an active role in the coming Apocalypse or a passive survivalist role:

> A cult that predicts that 'God will punish' or 'evil will be punished' indicates a more passive and less threatening posture than the cult that predicts that 'God's chosen people will punish...' As another example, the members of a passive group might predict that God or another being will one day liberate their souls from their bodies or come to carry them away. The followers of a more action-oriented group would, in contrast, predict that they themselves will one day shed their mortal bodies or transport themselves to another place.[40]

A cult that displays these characteristics may then produce three social-psychological components, referred to as the 'Lethal Triad', that predispose a cult towards violence aimed at its members and/or outsiders.[41] Cults in which members are heavily dependent on the leader for all decision making almost always physically and psychologically isolate their members from outsiders, the first component of the triad.[42] The other two components interact in the following way:

> '... **isolation** causes a reduction of critical thinking on the part of group members who become entrenched in the belief proposed by the group leadership. As a result, group members relinquish all responsibility for group decision making to their leader and blame the cause of all group grievances on some outside entity or force, a process known as **projection**. Finally, isolation and projection combine to produce pathological **anger**, the final component of the triad.'[43]

Of the nearly 1000 cults operating in the United States, very few present credible threats for millennial violence. Law enforcement officials should concentrate on those cults that advocate force or violence to achieve their goals concerning the endtime, as well as those cults which possess a substantial number of the distinguishing traits listed above.[44] In particular, cults of greatest concern to law enforcement are those that: (1) believe they play a special, elite role in the endtime; (2) believe violent offensive action is needed to fulfill their endtime prophecy; (3) take steps to attain their beliefs. Those factors may culminate in plans to initiate conflict with outsiders or law enforcement.

The violent tendencies of dangerous cults can be classified into two general categories – defensive violence and offensive violence. Defensive violence is utilized by cults to defend a compound or enclave that was created specifically to eliminate most contact with the dominant culture.[45] The 1993 clash in Waco, Texas at the Branch Davidian complex is an illustration of such defensive violence. History has shown that groups that seek to withdraw from the dominant culture seldom act on their beliefs that the endtime has come unless provoked.[46]

Cults with an apocalyptic agenda, particularly those that appear ready to initiate rather than anticipate violent confrontations to bring about Armageddon or fulfill 'prophesy' present unique challenges to law enforcement officials. One example of this type of group is the Concerned Christians (CC). Monte Kim Miller, the CC leader, claims to be one of the two witnesses or prophets described in the Book of Revelation who will die on the streets of Jerusalem prior to the second coming of Christ. To attain that result, members of the CC traveled to Israel in 1998 in the belief that Miller will be killed in a violent confrontation in the streets of Jerusalem in December 1999. CC members believe that Miller's death will set off an apocalyptic end to the millennium, at which time all of Miller's followers will be sent to Heaven. Miller has convinced his followers that America is 'Babylon the Great' referred to in the Book of Revelation. In early October 1998, CC members suddenly vanished from the United States, an apparent response to one of Miller's 'prophesies' that Denver would be destroyed on October 10, 1998. In January 1999, fourteen members of the group who had moved to Jerusalem were deported by the Israeli government on the grounds that they were preparing to hasten the fulfillment of Miller's prophecies by instigating violence.[47]

Ascertaining the intentions of such cults is a daunting endeavor, particularly since the agenda or plan of a cult is often at the whim of its leader. Law enforcement personnel should become well acquainted with the previously mentioned indicators of potential cult violence in order to separate the violent from the non-violent.

VIII. THE SIGNIFICANCE OF JERUSALEM

The city of Jerusalem, cherished by Jews, Christians, and Muslims alike, faces many serious challenges as the year 2000 approaches. As already evidenced by the deportation of various members of the religious cult known as the Concerned Christians, zealotry from all three major monotheistic religions is particularly acute in Israel, where holy shrines, temples, churches, and mosques are located. While events surrounding the millennium in Jerusalem are much more problematic for the Israeli government than for the United States, the potential for violent acts in Jerusalem will cause reverberations around the world, including the United States. The extreme terrorist fringes of Christianity, Judaism, and Islam are all present in the United States. Thus, millennial violence in Jerusalem could conceivably lead to violence in the United States as well.

Within Jerusalem, the Temple Mount, or Haram al-Sharif, holds a special significance for both Muslims and Jews.[48] The Temple Mount houses the third holiest of all Islamic sites, the Dome of the Rock. Muslims believe that the prophet Muhammad ascended to Heaven from a slab of stone – the 'Rock of Foundation' – located in the center of what is now the Dome of the Rock. In addition, when Arab armies conquered Jerusalem in 638 AD, the Caliph Omar built the al-Aqsa Mosque facing the Dome of the Rock on the opposite end of the Temple Mount. The Western (or Wailing) Wall, the last remnant of the second Jewish temple that the Romans destroyed in 70 AD, stands at the western base of the Temple Mount. The Western Wall has long been a favorite pilgrimage site for Jews, and religious men and women pray there on a daily basis. Thus, the Temple Mount is equally revered by Jews as the site upon which the first and second Jewish Temples stood.

Israeli officials are extremely concerned that the Temple Mount, an area already seething with tension and distrust among Jews and Muslims, will be the stage for violent encounters between religious zealots. Most troubling is the fact that an act of terrorism need not be the catalyst that sparks widespread violence. Indeed, a simple symbolic act of desecration, or even perceived desecration, of any of the holy sites on the Temple Mount is likely to trigger a violent reaction. For example, the Islamic holy month of Ramadan is expected to coincide with the arrival of the year 2000. Thus, even minor provocations on or near the Temple Mount may provide the impetus for a violent confrontation.

The implications of pilgrimages to Jerusalem by vast numbers of tourists are ominous, particularly since such pilgrimages are likely to include millennial or apocalyptic cults on a mission to hasten the arrival of the Messiah. There is general concern among Israeli officials that Jewish and Islamic extremists may react violently to the influx of Christians, particularly near the Temple Mount. The primary concern is that extreme millennial cults will engage in proactive violence designed to hasten the second coming of Christ. Perhaps the most likely scenario involves an attack on the Al-Aqsa Mosque or the Dome of the Rock. Some millennial cults hold that these structures must be destroyed so that the Jewish Temple can be rebuilt, which they see as a prerequisite for the return of the Messiah. Additionally, several religious cults have already made inroads into Israel, apparently in preparation for what they believe to be the endtimes.

It is beyond the scope of this document to assess the potential repercussions from an attack on Jewish or Islamic holy sites in Jerusalem. It goes without saying, however, that an attack on the Dome of the Rock or the Al-Aqsa Mosque would have serious implications. In segments of the Islamic world, close political and cultural ties between Israel and the United States are often perceived as symbolic of anti-Islamic policies by the Western world. Attacks on Islamic holy sites in Jerusalem, particularly by Christian or Jewish extremists, are likely to be perceived by Islamic extremists as attacks on Islam itself. Finally, the possibility exists that Islamic extremist groups will capitalize upon the huge influx of foreigners into Jerusalem and engage in a symbolic attack.

IX. CONCLUSION

Extremists from various ideological perspectives attach significance to the arrival of the year 2000, and there are some signs of preparations for violence. The significance of the new millennium is based primarily upon either religious beliefs relating to the Apocalypse/Armageddon, or political beliefs relating to the New World Order conspiracy theory. The challenge to law enforcement is to understand these extremist theories and, if any incidents do occur, be prepared to respond to the unique crises they will represent.

Law enforcement officials should be particularly aware that the new millennium may increase the odds that extremists may engage in proactive violence specifically targeting law enforcement officers. Religiously motivated extremists may initiate violent conflicts with law enforcement officials in an attempt to facilitate the onset of Armageddon, or to help fulfill a 'prophesy.' For many on the extreme right-wing, the battle of Armageddon is interpreted as a race war to be fought between Aryans and the 'satanic' Jews and their allies. Likewise, extremists who are convinced that the millennium will lead to a One World Government may choose to engage in violence to prevent such a situation from occurring. In either case, extremists motivated by the millennium could choose martyrdom when approached or confronted by law enforcement officers. Thus, law enforcement officials should be alert for the following: 1) plans to initiate conflict with law enforcement; 2) the potential increase in the number of extremists willing to become martyrs; and 3) the potential for a quicker escalation of conflict during routine law enforcement activities (e.g. traffic stops, issuance of warrants, etc.).

NOTES

1. This version of the Megiddo Report in HTML format was obtained from the Cesnur website (www.cesnur.org/testi/FBI_004.htm)
2. US Congress, Senate, Special Committee on the Year 2000 Technology Problem, Investigating the Impact of the Year 2000 Problem, 24 February 1996, pp.1–6.
3. Ibid, p.3.
4. Ibid., p.5.
5. Cliff Linedecker, *Prophecies for the New Millennium* (Lantana, FL: Micromags, 1999), pp.3–4.
6. Charles Bosworth Jr., 'Illinois Man Sought Start of Race War', *St Louis Post-Dispatch*, 15 March 1998.
7. Paul Duggan, 'From Beloved Son to Murder Suspect', *The Washington Post*, 16 Feb. 1999.
8. While he never claimed to be the book's author, the Apostle John was identified as such by several of the early church Fathers. Authorship is generally ascribed to him today.
9. This interpretation of the Book of Revelation is according to the Catholic Bible and a Catholic scholar that was consulted on the matter. However, there are other varying interpretations of the Book of Revelation within Christianity.
10. All symbolism was taken from *The Catholic Bible; New American Bible*.
11. Kerry Noble, *Tabernacle of Hate: Why they Bombed Oklahoma City* (Prescott, Ontario: Voyageur Publishing, 1998).
12. Robert Draper, 'Happy Doomsday', *Texas Monthly*, July 1997, p.74; Evan Moore, 'A House Divided: Tensions divide Abilene-area cult', *The Houston Chronicle*, 24 March 1996.
13. Evan Moore, 'A House Divided: Tensions divide Abilene-area cult', *The Houston Chronicle*, 24 March 1996.
14. John K. Wiley, 'Profile of Attack Suspect is Familiar and Frightening', *The Miami Herald*, 12 Aug. 1999.
15. Use of this term within militia circles became more common after President Bush starting using it to refer to the state of world affairs after the collapse of the USSR at the end of the Cold War and in the context of using international organizations to assist in governing international relations. The term **One World Government** is also used as a synonym for the New World Order.
16. James Wickstrom, 'Intelligence Update', October 1998, accessed at www.posse~comitatus.org.
17. See Fall 1998 edition of the Southern Poverty Law Center's *Intelligence Report*, 'Millennium Y2KAOS'.
18. William Pierce, 'The Millennium Bug and "Mainstreaming" the News', accessed at www.natvan.com.
19. Larry Pratt, 'The United Nations: Pressing for US Gun Control', accessed at www.gunowners.org.

20. There were 12 tribes of Israel but they were divided into two different kingdoms after the death of King Solomon. The northern kingdom was called 'Israel' and consisted of ten tribes and the southern kingdom was called 'Judah' and was comprised of two tribes. There is a record of the two tribes making up the southern kingdom, but the ten northern tribes were 'lost' after they were conquered around 722 BC by the Assyrians.

21. Jeffrey Kaplan, *Radical Religion in America* (Syracuse, NY: Syracuse University Press, 1997), p.47–48.

22. Michael Barkun, *Religion and the Racist Right* (Chapel Hill, N.C.: The University of North Carolina Press, 1997), 60.

23. Anti-Defamation League, Explosion of Hate, 15.

24. 'US Mulls Church Probe; Ties To Killings Investigated', *Chicago Tribune*, July 9, 1999.

25. 'Behind the Hate', *The Washington Post*, July 6, 1999.

26. Accessed at www.eagleflt.com.

27. Van Huizen lost re-election as commander of the MMCW in late 1997 to the more radical Joe Pilchak.

28. See 'Militias – Initiating Contact', *FBI Law Enforcement Bulletin*, July 1997, pp.22–26.

29. See Fall 1997 Southern Poverty Law Center's *Intelligence Report*, 'Rough Waters: Stream of Knowledge Probed by Officials'.

30. Linda Jones, 'Claiming a Promised Land: African-American settlers in Israel are guided by idea of independent Black Hebrew Society', *The Dallas Morning News*, 27 July 1997.

31. Ibid.

32. See Fall 1997 Southern Poverty Law Center's *Intelligence Report*, 'Rough Waters: Stream of Knowledge Probed by Officials'.

33. Jones, *Dallas Morning News*, 27 July 1997.

34. Ibid.

35. Ibid. In fact, in the community of Dimona where the BHI community resides, the Dimona Police Chief spoke in complimentary terms as to the group's discipline, leadership, and integrity.

36. Frederick C. Mish, ed., *Merriam Webster's Collegiate Dictionary 10th Edition* (Springfield, MA: Merriam-Webster, Incorporated, 1997), p.282.

37. Margaret Thaler Singer and Janja Lalich, *Cults in Our Midst: The Hidden Menace in Our Everyday Lives* (San Francisco, CA: Jossey-Bass Publishers, 1995), p.7.

38. Singer and Lalich, p.7.

39. Singer and Lalich, pp.8–9.

40. Carl J. Jensen, III, Rod Gregg and Adam Szubin, 'When a Cult Comes to Town', accessed from Law Enforcement Online.

41. Kevin M. Gilmartin, 'The Lethal Triad: Understanding the Nature of Isolated Extremist Groups', accessed at www.leo.gov/tlib/leb/1996/sept961/txt.

42. Carl J. Jensen, III and Yvonne Hsieh, 'Law Enforcement and the Millennialist Vision: A Behavioral Approach', accessed from Law Enforcement Online.

43. Ibid.

44. B. A. Robinson in 'Factors Commonly Found in Doomsday Cults', (www.religious tolerance.org/cultsign.htm.) identifies traits that provide a framework for analyzing cults. They include the following: (1) The leader preaches end of the world/Armageddon in 2000 or within a reasonable time frame before and after 2000; (2) the cult expects to play a major, elite role at the end time; (3) the cult has large numbers of firearms, explosives or weapons of mass destruction; (4) the cult has prepared defensive structures; (5) the cult speaks of offensive action; (4) the cult is led by a single male charismatic leader; (5) the leader dominates the membership through physical, sexual and emotional control; (6) the cult is not an established denomination; (7) cult members live together in a community isolated from society; (8) extreme paranoia exists within the cult concerning monitoring by outsiders and government persecution; (9) and outsiders are distrusted, and disliked. These factors are designed to leave out cults that

have unique end-time beliefs, but whose ideology does not include the advocacy of
force or violence.

45. Jeffrey Kaplan, *Radical Religion in America*, p.57.
46. Ibid., p.165.
47. Lisa Beyer, 'Target: Jerusalem', *Time Magazine*, 18 Jan. 1999.
48. Arabs refer to this site as Haram al-Sharif, which is Arabic for 'Noble Sanctuary'.
    Israelis refer to it as Har HaBayit, which is Hebrew for 'Temple Mount'. American news
    organizations almost always refer to it as the Temple Mount. Therefore, for the sake of
    simplicity and continuity, the term Temple Mount will be used in this report when
    referring to this section of Jerusalem.

Doomsday Religious Movements*

CANADIAN SECURITY INTELLIGENCE SERVICE
– Report # 2000/03 (December 18, 1999)

This paper uses open sources to examine any topic with the potential to cause threats to public safety or national security.

Introduction

Often overlooked in the discussion of emerging security intelligence issues is the challenge of contending with religious movements whose defining characteristic is an adherence to non-traditional spiritual belief systems. While only a small fraction of these groups could be considered Doomsday Religious Movements espousing hostile beliefs and having the potential to be violent, the threat they represent is evinced by recent events involving groups such as the American Branch Davidians, as well as Canada's Order of the Solar Temple. Japan's infamous Aum Shinrikyo is a textbook example, where the coupling of apocalyptic beliefs and a charismatic leader fixated on enemies culminated in a nerve-gas attack intended to cause mass casualties in the hope of precipitating a world war and completing its apocalyptic prophecy. By examining the many characteristics of these movements, this paper intends to discuss which types of groups could be prone to violence and which factors indicate a group's move to actualize this violence. The conclusions presented here are solely the result of a review of unclassified information available in the public domain.

Definitions and History

According to relevant literature, 'millennialism' is the belief that human suffering will soon be eliminated in an imminent apocalyptic scenario, ensuring that the collective salvation of humanity is accomplished. Millennialism is an enduring

---

* Reproduced with the permission of the Canadian Minister of Public Works and Government Services, 2002.

pattern in many religious traditions, and it has been reported that 35 percent of Americans believe that the Apocalypse will take place at some point. Cults throughout history have thought that critical dates will bring the fulfillment of their beliefs (e.g. Solar Temple members believe in the supernatural power of solstices and equinoxes). The year 2000 AD as the turning of the millennium is a central date in the doctrines of many modern cults.

Millennialist beliefs are shared by a variety of groups, but not all foresee a violent turning of the millennium; in fact, many see it as the catalyst for peaceful and harmonious change. Those groups which espouse violence have been called Doomsday Religious Movements in this paper for the purpose of clarity. The approaching year 2000 AD has stimulated millennial anxiety and heightened concern that its unfolding will bring an increase in potential threats by groups that would choose to assert their apocalyptic beliefs through violence.

Characteristics of Doomsday Religious Movements

Although the large number of groups which could be considered a Doomsday Religious Movement presupposes a variety of beliefs, there are some commonalities in both doctrine and action which can be delineated in order to anticipate which groups might pose a physical threat to public safety.

1. *Apocalyptic Beliefs*: Movements often believe in doctrines which are similar to that of mainstream religions, yet the convergence of some of these doctrines expressed through rites helps to shape a violent theological world view characterized by an inherent volatility.

Dualism – The belief that the world is fractured into two opposing camps of Good and Evil, which confers a profound significance on small social and political conflicts as evidence of this great cosmic struggle, and which could precipitate a violent response.

The persecuted chosen – Movements view themselves as prophetic vanguards belonging to a chosen elite but feel persecuted by wicked and tyrannical forces, which push the group to make concrete preparations to defend their sacred status.

Imminence – Because movements believe the apocalypse is unfolding before their very eyes, the 'last days' are experienced as psychologically imminent and pressure them to take immediate action to ensure their salvation.

Determinism – Since a group devoutly believes it will be the ultimate winner of the final battle, if it believes a catastrophic scenario is being actualized, the group may feel it has no choice but to try to trigger the apocalypse through violence.

Salvation through conflict / enemy eradication – As salvation depends entirely upon direct participation in the apocalyptic struggle, a group is always on the verge of anticipating confrontation, which justifies action to eliminate evil and eradicate enemies.

2. *Charismatic Leadership*: Millenarian beliefs are associated with volatility when embodied in and disseminated by charismatic leaders who wish to portray themselves as messiahs, identify the millennial destiny of humankind with their

own personal evolution and demonize opposition to their personal aggrandizement.

Control over members – Groups monopolize members' daily lives and circumscribe their belief systems within rigid doctrines, insulating them from the influence of broader social constraints. The leader is then well positioned to ask his followers to commit acts they would not normally engage in, albeit violent ones.

Lack of restraint – Leaders believe themselves to be free from religious and social laws, and operate in a social vacuum where there is a relative absence of normal institutionalized restraints to curb their whims. Physical segregation further distances the group from society's mores, where its own social code is established as the basis of all acceptable behaviour. Here authority can be exercised arbitrarily without restraint, a situation that facilitates violence.

Withdrawal and mobilization – While society is often repelled by or hostile to these groups, movements are also often suspicious of others. This tends to lead to their physical, social and psychological withdrawal, intensifying a leader's power and increasing the homogenization and dependency of the followers. When withdrawal is coupled with the group's expectation that it will face hostility and persecution, members often feel they must mobilize for 'endtimes' by acquiring weapons and securing defences.

3. *Actions by Authorities*: Violence is often not actualized until the group comes into contact with state authorities, which usually embody all that is evil for the movement and which must be vanquished in order for the apocalyptic scenario to be realized. Action on the part of state agencies will almost always elicit a reaction, which underlines the delicacy with which the situation must be handled.

Lack of comprehension – Authorities often fail to appreciate the leverage they have over doomsday movements, which depend upon them to fulfill their apocalyptic scenarios. Failure to fully comprehend this symbolic role often results in actions that trigger violence.

Unsound negotiation – Should authorities decide to intervene in a crisis situation, negotiators dealing with the movement must understand its belief structure, as ignorance of the minor differences between the beliefs of respective groups can have drastic outcomes.

Hasty action – Hasty actions can directly trigger violence on the part of the group by forcing it to act out its 'endtimes' scenario, especially when its grandiose apocalyptic scenario appears discredited under humiliating circumstances.

Spiral of amplification – Sanctions applied by authorities are often interpreted by a movement as hostile to its existence, which reinforces their apocalyptic beliefs and leads to further withdrawal, mobilization and deviant actions, and which in turn elicits heavier sanctions by authorities. This unleashes a spiral of amplification, as each action amplifies each reaction, and the use of violence is facilitated as the group believes that this will ultimately actualize its doomsday scenario.

The presence of these three factors (apocalyptic beliefs, charismatic leadership and actions by authorities), whether inherent to the dynamics of a Doomsday Religious Movement or in response to the actions that it engages in, translates into a predisposition towards violent behaviour.

The Threat to Public Safety

It is difficult to ascertain the potentially violent behaviour and threats to public safety which some movements could represent, since there exists little information about the demographics or attributes of these movements or their members in Canada. This is exacerbated by the ambiguity which surrounds Doomsday Religious Movements: their motives are often not initially comprehensible, their actors not readily identifiable and their methods are difficult to predict. Despite these difficulties, the inherent volatility and unpredictability of some millennialist cults is a cause for concern because any could pose a realistic threat to public safety almost overnight.

1. *Threat to Democratic Governance:* This threat emerges when movements associate abstract enemies with concrete state entities; when combined with volatile beliefs, this encourages a blatant disregard for the law and overt revolt against the state. The integrity of democratic governance is severely undercut because the methods of these groups end with attacks, subtle or not, on government credibility. A public perception emerges that the government cannot meet its primary raison d'être, namely, the protection of the people.

2. *Weapons Acquisition*
Firearms – In Canada, stricter gun control laws prevent an accumulation of weapons comparable to the US situation, where groups justify the stockpiling of firearms through their interpretation of the US constitutional right to bear arms. However, this does not preclude their acquisition through illegal channels, as demonstrated by the case of the Order of the Solar Temple (see below).
Explosives – The possession of explosives poses an equal, if not greater, threat than do firearms. Given this consideration, it is plausible that a sophisticated bomb-maker could focus on the mass murder of non-group members. Situated in the middle of a continuum of destructive capability, explosives possessed by groups represent mass murder waiting to happen.
Chemical and biological weapons – A still greater threat is the acquisition and use of chemical and biological weapons. It is feared that some doomsday-like groups may have mastered the production of biological agents, while the Aum cult manufactured and deployed chemical weapons. Marking the dawn of a 'New Age,' Aum's vast biological and chemical stockpiles included, respectively, significant amounts of botulinum toxin, one of the most powerful poisons, and hundred of tons of deadly sarin nerve gas ingredients. Although the chances that a group will both acquire and deploy these weapons are slim, the Aum case proves that it is within the range of possible action.

3. *Institutional Infiltration*

Politics – Bribery has been one costly method of building mainstream political support; the Aum cult allegedly bribed Russian officials in exchange for a series of 'favours'. Another potential threat lies in members who are already involved in the political process; the Solar Temple's roster included the mayor of a Canadian town and a provincial government official. The most direct political linkages concern efforts to exert direct influence over political processes. Both the Aum leader and the head of a Peruvian Doomsday Religious Movement, the Israeli Mission of the New Universal Fact (not associated with the Government of Israel in any way), have campaigned for electoral office.

Business – Businesses owned by groups can both facilitate weapons acquisition and drive membership growth; the Aum cult's multimillion dollar empire financed the purchase of weapons, justified the possession of ingredients for chemical and biological weapons, and provided a legitimate vehicle for widespread recruitment. Also, the position a member occupies in an established enterprise can augment the potential threat; several Solar Temple members were senior employees of a public utility, whose access to sensitive systems could have crippled the provision of a much-needed service.

4. *Criminal Activity*

Crimes against individuals – Crimes against individuals not affiliated with the state may indirectly enable the above threats. Documented crimes include successful attempts to 'silence' opposition from non- and ex-members, while alleged crimes finance weapons acquisition. These acts undermine the state's ability to identify and respond to dangerous groups, where the ultimate costs of such crimes are public safety and, thereby, the legitimacy of government.

Transnational criminal activity – The final category of threats pivots around alleged involvement in transnational crime. The Solar Temple purportedly laundered money and trafficked in arms and illegal drugs, while Aum Shinrikyo allegedly supplied illegal drugs to transnational organized crime syndicates. If these reports are correct, any possible threats to public safety are magnified.

Identifying the Threat

Doomsday Religious Movements often provide both verbal and tangible early warning signs that are symptomatic of a group's volatility and propensity for violence. The challenge for government and law enforcement is to note those early-warning signs as a group shifts from a 'preoccupation with enemies' to 'enemy eradication', i.e. from belief to action. Such early-warning signs include:

1. *Intensification of illegal activities* – This early-warning sign is most often a noticeable increase in the illegal procurement of weapons, which often attracts the attention of locals, and signals that the group may be making the final preparations for its destiny in the cosmic battle of all time. This occurred at Waco, Texas, before the confrontation with law enforcement agencies unfolded.

2. *Humiliating circumstances* – Should a group be humiliated to the extent that either its leader or apocalyptic scenario appears discredited, for example, if its prophecies fail to actualize by a set date or if group leaders are arrested on minor charges, then it may try to counter this defamation by violently introducing its vision.

3. *Relocation to a rural area* – This indicates both a physical and psychological withdrawal, which usually precipitates the strengthening of group solidarity and increased control over members. A relocation betrays a group's desire to carry out either the defence preparations or violent acts called for by its scripted scenario.

4. *Increasingly violent rhetoric* – This may indicate that the group has reached a level of critical 'fervour' and is ready to take the first step towards actualizing its rhetoric and triggering an apocalyptic scenario.

5. *Struggle for leadership* – Owing to the unstable nature of the leadership and the volatility of the group, any situation which threatens the leader's control could result in violence. Examples include the challenging of group beliefs by dissidents and the questioning of the leader's physical health. All of these put the power of the leadership in question, and, by extension, its fundamental apocalyptic vision.

Annex I presents a brief table summarizing the preceding characteristics and serves as a quick reference guide.

A Canadian Example – The Order of the Solar Temple

The Order of the Solar Temple was a group espousing millennialist beliefs which met the preceding criteria of a Doomsday Religious Movement. The Order had members in the US, Quebec, Switzerland and France; in 1994, fifty-four members committed mass suicide. The group was composed of several leaders who were very charismatic and expert public speakers, and who also had aggrandized beliefs about themselves. They believed in an imminent ecological apocalypse, where members were the 'chosen ones' to repopulate the earth after its demise, but not before they had been persecuted on the earthly plane by non-believers. Other attributes typical of a Doomsday Religious Movement were the high degree of control exercised over members, the promotion of bigamy within the group, and the physical withdrawal to a rural area. The alleged criminal activities of the Solar Temple (money laundering, drug and arms trafficking) were clear threats to public safety, as was the infiltration of political and business circles by several members.

The Solar Temple mobilized for their coming apocalypse by acquiring weapons and money. This prompted several high-profile investigations and arrests which could have hastened the suicide. This was an early warning sign: a humiliating circumstance running counter to their supposed glorious salvation before the onslaught of the apocalypse. Other events which could have enhanced the feeling of humiliation included: an investigation initiated by the public utility into the Order's infiltration of their company; the near bankruptcy of the Order and the loss of investor capital; then, negative media attention. Finally, other early-warning signs immediately preceded the mass suicide and signalled that their potential for violence could be soon realized: a recent change in leadership; the failing health of one of the leaders; and foreboding, violent statements made by members.

The violence of the incident left 48 people dead in Switzerland and five in Quebec. Had the group believed that its salvation was tied to a direct conflict with the 'enemy' and the leaders opted for 'enemy eradication' rather than escape via mass suicide, the risk to members of the public would have been serious.

Conclusions – Continuing Threats to Canada

The irrationality which underlines the threat posed by Doomsday Religious Movements constitutes a different threat to public safety than that posed by the calculated terrorism traditionally manifested in the last 50 years, usually in support of an identified political cause. One estimation indicates that there are 1,200 active cults throughout the world, and that roughly 400 subscribe to doomsday philosophies which foresee catastrophe on or around the year 2000. While it is not known which cults have the potential for violence, this does not imply that possible threats posed by Doomsday Religious Movements should be ignored, as they can quickly manifest themselves in a variety of forms. Rather, there clearly is a continuing threat potential, given the temporal inaccuracies of the turning of the millennium (various scientific and religious accounts offer competing evidence as to when the new millennium will actually begin) and the tendency for groups to be unpredictable and give early-warning signs of their potential for violence, as well as ambiguities in their structure, dynamics and attributes.

ANNEX I
THE APOCALYPTIC CULT CHECKLIST

Characteristics	Threats	Early Warning Signs
Apocalyptic Beliefs	*Democratic*	
* dualism	*Governance*	
* the persecuted chosen	*Weapons Acquisition*	
* imminence	* firearms	* Intensification of illegal
* determinism	* explosives	activities
* salvation through conflict	* chemical/biological	* Humiliating
Charismatic Leadership	weapons	circumstances
* control over members	*Institutional*	* Relocation to a rural
* lack of restraint	*Infiltration*	area
* withdrawal	* political	* Increasingly violent
Actions by Authorities	* business	rhetoric
* lack of comprehension	*Criminal Activity*	* Struggle for leadership
* unsound negotiation	* crimes against	
* hasty action	individuals	
* spiral of amplification	* transnational crime	

ANNEX II
REFERENCES AND SUGGESTED READING

Internet Addresses
The Center for Millennial Studies http://www.mille.org/
Cult Awareness and Information Centre http://www.caic.org.au/
AFF http://www.csj.org/
FactNet http://www.factnet.org/
Info-Cult http://www.infocult.org/
Ontario Consultants on Religious Tolerance http://www.religioustolerance.org/

Monographs
Bainbridge, William S. (1997). *The Sociology of Religious Movements*. New York: Routledge.
Bromley, David G. & Jeffrey K. Hadden, eds. (1993). *The Handbook of Cults and Sects in America*. Greenwich, CT and London: Association for the Sociology of religion and JAI Press.
Dawson, Lorne L., ed. (1996). *Cults in Context: Readings in the Study of New Religious Movements*. Toronto: Scholar's Press.
Gesy, Lawrence J. (1993). *Destructive Cults and Movements*. Huntington, IN: Our Sunday Visitor, Inc.
Introvigne, Massimo. (1996). *Les Veilleurs de l'Apocalypse: Millénarisme et nouvelles religions au seuil de l'an 2000*. Paris: Claire Vigne.
Kaplan, Jeffrey. (1997). *Radical Religion in America: Millennial Movements from the Far Right to the Children of Noah*. Syracuse, NY: Syracuse University Press.
Lewis, James R. (1998). *The Encyclopedia of Cults, Sects, and New Religions*. Buffalo, NY: Prometheus Books.
Miller, Timothy. (1991). *When Prophets Die: The Postcharismatic Fate of New Religious Movements*. New York: State University of New York Press.
Robbins, Thomas & Susan Palmer, eds. (1997) *Millennium, Messiah, and Mayhem*. New York: Routledge.
Saliba, John A. (1995). *Perspectives on New Religious Movements*. London: Geoffrey Chapman.
Scotland, Nigel. (1995). *Charismatics and the Next Millennium*. Hodder & Stoughton.
Stark, Rodney & William Sims Bainbridge. (1996). *Religion, Deviance, and Social Control*. New York: Routledge.
Storr, Anthony. (1997). *Feet of Clay – Saints, Sinners, and Madmen: A Study of Gurus*. New York: The Free Press.
Strozier, Charles B. (1994). *Apocalypse: On the Psychology of Fundamentalism in America*. Boston: Beacon Press.
Wilson, Bryan & Jamie Cresswell, eds. (1999). *New Religious Movements: Challenge and Response*. London: Routledge.

4

Events at the End of the Millennium: Possible Implications for the Public Order in Jerusalem

EHUD SPRINZAK, YA'AKOV ARIEL, URI NE'EMAN and AMNON RAMON

Internal Report Submitted to the Jerusalem Institute for Israel Studies

Confidential: Not for Distribution

September 1999

Executive Summary[1]

1. This research group found no evidence for a catastrophic terror act to be conducted in Jerusalem on the eve or shortly after the advent of the millennium. It consequently believes that the likelihood of such act is very small.

2. Conclusion no. 1 should be qualified by the two following considerations:

One) We may not have reached all the relevant information including secretive terror plans or well kept conspiracies.

Two) We cannot rule out a fluid and dynamic situation in which a millennium-related ecstasy will produce a catastrophic act in Jerusalem despite the lack of early evidence and visible preparations.

3. Due to the risks involved in conclusion no. 2, this report offers five categories of information and recommendations:

One) A series of potential (though largely unlikely) scenarios for disorderly acts in Jerusalem that range from catastrophic operations on the Temple Mount to riots and demonstrations in the city. Each scenario is followed by a set of early warning indicators.

Two) Detailed recommendations for a proper intelligence and security force deployment in order to detect and prevent potential acts of millennium-related disorder.

Three) A detailed list of potential sources of information on Christian millenarian organizations worldwide.

Four) A list of Israeli sites most vulnerable for millennium-related disruptive action, and a list of sensitive dates for exceptional religious events in the coming year.

Five) A broad appendix on Jerusalem on the eve of 2000 from the perspective of Christian groups that operate in and around the city.

Preface

The approaching end of the second millennium – according to the Christian count, which has been adopted by the entire modern world – is arousing anxieties and hopes among 'believers' who draw their faith from religious-eschatological sources as well as among various 'eccentrics.' The anxieties concern natural disasters, such as earthquakes, storms, and plagues, and a horrific war of Armageddon, a man-made calamity, which will 'purge' the land and its inhabitants of the 'evil' that has seized them; while the hopes are that the disasters will usher in a 'messianic age' when the world will be blessed by the reappearance of the 'son of God' – Jesus Christ – and the onset of a 'golden age.'

The disasters are liable to strike anywhere in the world, but the 'messiah' will appear only in the place where he lived and was active – in the Land of Israel. Therefore, the believers maintain that land will be an arena fraught with both terrible events and miracles of surpassing importance. As a result, Israel and the territories of the Palestinian Authority are liable to become a magnet for individuals with an apocalyptic frame of mind who will make a pilgrimage to the 'Holy Land' either to witness the events or to take an active part in them.

Most of the believers in the 'end of days' and in the 'coming of the messiah' who will come to Israel are naive and sincere people who will wish to be passive observers to the events and will comply with the orders of the law enforcement authorities. However, there may be a few who think that the rush to the 'end of days' should be 'speeded up' by means of actions that will 'hasten' and 'ensure' its arrival. Such actions could assume a variety of forms, ranging from attempts to sabotage places that are holy to the various religions, to public suicide – due to unbearable disappointment, among other reasons – and thus not only severely disrupt the orderly life of the Israeli and Palestinian publics and of the many foreign tourists, but also foment, in an extreme case, a political or diplomatic crisis with unforetellable consequences.

We need to bear in mind that the end of the millennium is also a time of symbolic significance to many people who do not expect far-reaching changes in human existence but want to combine a visit to the country with the special events that the various authorities are planning for the extraordinary occasion. Millions of tourists are expected to stream into the country next year, and both Israel and the Palestinian Authority are readying themselves to make their stay a pleasant one and to reap the economic fruits of the tourism boom. At the same time, we cannot ignore the possibility that the crush of tourists and other visitors at the holy places on the critical dates will create problems, and will certainly add to the already onerous burden of the law enforcement authorities should a critical event occur at one or more of the sites.

It should also be recalled that in early May 1999 the interim agreement between Israel and the Palestinian Authority expired – though the PA agreed to refrain from taking unilateral measures and to wait until after the elections in Israel for the negotiations to resume. Both sides are contemplating how to continue the diplomatic process, and it should be taken into account that in the absence of an agreement the Palestinian Authority is liable to declare unilaterally the establishment of a 'Palestinian state with Jerusalem as its capital.' Such a move if it occurs close to the end of the millennium or slightly afterward, could have the effect of pouring oil on already troubled waters.

This possibility exists with respect to an elected political authority, which accepts in principle the rules of the game that are followed in international relations. Yet, even if the PA acts responsibly and avoids taking unilateral steps, the tension between Israel and the Palestinians could still intensify. Extremists, from Hamas for example, could exploit the advent of the millennium and the events that will accompany it to perpetrate serious acts of terrorism in an effort to shock the world and the media, compelling them to focus their attention on the Middle East.

But in addition to Muslim and Arab fundamentalists and terrorists, others too, including 'believing' Christians and extremist Jews, either individually or in small groups, could, citing similar religious and political reasons, sow terrorism and destruction, disrupt normal life, and set back the processes of conciliation between the two peoples and the three religions by many decades.

Clearly, then, the study of the millennialist phenomenon has many facets. The main task and contribution of the present study, which was undertaken within the framework of the Jerusalem Institute for Israel Studies, lie not in the religious-eschatological sphere but rather are to be found in the day-to-day realm of security and protection. Thus, the purpose of the report is to spotlight individuals and groups that are prone to abnormal activity, and to identify in advance negative phenomena and worrying actions.

The aim of the authors is to assist the authorities responsible for maintaining law and order in whatever way they can to execute their mission of maintaining public order and ensuring public safety.

Worst-case Scenarios

Possible scenarios involving groups of Christian 'believers'

The scenarios dealing with possible activity by groups of Christian believers can be divided into three main types:

(a) Activity by a mission-driven **cohesive group** headed or led by a charismatic figure. All or most of the members of this group have prepared **consciously and openly** for the year 2000 and do not hide their intention of perpetrating an action, or a series of actions, which will change the course of events and the existing order with the aim of hastening 'the coming of the messiah.'

(b) Activity by a small mission-driven **cohesive group** operating as a close-knit team. The members of such a group have prepared long and *secretly* to carry out a shocking act that will foment the desired change.

(c) Activity by a **homogeneous group** which idolizes its leader, who, in the course of a visit to one of the holy places, suddenly feels that the holy spirit has descended on him and that he has been '**chosen**' to announce and bring forward the coming of the messiah. By the force of his charisma, he induces the group to perform extreme acts in order to 'hasten the end.'

It is proposed that the danger of the public order being disrupted in Jerusalem and at other trouble-prone places in 2000–2001 by Christian messianic *groups* be analyzed along a sequential line extending from catastrophic terrorist activity and friction to local disruptions of order caused by dense crowds of Christian pilgrims. The proposed scenarios are based on a worst-case analysis, and therefore each should be viewed as a small sequential line, which incorporates several additional possibilities.

Scenario No. 1: Christian catastrophic terrorism on the Temple Mount

This scenario focuses on North American groups belonging to the 'Christian Identity' school. These are *anti-Semitic*, racist, radical organizations based in the northwestern United States, which are convinced that the Jews and their allies control America. The Christian Identity groups, which are connected with and exert an influence on armed militias and on a large network of American 'hate organizations', bear a messianic character. As such, they have been convinced for some years that the Second Coming of the messiah will take place around the year 2000, when the world will also be purged of the wicked.

Thus, for quite a long time these groups have been preparing themselves for the end of the world, which they believe will occur after an Armageddon war in which the majority of humanity will be wiped out. Nuclear arms as well as biological and chemical weapons will be unleashed in the apocalyptic battle. Some of these groups live in isolated areas in Idaho, Montana, and Washington state, where they are accumulating arms and explosives, undergoing intensive arms training, and preparing for an all-out racial–religious war. One of the most popular end-of-the-world scenarios espoused by these groups is found in *The Turner Diaries* (by William Pierce writing under the pen name of Andrew Macdonald, 1978). This fictional work describes the last war in great detail, including the launching of nuclear missiles from Vandenberg Air Force base in California at Israel.

It is important to note that the apocalyptic visions of the Christian Identity groups, including the war Armageddon, are to materialize not in Israel but in the United States and do not entail any dramatic events in Jerusalem. Nor is there any indication that these groups have ever considered undertaking missionary or any other type of activity in the Land of Israel. The Christian Identity doctrine does not relate to the Jews as the 'chosen people' but as the 'mud people', a kind of premature attempt by God to create human beings before he created the white Aryans, who are the true Jews of the Scriptures, the descendants of the Ten Tribes.

The reason for the inclusion here of the Christian Identity groups as risk groups is their vast hatred of Jews and Israel and their awareness of the dramatic character of the millennium year in Jerusalem, perhaps also entailing the possibility that the war of Armageddon can be ignited easily in the city.

Even though it is very unlikely that any of these groups will try to operate in Israel, a possible scenario of this kind can be constructed:

(a) The charismatic leader of a Christian Identity group arrives at the rational conclusion that the most volatile place on earth, and the nearest to Armageddon, is Israel. Alternatively, this leader experiences a divine revelation in which he is given the task of initiating the end of the world by perpetrating an act of terrorism in Israel.

(b) The impulse to carry out a radical operation in Israel is heightened by the 'persecution' of the FBI, which frustrate the group's efforts to spark a world war. An action in Jerusalem, and more specifically on the Temple Mount, where Jews and Muslims clash, looms as an attractive possibility. The leader's thinking and planning is also nourished by the broad media coverage of the year 2000 events in Jerusalem, including a papal visit.

(c) The mission is assigned to a small squad from the group, which includes a demolition officer and a number of former US soldiers from the cult who have attended military refresher courses at the group's ranch in Idaho. Their operative plan is to enter Israel as part of a large group of pilgrims visiting the holy places.

(d) The group's members carry a large quantity of plastic explosives, which they conceal in double-bottom suitcases. They intend to purchase pistols from Muslim elements or via the underworld in Jerusalem.

(e) In Israel the members of the squad split off from the group of pilgrims with which they arrived and check into a hotel in East Jerusalem, which becomes their base as they begin to collect intelligence information for their operation on the Temple Mount. Their plan is to dress up as Muslims in long *galabias* beneath which a belt of explosives can be worn, join the Friday prayers, conceal themselves in a corner of Al-Aqsa Mosque after the services end, plant their hidden bombs in appropriate places, and detonate them afterward by remote control. Escape routes are planned but the squad members are also prepared to sacrifice themselves.

(f) Dry runs of the operation are carried out for two weeks and various technical problems are solved. As part of their preparations, the squad practices blending in with the Muslim worshippers and overcoming the language problem.

(g) On Friday evening, al-Aqsa Mosque (or the Dome of the Rock) is propelled into the heavens.

Early warning indicators

1. References in the group's literature to options for operating in Jerusalem and statements linking an upcoming Armageddon to activity in Israel.
2. Signs that the group is organizing to go to Israel.
3. The appearance in Israel of an advance contingent from the group, or of its leader.
4. Identification in Israel of signs that the group is preparing for its mission, including attempts to acquire weapons.
5. Reports by informants of recurring visits and observations made by pilgrims on the Temple Mount.

Scenario No. 2: Terrorist outburst by a fraction of a group

This scenario is based on a generalization and expansion of an actual event: the case of Dennis Michael Rohan, who in August 1969 burst into the plaza in front of Al-Aqsa Mosque and succeeded in setting the structure ablaze.

The fire, it will be recalled, triggered serious rioting on the Temple Mount, resulting in deaths, and generated fierce condemnations of Israel by the international community. Rohan was a member of the Australia-based Church of God, a charismatic evangelical group, and came to Israel as a volunteer on Kibbutz Mishmar Hasharon. A few weeks later he set out on his mission to purge the Temple Mount in order to prepare the ground for the building of the temple – a precondition for Jesus' return, in Rohan's perception. Rohan belonged to the extremist wing of the Church of God, which was far more messianic and radical than the mainstream. He was impelled to act by his deep disappointment that even though two years had passed since the Jews liberated the Temple Mount, the Israeli government had as yet taken no action toward demolishing the mosques there and building a new temple.

Rohan acted alone but displayed considerable sophistication. In order to prepare himself, he carried out an advance visit to the Temple Mount in which he familiarized himself with the details of the site. He carried the flammable material under his shirt and used a small pipe to spray them on the mosque.

After his trial, Rohan was deported to Australia on grounds of insanity. However, it is far from clear whether he was clinically insane or an eccentric radical believer who was defined as insane in order to spare the Israelis and the Palestinians further unpleasantness and mutual recriminations of the kind that followed the severe disturbances on the Temple Mount.

The scenario thus develops as follows:

(a) A respectable evangelical group about which no suspicions are harbored arrives for a visit to Jerusalem in 2000.

(b) Operating on the fringes of the large group are extremist, ultra-messianic circles which are not known to the authorities. While in Jerusalem these zealots become intensely radicalized because of their disappointment at the fact that Jesus has not materialized. Chafing at the bit to begin with, these believers become less patient with every passing day.

(c) A lone believer of the Rohan type, or a small group that is under the sway of this loner, secretly plans an unsophisticated sabotage operation, probably involving arson. To prepare for this, several observation visits to the site are made by the leader or the whole group.

(d) On the day of the operation, they come to the Temple Mount in the guise of innocent visitors, or perhaps dressed as Muslims, concealing the flammable material beneath their clothing in small plastic containers. Just as Rohan did (or perhaps after misleading the Waqf guards by a diversionary action) they set fire to Al-Aqsa Mosque.

Early warning indicators

1. The appearance in Jerusalem of a group of moderate evangelicals accompanied by radical fringe that does not accept the authority of the group's leader.

2. Extreme, messianic-driven behavior of the radical splinter group and its repeated visits to certain holy places, particularly the Temple Mount. A flow of information concerns catastrophic statements by members of the group in favor of sabotage to hasten the coming of the messiah.
3. Signs that members of the group or individuals are collecting and storing flammables or explosives.

Scenario No. 3: Activity by a Christian evangelical group on the Temple Mount

The third scenario focuses on Christian evangelical and messianic groups that are awaiting with hope the advent of Jesus and the great rupture that will destroy the world as we know it and herald mankind's redemption in 2000. These are philosemitic groups that take a positive view of Israel's role, including the role played by the messianic settlers in the territories. That identification, which in the past has generated deep friendship and political support for Israel against the Arabs and the Palestinians, is based on the belief that Israel's establishment followed by the Six Day War of 1967, and particularly the conquest of Jerusalem in that war, are events of Christian eschatological significance, heralding the second coming of Jesus and the final redemption.

It is important to note that in contrast to the Christian Identity organizations, many of which are armed and espouse an aggressively militant orientation, the evangelical groups are not violent and have no experience in political terrorism. Evangelical zealotry is overwhelmingly characterized by hypernomic religious behavior. Direct violent activity by such groups is thus of low probability, but it should be taken into account that they are liable to disrupt the public order on the Temple Mount even without resorting to violence, by intense praying, aggressive sit-in strikes and refusal to leave.

Another variation is an extreme scenario according to which such groups, or some of their members, might be induced to act by Jews who want to see a catastrophic action perpetrated on the Temple Mount. As is well known, some messianic Jewish groups seek the destruction of the Dome of the Rock ('the abomination') because it stands exactly on the spot where the third temple is to be built. In 1982 one of these groups, led by Yehuda Etzion, was ready to blow up the Dome of the Rock by itself. Although no Jewish groups are at present known to have concrete violent plans, some of them have not forsaken their dream of seeing the Temple Mount 'purged' of the mosques.

This scenario, then, is based on the quite hypothetical assumption that extremist Jewish groups, such as the Kahanists (followers of the slain Rabbi Meir Kahane) or others with a fixation on purifying the Temple Mount, will seek to take advantage of Christian messianic enthusiasm relating to the year 2000 and activate evangelical friends to carry out the sacred blast. The likelihood of this will increase if the Israeli-Palestinian negotiations on a permanent agreement (including the possible evacuation of settlements and Israeli concessions in Jerusalem) make progress and the Jewish messianic believers are seized by a despondent, even catastrophic, frame of mind. Aware of the close surveillance to which they and their supporters are subjected by the security services, they might

try to induce evangelicals who are not known to the authorities to perpetrate the
great act of sabotage for them.

The following scenario illustrates one model of a possible course of events:

(a) As part of their pilgrimage to Jerusalem, some members of a charismatic
    Pentecostal evangelical group visit the Temple Institute in the city; run by
    Rabbi Israel Ariel, the Institute's aim is to reconstruct with biblical and
    halakhic accuracy the instruments and utensils that were used for making
    sacrifices in the Temple. Some members of the group visited the institute in
    the past and were deeply impressed. The current visit leads to a series of
    meetings between messianic Jews and Christians at which views about the
    coming deliverance of the world are exchanged.

    Seeing the tremendous messianic fervor of their Christian interlocutors,
    the members of the Jewish group believe that it will be possible to persuade
    some of the more impassioned Christians to take action on the Temple Mount.
    The small circle of messianic Christians is in fact manipulated by the Jews into
    believing that God expects them to fire the first shot in the war of
    Armageddon.

(b) The task that is given to the small Christian group, which trains under the
    watchful eyes of the Jewish 'organizers', is to plant explosives in one of the
    Temple Mount shrines. The explosion itself will be triggered by the Jews via
    remote control. The Christians also undergo a brief course in sabotage
    techniques.

(c) The plan calls for the Christians to dress up as Muslims wearing *galabias*
    under which the explosives can be concealed. They will join the Friday
    prayers on the Temple Mount and afterward hide in one of the corners of Al-
    Aqsa Mosque or the Dome of the Rock, where they will plant the explosives.
    The members of the group do not intend to commit suicide, but driven by their
    belief that deliverance and the resurrection of the dead are at hand, they are
    ready for self-sacrifice if necessary.

(d) Dry runs of the operation take place over a two-week period during which all
    the technical problems are resolved.

(e) On Friday evening a huge explosion turns the Dome of the Rock into a heap
    of rubble.

A secondary scenario to the one described above is based on the idea of the 'two
witnesses.' According to the Revelation of John (Chapter XI), two witnesses are
to ascend to the Temple Mount and testify there before the people. Anyone who
tries to injure them will be put to death. After they have completed their testimony,
according to the vision, the 'beast' will arise from the depths of hell and kill them,
but after three and a half days (some say three and a half years) they will return to
life. This vision could become the basis for concrete action by extremist
millenarian Christians and by extremist Jews who will 'recruit' naive Christians to
execute a 'provocation' of this type.

As noted, the possibility also exists of overt action, initially nonviolent, such
as a demonstration or a sit-down strike, which will generate friction with the Waqf
officials and the Muslim public, triggering an outburst of emotions, severe rioting,
and loss of control.

Early warning indicators

1. Enthusiastic statements in the group's literature about imminent redemption in Jerusalem.
2. Members of the group forge intense ties with Jewish groups that are active with regard to the Temple Mount.
3. Severe radicalization within the Israeli extreme right caused by progress in the peace negotiations and identification of signs of despair within the Temple Mount groups.
4. Indications of operative meetings between the Christian evangelical group and extremists in the Temple Mount organizations.
5. Agents report on meetings and operative plans.

Scenario No. 4: Attempted suicide in Jerusalem

The fourth scenario relates to new and as yet not fully established Christian groups. These groups are relevant here because they believe that Jerusalem is the connecting link in the contact that is expected in 2000 between heaven and earth and between believers and God. Some groups believe in aliens and in objects from space on which Jesus will arrive, or which will carry the believers aloft in a storm. The groups usually have a charismatic leader who is in total control of the members' life and belief. The followers are deeply isolated from the external world, including their families, and are so dependent on their leader that they are ready to take their lives at his command in order to gain redemption. Past groups belonging to this category include the Solar Temple; Heaven's Gate, the Concerned Christians, and perhaps also the Davidians (followers of David Koresh). Such groups may come to Jerusalem in 2000 in order to seek deliverance and commit collective suicide if that does not occur. Although such an act is not comparable to an attack by external groups on religious shrines, the Israeli authorities clearly have no interest in its occurrence. Moreover, it is possible that the authorities' efforts to prevent acts of despair could spark clashes between these groups and the police, resulting in a heavy loss of life, as occurred in Waco, Texas.

A possible scenario could unfold as follows:

(a) An American (or Korean, or European, or South American) religious group arrives in Israel with one-way tickets and members burning their passports. The head of the sect assures the believers that the end of the world is at hand and that Jesus will arrive immediately after the advent of the new year borne by a meteor in order to redeem mankind. In the meantime, prayer and spiritual purification must be undertaken to prepare for his arrival. At the same time, the members of the group are warned about the possible presence of the Antichrist, the representative of Satan, who is liable to disrupt the final stages of the redemption.

(b) Aware of searches and other preventive activities of the Israeli police, the group's leaders instruct members to maintain a low profile, hide in both new and old Jerusalem, and prepare for possible disruptions of their activity. The heads of the group rent a house around Abu Dis, a Palestinian village just east of Jerusalem, and manage not to attract undue attention. Members of the cult are given poison capsules, to be taken in case of emergency. The group's leader and some of his assistants obtain a number of firearms illegally.

(c) As the new year approaches, the messianic tension within the group mounts steadily. The leader delivers fiery sermons promising that redemption is at hand. The presence of tens of thousands of pilgrims in Jerusalem only heightens expectations. Group members are convinced that the end is near.

(d) Nothing happens during or after the arrival of the new year and the pressure within the group rises dramatically. The leader, who promised imminent redemption, is under particularly heavy pressure. The result is that he reinforces his pledge that the end of the world is imminent and the group prepares to take the first step to spur the coming of the messiah who, they believe, is already at the door. The group shows signs of early preparation for collective suicide.

(e) The police find out about the group and are gearing up for action. The residence of the group – they are all now under one roof – is placed under continuous surveillance. A few members discover the surveillance team but are instantly arrested.

(f) A violent clash erupts between the security forces and the other members of the group, during which most of them commit suicide while the others are subdued with loss of life on both sides.

Early warning indicators

1. Identification of a group headed to Jerusalem via the written or electronic media; complaints of anxious relatives; catastrophic statements by members.
2. The group's charismatic leader talks about an imminent end of the world.
3. Purchase of one-way tickets to Israel and reports about plans to burn passports upon arrival.
4. Signs of mounting messianic and fatalistic tension within the group.
5. The group isolates itself from the world and from its immediate surroundings and prepares obsessively for the end of the world.
6. Information about poisons, weapons, and explosives in the group's possession.

Scenario No. 5: Aggressive proselytizing

The fifth scenario focuses on Christian evangelical groups or Judeo-Christian sects (such as Jehovah's Witnesses, Jews for Jesus, etc.) that come to Jerusalem for the millennium year events and in expectation of Jesus' imminent revelation. Stirred by powerful emotions and by the belief that when the day comes the Jews, too, will grasp the meaning of Christian redemption (which will be vouchsafed even to non-Christians who understand and identify with the act), they undertake missionary activity in Jerusalem. Their activity is nourished also by the belief that the conversion of the Jews will pave the way for the Second Coming. The scenario of disruption to the public order unfolds as follows:

(a) A Judeo-Christian group (Jehovah's Witnesses, perhaps) distributes Bibles and Christian pamphlets promising redemption. Missionaries who are 'filled with love' wander the streets of Jerusalem and particularly the disadvantaged neighborhoods, trying to persuade anyone who will listen that the great moment is at hand. The presence of tens of thousands of pilgrims in the city creates a broad panorama for this missionary activity and also creates the mistaken impression that it is taking place on a massive scale.

(b) In the ultra-Orthodox quarter of Me'a She'arim and among the Eda Haredit sect there is mounting anger over what appears to be a missionary assault on Jerusalem. An ongoing series of special prayers and lamentations begins, and savage lampoons appear on the walls of the ultra-Orthodox areas against the missionaries, 'may their names be blotted out' for 'corrupting the souls of the young' and 'threatening our existence, heaven forbid.'

(c) Members of the ultra-Orthodox Yad Leachim group, which seeks to root out desecration of this kind, place the missionaries under surveillance and report to their rabbis about the imminent danger of forced conversion. Large-scale demonstrations are organized calling on the government to put a stop to the influx of Christian pilgrims and preserve Jerusalem.

(d) The 'commando unit' of the Eda Haredit (led by Yehuda Meshi-Zahav) decides to act and carries out a number of night raids on the missionaries and on other Christian groups, which are not engaged in proselytization. Apartments are torched, young men and even women are beaten up. A huge public outcry goes up. The extensive coverage in the international media causes a severe drop in tourism to the city.

Early warning indicators

1. High-visibility missionary activity.
2. Outcries and protests by the ultra-Orthodox.
3. Information on the increasing involvement of Yad Leachim.
4. Lampoons condemning the missionaries appear on walls of Me'a She'arim.
5. Public warnings by rabbis and anti-missionary rulings issued by the Badatz (ultra-Orthodox rabbinical court).
   (A similar scenario could be developed with regard to the Muslims in East Jerusalem.)

Scenario No. 6: Disruption of the public order due to a crush of visitors and overcrowding that goes out of control

This scenario does not involve either political or religious violence. It has to do with sheer overcrowding, the authorities' inability to control several large groups of pilgrims simultaneously, and dangerous situations of a crush in narrow places such as the Via Dolorosa or the Church of the Holy Sepulcher. The scenario relates to a mass panic in a situation of severe overcrowding, with people who are trying to flee being trampled beneath the onrushing crowd.

Early warning indicators

Overbooking in hotels in various parts of the country, overcrowding and chaos at Christian tourist sites, and international reports about occurrences of disorder in Jerusalem and other sacred sites.

Scenarios involving a lone Christian 'believer'

Two basic scenarios suggest themselves in this connection:

- In one, a believer experiences a 'revelation' in his regular place of residence and then embarks on a pilgrimage to the 'Holy Land' in order to execute the will of God as he was commanded.
- The second scenario involves a believer who is moved by his experience at a holy place to commit aberrant acts – the 'Jerusalem syndrome.'

Scenario No. 7: The 'lone believer'

Among the tens of thousands of Christian evangelical faithful who are organizing to make pilgrimages to the holy places is a group from Atlanta, Georgia. Its leader is a young cleric in his early thirties who had experienced a 'revelation' while serving as a soldier in the Gulf War. After the war, the priest, who served in the army as a demolition expert, began to feel that he must devote his life to correcting his ways and the ways of the world. Since his discharge he has devoted himself to studying the Scriptures and helping distressed youngsters. His activity, his way of life, and his charismatic personality have gained him respect in his community, and a group of young whites and blacks view him as a spiritual mentor whose word is law.

The approaching millennium and the recent events in Iraq led the young cleric to believe that on or around Christmas 2000; extraordinary occurrences can be expected in the region, centering around an attempt by the 'Satan' Saddam Hussein to destroy the Christian holy places in the Holy Land. Neither the US administration nor the governments of the Middle East, including Israel, are aware of this terrible danger.

In order to shake the authorities out of their complacency and alert them to what lies in store, the cleric concludes that he and a select group of followers have no choice but to commit collective suicide at one of the stations on the Via Dolorosa on a suitable date in December 1999.

As an experienced army man, he knows that if his plans are exposed prematurely they will fail, and therefore keeps his idea strictly to himself. He arrives in Israel around the middle of December with his group in the guise of innocent pilgrims and they lodge in a hotel in or around Jerusalem. After visiting various sites in the city, he decides on the place and sets the date for the suicide.

On the appointed day he leads his group to the chosen site and sets himself ablaze, calling on the others to follow suit.

A more reasonable scenario involves a pilgrim who falls victim to the 'Jerusalem syndrome.' While visiting the Temple Mount he goes out of his mind and runs amok, clashing with the Waqf guards, sparking an outburst of passions and a mass disturbance. Possibly this act could also lead to violent activity such as arson or shooting (as in the cases of Michael Rohan and Allen Goodman).

Early warning indicators

Probably there will be none, apart perhaps from reports by field informants about recurrent wandering about by a suspicious pilgrim.

Scenario No. 8: Disruption by radical nationalist and fundamentalist movements

The scenarios in this case derive from the assumption that the masses of tourists who will visit the holy places in order to view and take part in the events of the year 2000, and the accompanying worldwide media coverage, could spur nationalist and religious-fundamentalist terrorists to act. Their purpose would be to draw the world's attention to their existence, both in order to advance their causes and to disrupt and thwart the diplomatic process between Israel and the Palestinians, which they abhor.

The perpetrators of terrorist acts of this kind could be:

(a) Palestinian religious fanatics from Hamas or Islamic Jihad.
(b) Lebanese Shiite religious fanatics from the Hezbollah organization, or Shiites of other nationalities who are recruited for the mission by the organization.
(c) Jewish religious fanatics.
(d) A lone Muslim or Jewish fanatic.

Among the operations that extremists of this kind are liable to carry out:

(a) Terrorists attack a holy place during a mass gathering by detonating a bomb planted there earlier using a remote, automatic mechanism.
(b) A terrorist suicide squad attacks a holy place during a mass gathering by blowing themselves up or opening fire on the crowd.
(c) A large-scale terrorist attack is perpetrated at a site of special sanctity when it is closed to the public by means of arson or a powerful explosion, which destroys the site or damages it irreparably.

Early warning indicators

Informants reporting of unusual and intense frenzy, and secretive mobilization.

Scenario No. 9: Potential attack by an Islamic group

It is difficult to ignore the attraction that huge crowds of Christian pilgrims in Jerusalem will have for radical terrorist groups such as Hamas and Islamic Jihad. The possibility (albeit a faint one) exists that they will detonate a bomb in a large crowd of pilgrims in order to embarrass Israel and tarnish its name while also undermining the potential atmosphere of peace and conciliation. This scenario could become more concrete if significant progress is made in the peace process and the radical groups that oppose any change conclude that the only way to stop the process is by means of horrific acts of terrorism. In this situation we cannot rule out a parallel initiative by a Jewish messianic group which has been unsuccessful in its efforts to recruit Christian volunteers for an operation on the Temple Mount.

Indicators

Information from informants or undercover agents about intentions.

Organizing Undercover Intelligence Activity

It is axiomatic that in order to deploy optimally for the events under consideration here, the first order of business is to organize undercover intelligence activity. Whether in connection with the events being planned by the official religious agencies in Israel and the Palestinian Authority, or in connection with possible negative actions that religious extremists, whether individuals or groups, will try to perpetrate, undercover activity and surveillance has three goals in the run-up period to the millennium:

(a) To preempt any attempt to exploit the 'millennium period' in order to further the dreams and ambitions of the various fanatic elements and to prevent, as far as possible, any effort to disrupt the normal course of life in the coming two or three years.

(b) To deploy optimally in order to forestall disruptions to the events being planned by the official bodies.

(c) To reduce damage resulting from events that spin out of control and to minimize the consequences of actions and operations that various fanatics will succeed in carrying out despite the preventive efforts.

The purpose of this organizing will be to:

(a) Obtain relevant prior information about violence-prone groups and individuals. With this information, it will be possible to implement multilayered preventive and protective measures to prevent these groups or individuals from entering Israel, uncover their attempts to position themselves in the country, block their efforts to carry out their plans, and of course ensure that they do not get close to sensitive sites at or near which they intend to act.

(b) Improve and sharpen the ability of the responsible law-and-order enforcement authorities to make prior identification of aberrant individuals and negative phenomena.

(c) Train professionals to acquire expertise in the way of life, culture, and language of millenarians. These experts can then be attached at any time to the available skilled task forces to ensure optimal handling of extremists should they succeed in taking over an arena or seizing a group for bargaining purposes.

All this, of course, needs to occur in addition to and above and beyond the optimal operational deployment of the forces that are responsible for preserving law and order during routine periods and ahead of and during planned public events.

Obtaining Advance Information

Obtaining relevant advance information entails comprehensive collection activity mainly in the arenas in which the target groups and individuals are likely to originate – that is, primarily the United States and Canada, though also certain countries in Europe, South America, and the Far East, where active messianic movements exist, or where specific groups are known to live in expectation of 'the end of the world.' Collecting information about such groups is of course the responsibility of the security agencies in these countries, and therefore the Israeli security bodies – the police, the Shin Bet (General Security Service), the Mossad espionage agency, and the Prime Minister's Anti-terrorism Adviser – should be in contact with the security and intelligence authorities in the relevant countries and urge them to take action. Special importance in this connection attaches to the security authorities in Jordan, the Palestinian Authority, and of course the United States. However, it is precisely in the United States, where most of the 'messianic' groups are concentrated, that the ability of the authorized body, the FBI, to act, collect information, and conduct investigations is limited; other avenues should therefore be tried.

It is important to point out from the beginning that even though the messianic-Christian scenario anticipates riots, acts of violence, and various shock events as 'heralding' the 'coming of the messiah', the overwhelming majority of the Christians who believe in the messiah are law-abiding citizens. These broad publics object to the use of violence and certainly to terrorism. In addition, it needs to be said that while the eschatological anticipation of certain millenarian groups is that the Jews will rebuild the Temple before the advent of the messiah, only a very few will be willing to resort to violence and illegal acts in order to hasten that development.

Moreover, the conclusion reached by those who are familiar with and knowledgeable about the mainstream Christian messianic movement in the United States is that many of its adherents, including spiritual leaders, will be ready to cooperate in surveillance activity over the militant groups and to convey to the responsible law-and-order authorities any information that may obtain, or already possess, about them.

That said, we recommend that special attention nevertheless be paid to two types of groups: 'post-Christian' and 'latter-day':

Groups that believe in a connection between UFOs and the end of days

Although these are not regular Christian groups, they make considerable use, surprisingly, of Christian imagery to express their messianic hopes. Bizarrely, some of these groups identify Jerusalem as the concrete meeting point between heaven and earth, or between mortals and God. One of the largest and best known of these groups is the Raelians, whose center is in Montreal, Canada. The Raelians expect Jesus to appear in Jerusalem mounted on a UFO. The critical date for the Raelians is not the year 2000. As has recently become apparent, they plan to build an 'intergalactic space embassy' in Jerusalem in expectation of Jesus' coming.

The Raelians have become a subject of research interest. Like every self-respecting group of this kind, they have a Web site (www.rael.org). We do not know whether they have representatives in Jerusalem but would not be surprised to find that they do.

End-of-days groups that grasp and analyze human history in racist terms

Most of the groups in this category, apart from pronounced exceptions such as the International Church of God, are influenced by the approach of British Israelism, which rejects the authenticity of the Jews and does not assign Jews or Jerusalem a positive role in the messianic age. These are racist, anti-Semitic groups, which believe that the members of the white race in America are the true Jews of the Scriptures. As such, it is very unlikely that they will plan to carry out anything in Jerusalem. On the other hand, because they are violent and are preoccupied with the end of days, the coming of Jesus, and the final deliverance, they cannot be ignored.

Monitoring and studying these groups involves tactics different from the surveillance of philo-Semitic and premillennialist groups. There are no pro-Israeli groups in the milieu of the racist, anti-Semitic organizations, which will supply 'inside' information. Most of these groups have Web sites where their ideas and some of their plans are spelled out; for example, Christian Identity Online: www.cris.com/-Chrisdent/. The monitoring groups described below are among those that devote much of their attention to these groups.

The following are several concrete proposals for collecting information and monitoring the activity of the radical groups in the United States:

1. Individuals in radical groups

Astonishingly enough, one of the most promising sources of information about developments in the militant, radical groups is the groups themselves. Of course, we need not assume that the radical organizations will be ready to expose their plans and their internal activities to researchers or to academics that are monitoring them. However, experience shows that there are people within the messianic movement and its various groups who are in possession of a wealth of internal information about individuals and organizations who are more extreme than they are. Although these people do not themselves support radical-militant viewpoints, they frequently meet with radical leaders and activists, or know others who are in contact with them.

Potentially promising in this connection are leaders and activists of Pentecostal, messianic, or prophetic groups, who have almost certainly been, or will be, in contact with those who seek to hasten the advent of the 'end of days.'

In the United States, such individuals include:

(a) Rev. John Hagee, John Hagee Ministries, San Antonio, Texas
    John Hagee is a premillennialist Dispensationalist evangelical. His messianic faith makes him a supporter of Israel (he supported the Netanyahu government), and he would probably be willing to share what he knows with an Israeli-American investigator.

(b) Chuck Smith, Calvary Chapel, Costa Mesa, California
    Chuck Smith, who advocates the building of the Temple, is a charismatic personality on the same scale as Hagee. He sponsored research on the Temple Mount in the early 1980s. Smith was in contact with Jewish groups that aspire to build the Temple and he may know about less overt attempts along these lines.

(c) Lambert T. Dolphin, Santa Clara, California
    Lambert Dolphin is a physicist and archeologist who heads the Science and Archeology Team. He is known as an avowed premillennialist who in the 1980s tried to identify the exact location of the Temple using sophisticated geophysical methods.

(d) Zola Levitt, Dallas, Texas

Zola Levitt is an evangelist and author who has written a number of books bearing a prophetic-messianic character about the future of Israel and the Middle East. Like other evangelicals, he considers himself a loyal friend of Israel.

(e) Jack Van Impe, Jack Van Impe Ministries

Jack Van Impe is a well-known televangelist. In his appearances he focuses on messianic themes and is known to support Israel. He frequently cites current events in Israel and the Middle East as signs from heaven about the approaching messianic age.

(f) Hal Lindsey

A well-known evangelist, theologist, and author of popular best sellers. He usually visits Israel twice a year. In his conception, Israel plays a central role on the road to redemption.

In Israel:

(a) The King of Kings Congregation and its leader, Rev. Wayne Hilsdan

This is a fairly large charismatic Pentecostal congregation in the center of Jerusalem, many of whose members are temporary residents who hail from various countries. The congregation espouses a premillennialist messianic belief, though its leaders feel obliged to try to moderate such 'messianic fervor' and to suppress any attempt to further messianic hopes by means of immediate action. This approach was given striking expression during the Gulf War, which many premillennialist Christians interpreted as being fraught with eschatological meaning.

In his sermons at the time, Hilsdan did not rule out the eschatological significance of the events, but told his congregation in no uncertain terms not to treat the messianic situation on a personal and immediate level and to avoid taking action intended to hasten the end of days. (A former priest of the congregation, Ray Ganon, who now lives and works in the United States, might be a useful source of information about current developments in the congregation.)

(b) The Church of God

This premillennialist Pentecostal community which is active among Israeli Arabs and in East Jerusalem and the West Bank. Its leaders are very knowledgeable about the charismatic evangelical arena in East Jerusalem and attentive to individuals and groups there that are expecting the coming of the messiah.

(c) Charismatic groups with a 'prophetic' orientation

Ruth Heflin leads one of these groups, which have its headquarters in the Sheikh Jerrah neighborhood of East Jerusalem. This group, whose origins lie in Texas, has been active in Jerusalem for about twenty years and is in touch with various charismatic groups, including some that have recently arrived in the city.

(d) Newer and less-established groups in El-Azzariya and A-Tur

One of these groups, which is religiously homogeneous, is led by Brother Solomon and belongs to the House of David, which split from the Seventh

Day Adventists. A second group, headed by Brother David and Sister Sharon, consists of a broad range of evangelicals of all stripes.

2. Scholars and researchers in the field

A number of scholars and researchers who specialize in the study of radical messianic groups are in possession of extremely valuable information about those organizations. Some of them have also formed friendships based on mutual trust with many of the activists and with others that are close to the groups. In the course of their work, these researchers have listened to sermons of various kinds, heard stories that are not intended for public consumption, and had access to sensitive documents. Each of them is deeply and intimately acquainted with certain groups. Field researchers whose work has brought them into close contact with radical messianic groups include:

* Prof. Jeffrey Kaplan, University of Alaska at Barrows
* Prof. Michael Barkun, Syracuse University
* Prof. Susan Palmer, Concordia University
* Prof. Benjamin Beit-Hallahmi, University of Haifa

We strongly recommend getting in touch with these individuals through an Israeli scholar who is well versed in the subject and asking them to provide any information they might have pertaining to potential dangerous activity or intentions of members of the messianic groups.

3. 'Cult-watch groups'

A number of bodies are interested in the phenomenon of new religions, which used to be called 'cults' before the advent of the 'politically correct' age. The 'cult awareness' or 'cult watch' groups, which have set themselves the task of mapping and cataloguing the religious movements, are impelled by a variety of motives. Some of them espouse a conservative evangelical outlook and are deeply suspicious of the appearance of every new religious movement. In any event, the information they collect is extremely valuable. Among the best known of them:

* The Spiritual Counterfeits Project – a distinctly conservative evangelical group.
* The Southern Poverty Law center – a group also known by the name of its founding organization, the Morris Dees Center. It publishes a magazine called 'Klan Watch.'
* The Christian Research Center in Southern California – another evangelical group.
* Research and Information Service – based in Milwaukee, Wisconsin.

Groups with a more secular approach that are active in the fight against racism and anti-Semitism include:

* The Center for Democratic Renewal.
* The Political Research Associates.
* And in particular the Anti-Defamation League (ADL), the largest and best connected of the groups, with branches across the United States.

Investigators specializing in these fields can make contact with the centers and organizations cited above and ask them to pass on information about messianic groups that intend to come to Jerusalem and about what they plan to do in the city. It is more than likely that they will accede willingly to such requests and even be happy to help by sharing the information in their possession. It should be noted that some groups of cult watchers are operated by the Church of Scientology, which is itself, a new religious movement. Thus, the American Family Foundation and the Cult Awareness Network, which began as groups of concerned citizens, are now effectively run by Scientologists. They too may be willing to share relevant information about dangerous elements within the radical organizations.

4. Internet sites, books, audio tapes

Various millenarian individuals and groups, as well as esoteric religious cults and personalities that focus on visions of the 'end of days', use written and oral means to try and gain adherents. One of the channels they make use of is the Internet. An intelligent survey of relevant Internet sites will undoubtedly turn up information that will be useful both for understanding the phenomenon and for coping operatively against target groups and individuals. Books on these subjects also contain a wealth of information. A key means of the dissemination of messianic ideas is via tapes made by preachers and spiritual leaders who allow themselves to speak freely and express their inner thoughts when addressing supporters and their own congregations. Most of the messianic congregations sell audiotapes of such sermons, which often contain interesting material.

Chat groups on the Internet. Already today there is a site through which millennialist Christian groups can communicate in real time, and it should be monitored: www.netpgi.com.

5. Research encounters

Academics and research institutes in Israel which deal with this field, such as the Jerusalem Institute for Israel Studies, can organize research encounters on relevant subjects with the participation of American and European experts for an exchange of findings, viewpoints, and assessments. Officials of the Israeli defense establishment could also be invited to attend such gatherings as passive observers, as they might learn a thing or two, which eluded them despite their best efforts.

Utilizing the Advance Information

The collection efforts described above will likely produce a small list of mischief-prone groups and individuals that should be barred from entering Israel. Some of them will try to enter by air and thus purchase tickets from various airlines. Organized groups may even charter planes. Since a large proportion of the tourists expected for the millennium year will come from countries in which millenarians operate, and whose citizens do not need a visa to enter Israel, there will be no way to stop target individuals until they actually board the plane for the flight or at the entry points to Israel itself.

It is no simple matter to check closely passengers boarding planes or entering the country according to 'blacklists', but this must be done as an initial preventative step at every possible airport. A reasonable interrogation of passengers at departure terminals before they board their plane can identify suspects, and this is certainly the case at the border and customs control checkpoints in Israel. To facilitate such checks in Israel, passenger lists should be obtained from the airlines in question and perused before the plane land. A luggage check of all Israel-bound passengers in order to discover possible explosives will be routinely undertaken at the departure airports.

Some of the tourists who enter Israel in 1999–2000 will do so via land from Jordan directly into the country or in a second stage, after visiting the area of the Palestinian Authority. Consequently, the Israeli security authorities must arrange for close cooperation with Jordan and the PA in order to prevent the entry of known millenarian activists not only into Israel but also into PA territory. This is crucial because some of the Christian holy places are now in PA-controlled areas, and as far as is known large-scale events are being planned for them as part of the millennium celebrations. Invaluable help in this regard could be obtained from both the Muslims' Waqf apparatus and from the established churches in the areas of the PA which safeguard the holy places there and are involved in planning the events.

Getting Information in Real Time

The security system at Israel's entry ports cannot cope with individuals who are not identified in advance as potential troublemakers. We should also take into account the possibility that perfectly innocent tourists may undergo unusual experiences while in Israel, succumbing perhaps to the famous 'Jerusalem syndrome.' A mechanism is therefore necessary in order to collect information about individuals and groups that display odd behavior in Israel itself. The police and the Shin Bet certainly have networks of informants who report to them about suspicious behavior in their work environment, and it stands to reason that the security officers of hotels are among these informants. All such informants should be briefed on the necessity of reporting also about strange behavior by guests proximate to religious events. In addition, the network of informants should be expanded to include tour guides and ushers at the holy places, if they have not already been activated.

Special attention should be given to cementing ties with representatives of the evangelical institutions and organizations that operate in Israel on a permanent basis. These clerics are well informed about and involved with pilgrims and most of them are capable of identifying incipient aberrant activity and dangerous behavior. Such functionaries are likely to prefer contact with the civilian rather than the police level, and their preference should be respected.

A worst-case analysis must assume that a few fanatics who intend to act in Israel during the millennium year will have military or other operational experience. As such, they will endeavor to collect operational information in the field well before the prospective date of their action. These individuals will likely come to Israel to collect the relevant information and then return home to continue their planning.

Individuals who visit Israel, leave the country, and then return after a brief period, should be marked as 'suspicious' and be reported to the authorities.

An additional method that is desirable, and indeed vital, for collecting information in real time is by means of photography, with the picture then transferred (by line or wireless) back to the command and control levels. Our recommendation is to consider this method at specific sites such as the Temple Mount, the Via Dolorosa, or the Church of the Holy Sepulcher – places where serious overcrowding will occur and where it will therefore be difficult to move about and obtain a reliable overall picture of events only from eye-witnesses and security personnel who are in the field, particularly in the case of a critical event.

Enhancing and Sharpening Identification Capability

Enhancing the identification capability of the security forces and sharpening their ability to spot in real time individuals or squads that are behaving strangely and suspiciously, entails a complex learning process but a necessary one, at least for the command levels. Inculcating this knowledge in police officers and commanders in the other security forces that will assist in maintaining law and order in public places and at sites with a 'millenarian profile' will include:

- Lectures and briefings by experts.
- Verbal and, if possible, visual description of apocalyptic events that have occurred in the past, and an analysis of the phases through which they developed.
- 'War games' based on possible future scenarios (more on this below).

Training Negotiating Teams

Security officials are aware of the need to train negotiating teams who will be familiar with the way of life, culture, lexicon, expressions, and symbols of the apocalyptic groups, and such training is already underway with the assistance of experienced personnel.

Operational Organization

The security forces have ways and means (special units, transportation and communications means, command and control centers) to cope with anticipated events as well as with unexpected developments and events that lurch out of control.

In this connection, we have one concrete operative proposal and two purely procedural recommendations:

- It must be considered highly probable that among the hundreds of thousands of Christian pilgrims who will visit Jerusalem during the millennium period there will be a few thousand 'eccentrics', at least hundreds of mentally deranged individuals, and quite a few healthy people who will be so overwhelmed by their encounter with the city that they will fall prey to the 'Jerusalem syndrome', identify with a well-known biblical figure, and begin to 'prophesy.'

It is both possible and desirable to enable many of these individuals to express themselves in a controlled and harmless manner by setting up a platform on which they can say their piece. Such a platform or 'stage' should be located at an appropriate site, for example at a 'neutral' location such as on the Mount of Olives overlooking the Temple Mount. This can provide a reasonable psychological release for those who feel the need to address an audience of pilgrims while also enabling the authorities to identify and control eccentrics and in particular to furnish those who are responsible for keeping order with an effective instrument by which to neutralize possible damage by this population at other places. The pilgrims' 'Hyde Park' will become a tourist attraction and, if properly supervised, will not cause any harm.

- To mark the dates of the religious events of the different branches of Christianity, Islam, and Judaism during the coming two years.
- To define the violence-prone sites and field conditions, clarify and mark their problematic points in order to prepare operational responses, and drill special task forces to take action at them if needed.

Unfortunately, this is not enough. The near future, which includes the period of 2000–2001, will very likely be highly significant not only for believing Christians but also for the political future of the region due to the onset of negotiations between Israel and the Palestinians on a permanent settlement, the possible establishment of a Palestinian state, the renewal of the negotiations with Syria, an Israeli withdrawal from Lebanon, and more. These are controversial, highly charged issues for the Jewish and the Palestinian public alike. Possibly, therefore, extremists from both communities may try to torpedo the negotiations by acts of terrorism, including attacks on religious targets and not only on dates of religious significance. It follows that the coming millenarian period will be influenced not only by events related to the agenda of the turn of the millennium, but also by developments related to the Israeli-Palestinian diplomatic agenda and by the political struggle between the two communities.

With the aim of reducing the uncertainty stemming from the complexity of the problems and to facilitate, even slightly, the security forces' deployment in the face of the unknown, the following sections offer:

- A number of worst-case scenarios liable to be fomented by extremists.
- A calendar of expected religious and political events in 1999–2001.
- A list of sites that could be targeted by extremists of various stripes.

Likely Targets that Require Special Attention

Jerusalem: Temple Mount, Church of the Holy Sepulcher, the stations of the Via Dolorosa, Mount of Olives (particularly the churches dedicated to Jesus' ascension to heaven), Gethsemane, the tomb of Lazarus in El-Azzariya, the Garden Tomb (sacred to some Protestant groups), the room of the Last Supper on Mount Zion (this site is under the authority of the Religious Affairs Ministry).

Nazareth: Basilica of the Annunciation, Mary's spring (events at these sites could affect the tension between Muslims and Christians in Nazareth).

Meggido: Armageddon, site of the final battle between Jesus and the Antichrist.

Hebron: Around the Tomb of the Patriarchs (Cave of Machpela), which is a constant focus of tension between Jews and Muslims.

Bethlehem: Around the Church of the Nativity (under the responsibility of the Palestinian Authority).

Baptismal sites: The Jordan River near Jericho, 'Yardenit' near Degania, the shore of Lake Kinneret (Sea of Galilee) near Capernaum or Tabha.

Key dates in 2000

Sept. 24 – Oct. 3, 1999 – Jewish Sukkoth festival coinciding with the Tabernacles festivities being organized by the Christian Embassy in Israel.

Dec. 24–25, 1999 – Christmas for Catholics and Protestants. Important events in Bethlehem, Jerusalem, Nazareth.

Dec. 31, 1999 (Friday) – The last day of the second millennium and also (apparently) the last Friday of the Muslims' Ramadan holy month. Events in Bethlehem, Jerusalem, Nazareth.

Jan. 1, 2000 (Saturday) – New Year's Day. The 'Jubileum' organization is scheduled to hold events marking this day with an ecological emphasis, arranged by a special body connected with the Society for the Protection of Nature in Israel.

Jan. 6–7, 2000 – Christmas celebrated by the Eastern Orthodox churches. Epiphany for Catholics and Protestants.

Jan. 18–19, 2000 – Armenian Christmas.

Jan. 20, 2000 – Orthodox Epiphany.

March 24–25, 2000 – Annunciation Day for Catholics and Protestants (possible papal visit). Center of events: Nazareth.

April 16, 2000 – Palm Sunday for Catholics and Protestants. Processions from the Mount of Olives to the Church of the Holy Sepulcher.

April 19–26, 2000 – Jewish Passover festival.

April 21, 2000 – Good Friday for Catholics and Protestants.

April 23, 2000 – Easter Day for Catholics and Protestants. Center of events: Jerusalem.

April 30, 2000 – Orthodox and Armenian Easter.

June 1, 2000 – Ascension Day for Catholics and Protestants (centering on the Mount of Olives).

June 8, 2000 – Ascension Day for Orthodox and Armenian churches.

June 11, 2000 – Pentecost (Jewish Shavuot) for Catholics and Protestants (center of events: Mount Zion in Jerusalem).

June 18, 2000 – Pentecost (Jewish Shavuot) for Orthodox and Armenian churches.

Oct. 13–20, 2000 – Jewish Sukkoth festival, Tabernacles festivities of Christian Embassy.

Dec. 24–25, 2000 – Christmas for Catholics and Protestants.

Jan. 1, 2001 – New Year's Day.

Jan. 6–7, 2001 – Orthodox Christmas.

Jan. 18–19, 2001 – Armenian Christmas.

APPENDIX

Jerusalem on the eve of 2000: The situation from the viewpoint of the Christian groups operating in the city

A. Preface

Some five months ahead of 2000 and the events surrounding that date, confusion and bewilderment prevail among the Israeli public, the media, and some policy-makers at the different levels of government about what to expect in this special year. The former indifference and non-awareness that characterized the Israeli society's attitude toward the meaning of the year 2000 for Christians have now given way to hysteria which is fed by fears some of which are totally groundless. One cause of the panic is the large number of expected tourists and pilgrims being bandied about (the figures range from two to six million pilgrims) – which will cause overcrowding at the important Christian sites, a shortage of hotel rooms, huge lines at the airport and vast traffic jams on the main roads – an influx of eccentrics and 'nut cases' of various kinds into Jerusalem, an epidemic of the 'Jerusalem syndrome', the arrival of Christian cults (such as Concerned Christians) intent on committing collective suicide or demolishing the Muslim sites on the Temple Mount, and anxiety over the possible massive entry of Christian pilgrims from the Second and Third Worlds who will remain in the country and join the labor force, and more.

The purpose of this appendix is to dissipate some of the fog surrounding the 2000 events by analyzing the approach of the local and international Jerusalem-based Christian bodies to the year 2000 and its implications. Such an analysis will hopefully produce a more balanced view of what to expect and thus also indicate the preparations that are required by the Israeli administration.

B. The theological meaning of the year 2000 to the Catholic Church

Surprisingly, no special preparation or other activity is discernible among the majority of the local churches ahead of 2000. These churches are in fact very far from harboring an apocalyptic frame of mind that envisions far-reaching events such as the end of history, the advent of the 'end of days', or the beginning of human redemption on a particular date. Indeed, clerics who are permanent residents of Jerusalem are showing reservations about the 'festival' and the fuss being made over the special year.

That 2000 has been marked as a special year is above all due to the viewpoint and activity of Pope John Paul II and the Catholic Church. The Catholic Church considers 2000 to be a 'Jubilee Year' in the biblical sense. The Torah designates such a year (which occurs every fifty years) as a period of sabbatical and of freedom for the slaves and the land; the Pope has declared it a year of special grace and an occasion for spiritual contemplation and renewal.

According to the Catholics, 2000 is a special Jubilee Year marking the revelation of Jesus, the incarnation of God, who came to redeem mankind – like the slaves who are released in the biblical Jubilee Year. At the Pope's directive, the year should be devoted to soul-searching, forgiveness, spiritual renewal, dialogue, and reconciliation within Christendom and throughout the world. By the same token, special importance attaches to dialogue with Judaism and with Islam in the Holy Land.

Pilgrimage to Rome and to the Holy Land, as recommended by the Pope in his encyclical of November 1994, will enable pilgrims to achieve spiritual and religious renewal by becoming acquainted with the roots of Christianity in its birthplace. The pilgrim who visits the Holy Places, walks in the footsteps of Jesus and of the heroes of the Old and New Testaments, and gets to know first-hand the roots of his faith, obtains special grace and forgiveness. In any event, it is important to emphasize that this is an inner and very personal experience of the pilgrim, which has no external expression in the life of the individual or the community and does not in any way involve an apocalyptic outlook. The other established churches do not attribute any special theological meaning to the year 2000. Indeed, some Protestant groups object to setting the year 2000 as the two thousandth anniversary of Jesus' birth, as modern research has found that he was probably born four years earlier.

C. Approaches of the local established churches

The Greek Orthodox Patriarchate, which considers itself the senior and longest-standing Christian body in Jerusalem – the successor to the ancient Byzantine church – is not showing any unusual enthusiasm for the expected events in connection with the year 2000; rather, it seems to have been dragged into activity by the worldwide interest in the millennium and the activity of the Catholic Church. The Patriarchate is taking part in the interchurch conference that is scheduled to conclude the preparations and is working to renovate and open to the public holy places and churches which are under its authority (in this connection, it is particularly important to emphasize its cooperation with the Armenians and the Franciscans – the latter are the representatives of the Catholic Church – in the renovation of the Church of the Holy Sepulcher). Churches that were closed to the public for many years (in Jaffa, at Capernaum, at Shepherds' Field in Beit Sahour, and elsewhere) have been renovated recently and opened to the general public. Preparations are also underway to accommodate a larger number of Orthodox pilgrims than usual between the Orthodox Christmas on January 6, 2000, and Easter 2001. The Patriarchate plans to put up pilgrims who cannot find accommodation in hotels and hostels in private homes in and around the Old City. Invitations have been sent to the Orthodox Patriarchs and to the heads of the states in the Orthodox world (Russia, Romania, Bulgaria, Greece, Serbia, and others) to visit Jerusalem for Christmas 1999. The Patriarchate hopes that a high-level delegation will in fact arrive for the celebrations.

Israeli tourism officials are looking forward to the arrival of Orthodox pilgrims from the developed countries as well, particularly from North and South America. The Israeli authorities are not enthusiastic about the arrival of poor pilgrims from Russia and Romania, as some of them may try to stay in the country and look for work.

The Armenian Orthodox Patriarchate, which has important rights at some of the key holy places, is taking a line similar to that of the Greek Orthodox Patriarchate, though its activity is directed exclusively at Armenian communities. The Patriarchate is renovating and preparing accommodations for pilgrims in the Armenian Quarter of the Old City and is planning a number of events (including concerts) for 2000. Important celebrations will likely take place in 2001 to mark the 1700th anniversary of Armenia's conversion to Christianity, and are expected to attract pilgrims from Armenian communities abroad (mainly from the United States and possibly from Armenia itself). A similar pattern of activity ahead of 2000 (mainly in the form of renovations and preparations for a larger number of pilgrims than usual) is also discernible among the three small Monophysite churches (Coptic, Ethiopian, and Syrian) and among the established Protestant churches (Episcopalian, Anglican, and Lutheran).

The exception in terms of preparations for year 2000 is the local Catholic Church (sometimes known as the Latin Church). The Catholics, and particularly the monastic orders which it operates through the Franciscans – the custodians of the holy places – are the moving force behind the preparations for the Great Jubilee decreed by Pope John Paul II six years ago. The Catholic Church is also the major sponsor of interchurch cooperation in an ecumenical spirit, as demonstrated in the renovation of the dome of the Church of the Holy Sepulcher and on the Internet site of the Christian Information Center, which is run by the Franciscans on behalf of all the recognized churches in Jerusalem. It is also the Catholics who are conducting the negotiations with Israel, the Palestinian Authority, and Jordan over the preparations for the mass influx of pilgrims. The Franciscans are also developing the holy sites under their supervision. Among other projects, they are building a large hall in Bethlehem (adjacent to the Church of the Nativity) and carrying out renovations at their center in the St. Salvador Monastery in the Old City of Jerusalem. They also intend to prepare camping sites in Galilee and around Bethlehem. This intense activity is based on the assessment of the Catholic Church that most of the pilgrims in 2000 will be Catholics, in response to the Pope's call. Tourism officials also accept this assumption.

The close relations between the Catholic Church and the Palestinian community are seen also in the emphasis being placed on the importance of the local Christian community – 'the mother of the churches', according to written material issued by the Catholic Church ahead of 2000. The Catholic Church is calling on pilgrims who visit the Holy Land to show solidarity with and assist the local community, which finds itself in dire straits, caught between the pressures of the Israeli occupation and the fundamentalist Islamic movement. If the Holy Places are perceived by the Church as 'the fifth Gospel', in that they help pilgrims identify with the fate of Jesus, the encounter and identification with the local Christians, who are considered the descendants of the first Christian congregation of Jesus' disciples, constitute a kind of 'sixth Gospel' which shows pilgrims an exemplary model of steadfast clinging to the Holy Land despite the many obstacles.

D. The approach of established international Christian bodies

1. The most active and important international body in connection with the events of year 2000 in the Holy Land is the Holy See, which is intensively urging the local Catholic Church to prepare for the advent of the third millennium. To date, the Vatican's involvement is discernible in two crucial areas: deployment for the expected large wave of pilgrims and the probable papal visit.

Papal activity ahead of 2000 began with the encyclical issued on November 10, 1994, entitled 'Tertio Millennio Advenientem' (Advent of the Third Millennium), which was addressed to Catholic bishops, clerics, and the community of the faithful. The encyclical dealt primarily with the spiritual preparations of believers for the Jubilee Year, calling on them to engage in deep soul-searching, recognize past sins, work for the unification of Christendom and for the dissemination of social justice in the spirit of the biblical Jubilee, and to remember the martyrs (including those of the twentieth century).

To imbue the year 2000 with a special character as a period of spiritual renewal, the Pope set a three-year track of preparation for the Jubilee Year based on the Holy Trinity: 1997 was devoted to the figure and doctrine of the Son (Jesus), 1998 to the Holy Spirit, and 1999 to the deeds of the Father. The quest leading up to God the Father was intended to lead the believer to repentance, purification, and spiritual renewal in 2000. In this connection, the Pope noted explicitly that 'the celebration of the Great Jubilee will take place simultaneously in the Holy Land, in Rome, and in the local churches around the world.' This was a crucial text in that it placed the Holy Land (and Jerusalem in particular) at the head of the pilgrimage sites, within a highly meaningful religious and historical context of repentance, atonement for transgressions, and forgiveness through divine grace.

Four years after issuing the encyclical, the Pope stated, in a special bulla, published on November 29, 1998, that the special Jubilee Year would begin on Christmas Eve 1999 with the opening of the holy door in the basilica of St. Peter's in the Vatican, a few hours before the start of the celebrations in Jerusalem and Bethlehem, and would conclude at Epiphany on January 6, 2001.

Pursuant to a tradition which has its origins in the Jubilee Year of 1300, during the term of Pope Boniface VIII, the current Pope noted three features of the Jubilee Year: pilgrimage, the opening of the holy door, and indulgences. Indulgences will be granted, among others, to pilgrims in Rome and in the Holy Land (particularly to those visiting the Church of the Holy Sepulcher, the Church of the Nativity in Bethlehem, and the Basilica of the Annunciation in Nazareth); they will include absolution for punishment in this world which was meted out for sins that were forgiven through the sacrament of the confession. The papal encyclical and bulla thus form the ideological basis for the Vatican's promotion of pilgrimage to the Holy Land. Pilgrimages are being organized by, among others, the Vatican's official travel firm, Opera Romana, whose manager, Msgnr. Liberio Andreatta, paid several visits to Israel. This firm will likely be one of the major companies bringing Catholic pilgrims to Israel.

Exaggerated estimates ranging from four to even six million pilgrims and tourists expected to visit Israel in 2000 have been voiced, but a more realistic number is between 2 to 3.1 million. The political and security situation, and the general atmosphere that will prevail in the Middle East in the wake of the Israeli election results will have a major effect on the scale of pilgrimage, as will a possible papal visit. If the realistically optimistic projections of 2.5 to 3.1 million tourists in 2000 prove accurate, difficulties can be expected in absorbing them (traffic jams, crowding at popular sites, overbooking, etc.). Exaggerated reports that speak about incredible numbers of tourists and serious overcrowding in the Holy Land are liable to deter visitors and cause serious harm.

The first third of 1999 saw an increase of 13 percent in incoming tourism to Israel (as compared to the same period in 1998), which according to the Ministry of Tourism suggests an approaching peak period. However, it is clear that Israel's security and political situation will have a decisive impact on the scale of pilgrimage in 2000 and perhaps in 2001 as well. Already now there is crowding at certain times in the Church of the Holy Sepulcher, and for the first time the heads of the churches have agreed to the establishment of a police station next to the church, to help cope with the crowds in 2000. In any event, it is important to emphasize that the Catholic pilgrims who visit the Holy Land in the wake of the papal encyclical will not be imbued with an apocalyptic frame of mind. Most of them will arrive in groups organized by established Catholic institutions. Thus, the Catholic pilgrims are not expected to constitute a significant danger to the public order, other than overcrowding at holy sites if the optimistic forecasts about the number of pilgrims prove correct.

Nor is it clear whether the Pope will visit in 2000. True, John Paul II has declared on many occasions his strong desire to visit the Holy Land and the neighboring countries (Lebanon, Iraq, Syria, Egypt and Sinai) during the Jubilee Year. He has expressed his wish to visit the important places cited in the 'Old Testament' and the New Testament, which are connected with the activity of Abraham, Moses, Jesus, and St. Paul. He has also mentioned that he would like to meet with Jewish and Muslim religious leaders at places of symbolic meaning for the three religions, such as Bethlehem, Jerusalem, and Mount Sinai, in order to promote an interfaith dialogue. Further to these intentions, reports from various sources in recent months say the Pope has accepted the invitation of Israel and the Palestinian Authority. He will visit the Holy Land from March 21–25, 2000, in conjunction with the Festival of the Annunciation; or, according to a different source, toward the end of 2000. To date, though, the Vatican has not officially confirmed these reports. Confirmation of the visit will probably not be forthcoming until the political-diplomatic situation in the Middle East and in the Holy Land becomes clear in the wake of the Israeli elections of May 1999, particularly with regard to progress in the peace process. Naturally, the Pope's health could also have an effect on the visit. A papal visit to the three holy cities – Bethlehem, which is under the control of the Palestinian Authority; Jerusalem, which is at the center of the dispute between Israel and the Palestinians; and Nazareth, where serious clashes between Muslims and Christians occurred recently – is politically and diplomatically an extremely complex exercise. The question of who will host and escort the Pope during his visit to Jerusalem, and particularly in his visits to the holy places in the Old City and on the Mount of Olives, exemplify the many problems involved in a papal visit. Nevertheless, if there is an improvement (even at the symbolic level) in the atmosphere in the Middle East due to progress in the peace process, the Pope, who is very eager to visit the Holy Land, will in fact make the visit.

A visit by the Pope can of course bring about an increase in the scale of Catholic pilgrimage to Israel. It will also be a major international media event and could therefore 'invite' radical groups or individuals, whether Muslim or Christian (in particular from the milieu of Christian Identity activists), to try to disrupt the visit. Festive dramatic meetings in

Jerusalem between the leaders of the three monotheistic religions during the Jubilee Year in an atmosphere of the 'end of days' could constitute a particularly desirable target for extremists.

2. Other established international Christian bodies (apart from the Vatican) that could have an effect on the events of 2000 are the Orthodox Churches in Russia, Romania, Greece, and Bulgaria, as well as Orthodox communities in the West. Visits to the Holy Land by their leaders at Christmas or Easter could bring about pilgrimage on a more intensive scale. Russia and Romania are potential sources of mass pilgrimage, but the cost of the visit will likely deter many prospective pilgrims from those economically impoverished countries. Pilgrimage from these countries also brings acutely to the fore the question of Israeli policy toward pilgrims who may stay in the country and try to enter the labor market. Similar apprehensions and dilemmas exist with regard to pilgrims from Third World states such as Ethiopia, Ghana, the Philippines, and others.

3. As for the established currents in the Protestant world, or those who broke with it (such as evangelicals, Lutherans, Methodists, Northern Baptists, etc.), apocalyptic thought does not occupy an important place in their religious outlook and they are not engaged in any special activity ahead of 2000. Many of these groups are aware of the problem entailed in dating year 0 as the birth of Jesus (most historians now believe he was born between 7 and 4 BCE), hence also in specially marking the year 2000. In the light of previous 'disappointments', some of the Protestant and other groups also object to setting dates for the end of history and the onset of the millennial kingdom. Others among them emphasize the personal experience of being 'reborn' and reject the idea of collective redemption for all mankind. Against this background, the disinterest of these groups in the year 2000, and consequently in visiting Israel in that year, becomes understandable. No significant increase in pilgrimage by these currents and groups is therefore to be expected, although it is possible that the round year will attract more visitors than usual (assuming a situation of quiet and relative security in the Holy Land and the Middle East).

E. The approach of the fundamentalist evangelical Protestants

The approach of these groups, which are sometimes identified with the evangelical camp (though it includes many diverse groups), is based on the perception of the Bible and the New Testament as the word of God and as the absolute truth which guide the way of life of the individual and the community and reflect God's plans for the current age and the age to come. Large parts of the evangelical camp – which currently numbers between 60 and 90 million believers in the United States, Latin America, and parts of East Asia – maintain a Christian messianic belief in the imminent return of Jesus as the redeemer and the establishment of the millennial kingdom in which Jesus and 'the elect' will rule until the final redemption at the end of history.

Christian messianic belief has several versions, though the dominant version among contemporary evangelicals is Dispensationalism. According to this conception, which rests on verses from the Holy Scriptures (particularly the Book of Daniel and the Revelation of John), history is divided into periods, each of which contains a divine plan for mankind. We are living at the end of the penultimate age, before the millennium, meaning the thousand-year reign of God's kingdom on earth.

The appearance of the messiah is expected in two stages. In the first stage, known as 'the rapture', the true believers – those who have experienced an inner religious experience and been born again – will be 'swept up' into heaven, where they will meet Jesus and stay with him for seven years. Earth in the meantime will experience 'the great tribulation' in the form of plagues, earthquakes, volcanic eruptions, wars, and a regime of terror.

The Jews and the Jewish people will have a key role to play in the interim period, according to this conception. They will return to their land prior to or at the outset of the messianic event in order to establish a Jewish state in accordance with the vision of the 'return to Zion' of the biblical prophets. During the seven-year period the Jews will bring forth a leader who will pose as the messiah – the Antichrist. They will build the temple and renew the sacrificial practices under the leadership of the Antichrist. He will persecute those Jews who begin to recognize Jesus as the true messiah. The seven years will end with a series of invasions of the Land of Israel, including an invasion by a northern country called Rush (which until 1990 was identified with the Soviet Union). The invaders will be crushed in the battle of Armageddon (the famous Har [=Mount] Meggido), and immediately after the final invasion the messiah will reappear, together with his true believers, eradicate the government of the Antichrist, and establish his government of justice on earth for a thousand years. Jerusalem, the capital of the revivified Kingdom of David, will become the capital of the entire world. The Jewish people – the chosen people – will reside in its land and assist the messiah in establishing his kingdom throughout the world. Another role of the Jewish people will be to ready humanity for the utopian age, which will begin only after the conclusion of the thousand-year kingdom. Then the Son and the Father will reign together and totally eradicate sin and death.

This general messianic conception, which is shared by many evangelical groups, has several versions, which are prone to change in accordance with the specific current reality as seen through the prism of the messianic vision. Many groups believe that we are on the brink of the new messianic age of the millennial kingdom, though only a small minority among them believe that 2000 is the year in which the messianic scenario described above will begin. The dominant conception among these minority groups is that God will foment the vision they are expecting to materialize without human intervention. Others, who apparently constitute a tiny minority, are ready to carry out certain acts (generally of a passive character) which they believe can hasten the end, such as activity (largely in the sphere of publicity and perhaps also in terms of financial support) to bring about the building of the temple on the Temple Mount by the Jews.

These distinctions among the different groups are extremely important in order to refute the simplistic monolithic approach toward the entire evangelical camp. It is important to emphasize that the vast majority of the evangelical Christians who will come to the country are law-abiding, peaceful pilgrims who support Israel (precisely because of their messianic religious view). On the fringes of the fringes of these groups, there are some individuals who may try to harm themselves (by means of suicide, as intended by the Concerned Christians) or injure others (as yet we have no evidence of plans of this kind).

There are no precise estimates concerning the scale of the evangelical tourism that can be expected in 2000, though several major events are planned for the Jerusalem Convention Center. Some is organizing of these gatherings, whose meetings attract participants from the whole evangelical spectrum. The major events planned by the Embassy include the Tabernacles gathering (September 24–October 3, 1999), which will have a particularly festive and grand character, and a special production of Handel's 'Messiah' to coincide with Christmas 1999. The Fourth Christian Zionist Congress, who was planned by the Christian Embassy, has been postponed from March 2000 to February 2001 – the first year of the new millennium – because of the expected papal visit.

A relatively large number of groups will arrive within the framework of an organization called 'Jerusalem 2000', which was organized by the Millennium Council and has published a declaration about the formation of a world leadership and the dissemination of the Christian gospel in the evangelical spirit from Jerusalem in 2000. Signatories to the declaration include the well-known televangelists Jerry Falwell and Pat Robertson. Among the groups scheduled to visit the country are the Full Gospel Baptist Azu Fellowship, CBN 700 Club, Feast of Pentecost, Korean Church Association, Church Fellowship, Church of God in Christ, National Baptist Convention, and others. The Third World Leadership Summit is scheduled to take place in Israel from August 14–23, 2000.

According to reports of the Convention Center, 12 festive events are scheduled to take place there in connection with the year 2000, with the participation of 33,000 pilgrims. Most of these events will be held by evangelicals (among the expected events: a conference of the

Charismatic Church of Hungary and the United States, events organized by the Christian Embassy, and others).

The security situation in the Holy Land and in the Middle East in general will undoubtedly affect the scale of evangelical tourism, but given the pro-Israel approach of many of these groups, most of them will probably arrive even if there are negative developments in the area.

F. Evangelical groups operating in Jerusalem

A number of organizations exist in Jerusalem, representing different approaches and methods of operation within the evangelical camp toward the Jewish people and Israel.

One approach, which is represented by the Bridges for Peace organization, holds that the covenant between the Jewish people and God is eternal and inseparable. Even when the Jewish people were exiled from its land, God did not violate the covenant. As the Scriptures say, He promised to let the Jews return and establish their state. The return of the Jews to their land and the establishment of the State of Israel are viewed as evidence to the special bond between God and the Jewish people.

The role of the Christians, according to this view, is to assist the return to Zion just as the Persians assisted their neighbors the Jews to return to the Land of Israel following the declaration by Cyrus the Great. They therefore help new immigrants, needy families, the elderly, and Holocaust survivors by providing foodstuffs, blankets, clothing, toys, and so forth. The organization, which has its headquarters off Hanevi'im Street (Street of the Prophets) in downtown Jerusalem, operates a warehouse for the distribution of food and clothes in the city's Talpiot neighborhood.

This organization rejects completely attempts to proselytize among the Jews. Despite its belief that redemption is possible only through belief in Jesus, its members maintain that the covenant between God and Israel existed before Jesus appeared in the world. Therefore in a mysterious way the Jews do not need any other faith and no attempts should be made to convert them. The organization's members also devote themselves to studying the Jewish roots of Christianity, promote a dialogue between Christians and Jews, and take clear-cut pro-Israel positions, which are less extreme than those of the Christian Embassy (see below). Its publications make no reference to any special activity related to the year 2000.

A somewhat different approach to the role of the Jews and of the State of Israel is taken by the International Christian Embassy, which is the largest and best-known 'Christian Zionist' group operating in Israel. The ICE, which was established to compensate Israel for the removal of the foreign embassies from Jerusalem in the wake of a resolution by the United Nations Security Council (which came in reaction to the enactment of the Basic Law on Jerusalem by the Knesset in 1980), represents mainly charismatic evangelical groups from the United States, Europe, and South Africa. It is extreme in its attitudes toward Israeli politics, even by comparison with the approach taken by pro-Israel evangelical groups (although since the resignation of William van der Hooven as the organization's head its public statements have become more moderate).

The ICE believes that 'Israel's miraculous rebirth as a nation in 1948 and the return of the Jews from the four corners of the world to their biblical home are signs that the time is ripe for the return to Zion.' In the ICE's view, the Bible assigns the Jews have 'a special role. God has returned them to the land of Israel in order to establish a new covenant with them which will bring about their spiritual renewal.' The implication is that, as the ICE expects, the Jews will ultimately recognize Christianity as the true faith, which will be one of the signs that redemption is at hand. The ICE does not pretend to know when this will take place and therefore abstains from missionary activity (they are also aware of the Jewish and Israeli sensitivity regarding such activity).[2]

The ICE, which is headquartered in a magnificent building at 20 Rachel Imeinu Street, runs a number of pro-Israel projects. These include providing financial aid for new immigrants and needy families, boosting Israel's image in the international media by means of bulletins and journals, disseminating the idea of support for Israel within Christendom, and other activities. The ICE is also known for the huge assemblies it organizes during the Sukkoth festival (Tabernacles), when thousands of evangelical pilgrims cheer wildly at the Prime Minister's speech.

As the most important evangelical body in Israel, the ICE is organizing a series of events in connection with 2000, as mentioned above. Its written material is vague about the meaning of the Jubilee Year, citing a variety of viewpoints concerning its importance: 'There are some who view it as the advent of a new prophetic age, for others it marks the progress of mankind across twenty turbulent centuries, for two billion Christians it is the 2000th Jubilee of the birth of Jesus Christ.'

The episode of Israel's expulsion of the Concerned Christians group, which Israeli media reports mistakenly linked with the ICE, prompted the ICE to issue a press release which drew a distinction between that cult and others like it, and the large majority of Christian pilgrims, particularly those who visit with the help of the ICE, which the communique described as a peaceful, pro-Israel group. The ICE also assisted the police to uncover the cult by arranging a meeting between the police and the mother of one of the cult's members (who had approached the ICE to help her find her daughter). Thanks to information the mother gave the police about some of the cult's members, those who were in Israel were identified.

That event shows the importance of the ICE and similar groups as junctions at whom considerable information collects about problematic groups and individuals. The ties with the ICE are important to the police also as a channel for making contact with members of the problematic sects and cults if necessary.

Two other organizations that are active in Jerusalem are the Casperi Center and the Christian Friends of Israel. The Casperi Center seeks to create closer ties between Scandinavian and German pilgrims and Israel, and actively assists the messianic congregations in the country, which have about 3,000 members. They do not flinch at conducting missionary activity among the Jews based on the approach that such activity is needed above all in the Land of Israel in order to show the Jews the right road. The Christian Friends of Israel, like the International Christian Embassy and Bridges for Peace, operate various projects for the needy in Israel.

In addition to these groups, which show a distinctly pro-Israel attitude, several other groups, bearing a premillennialist evangelical character are also active in Jerusalem:

- The King of Kings congregation led by Wayne Hilsdan is located at 24 Ben Maimon Street. The group runs a college for Bible studies and a center for young people called 'Victory Arch' at 1 Dorot Rishonim Street in downtown Jerusalem. The members of this 'messianic' congregation consist of Jews and Christians from various countries.
- The Church of God, which operates on the slopes of the Mount of Olives near the Commodore Hotel, is led by Peter Ousman. Its activity is carried out mainly among the Arab sector.
- The Mount Zion Fellowship has its headquarters in Rajib Nashishibi House in the Sheikh Jerrah neighborhood of East Jerusalem. Headed by the 'prophetess' Ruth W. Heflin, this group originated in Texas and has been operating in Jerusalem for 20 years.
- Another messianic group which includes members of Jewish and Christian origin meets at St. Paul's Church on Shivtei Yisrael Street near the Old City.

None of these groups is driven by an apocalyptic frame of mind, but our recommendation is to maintain ties with them in order to obtain information about problematic groups or individuals.

G. The groups in A-Tur and Al-Azzariya

On the eastern slope of the Mount of Olives, in the area of A-Tur and Al-Azzariya, there are two groups headed by leaders called Brother David (and his assistant Sister Sharon) and

Brother Solomon, who are awaiting the Second Coming of Jesus on the Mount of Olives. Most of the members of these groups, each of which has no more than a few dozen believers, are in the country illegally. Brother David and some of his people do not have passports (making it extremely difficult to deport them). His group consists of a broad variety of evangelicals from different currents who rent rooms and apartments in the two villages. The group also maintains a few apartments, which they rent on a short-term basis to visiting evangelical pilgrims.

So far there have been no clashes between them and the surrounding Palestinian population or the security forces. This group also distributes clothing to residents of the villages in order to maintain good relations with them.

The group of Brother Solomon is part of a larger organization called the House of David, which split from the Davidians, who in turn broke away from the Seventh Day Adventists. Although David Koresh was also a Davidian, there is no connection between that group and the Jerusalem group. Its leader has been engaged in 'end of days' calculations since the 1970s and gives the impression of being moderate.

There are apparently also a few 'eccentrics' in Brother David's group. Its membership has dwindled in recent months, probably because of pressure exerted by the authorities regarding the illegal presence of some of the members. Brother David has apparently moderated his views to some degree and says he has good relations with the Jerusalem police.

H. The messianic Jewish groups

In the light of the events that are expected in 2000, it is of special interest to monitor these groups and various evangelical organizations that maintain ties with them. To date the groups in question have not displayed unusual activity apart from placing ads in the press and distributing missionary material.

The messianic congregations (some of them consisting of members of Jewish and Christian origin) are under close surveillance by ultra-Orthodox organizations (such as Yad Leachim), which sometimes subject them to violence.

The major congregations in Jerusalem operate in Christ Church near the Church of the Holy Sepulcher, at 56 Hanevi'im Street, at the Baptist Church, and in Beit Netiveha on Hanarkis Street. In March 1999 two firebombs were thrown into the home of Yosef Sholem, one of the leaders of the Beit Netiveha congregation, and the bookstore of the Baptist Church (where a Jewish messianic group also worships) was set ablaze. A 'pogrom' that was perpetrated in November 1998 in an apartment in the ultra-Orthodox Me'a She'arim neighborhood, which was rented by two Christian women, was also directed against missionary activity, although the two women were not engaged in such activity. Such attacks by fiercely anti-missionary ultra-Orthodox groups or individuals, which are also aimed at the Christian community in general, could have an adverse effect on Christian tourism to the Holy Land and seriously damage Israel's image. We recommend that contact be maintained with the messianic congregations in order to obtain information about problematic individuals or groups and also to safeguard them against violence by ultra-Orthodox Jews.

I. Conclusion

As the above survey shows, the Christian churches and congregations in Jerusalem show a wide range of attitudes toward the year 2000. Given the fact that the radical millenarians are a minuscule minority in the Christian world and have no representation in Jerusalem, the probability that these groups will perpetrate violence in the city is very low. Good relations with the evangelical, Pentecostal, and Jewish messianic groups that are represented in Jerusalem can be a key source of information about dangerous individuals and groups that may make contact with the Jerusalem groups.

More concrete threats to public safety in Jerusalem, particularly around the Old City, lie in the crowding that is expected around the Church of the Holy Sepulcher, the papal visit – which will generate a host of security and political problems – and perhaps also in violence against suspected missionaries by ultra-Orthodox Jews.

Special attention should be paid to the groups of Brother David and Brother Solomon around A-Tur and Al-Azzariya. Efforts and resources should be directed toward collecting intelligence information about them and about problematic individuals who are attracted to them, ahead of formulating policy and deciding on measures to take in connection with them and with similar groups that may arrive in the country during the coming year. The forthcoming Sukkoth festival (late September-early October 1999) and the Tabernacles festivities being organized by the International Christian Embassy at this time – which are expected to attract a larger number than usual of evangelical pilgrims – will be an important test period. The events that occur in this period, which some evangelicals consider a propitious time for the Second Coming of Jesus, may be a portent of things to come in 2000.

About the authors

Ehud Sprinzak
Former professor of political science at the Hebrew University of Jerusalem, now Dean of the Lauder School of Government at the Interdisciplinary Center in Herzliya. Expert on terrorism and radical groups and on illegalism in the Israeli political system.

Uri Ne'eman
Former official of the defense establishment. Has dealt with the Israeli-Palestinian conflict, the Middle East, and the international arena.

Ya'akov Ariel
Professor of the study of religions at the University of North Carolina. Expert on modern Christianity who specializes in evangelical Christianity.

Amnon Ramon
Researcher at the Jerusalem Institute for Israel Studies and at Yad Ben-Zvi. Specializes in Christianity in Jerusalem during the modern era.

NOTES

1. This executive summary was not included in the original report, but was prepared by Dr Sprinzak at the request of General (res.) Ami Ayalon, Head of Israel's Domestic Security Service (Shin Beth), before the oral presentation of the report to the Service's General Command.
2. Ariel, *Ibid.*, p.30.

SCHOLARLY ANALYSIS OF THE
THREE MILLENNIUM REPORTS

5

Project Megiddo, the FBI and the Academic Community

MICHAEL BARKUN

Project Megiddo attracted significant media attention from the moment its existence was revealed by *USA Today* in October 1999.[1] Interest was not, however, limited to the mass media, nor was it entirely the product of end-of-millennium anxieties. Rather, *Megiddo* also attracted substantial attention among scholars – more, certainly, than would have been expected of a slim government report.

The academic interest in *Project Megiddo* was in part a function of its ambitions, for it sought to cover a substantial portion of the American religious terrain. However, the principal reason it drew the attention of scholars was because of the anguished relationship between the academy and the Federal Bureau of Investigation concerning the Bureau's perception of religious groups. That friction was a product of the Branch Davidian siege, six years before the release of *Project Megiddo*.

Although *Project Megiddo* was produced by an FBI division uninvolved at Waco, and by individual authors who, as far as I know, played no role in those events, the document was inevitably read against the background of the Branch Davidian debacle. While Waco forms an important part of the context in which *Megiddo* was evaluated, that is not the whole story, for the relationship between the FBI and scholars of religion particularly, underwent significant changes between 1993 and 1999.

It is my purpose here, therefore, to examine a number of those developments: scholarly reactions to Waco; post-Waco changes in FBI

organization and practice, notably through the creation of the Critical
Incident Response Group (CIRG); the evidence of changes seen during
the Montana Freemen standoff; and the developing relationship between
the Bureau and the American Academy of Religion (AAR).

Waco and the Utilization of Outside Consultants

Although the disastrous conclusion of the Branch Davidian siege had
multiple causes, a major problem was the narrow range of outside
information and advice upon which the FBI drew. As the subsequent
Department of Justice investigation revealed, the Bureau solicited the
views of at least 13 external experts. However, they were weighted
heavily toward individuals with expertise in psychology and forensic
psychiatry. Only slight use was made of religion scholars, and it appears
that no effort was made to contact the leading expert on the Branch
Davidians, Bill Pitts, although he was on the faculty of Baylor
University in Waco.[2]

The result of this skewed distribution of experts was that most of the
advice received emphasized David Koresh's alleged psychopathology.
Scarcely any took the group's doctrines seriously or suggested that the
Davidians were competent to make decisions for themselves.

An attempt to repair these omissions was made after the fact, when the
departments of Justice and Treasury jointly asked a new set of experts to
evaluate 'federal law enforcement's capacity to handle … analogous
situations that may arise in the future'.[3] Among those whose views were
solicited were two religion scholars, Nancy T. Ammerman and Lawrence
E. Sullivan. Both submitted extensive comments, in which both criticized
the lopsided advice sought during the standoff and made recommendations
for changes in Bureau procedures for gaining outside expertise.

Ammerman noted that during the Branch Davidian crisis, the FBI
'failed to consult a single person who might be recognized by the social
science community as an expert on the Branch Davidians or on other
marginal religious movements'.[4] Sullivan observed that 'ignorance
about religion could have harmful consequences, and actions based on
lack of knowledge can trigger unwanted harmful reactions which might
otherwise be avoided, if the religious context and motives for those
reactions were better understood beforehand'[5] – a relationship that
might seem obvious, but was apparently contrary to longstanding
institutional practice among law enforcement agencies.

Ammerman's and Sullivan's recommendations advocated that new bridges be built to the academic community. Ammerman regarded it as 'essential that behavioral scientists inside federal law enforcement and behavioral scientists in the academic community forge expanded working ties'.[6] She appended to her report a letter from the Society for the Scientific Study of Religion which listed a dozen of the organization's members who might provide needed perspective on religious issues in the future. Sullivan, for his part, urged law enforcement 'to close their knowledge gap about religion', and pointed out that religious studies and related fields constituted untapped resources for law enforcement.[7]

All too often, post-crisis studies, investigations and recommendations turn out to be ritual acts that have little effect because of institutional inertia. In this case, however, change came quickly, in no small measure because the urgings of scholars intersected with organizational change in the FBI.

The Critical Incident Response Group (CIRG)

The resources assembled by the FBI at Mount Carmel were immense, with an average of 258 Bureau agents and staff present at any given time.[8] Nonetheless, they were assembled on an ad hoc basis, from throughout the organization, since in 1993 the Bureau had no centralized crisis-management capability. That, in turn, led to the lack of a coherent approach to problems such as those posed by the Branch Davidian standoff. As the Department of Justice's subsequent investigation revealed, there were intense clashes of viewpoint between the tactical commander and those conducting negotiations, whose efforts to secure withdrawal from the compound were undercut by the commander's desire to place pressure on the Davidians.[9]

Among the less well-known 'fallout' from the Waco debacle was a reorganization of the FBI's resources in order to better respond to crisis situations. In 1994, the Bureau established the Critical Incident Response Group (CIRG), whose mission was to 'integrate tactical and investigative resources and expertise for critical incidents which necessitate an immediate response from law enforcement authorities'.[10] Such incidents include terrorist acts, prison riots and hostage-takings, as well as barricaded armed groups. CIRG brought together capabilities for research, training, negotiation, and other functions that had previously been fragmented. Although much of the early development of negotiation capability had been directed at hostage situations, it quickly became evident after Waco that hostage-taking needed to be distinguished from incidents which involved barricaded subjects. Assumptions that many of the Branch Davidians were 'hostages' were clearly incorrect; hence techniques needed to be developed for situations in which those within a building or compound had shut themselves up voluntarily. Such techniques emphasize the establishment of trust and rapport between negotiators and subjects rather than an adversarial relationship.

The creation of CIRG did not by itself, however, alter the relationship between the Bureau and the scholarly community – a relationship still historically grounded in fields such as criminology and forensic psychiatry. However, at the urging of then-Attorney General Janet Reno, CIRG began to explore ways in which it might broaden its contacts with academia.

The first step in doing so was the creation of a Special Advisory Commission to CIRG, chaired by Vamik Volkan, a psychiatrist at the University of Virginia with a long record of pioneering work in the relationship between conflict and culture. In fall 1995, I was asked to join the Commission. The other members were Joseph Krofcheck, a psychiatrist with Yarrow and Associates; Elizabeth Marvick, a political scientist; Gregory Saathoff, a psychiatrist at the University of Virginia; Stephen Sampson, a psychologist at Georgia State University; Allen Sapp, a criminal justice expert at Central Missouri State University; and Robert Washington, a sociologist at Bryn Mawr College. The Commission met at the FBI Academy in Quantico, Virginia, in late 1995 and early 1996. The Commission's report, submitted in February 1996, recommended that CIRG have a multidisciplinary advisory group available, and have on staff individuals able to serve as links between the advisors and operational personnel.[11] Sooner than the Commission had imagined, the opportunity would arise to begin building these bridges, for unknown to the Commission, CIRG was already planning the Montana Freemen operation.

The Montana Freemen Standoff

The Freemen were a 'Christian patriot' group near Jordan, Montana, whose members included Christian Identity believers and schismatic

Mormons. They had a long history of friction with individuals in the surrounding area, and in September 1995, took over a 960-acre ranch. Pursuant to indictments handed down in December, the FBI arrested two Freemen outside the ranch on 25 March 1996. The remaining members of the group, many of whom were also under indictment, were armed and well provisioned. Although the Freemen lacked a charismatic leader, in other respects they resembled the Branch Davidians: a religious group (but in this instance one with pronounced anti-government views), that had physically isolated itself, and seemed prepared to defend itself with armed force if necessary.

The complex story of the episode will not be recapitulated here.[12] However, two points are pertinent to the present discussion: First, the FBI/CIRG operation was conducted with great restraint and with an emphasis on peaceful resolution. Although the standoff lasted from 26 March to 13 June, no shots were fired, and in the end the Freemen surrendered to authorities. Second, the Bureau reached out to religion scholars throughout the operation. Those consulted included Phillip Arnold, Jean Rosenfeld, Catherine Wessinger, Michael Webster (a psychologist) and myself. I maintained contact with Bureau personnel by phone, mail, and fax through April 1996. By May I was involved in a teaching commitment in London, which made it impossible to fulfill a request to go to Montana, although I remained in telephone contact, and other consultants did journey to the site. One of those was Phillip Arnold, whose presence was a measure of how significantly FBI practice had changed. At the time of Waco, three years earlier, a request by Arnold and his colleague, James Tabor, to play a role was rebuffed.[13]

While it is difficult to establish the significance of our role in an operation so long and complex, the tactics and resolution were clearly consistent with the advice we gave. More importantly, the successful outcome validated CIRG's intention to approach crises in a new way.

CIRG and the AAR

Although the Montana Freemen case was dramatic, the relationships between CIRG and scholars at the time were necessarily ad hoc and short-term. They ended when the group came out. Despite its success, therefore, the Montana case left open the issue of a more structured relationship, which had yet to be effected. Since the catalyst for change was the Waco affair, and in view of the recommendations made by

Nancy Ammerman and Lawrence Sullivan, in 1994 the Department of Justice contacted the American Academy of Religion (AAR) requesting that it help 'educate federal law enforcement agencies about religious groups'.[14] In response, the AAR invited an FBI agent to attend a session at the 1995 annual meeting in Philadelphia, devoted to the Oklahoma City bombing, which had occurred the preceding spring. I participated in that session, with, among others, Eugene Gallagher, and had a brief meeting with the agent afterward. Agents also attended the 1996 and 1997 annual meetings to hear papers that appeared to be relevant, but such involvement proved relatively unproductive. There were not always papers that addressed matters the Bureau was interested in, nor did such visits provide a chance for agents to communicate effectively with scholars.

Links to the AAR were closely tied to the report of the Volkan Commission. One of its recommendations had been the appointment of an individual to link the FBI with outside experts. In August 1996, Gregory Saathoff was named to that position. Although he bore the title of 'conflict resolution specialist', it was understood that he would facilitate connections with scholars in fields previously ignored by the Bureau.

In that capacity, he attended the November 1996 meeting in New Orleans. Catherine Wessinger of Loyola University in New Orleans arranged a private session with religion scholars in which Saathoff could explore the needs of law enforcement. He also met with two AAR officials: Barbara De Concini, the executive director, and Steve Herrick, the director of external relations. On the basis of these contacts, Saathoff saw the AAR as a principal forum for future contacts between the Bureau and the academic community.

In addition to his FBI position and his faculty post at the University of Virginia, Saathoff also serves as executive director of the Critical Incident Analysis Group at Virginia (CIAG). CIAG is the outgrowth of a conference held at Michigan State University in 1994, which brought together law enforcement personnel and scholars in reaction to the Waco debacle. After CIAG's transfer to the University of Virginia, it has continued to organize conferences that bring together academics and persons in the public sector, including a significant number of present and former FBI staff.[15]

Beginning in 1999, AAR annual meetings became the venue for contacts between scholars and FBI representatives. These sessions – 14 in all in 1999–2000 – were by invitation only and were often not listed in the conference program. The CIRG attendees came primarily from two of its components, the Crisis Negotiation Unit and the National Center for the Analysis of Violent Crime. The number of non-FBI participants varied. For example, in both 1999 and 2000, I gave presentations on extremist groups to the agents attending and responded at length to their questions. There were other sessions with as many as 15 or 20 scholars present. At the 2000 meeting in Nashville, FBI agents presented a simulated crisis negotiation with a barricaded religious believer, so that the academic audience could observe FBI negotiation techniques, as well as understand the pressures that might face outside consultants.[16] Plans are underway for a similar simulation, open to the AAR membership, at a future annual meeting.

AAR meetings, however, have not been the sole venue for contacts. In 1998, Saathoff arranged with Massimo Introvigne for a meeting of scholars and CIRG personnel in Fredericksburg, Virginia. Those attending included not only Americans but a number of Europeans, indicating that the incorporation of scholarly expertise was to be an international initiative. It involved, in addition to Introvigne, Eileen Barker, Jean-Francois Mayer, Susan Palmer and Ian Reader.

The Fredericksburg meeting was held a month before a conference in Jerusalem to which American and Israeli religion scholars and law enforcement officials had been invited, including CIRG personnel. Noting the Fredericksburg conference, members of the Bureau's Counter-terrorism Unit expressed interest in also attending the Jerusalem meeting. Invitations were arranged, and as a result, several of the *Project Megiddo* authors went to Jerusalem, together with their CIRG colleagues.

For the most part, however, the agents participating in AAR sessions have come from CIRG. But the 1999 annual meeting in Boston was an exception. Building on the experience of the Jerusalem conference, three analysts from the Counterterrorism Unit who had participated in the drafting of *Project Megiddo* agreed to attend. Richard Landes, director of the Center for Millennial Studies at Boston University, organized a closed session on the campus at which the *Megiddo* authors discussed the report in a conversation with an invited audience. While the details of the discussion were off the record, the session was characterized by both frankness and mutual respect. Although some academics present dissented from the report's tone or conclusions, the participants found a surprising amount of common ground.

The meeting was particularly valuable, inasmuch as none of the academics attending had been consulted during *Megiddo*'s drafting. Indeed, it is not clear whether the authors had consulted anyone outside the Bureau. The redacted text (reprinted as an appendix to this issue) cites only open, published sources. It is, I think, a realistic inference that one effect of the Boston meeting was to impress upon the writers how their effort might have been different had they sought the views of scholars.

The FBI and the Academy

Turnover in government occurs far more frequently than at universities. Transfers, promotions and retirements take FBI personnel out of crisis management far more rapidly than similar changes in the university world. Academics whose rank, institutional affiliation or work status changes, remain available as advisors, but agents who move to another unit of a complex organization or who shift to the private sector, are instantly removed from crisis management. In light of this, it has been particularly heartening that the contacts with the academic community have enjoyed strong support from the CIRG Special Agents in Charge (SACs): Robin Montgomery, who served from CIRG's creation in 1994 to 1997, and Roger Nisley, the SAC from 1997 to 2001. There is every reason to believe that the new SAC, Stephen Wiley, will continue this pattern. Beyond changes at the unit level, however, higher-level personnel shifts may also have an impact. A new Attorney General and FBI Director assumed office, and quickly faced the terrorist attacks of September 11, 2001.

The relationship between the FBI and the academic community is still in its infancy, at least concerning disciplines that have no historic relationship to law enforcement. Criminology and forensic psychiatry, for example, are fields with long histories of involvement with law enforcement agencies. As a result, relationships have formed, utility no longer needs to be constantly validated, and the 'comfort level' is high. But in areas such as religious studies, sociology, and political science none of these exists. There are no longstanding personal ties, potential consumers of scholarly knowledge are often skeptical of its usefulness, and as a result, neither party may be wholly comfortable with the other.

These sources of stress are exacerbated in crisis situations, which generally provide the context in which partnerships are supposed to be formed. From the standpoint of the endurance of those partnerships, it is the worst possible setting in which parties from separate cultures without previous histories of collaboration are supposed to work jointly. Thus it becomes necessary to develop forms of interaction in non-crisis settings that will allow productive communication in future crises.

For these reasons, the involvement of scholars needs to constitute more than names on a Rolodex, who might be called as necessary. Unless personal trust has already been established, the advice proffered is unlikely to be taken seriously.

Fostering such cooperation is a delicate matter. On the one hand, those to whom advice is rendered need to have confidence in those who render the advice. At the same time, academic consultants must maintain their own independence. The advice of co-opted scholars may not be worth having, since they have lost precisely the freshness of perspective that makes their advice valuable. Put another way, if consultants get co-opted, an agency might be better off retaining its own in-house experts. But the desire to cultivate relationships with external academics is predicated on the belief (surely correct) that outsiders can provide assistance that insiders cannot. Unfortunately, there are few established ground rules for securing the right balance between independence and collaboration.

During the Montana Freemen affair – the only crisis situation in which significant use was made of scholars – I was struck by the ad hoc, undefined character of consultants' roles. Those of us who had participated in the Volkan Commission deliberations had concentrated on mechanisms for inserting new forms of expertise into crisis management. We had neither the time nor the mandate to explore the norms that ought to govern the behavior of outsiders in law enforcement operations. This remains uncharted territory, and significant unresolved issues of role definition remain.

There is, for example, the gap between scholars' desire to slowly weigh evidence and reflect, and practitioners' needs for immediate action. This is less true where the primary goal is analysis, as it was in *Project Megiddo*, than in situations in which, for example, governmental authority confronts an armed political or religious group. In such a situation, time for reflection may be an unaffordable luxury. There is also the issue of secrecy versus openness. To what extent are scholars who are called in by law enforcement agencies constrained from revealing what they may learn? The constraints may range from those connected with information derived from non-open sources, such as informants; to limitations imposed by the need to protect opportunities for prosecution. On the other side, it is unlikely that the best expertise will be available if those possessing it find that they must accept a regime of unlimited secrecy.

Unfortunately, at the present time there are no formal guidelines governing the relationship between the FBI and outside academic consultants. In their absence, the two parties can easily develop incompatible role conceptions without intending to do so. An attempt to place a panel on this subject on the 2000 AAR annual meeting program was not successful. It is possible, of course, that rules will evolve naturally, but given the episodic nature of the contacts, that is by no means assured. There is, instead, a need for mutually agreed upon norms. Although this is not the place to try and develop such norms, let me suggest some areas where the need appears greatest.

One area that needs to be more clearly structured concerns the use of information. Both the FBI and at least some scholars possess confidential information. The Bureau's non-public sources are well known, including reports from informants, undercover agents and court-ordered phone taps. But academics, too, often possess confidential information, particularly as a result of participant observation and interviewing, where the researcher has made implicit or explicit promises of confidentiality to those he/she is studying. While these assurances can be overridden by a court order (for example, by subpoena, since there is no legal privilege for researchers), in its absence, a binding ethical obligation remains. Within university settings, this obligation has become 'legalized' through the oversight of Institutional Review Boards (IRBs) for research that involves human subjects. The informed consent required by IRBs imposes special constraints on scholars who might be consulted by law enforcement. Hence some academic researchers may face a conflict between what law enforcement agencies wish to know and the guarantees they have given to their subjects.

At the same time, a crisis is likely to be seen by academics who are consulted as a potential research situation. How far 'inside' an incident they get can vary from case to case, but they may well come upon data that they would not ordinarily see: non-public documents, conversations among law enforcement personnel, and negotiations with barricaded groups, for example. Then there is, necessarily, their own experience, since as consultants they become participants in the situation. It is not at all clear what may or may not subsequently be done with such information. If such participation by scholars amounts to an open-ended commitment never to write about the situation, providing advice is not likely to be very attractive. By the same token, some level of discretion is presumably called for, although scholars and agencies may have quite different ideas about how much.

To date, the use of social science expertise by the FBI has been the special province of CIRG. Those concerned with domestic terrorism, including the authors of *Project Megiddo*, have been less influenced by the bridge-building described here. Such compartmentalization is hardly surprising in a large and complex bureaucracy.

There is thus, in the end, a 'two-cultures' problem. The FBI, like many government agencies, encourages loyalty and teamwork. Academia, on the other hand, fosters individuality and skepticism. These divergent values are exhibited across a broad range of government–academic interactions. The shifting relationship in the case of the FBI and religious studies is merely one instance of a broader class. However, measured against the situation that existed at the time of Waco, in 1993, present arrangements, incomplete though they are, constitute extraordinary progress.

NOTES

I am most appreciative of Gregory Saathoff's willingness to read and comment on an earlier draft. I am also grateful to Jeffrey Kaplan for his insightful suggestions. However, I bear sole responsibility for any errors of fact.

1. 'FBI: Militias a Threat at Millennium', *USA Today* (20 Oct. 1999).
2. *Report to the Deputy Attorney General on the Events at Waco, Texas February 28 to April 19, 1993*, redacted version (Washington, DC: Department of Justice, 8 Oct. 1993).
3. *Recommendations of Experts for Improvement in Federal Law Enforcement After Waco* (Washington, DC: Department of Justice 1993), p.1 of 'Memorandum' from Philip B. Heymann and Ronald K. Noble (this volume is not consecutively paginated).
4. *Recommendations of Expert*, p.1 of the Ammerman memo.
5. *Recommendations of Experts*, p.14 of the Sullivan memo.
6. *Recommendations of Experts*, p.9 of the Ammerman memo.
7. *Recommendations of Experts*, p.14 of the Sullivan memo.
8. *Report to the Deputy Attorney General*, p.10.
9. *Report to the Deputy Attorney General*, pp.139–40.
10. CIRG homepage, (accessed 26 March 2001).
11. *Commission Report, Select Advisory Commission to the FBI's Critical Incident Response Group*, Feb. 1996.
12. See for example Jean E. Rosenfeld, 'The Importance of the Analysis of Religion in

Avoiding Violent Outcomes: The Justus Freemen Crisis', *Nova Religio* 1/1 (Oct. 1997), pp.72–95.
13. James D. Tabor and Eugene V. Gallagher, *Why Waco? Cults and the Battle for Religious Freedom in America* (Berkeley, CA: University of California Press 1995), pp.13–14.
14. Steve Herrick, 'New Religious Movement Scholars Watch FBI Simulate a Crisis', *Religious Studies News* 16/1 (Feb. 2001), pp.5–6.
15. The CIAG website is www.faculty.virginia.edu/ciag.
16. Herrick, 'New Religious Movement Scholars Watch FBI Simulate a Crisis' (note 14).

Questioning the Frame:
The Canadian, Israeli and US Reports

EUGENE V. GALLAGHER

The predictive value of the Canadian Security Intelligence Service (CSIS), Jerusalem Institute for Israel Studies (JIIS) and US Federal Bureau of Investigation (FBI) reports was never high and has steadily diminished. Nonetheless, the reports disclose much about how law enforcement agencies and their consultants framed the topic of millennial violence. The writers of the reports faced substantial and sometimes divergent challenges in gathering, interpreting and evaluating information. For example, the CSIS and FBI had to rely on open sources, while the JIIS directly recommends 'undercover intelligence activity'.[1] More telling than how the reports gathered information, however, is what they did with it. The ways in which the reports sifted through the collected information, sorted it into analytical categories, and situated it in specific interpretive contexts often depend upon largely unvoiced assumptions about several fundamental topics, including the nature of millennialism itself. On three particular topics the reports are especially revealing: the focus on the year 2000, the connections between millennialism and violence, and the treatment of Jerusalem as a central focus of biblical millennialism.

The Year 2000

The reasons for focusing on the year 2000 are not fully articulated in the reports.[2] Assertions about the potential for violent millennial outbursts are not supported by detailed quantitative or qualitative evidence; instead, the reports appeal more to a general *zeitgeist*. But it is easy enough to identify likely influential factors. The 1990s featured several violent episodes involving millennial groups. In 1993, encounters between the Branch Davidian Adventist sect and agents of the US Bureau of Alcohol, Tobacco and Firearms and the FBI left four federal agents and 80 members of the group dead. In five separate incidents between 1994 and 1997, 73 members of the Order of the Solar Temple died either by their own hands or at the hands of their fellow believers in Quebec, Switzerland and France. In 1995, members of the Japanese millennial group Aum Shinrikyô injured more than 5,000 people and killed 12 by releasing sarin gas in the Tokyo subway. In 1997, 39 members of the group known as 'Heaven's Gate' committed suicide, with another to follow later in that year and one in 1998.[3] Those events also fed the amorphous but persistent international anti-cult movement which, taking the 1978 mass suicide and murder of nearly 1,000 people at the Peoples Temple's community in Jonestown, Guyana, as its primary model, had long associated 'cults' with violence.[4] Throughout its history, the anti-cult movement has aggressively marketed its 'expertise' to both media outlets and law enforcement agencies and its influence is evident in the reports.[5] Finally, the concern about widespread computer malfunctions at the dawn of the year 2000 also influenced the reports' focus on the chronological millennium.

Their concentration on the relation of millennialists to widely used chronological systems, however, led the reports to downplay the power of the internal logic of millennial systems to make virtually any date a crucial one. Although the dawning of a new millennium is indelibly aligned with significant events in Christian history because of the Christian origins of the common calendar, the particular calendar of any millennial group or individual need not, and most likely will not, coincide with the secular calendar used by a specific society. An individual's or group's millennial calculus takes into account multiple variables, many of them qualitative and subject to continual re-interpretation. Lack of access to power, prestige, material goods, moral stature, or other tangible or intangible 'goods', the experience of disaster, the recognition of divine inspiration, and many other factors shape millennial thinking more profoundly than numbers on a calendar.[6] In fact, the re-calculation of the time of the end has been a prominent theme in Western millennial thought at least since the time of the book of Daniel in the second century BCE.[7] But the calendar doesn't drive millennial thought; millennial thought drives the calendar. Since millennial thought is about the making of a new society, a new moral order and a new human being, or, as Norman Cohn's well-known characterization has it, immediate, collective, total, this-worldly salvation,[8] it operates with a distinctive logic that separates it from the routine observation of transitions in a secular calendar from one day, week, month, or year to another.

There are passages in the reports that seem to signal an awareness that millennialism is not necessarily linked to specific dates on a common calendar. The CSIS report concludes that 'there clearly is continuing threat potential, given the temporal inaccuracies of the turning of the millennium … and the tendency for groups to be unpredictable and give [no] early-warning signs of their potential for violence, as well as ambiguities in their structure, dynamics and attributes.'[9] The concluding appreciation of the fluidity, ambiguity and unpredictability of millennial groups, however, might better have served as a starting point. If millennial groups are changeable and if the motivations of their members spring directly from their experiences and perceptions, a general analysis that strives to associate many of them with a single date is likely to miss significant variations and nuances. Some of that diversity is nicely captured in the appendix to the JIIS report, which underscores the variety of Christian attitudes toward the year 2000. In general, however, the reports did not conclude from their recognition of the differences among millennial groups that their particular 'millennial calendars' could be equally diverse. At the least, the reports should have acknowledged that the year 2000 had no *universally* compelling force for millennial groups. It was not *necessarily* significant for any of them, since they primarily determined significance not from the secular calendar but from the pronouncements of prophetic figures, passages from authoritative texts, and their own readings of the 'signs of the times'. By narrowing the focus to the year 2000, the reports misconstrued both the relationship of millennialism to the common, secular calendar and, as a result, the nature of millennialism itself. Both flaws, most pronounced in the FBI document, could have serious consequences, particularly if they were to lead law enforcement to conclude that millennial activity and any millennial threats are now in the past. Millennial activity is not primarily a calendrical phenomenon, but an ever-present possibility. Its primary motivating factors are intellectual, moral, social and existential, rather than chronological.

Millennialism and Violence

The connection between millennialism and violence has been cemented in public discourse by the anti-cult movement's privileging of the

examples of Jonestown and then the Branch Davidians, the Order of the
Solar Temple, Aum Shinrikyô, and Heaven's Gate. Freelance anti-cult
activist Rick Ross, for example, argues that 'the most important concern
today is not simply who might be somewhat "cultic" in their devotion
now or historically, but what groups might represent potential problems
regarding personal or public safety, that is, groups that are potentially
unsafe and/or destructive'.[10] Margaret Singer put it more succinctly,
claiming that 'Waco was a replay of Jonestown'.[11] That highlighting of
a handful of examples out of literally thousands begs further
explanation.[12] Yet there is little in the anti-cult literature that explains
precisely why those particular cases are supposed to be exemplary; just
what they are intended to be examples of, and what types of
generalizations they can support. Thus, they devolve into a random
collection of the most frightening examples.

The FBI report bears traces of similar thinking. It ignores the
dynamic interaction of leaders and followers that characterizes any
social movement and instead endorses the notion of the all-powerful
leader that dominates anti-cult polemics. It claims, for example, that 'the
potential for violence on behalf of the members of biblically-driven
cults is determined almost exclusively by the whims of the cult leader'.
Anti-cult arguments may also have shaped the FBI report's taxonomy of
groups, which separates 'apocalyptic cults' from Christian Identity
groups, white supremacists, militias and Black Hebrew Israelites. The
artificial and untenable distinction between groups motivated by
religious ideas and those motivated by 'New World Order' conspiracy
theories also suggests the absence of a clear set of principles for
classifying groups and lack of awareness of the migration of ideas and
explanatory constructs from one milieu to another.

The JIIS report focuses on developing a series of 'worst-case
scenarios', ranging from catastrophic terrorist actions to disruptions
caused by overcrowding at holy sites. While the detail of the scenarios
makes them gripping reading, it mutes some of their common themes
and submerges the theoretical orientation of the report. There is also
some tension between the report's emphases. On one hand, it echoes the
standard anti-cult position in devoting particular attention to the
charismatic leader or 'lone believer' as a likely primary catalyst for
violence. The report asserts, for example, that new or not fully
established Christian groups 'usually have a charismatic leader who is
in total control of the members' life and belief'. On the other hand, the

report identifies several kinds of interactions between millennialists and foreign law enforcement agencies, Israeli authorities, or Ultra-orthodox Jews as dynamic factors that could lead towards violence. But the report never integrates its emphases on leadership and situational factors into a single model of how millennial groups operate.

The implicit theoretical frameworks and internal contradictions of the reports complicate any attempts to investigate potential connections between millennialism and violence, though the reports' very existence, choices of examples, and rhetoric presume such connections. For example, the JIIS report's opening observation that the likelihood of 'a catastrophic terror act [being] conducted in Jerusalem ... is very small' exists in some tension with the seven ensuing pages of vividly detailed, though 'largely unlikely', worst-case scenarios. Since there is a convergence of the interests of both law enforcement and scholars on this topic, a review of a few recent scholarly attempts to investigate the potential links between millennialism and violence can highlight alternative frameworks. In *Apocalypse Observed* John R. Hall and his co-authors persuasively reject the 'cult essentialism' that explains everything by reference to supposedly universal internal dynamics of contemporary millennialist groups. In its place they demonstrate the distinctiveness of individual groups and show how the interaction of a movement and its 'cultural opponents' is the key to understanding outbreaks of violence. Hall also identifies two different apocalyptic types. The 'warring sect', under which he classifies the Peoples Temple, the Branch Davidians and Japan's Aum Shinrikyô, pursues a climactic struggle against the forces of evil. Under a second type, the mystical apocalypse of deathly transcendence, Hall includes both the Order of the Solar Temple and Heaven's Gate. Hall concludes with a caution about how law enforcement itself may contribute to the problem. He observes that 'the strong relationship between state-cultural opposition and outcomes of violence underscores how problematic state action becomes in the view of apocalyptic sectarians when it seems to take the side of cultural opponents under the glare of hostile media coverage'.[13]

Relying in part on Hall's stress that 'cultural opponents' often catalyze violence between millennialists and the world outside their group, Catherine Wessinger identifies three types of millennial groups: fragile, assaulted and revolutionary. Factors that can make a group fragile include instability in the leadership, manifest failures to progress towards the millennial goal, and external pressure from opponents; fragile groups may either implode into violence directed against themselves or explode in conflicts with those outside. Assaulted groups either actually are or believe themselves to be besieged by opponents; they may prepare for what they see as an inevitable conflict and may well fight back if attacked. Revolutionary groups may devise intricate and detailed plans for attacks on their perceived enemies, will favor a violent rhetoric, and sometimes may actually act on their plans.[14] Hall and Wessinger share an emphasis on violence as the outcome of specific kinds of interactions, rather than an inherent potential of some groups. Their analysis is most directly echoed by the CSIS report's discussion of the consequences of actions by the authorities. It notes that 'violence is often not actualized until the group comes into contact with state authorities' and that 'action on the part of state agencies will almost always elicit a reaction.' That overlap suggests the possibility of fruitful analytical cooperation between scholars and law enforcement officials. In fact, the scenarios formulated by the JIIS report, or something like them, could provide an interesting and helpful framework for such an exercise.

Only the CSIS report, however, draws pointed conclusions for law enforcement from the analysis of violence as the product of interaction between millennialists and their opponents. It reminds its readers that 'authorities often fail to appreciate the leverage they have over doomsday movements, which depend upon them to fulfill their apocalyptic scenarios'. Specifically in the case of groups that focus on authoritative texts, law enforcement has a double leverage. In biblical apocalypticism, for example, millennial messages are generated through the triangular interrelationships of text, interpreter and context. While the text remains fixed, the interpreter and the context can always change. Through interaction with interpreters and manipulation of the context, law enforcement has the potential to shift situations away from potential violence and towards peaceful resolution. Law enforcement officials will not be able to capitalize on those possibilities, however, if they adopt the view that specific groups are inherently prone to violence. For law enforcement 'cult essentialism' is a self-limiting, or even self-defeating, position because it fosters the perception that outsiders are drastically constrained in their ability to alter the course of events. In contrast, the interactionist model described by Hall and Wessinger enlarges the possibilities for positive intervention in any encounter with millennialists.

Recognizing the malleability of the situation, however, in no way guarantees a successful outcome. The CSIS report rightly reminds law enforcement that 'negotiators dealing with the movement must understand its belief structure, as ignorance of the minor differences between the beliefs of respective groups can have drastic outcomes'. Robin Wagner-Pacifici has effectively captured the nuances of conflicts between millennial groups and outsiders in her analysis of the standoff as a social situation. She notes a particular paradox 'that while all participants have committed themselves to the situation (with highly variable degrees of freedom) they have, in a profound sense, committed themselves to *different* situations'.[15] Consequently, she argues that 'the action driving the parties of a standoff to a standoff state and out through the other side of it is primarily a project of interpretation'.[16] All of the parties in a standoff are involved in interpreting statements and actions, calibrating their responses, and assessing their consequences. While it may appear static, the standoff is actually a very fluid situation. Accordingly, analysis of any individual's or group's potential for violence always needs to be context-specific, deeply attentive to the particular beliefs and convictions at play, fully aware of multiple perceptions of the situation, and cognizant of how matters may change over time. The closer the reports come to adopting the view that certain groups are inherently liable to commit violent acts, the further they move away from the kind of nuanced analysis of specific situations that the interactionist model recommends.

Another issue related to the connections between millennialism and violence concerns the relationship of rhetoric to action. The FBI report states that 'in light of the enormous amount of millennial rhetoric, the FBI sought to analyze a number of variables that have the potential to spark violent acts'. Although the FBI was correct to note that millennial beliefs are very often expressed in dramatically violent language, the extent to which that language has the ability to 'spark violent acts' remains to be investigated.[17] Jeffrey Kaplan, for example, has emphasized that most millennial rhetoric is just that. Noting how infrequently violent millennial rhetoric inspires violent actions on the part of millennialists, he suggests that 'watching is what millenarians do best', and proceeds to distinguish rhetorical, defensive, and revolutionary forms of violence.[18] In addition, episodic violence is only sometimes related to the programmatic goals of the group, as it was, for example, with the activities of The Order in 1983–84.[19] Defensive violence could occur in either the fragile or the assaulted groups that Wessinger describes. For example, she identifies the Peoples Temple in its final, Jonestown phase as a fragile group that turned its violence inward when

it despaired of reaching its millennial goal. In contrast, she sees the
Branch Davidians as an assaulted group that reacted violently to a
military raid by the Bureau of Alcohol, Tobacco and Firearms. Kaplan
also singles out a factor that can easily be ignored. In his view, the 'self-
perception as a tiny and powerless band of the faithful acts as a powerful
check on the catalyzation of violence. Millenarians are no fools. They are
canny judges of the prevailing balance of forces.'[20] Taken together, recent
scholarly considerations of millennialism and violence provide a much
more subtle understanding of millennial language and its relation to
action than is evident in any of the reports. They also suggest that
prolonged intensive conversations between law enforcement officials
and scholars on topics of mutual interest would certainly be beneficial to
law enforcement and probably to the scholars as well.

Jerusalem and the Bible

The JIIS report is understandably focused on millennial activity in
Jerusalem, and even though some of its details may now be dated, it
offers a rich account of the sites and actors that may come into play in
millennial scenarios. The FBI report also devotes substantial attention to
the city as a potentially volatile site. The importance of Jerusalem in
both reports highlights the international character of many millennial
groups. Wherever they are headquartered, they are often able to draw
adherents from many disparate places of origin, and they also easily
move themselves or at least some adherents across national
boundaries.[21] While the magnetic attraction of the many holy places,
shrines, churches and mosques in Jerusalem and throughout Israel
cannot be ignored, the reports fail to address another aspect of sacred
geography. The propensity of religious groups in the broad biblical
tradition to superimpose elements from the biblical landscape over
virtually any territory is succinctly exemplified in Branch Davidians'
decision to name their property 'Mount Carmel'. That name is derived
from the story in I Kings 18:1–46 where, on Mount Carmel in Israel, the
prophet Elijah demonstrated the power of Yahweh and the truth of his
prophecy in a contest with prophets of Baal. For the residents of Mount
Carmel, their community demonstrated the truth of David Koresh's
prophecy and the reality of the God they worshipped.[22] The significance
for law enforcement of 're-used' biblical place names is that officials
should expect to encounter in virtually any place the same intense

devotion, surging emotions and fervent willingness to defend or liberate sacred places that they see in Jerusalem. Just as millennial groups can develop their own distinctive chronologies that are not governed by the secular calendar, so can they develop sacred geographies that are governed by their own distinctive logics. Potentially any place, no matter how nondescript in the view of outsiders, can become sacred. If law enforcement officials were to cross the boundaries of sacred space, intentionally or unintentionally, their actions could easily be interpreted as transgressing divine commands, polluting religious purity, or assaulting an entire world view. Such provocative actions are possible not only in Jerusalem, whose sacred character is widely recognized, but in literally any place that a group identifies as its own sacred ground. Just as the turning of the secular millennium should not lead law enforcement to decide that millennial activity will necessarily wane, so should the focus on Jerusalem and Israel as ground zero for the millennium not keep them from realizing that any place can become the focus for millennial activity.

Jerusalem and other sites in Israel are important in many millennial scenarios because of their roles in the sacred narratives in the Old and New Testaments. Yet none of the three reports offers a sophisticated analysis of the roles of the appropriation and interpretation of scripture in millennial movements. The CSIS report is virtually silent on the subject, and the JIIS report limits its discussion to a brief paragraph on the 'two witnesses' scenario from Revelation 11. Although the FBI report is more alert to the importance of scripture in Christian millennialism, its exclusive focus on the New Testament's book of Revelation leaves out many other texts that have contributed to millennial scenarios. For example, the account of the 'rapture' in the apostle Paul's first letter to the Thessalonians (c. 50 CE) has long excited the imaginations of millennialists with its vivid image of all of the faithful, both living and dead, rising to meet the Lord in the air.[23] The 'little apocalypse' in chapter 13 of the gospel of Mark, along with its parallel passages in Matthew and Luke, has also been a fertile source of apocalyptic imagery. Many other texts can also come into play, including passages from the Psalms and Prophets in the Hebrew Bible. The assertion of the FBI report that 'to understand many religious extremists, it is crucial to know the origin of the Book of Revelation and the meanings of its words, numbers and characters' both constricts the reader's focus and only scratches the surface of the resources available to biblical millennialists. It misleads because it fosters the impression that there are stable meanings to the 'words, numbers and characters' of Revelation. Though defensible in a general sense, that statement fails to appreciate how individual items derive their meaning from their position in a system of millennial thought. For example, the meaning of the rider on the white horse in Revelation 6:1–2 may only become clear when that passage is read in light of Psalm 45 and other texts, as is the case in David Koresh's exegesis of the passage.[24] Because millennial messages are created through the interplay of text, interpreter and context, the same texts cannot be presumed to carry precisely the same meanings in different contexts, and, as with all exegesis, small differences can have large consequences.

A prominent characteristic of biblical millennialism is the construction of elaborate mosaics of 'proof texts' taken from many different parts of the Bible, rather than the rote application of a single text to a specific situation. One of the tests of an effective interpreter, then, becomes his or her ability to marshal an abundance of biblical citations to address the particular 'signs of the times' that an apocalyptic group observes. The ingenuity of the interpreter lies in the ability to see a fit between the perceived state of the world and the resources provided by the textual tradition. That process never really stops; even when a persuasive alignment between text and situation is identified, there is always room for refinements, re-calibrations and re-considerations. Because the situation itself is fluid, the demand for new interpretations and the revision of old ones will never cease until the millennium actually does arrive. The reports therefore need to re-conceive biblical interpretation as a dynamic process that can draw upon the entire Bible and is sensitive to even small changes in context. Rather than depending solely on 'the whims of the cult leader', biblical interpretation is constrained by an audience's open access to the same book. With every comment on the text, an interpreter's authority can be augmented or diminished in the eyes of the audience. Authority in biblically based millennial groups is perpetually under construction, always with reference to the biblical text. Law enforcement officials, who are attentive to the ebb and flow between an interpreter of the sacred texts and his or her audience and aware of the necessarily tentative and contextual nature of any particular interpretation, can therefore seize the possibility of influencing both the interpreter and the context in ways that diminish the potential for violence. In general, the reports need to recognize more fully how fluid and shifting the interpretation of any authoritative text can be; that awareness would open up many more avenues for positive interaction than an image of texts as having single, fixed meanings that are simply conveyed to an audience. In millennial groups interpretation of authoritative texts can easily become the primary form of leadership. Thus it becomes crucial for law enforcement officials to have an accurate and subtle grasp of the multiple strategies of interpretation that can be employed within a group that focuses on the biblical message.

The fourth scenario described in the JIIS report provides an example of how interpretive flexibility might come into play. Its plot features a new Christian group headed by a charismatic leader with virtually total control over the followers. The report envisions the group arriving in an Israel already at a high pitch of apocalyptic excitement. The leader, feeling heavy pressure to validate his own prophecies, desperately reasserts the imminence of the End even when nothing happens at the turn of the year. The report anticipates a violent denouement when a clash between security forces and the edgy members of the group ends in loss of life on both sides. While the JIIS report attributes more fervor than flexibility to the group, there are many instances in the history of millennialism where disappointment leads to reinterpretation and subsequently to transformation or eventual dissolution of a group rather than greater fragility and increased propensity for violence. The history of the Millerites in the nineteenth-century US is a case in point. After substantial labor in the interpretation of the Bible, William Miller concluded that the Second Coming of Christ would occur sometime between 21 March 1843 and 21 March 1844. When it did not, Miller neither gave up his convictions nor turned to violence. He simply adjusted his interpretation of the date from the spring to the fall, focusing instead on 22 October 1844. The failure of Christ to return on that date provoked among Miller's followers the 'Great Disappointment', but the Millerite hope for the dawning of a new millennium was not extinguished and within a few years took new shape in the nascent Seventh-Day Adventist movement. As the case of the Millerites shows, leaders and followers alike are often unwilling or even unable to abandon their most cherished hopes; they can persistently strive to adjust their predictions to suit their desires. When they are working with a rich and multi-faceted collection of authoritative texts like the Christian Scriptures, skilled interpreters can frequently find ways to keep hope alive even after multiple disappointments. The JIIS scenario is indeed a worst-case analysis; as presented, it shortchanges the flexibility that a leader can claim, and that followers can acknowledge, in the interpretation of holy texts. Unfulfilled prophecies need not beget violence, and in most cases they don't. Internal factors, such as the exercise of exegetical ingenuity, can lead a group away from climactic confrontations by thoroughly re-shaping the group's perception of its own situation. Authoritative and textually persuasive re-interpretation of their millennial scenario can lead a group to wait peacefully for another, more distant, millennial dawn.

Conclusion

All three reports are all marked by the purposes for which they were created. As the secular millennium fades from view, they remain the most current indicators of how some government agencies and their consultants think about millennialism and especially its ability to inspire violent actions. They display an understanding of the topic that is uneven and evidently subject to the pushes and pulls of different interest groups. Despite a deepening relationship between some scholars of millennialism and the FBI and in part because of agency prohibitions against prior consultation, the *Project Megiddo* report remains largely uncritical in its appropriation of anti-cult polemics. That literature depends so strongly on a single model of the virtually omnipotent 'cult leader', the bamboozled followers who are easily led, and the high potential for violence, that it virtually precludes any possibility of understanding violence as the product of discrete interactions, authority as a volatile quality subject to constant testing, and millennial groups as continually changing as they seek the perfect understanding of the signs of the times in their own authoritative sources. Both law enforcement, and the public safety that it strives to ensure, are ill-served by such a cramped view of the nature of millennialism. For example, the JIIS report's recommendation that authorities compile 'a small list of mischief-prone groups and individuals that should be barred from entering Israel' presumes an inherent stability of both groups and leaders that is undermined by the emphases on dynamism and interaction in its own 'worst-case scenarios'. Also, while it may deter millennial violence on the local level, it may also simply displace it, in an exacerbated form, to another locale.

The turn of the secular millennium, while potentially important, was certainly not the only time that a group might envisage a new heaven and new earth; the possibility of violence is not inherent in some groups like a genetic marker; and a new Jerusalem in a hitherto unexpected location is as likely to become ground zero for some group's millennial vision as are the Western Wall and the Dome of the Rock. Millennialism is more diverse and unpredictable than the reports imply, and thus demands the constant attention of both scholars and law enforcement officials.

NOTES

1. The FBI report makes no direct statement about sources.
2. *Project Megiddo* simply notes that 'the year 2000 is being discussed and debated at all levels of society', while the JIIS report notes that 'the approaching end of the second millennium – according to the Christian count, which has been adopted by the entire modern world – is arousing anxieties and hopes among "believers" who draw their faith from religious-eschatological sources as well as among various eccentrics'. The CSIS report notes that 'the approaching year 2000 AD has stimulated millennial anxiety and heightened concern that its unfolding will bring an increase in potential threats by groups that would choose to assert their apocalyptic beliefs through violence'.
3. For analysis and interpretations of those events see Catherine Wessinger, *How the Millennium Comes Violently: From Jonestown to Heaven's Gate* (New York: Seven Bridges Press, 2000) and John R. Hall *et al.*, *Apocalypse Observed: Religious Movements and Violence in North America, Europe, and Japan* (New York: Routledge, 2000).
4. On the anti-cult movement see the material on the website maintained by Prof. Jeffrey Hammond of the University of Virginia at http://religiousmovements.lib.virginia.edu.
5. For an example of marketing anti-cult 'expertise' see James D. Tabor and Eugene V. Gallagher, *Cults and the Battle for Religious Freedom in America* (Berkeley, CA: University of California Press, 1995), pp.93–96.
6. See Kenelm Burridge, *New Heaven, New Earth: A Study of Millenarian Activities* (New York: Schocken, 1969); Michael Barkun, *Disaster and the Millennium* (New Haven, CT: Yale University Press, 1974); Norman Cohn, *The Pursuit of the Millennium: Revolutionary Millenarians and Mystical Anarchists of the Middle Ages* (New York: Oxford University Press, 1970); and Cohn, *Cosmos, Chaos, and the World to Come: The Ancient Roots of Apocalyptic Faith* (New Haven, CT: Yale University Press, 1993).
7. See Daniel's reinterpretation of Jeremiah's 70 years to mean 70 weeks of years in Daniel 9:24. On Daniel in general see Cohn, *Cosmos, Chaos* (note 6), pp.167–75. Daniel associates the time of the end with the reign and activities of the Syrian king Antiochus Epiphanes. Mark 13:14 borrows language from Daniel 9:27, 11:31 and 12:11 ('the abomination of desolation') to express the idea that the end will come around the year 70 CE. On Jesus and millennialism see Dale C. Allison, *Jesus of Nazareth: Millenarian Prophet* (Minneapolis, MN: Augsburg Fortress, 1998). For a selection of recent attempts to set the date see the website of the Ontario Consultants on Religious Tolerance: www.religioustolerance.org.
8. See Norman Cohn, 'Medieval Millenarism: Its Bearing on the Comparative Study of Millenarian Movements', in Sylvia L. Thrupp (ed.), *Millennial Dreams in Action: Studies in Revolutionary Religious Movements* (New York: Schocken, 1970), pp.31–43.
9. Word in brackets added for logic and sense.
10. www.rickross.com, FAQ, p.1.
11. Margaret Thaler Singer with Janja Lalich, *Cults in Our Midst: The Hidden Menace in Everyday Life* (San Francisco: Jossey-Bass, 1995), p.28.
12. It is very difficult to get an accurate and stable census of the number of 'cults' active at any one time, in large part because of the vague definitions of the term in popular usage. The FBI report mentions 'nearly 1,000'.

13. Hall, *Apocalypse Observed*, 201.
14. See Wessinger, *How the Millennium*, pp.12–29. See also Wessinger, 'Millennialism With and Without the Mayhem', in Thomas Robbins and Susan J. Palmer, *Millennium, Messiahs, and Mayhem: Contemporary Apocalyptic Movements* (New York: Routledge, 1997), pp.47–59; and Wessinger (ed.), *Millennialism, Persecution, and Violence: Historical Cases* (Syracuse, NY: Syracuse University Press, 2000).
15. Robin Wagner-Pacifici, *Theorizing the Standoff: Contingency in Action* (Cambridge: Cambridge University Press, 2000), p.7; her emphasis.
16. Ibid., p.19.
17. For analyses of millennial rhetoric see Stephen D. O'Leary, *Arguing the Apocalypse: A Theory of Millennial Rhetoric* (New York: Oxford University Press, 1994) and Barry Brummett, *Contemporary Apocalyptic Rhetoric* (New York: Praeger, 1991).
18. See Jeffrey Kaplan, *Radical Religion in America: Millenarian Movements from the Far Right to the Children of Noah* (Syracuse, NY: Syracuse University Press, 1997), p.168, passage quoted, pp.55–7, 65 for the types of violence. See also Eugene V. Gallagher, 'Cults', in Ronald Gottesman, *Violence in America: An Encyclopedia* (New York: Scribners, 1999), pp.364–8 for a distinction between rhetorical, episodic, programmatic and defensive forms of violence.
19. On The Order see Kevin Flynn and Gary Gerhart, *The Silent Brotherhood* (New York: Signet, 1990) and Kaplan, *Radical Religion* (note 18), pp.61–7.
20. See Kaplan, *Radical Religion* (note 18), p.171.
21. For example, the Branch Davidians, though located in rural farmland outside Waco, Texas, had members from Great Britain and Australia, among other places. Their leader, David Koresh, experienced a profound religious transformation while visiting Jerusalem. The Concerned Christians group moved from Denver to Israel before they were expelled by wary Israeli authorities. Aum Shinrikyô was active in Russia. Examples could easily be multiplied.
22. On the Branch Davidians' Mount Carmel see Tabor and Gallagher, *Why Waco* (note 5), pp.32–3, 37–8, 210–11. See also Belden C. Lane, *Landscapes of the Sacred: Geography and Narrative in American Spirituality* (New York: Paulist Press, 1988).
23. See 1 Thessalonians 4:3–18, esp. 16–17: 'For the Lord himself will descend from heaven with a cry of command, with the archangel's call, and with the sound of the trumpet of God. And the dead in Christ will rise first; then we who are alive, who are left, shall be caught up together with them in the clouds to meet the Lord in the air; and so we shall always be with the Lord.' On the motif of the rapture see Paul Boyer, *When Time Shall Be No More: Prophecy Belief in Modern American Culture* (Cambridge, MA: Belknap Press, 1992), pp.9–10, 254–60.
24. See the treatment of Revelation 6:1–2 in David Koresh's unfinished manuscript on the seven seals of the book of Revelation in Tabor and Gallagher, *Why Waco* (note 5), pp.197–203.

Ten Comments on Watching Closely the Gaps Between Beliefs and Actions

BENJAMIN BEIT-HALLAHMI

One

Attempts to forecast future developments in the short or long term are not just a common human pursuit, but an evolutionary necessity fraught with risks and anxieties. They may be guided by a variety of considerations, but any thought about the future, for any human consciousness of fate and nature, must bring up intimations of mortality above all else. John Maynard Keynes is famous, for, among other things, telling us that 'In the long run we are all dead',[1] but we should point out in fairness that the next sentence, which is quite relevant to our discussion here, is: 'Economists set themselves too easy, too useless a task if in tempestuous seasons they tell us that when the storm is long past the ocean is flat again.' So what the world expects from us in our role as scholars and experts is indeed more specific forecasts in both the shorter and the longer term. We may all be dead in the long run, but the world will not die with us, and what we are, and should be, concerned about is more than just our private fate. Mortality becomes naturally salient as we discuss, and even try to forecast, lethal violence and the phenomenon of individuals who are ready to kill, and be killed, for their beliefs. Our trepidation naturally grows, and it should, when we are put in positions of responsibility and decision-making. Then, our inevitable and repeated failures cause even more consternation.

Two

Occasions which give rise to attempts at forecasting may have to do with both practical concerns and magical thinking. Our Western calendar has no objective meaning, but subjectively we think of it as a powerful partner in our lives, full of fateful authority.

It was not only recently that the year 2000 caught the imagination of serious scholars. Back in 1964, the American Academy of Arts and Sciences set up the Commission on the Year 2000, chaired by Daniel Bell, an eminent sociologist. Some of the Commission's output was published in 1967. Reading these fascinating articles, written almost four decades ago, is highly recommended.[2] We can see that these experts were quite daring. De Sola Pool firmly held that there would be 'no nuclear war within the next fifty years'.[3] So far, so good; but he also predicted that 'In the period 1965–1970, Mao Tse-tung and De Gaulle will die',[4] and that 'Major fighting in Viet-Nam will peter out about 1967; and most objective observers will regard it as a substantial American victory'.[5] Deaths and wars are clearly the hardest to predict.

Kahn and Wiener (1967) were able to predict the coming of computers into our homes and offices, but were otherwise too optimistic in terms of assuming great breakthroughs in easily accessible technology. The point is not to poke fun at wrong predictions. Quite the contrary. I think that what was done by the Commission on the Year 2000 in the 1960s showed brilliant minds at work, as well as the inability of the same minds to forecast significant events in human history.

Can catastrophes be predicted? By definition they are unexpected, and this is part of their essence, because any level of preparation and preparedness reduces their impact. Our wish to predict events 'in the real world' is understandable. We are getting tired of merely reacting to events which are sometimes truly horrifying, and haunted by our failures to understand, and our feeling of helplessness in the face of a series of disappointments and shocks may push us in the direction of further predictions.

In the case of the year 2000 millennium complex, a consensus of concern was reached by various governments, which led to many acts of preparation and readiness. We were faced with two questions. First, whether anything violent would happen, and then who would be involved. The Millennium assignment, given to the writers of the three reports under study was, assuming the expectation or probability of millennium violence, to identify groups at high risk for violent acts. As we all know, the overall success was limited, as the basic expectation fortunately proved wrong. Beyond that, we can point to further faults and limitations in the three reports.

This consensus in the media and among some government leaders around the world first focused on disasters caused by deviant religious groups, which were later tied to the fantasy of widespread technological failures because of the Y2K computer problems. This combination of imagined catastrophes, coming from the direction of past burdens (i.e. religion) and future achievements coming closer (i.e. advanced technology) can be interpreted as a reaction to our collective anxiety about a fast-changing world, which makes us all increasingly insecure.

When assessing risks in the real world, those in positions of responsibility can take few chances. The quantitative and qualitative marginality of high-intensity religious movements and their membership, which is clearly in evidence, does not guarantee an absence of serious threats. Even a totally marginal group, or just one individual, may inflict horrific damage on society. Thus, being extremely cautious, planning for a worst-case scenario, or being in actual panic when the responsibility is in your hands seems reasonable. The Israeli report describes the case of Dennis Michael Rohan, who in 1967 set fire to the al-Aqsa mosque in Jerusalem, which proves that one individual may cause untold damage.

Three

Looking back, with no *schadenfreude* and some hindsight, at the pre-2000 reports, we can see that our collective attempts to predict have failed. Not only that, but the basic assumption about the millennium effects was unfounded. The case of the panic around the year 2000 seems to be wrong theoretically and statistically. Round-numbered dates are not more likely to be tied to violence, and movements do not appear and develop in response to some date expressed in round numbers. The millennium idea, whatever its historical significance in some Christian movements, has lost much of its power. Millennium as an idea and a dream remains alive, but it is as divorced from action as most other religious beliefs in a secular society.

The reliability and scholarly quality of the reports are found to be quite uneven. Thus, on the first page of the FBI *Project Megiddo*, a claim is made that the millennial term 'Armageddon' is a Hebrew word. Even if the Book of Revelation is cited as an authority, the word is

Greek. Speakers of Hebrew will be amazed to hear such a claim, because the word does not appear in any Hebrew dictionary and will be recognized immediately by any native speaker as foreign.

The most egregious error in *Project Megiddo*, however, is the discussion of a group referred to as 'Black Hebrew Israelites'. There have probably been, over the past 100 years, scores of 'Black Hebrew' groups (i.e. African-Americans claiming to be Jews or the only real Jews), just as there have been scores of 'Black Moslem' groups.[6] Out of this multitude, two groups were selected and connected, even though there has never been any real connection between them. The description of the 'Hebrew Israelites' in the document shows very limited knowledge of their history and origins, together with errors in names and dates. Even if members of the groups under discussion have been violent, and even if some of them have long criminal records, this had nothing whatsoever to do with the millennium.

In short, the FBI gets an 'F' on this section of the report, which raises doubts about the quality of the whole effort. *Project Megiddo* seems to rely excessively on newspaper clippings, collected by FBI agents all over the United States. I would respectfully suggest that FBI agents consult not just newspapers, but also encyclopedias, research literature, Internet sites or even live scholars next time they do a report on religious groups.

The Israeli report gets high marks in terms of scholarship, because scholars had a leading hand in its preparation, and is chock-full of interesting information about many marginal groups and individuals. This is noteworthy especially because the Israeli context of millennium apocalyptic predictions is that of a culture in which thinking about 'Christianity' today (an abstraction with little meaning to scholars) is dominated by fantasies, suspicion and prejudice. Most Israelis know very little about the history and beliefs of Christian denominations, and we cannot blame them for that. Israelis are just as ethnocentric as members of other cultures. What does the average European know about Islam or Judaism? When you read the Israeli media, you encounter such figures as the Pope who 'heads Christianity'. Most Israeli politicians and law enforcement officials do not know more than that.

The Israeli context of millennium violence predictions is one of a permanent war situation, including both terrorism and conventional warfare. The state of Israel, a settler-colonialist enterprise in the midst of Arab West Asia, has been facing more and more resistance on the part of the indigenous Palestinian population.[7] The predictions of millennium violence were naturally perceived as an added burden on local security forces facing other serious threats. Because of habitual vigilance, the policy adopted was of zero tolerance for 'false negatives' and high tolerance for 'false positives', i.e. erring on the side of caution.

The Canadian report is obviously the work of serious scholars, who present a general theory of apocalyptic groups, their belief systems, and their behavior. We can take issue with the report's implications for law enforcement (it seems to suggest that treatment of these groups should 'avoid humiliation', and this may rule out most law enforcement activities), but given its brevity it gives us the most knowledge and thinking per page.

Having made these *ex cathedra* judgments of these reports, the issue is not judging with hindsight the noble failure of the pre-2000 millennium risk reports, but drawing lessons that involve the larger community of those watching with interest or with concern contemporary religious movements. We are all in it together, scholars and those in positions of public responsibility who are trying to make practical assessments. These reports, and our collective failure to assess the millennium risks, should be viewed in the context of the social sciences in general, and of other cases of success and failure in predicting violence in religious groups.

Four

The mission of the human sciences, ever since the days of Condorcet, has been that of finding regularities and reaching generalizations. Any generalization is a prediction, and we aim at being able to forecast actual behavior at both individual and social levels, ranging from specific acts to social and historical trends.[8] We still most often study specific past events, but then we generalize from them to assume future developments.[9] The limits on our ability to predict human behavior both in general and in specific cases are well known. Clinical psychologists can make some pretty good predictions in terms of statistical generalizations. A particular profile on an exceptionally useful personality test (the MMPI-2) enables us to predict that an individual with a particular profile is likely, with a 90 per cent probability, to run into serious trouble, and most probably has done so already. However, there are 10 per cent of cases where this is not going to happen, because of personality and environmental interactions. And we don't know, of course, who is going to be in the 10 per cent group. In some situations we have no choice, and we are required to offer not just general discussions of the laws of nature, but specific judgments, when the goal is not to reach generalizations, but to make clear-cut decisions. Thus, the individual in question is not going to be hired for any job requiring responsibility, unless closely supervised (in some kind of a sheltered workshop, for example).

What we, as experts, are being asked to do in the face of perceived threats is not just develop evaluations or predictions, but reach specific risk assessments. Risk assessment (RA) is a way of learning about threat sources, through vigilance and scanning, which are behaviorally associated with ambiguous threat situations. Labeling an object or situation dangerous involves a prediction that given the presence (or absence) of certain well-defined conditions an object poses a likely threat of harm to another.[10] We judge risk on the basis of past behavior or on the basis of special diagnostic signs.

Following risk assessment we can move to risk management, which involves the necessary practical steps to minimize damage. This is most often done in psychiatric and legal settings, where psychiatric predictions of future dangerousness represent the single most significant factor in the commitment of the mentally ill and in the treatment of incarcerated offenders.[11]

Decisions regarding danger are often grounded in judgments of beliefs and likely actions. In psychiatric diagnosis, individuals are often judged on the basis of the beliefs they express. A diagnosis of paranoid schizophrenia is often based on statements made by an individual, which reflect, in our judgment, a delusional belief system. The question in risk assessment is whether this belief system will lead to actions dangerous to the self or others. Here examining the gap or the connection between beliefs and actions is quite complicated. Usually delusional beliefs in the case of an individual do not imply specific action, unlike some religious ideas.

Specific symptoms are sometimes good predictors of risk. Compliance with command hallucinations, a relatively common phenomenon which may accompany schizophrenia, may be the cause of serious violence. We know that this risk grows when the source of these commands is given an identity. It has been found that the dangerousness of the commands was a function of the environment, and individuals tended to experience less violent commands in hospital than those experienced elsewhere.[12] Thus, it is clear that hospitalization does indeed reduce the risk of violence by those who experience command hallucinations. Knowing this, we can decide on guidelines for action. Any individual with command hallucinations attributed to one identity (God, my dead grandmother) is a good candidate for hospitalization.

Five

There are two psychological problems we are faced with. We are unable to assess the gap between belief and action, and the gap between psychopathology and performance, except in the most extreme cases. One specific aspect of the problem of predicting behavior is that of the gap between beliefs and action. When and how do beliefs lead to action? We know that most often beliefs predict other beliefs, rather than actions.[13] Assessing when people are going to act on their beliefs is one of our greatest challenges. Religion is defined through a unique system of beliefs that more and more often do not lead to action. Secularization can be measured and assessed through the growing distance between beliefs and acts.

Looking at the case of a particular religious group, our diagnostic and predictive efforts are severely hampered by the complexity of interactions between beliefs, individual members, leadership, and the surrounding environment. The most important ingredient in evaluating the potential for violence is knowledge of the intentions and capabilities of group leaders and members.

Within the psychological (hypothetical) systems of individual personality and individual psychopathology in which we analyse our observations of individuals and especially group leaders, one prominent issue is that of the limitations psychopathology puts on performance. In plain English, if you are really insane, your ability to carry out more complicated acts of destruction, or self-destruction, must be limited. Still, we see cases of religious leaders where presumed insanity still leaves much room for successful leadership and organizational talent, as well as fairly sophisticated acts of violence, which involve planning and preparation.[14]

Six

All our observations take place within the historical context of
secularization, a process through which both society and individuals
have moved away from the dominance of religious institutions and
religious ideation. In traditional cultures religion is experienced in the
collective sphere. The possibility of choice and preference in individual
religious identities is a modern phenomenon, interpreted as a symptom
of the decline of religion as an institution. In most traditional societies,
religion is not a matter of choice, but of birth and of automatic
acceptance.

The context of secularization and modernity means the privatization
of religious beliefs and religious activities. It is easy to prove that in all
industrial societies today, religion, which was once uniform,
collectivistic, public, ascribed and inherited, is today pluralist,
individualistic, privatized, achieved, and often freely chosen.
Privatization is the most important change, overriding all other
dimensions. Organized religious activities become part of civil society,
and often take on the characteristics of leisure-time pursuits. Religious
beliefs survive and are commonly expressed, but they are rarely tied to
action or to collective action. A common claim in the age of
secularization is that religious assertions are only symbolic,
metaphorical or abstract. This tends to make us underestimate their
ability to motivate and to discount any risks stemming from religious
belief systems.[15]

Human history, until recent centuries, was filled with religious
violence, but in our secularized mindset the age of the wars of religion is
over. The connection between religion and violence, once quite intimate,
has become remote. What we observe next to us from Moscow to San
Francisco is a new and improved model of a defanged Christianity. Since
the eighteenth century we have been fighting about national liberation,
economics, and equality: all respectably secular causes. Secular
ideologies, as we all know, can be no less lethal than religious ones, but
today in the West we are ready to accept democratic ideals as the right
justification for violence as the last resort. 'The tree of liberty must be
refreshed from time to time with the blood of patriots and tyrants', wrote
Thomas Jefferson in 1787, and we all admire him for that.

We identify wholeheartedly with the violence of the oppressed as
they fight for their universally acknowledged rights.[16] Indeed, most wars

in the twentieth century were fought for the secular causes of national liberation, revolution and counter-revolution. Religion in the First World has become non-violent, even pacific. The truth is that we don't expect violence to arise out of religious beliefs, because we expect religiosity to have a limited impact on behavior outside of clearly religious settings. Glock (1962) suggested five dimensions for the measurement of religiosity: ideological, ritualistic, intellectual, experiential and consequential.[17] The so-called consequential dimension of religiosity was soon dropped by Glock himself[18] and is usually absent from the literature dealing with the behavior of believers.[19]

Whenever, and wherever, religion in the West manifests itself in a form which is more than a matter of private faith, it is defined in most Western societies as disruptive, and judged to be marginal and deviant. Any religious conflict is perceived as merely atavistic.

We are collectively shocked by the return of religion as motive for political and violent actions. It seems that a pre-modern monster has come out of the depths to haunt us. Incidents of self-castration and ritual suicide today (see below) bring to mind ideas and practices of much earlier times and of cultures seemingly vanished. Ideals of purity and devotion have always led believers to acts of self-mutilation and martyrdom. We admire those acts from afar when we read about them in holy scriptures, but are shocked to witness them up close today.

Some may argue that religion, even today, is a complex area of human behavior, where predictions are harder to make than in other areas. This argument can be tested against the record of the academic study of religion over the past century. What we discover is that there are a few things we can say with some certainty about religious individuals, and there are a few things we can say about individuals and groups following religious orthodoxy and fundamentalism. Studies done all over the world since the Second World War have shown that religious orthodoxy (in any tradition) is tied to a particular pattern of attitudes and political behaviors.

Fundamentalism, as an expression of religious orthodoxy, not surprisingly, has been tied to political conservatism, authoritarianism and prejudice.[20] This combination of political and social attitudes with religious beliefs is an ideological complex that characterizes and animates fundamentalist groups. It is about a confrontation with modernity, and a strategy which not only rejects any accommodation, but contains a clear, utopian vision for reconstructing society. This is a vision of decline, degeneration and renewal. In the case of fundamentalism, we expect the gap between to narrow considerably.

Seven

Because in the case of the 2000 millennium, contrary to expectation, no religious groups erupted in violence, let us look at cases where violence did erupt, to our collective surprise and shock. We can look at some well-publicized cases of violence in new religious movements (NRMs) and examine the issue of knowledge, assessment, and prediction in those cases. Violence in new religious movements is, of course, much more limited than that perpetrated by old religions over the ages, but it shocks us because we presumably live in the age of secularization in the First World, and eruptions of religious violence seem like unwelcome visitations from the Third World or from the Western past.

We need to discuss here the NRM phenomenon in some detail, first because the groups mentioned in all three reports were NRMs. New religious movements will be defined here as any groups founded after the year 1800. These groups exhibit a pattern of traditional, possibly pre-modern, or at least pre-secularized, religiosity within modern societies. The common denominator which unites researchers working on new religious movements (myself included) is their deep curiosity about high-ego-involvement, high-impact religion.[21]

There have always been two types of religiosity. One involves nominal or superficial identity commitment; the other is characterized by high intensity, and leads to ecstasy and sacrifice.[22] Modern scholars of religious behavior have been observers and collectors of high-intensity religious behaviors, following the example of such pioneers as William James, who collected cases of dramatic conversions. We try to explain exceptional behaviors and amazing events, believing that they can tell us something about religiosity in general, which most of the time has nothing amazing about it. We gasp and stare as we witness the devout, the zealots and the fanatics, and our voyeurism is amply rewarded.

NRMs have been viewed as laboratories or as natural experiments for testing hypotheses about human behavior in general (Festinger *et al.*, 1956),[23] or about charismatic leadership and violence (Robbins and Palmer, 1997).[24] Since the late 1970s, scholars doing research on active NRMs have worked in the shadow of several well-publicized NRM tragedies: Peoples Temple, Nation of Yahweh, the Branch Davidians, Aum Shinrikyô, the Solar Temple and Heaven's Gate.

Have we been able to predict or explain events when NRMs erupt in violence? There have been several well-known cases, starting in the 1950s, and they are worth looking at.[25] What did we know and what did we predict in cases of earlier NRM disasters? In each case we had some evidence of commitment to beliefs which may lead to violent action, destructive either to group members and/or to others, but we were unable to predict and assess intentions and estimate the real gap between beliefs and actions. Even when we had rumors and allegations, no one could have imagined the events that were eventually to unfold.

The record will show that in past cases of NRM tragedies since 1970, some early warnings were given. In all of these cases, early warnings about the potential for violence were given by relatives of group members, ex-members, some media sources, and some government officials. Scholars were never among those who were able to sense coming disasters, though we should point out that scholars had very little knowledge of the inner workings of the Peoples Temple in Jonestown or the Branch Davidians in Waco.

In the case of the Peoples Temple, there were warnings in 1977, which reached the California media. Relatives of members and some ex-members described Jim Jones in more than just unflattering terms. Before 1978 there were reports of rehearsals for mass suicide in the Peoples Temple. There were very serious accusations, but still no one could have predicted what happened in November 1978. It should be pointed out that the Peoples Temple never attracted academic attention before the November 1978 events.

The Heaven's Gate case is especially instructive because this particular group, which received public attention only in 1997, had been the subject of scholarly attention since the 1970s. Also known as Bo and Peep, or the Higher Source, this group was started in 1975 in Los Angeles by a former music professor, Marshall Herff Applewhite (1932–97), and a registered nurse, Bonnie Lu Trousdale Nettles (1928–85). They called themselves Bo and Peep, and were also known as Winnie and Pooh, Chip and Dale, Do and Ti, 'the Him and the Her', or 'the Two', in reference to a New Testament prophecy about two witnesses.

The group's doctrine was known as Human Individual Metamorphosis (HIM), aiming at the liberation of humans from the endless cycle of reincarnation. The leaders claimed that they would fulfill an ancient prophecy by being assassinated and coming back to life three and a half days later. Following the resurrection, they would be lifted up by a UFO to a divine kingdom in outer space. Followers agreed, in preparation for the outer space journey, to get rid of most material possessions and worldly attachments, including family and work. Members wore uniform clothing and identical haircuts. Marriage and sexual relations were forbidden.

Members traveled around the United States recruiting new followers and proclaiming their prophecies. Followers were promised immortality, androgeneity, and perfection, provided they followed the rules and ideas provided by the leaders. Bonnie Nettles died of cancer in 1985, and then the group started operating in complete secrecy. Applewhite told his followers that Bonnie Nettles was actually his divine father. In 1993, calling itself Total Overcomers Anonymous, the group published an ad in *USA Today*, inviting people to join.

In late March 1997, 39 members, including Applewhite, committed suicide in Rancho Santa Fe, California, by ingesting barbiturates and alcohol. They were found lying on bunk beds, wearing cotton pants, black shirts, and brand-name sneakers. Most of them were covered with purple shrouds. They all carried on them passports and drivers' licenses, as well as small change. The victims ranged in age from 26 to 72, but 21 were in their forties. There were 21 females and 18 males. In videotaped statements read before committing suicide, members stated that they were taking this step in preparation for an expected encounter with extraterrestrials, arriving in a spaceship following the Hale-Bopp comet. It was discovered after their deaths that some of the male group members had been castrated several years before.

In the case of the Heaven's Gate tragedy, scholars did have some relevant information, since the group attracted scholarly attention quite early in its history.[26] Back in 1993, I was able to report the following:

> The leaders claimed that they would fulfill the ancient prophecy by being assassinated and coming back to life three and half years later. Following the resurrection, they would be lifted up by a UFO to the divine kingdom in outer space. The followers agreed, in preparation for the journey, to get rid of most material possessions and worldly attachments, including family and work ... no further details are known, since the group has been operating in complete secrecy.[27]

As we can see, I had accurate information about all the ingredients for the eventual mass murder/suicide which took place in March 1997. All the ingredients, that is, save one, and the most important one: and that is the leaders' intentions. There was no way we could have known about intentions without having a direct intelligence source close to the leader.

Turning to another murder/suicide case, the brief history of the Order of the Solar Temple by Hall and Schuyler[28] ties us immediately to the real world of salvation hustlers and their victims. Here members of the francophone bourgeoisie in Canada and Western Europe, in scenes which could have been staged by Luis Bunuel and Federico Fellini, seek escape by any means from their lives of quiet desperation. There's not only demand, but also some supply, and various con artists are right there to take advantage of the growing market. The group's two leaders, Joseph DiMambro (1924–94) and Luc Jouret (1948–94) had between them a wide repertoire of fraudulent practices, from bad checks to homeopathy. The official belief system of the group, combining claims about 'ancient Egypt', 'energy fields', reincarnation, and the 'Age of Aquarius', is so widely offered in hundreds of groups all over the world as to be banal and harmless. Most of those who make a living marketing this rather used merchandise will never commit violence. But this was a high-involvement group, not just a club built around a series of lectures.

In 1993, the Order of the Solar Temple became the target of police attention (for illegal weapon charges) and of some sensational media reports in both Canada and Australia. In July 1993 Luc Jouret and two associates received light sentences from a judge in Quebec for their attempts to buy pistols equipped with silencers. The early warnings were not heeded. The most sensational media reports, calling the Solar Temple a 'doomsday cult', turned out to be on the mark. In the early 1990s the group attracted some attention by scholars in both Switzerland and Canada.[29] In 1994 and 1995, 68 individuals died in murder/suicide rites in Switzerland and Quebec. It's possible that DiMambro, terminally ill, wanted to take as many with him as he could when he left this vale of tears. It is clear that many of the dead at this going-away party were murdered, some for revenge, while others were willing victims. Of course, Jouret and DiMambro were more than just hustlers. It is likely that they actually believed at least in some of the ideas they propagated.[30] And who could have known that those beliefs, bizarre as they may seem to us, would lead to a mass murder/suicide?

The Aum Shinrikyô case in Japan is different from other NRM disasters we have described. Here we are not dealing with prediction, but with diagnosis and postdiction. Can either scholars or law enforcement agencies recognize a case of a clear and present danger staring them in the face? The movement known as Aum Shinrikyô was notorious in Japan long before the well-known 1995 terror events. The movement's belief system made it likely to attract less than friendly attention. Children in its schools were taught to regard Adolf Hitler as a living hero, and its official publications carried stories of the Jewish plan to exterminate most of humanity.[31] We know today that Japanese authorities were actually not just overly cautious, but negligent and deferential, if not protective, regarding criminal activities by Aum, because of its status as an NRM. 'Some observers wonder what took the Japanese authorities so long to take decisive action. It seems apparent that enough serious concerns had been raised about various Aum activities to warrant a more serious police inquiry prior to the subway gas attack.'[32] Based on what we know today, the group can only be described as extremely and consistently violent and murderous. 'Thirty-three Aum followers are believed to have been killed between ... 1988 and 1995... Another twenty-one followers have been reported missing.'[33] Among non-members, there have been 24 murder victims. There were at least nine germ-warfare attacks by Aum Shinrikyô in the early 1990s, most of which had no effect.[34] A triple murder case in 1989 and another poison gas attack in 1994 which killed seven were committed by the group, as well as less serious crimes which the police were not eager to investigate.[35]

Nor is it likely that this lethal record (77 deaths on numerous occasions over seven years) and other non-lethal criminal activities were the deeds of a few rogue leaders. Numerous individuals must have been involved in, and numerous others aware of, these activities. The Japanese authorities, as of May 1998, had charged 192 Aum Shinrikyô members with criminal activities.[36] Since then, many have been convicted and sentenced for capital crimes.

In May 1995 Japanese law enforcement authorities were finally realizing that Aum Shinrikyô was indeed quite violent. They were collecting evidence linking the group to the March 20 poison gas attack which killed 12 commuters on the Tokyo subway, and preparing what they thought was a strong case. Then they discovered, to their utter surprise, that they were under attack from an unexpected direction. Four

Americans arrived in Tokyo to defend Aum Shinrikyô against charges of mass terrorism. Two of them were scholars, J. Gordon Melton and James R. Lewis, whose names are well known among NRM scholars, thanks to their many scholarly activities. Melton, arguably, is one of the world's leading experts on NRMs.

On this trip they were acting as both super-sleuths and as self-styled defenders of religious freedom. They stated that Aum Shinrikyô could not have produced the sarin gas used in the attack, and called on the Japanese police not to 'crush a religion and deny freedom'. These statements, made at two news conferences, were met with open disbelief in the Japanese media. The fact that all travel expenses for the US experts were covered by Aum Shinrikyô did not help either.[37] Later, one of the US visitors published an account of the 1995 gas attack, which claimed that the North Korean secret services were behind it.[38]

What we realize is that both J. Gordon Melton and Japan's law enforcement agencies shared a similar, if not identical, evaluation bias. Until 1995 authorities in Japan assumed that a religious group was unlikely to be engaged in criminal and violent activities. Melton arrived in Japan, after contacting the Aum Shinrikyô organization and offering his help, assuming that the group was a victim of bias against religious minorities. This is an example of a clear failure by a scholar caused by both limited knowledge and poor judgment. The scholars coming from the USA had no first-hand knowledge and did not speak Japanese. Moreover, they were ready to ignore the evidence already available at the time of their arrival. This rush to judgment, in this case exculpating the suspects, is exactly what the visitors were accusing the Japanese authorities of doing. What may be regarded as the unethical practice of scholars accepting money from NRMs, such as Aum Shinrikyô, naturally adds to a positive evaluation bias.[39]

In every case of NRM disaster over the past 50 years, starting with Krishna Venta,[40] in addition to the untimely deaths involved, we encounter a hidden reality of madness and exploitation: a totalitarian, psychotic reality. Inside these groups paranoia reigned, while many outside observers demonstrated an extreme absence of suspicion. Following the Waco tragedy we have much knowledge about everyday life in the Branch Davidians, just as we have gained some insider views of the other NRMs involved in violence. Not only that, but it is now unfortunately quite clear that without these horrendous tragedies we would have never known about the reality of backstage life among the

Branch Davidians, Solar Temple, the Peoples Temple, Aum Shinrikyô and Heaven's Gate. Of course, most religious organizations are undemocratic by definition (and by claimed revelation), but in recent times not all have been totalitarian dictatorships. These groups were totalitarian organizations where exploitation and violence were inherent.

The dynamics we discover in these social movements are not just of ideological and organizational totalism, but of totalitarianism and fascism. Exposing the inner workings of these NRMs revealed leaders more deranged than anybody could imagine, at the head of a small-scale dictatorship system similar to the well-known dictatorships of the twentieth century. The questions we ask about these groups should be similar to the ones raised about historical twentieth-century regimes.[41] We are now better informed about the leaders that have been exposed, but this invokes some sobering thoughts about leaders in groups whose inner workings are still hidden from our view.

What have we learned from these three cases of murder/suicide (the Peoples Temple, Solar Temple, and Heaven's Gate) and from the one case of mass terrorism? Can we speak of clear diagnostic signs? In the murder/suicide cases, ideas about extraterrestrials and spaceships were present, but there are have been hundred of groups where such beliefs never led to any violent actions.[42]

Could scholars have done better with much better intelligence? We need reliable information and we need good interpretation. We are all likely to make errors in judgment because of our various biases. Even if we have data, the problem, as we have seen, may lie in evaluation bias. In the case of most NRMs, we have not failed in prediction, because we actually had very little information. Where we had some information we failed only because of bias and our optimistic mindsets. Our collective mindset in observing NRMs has been one of attributing, if not noble, then at least positive or harmless motives and beliefs to religious groups and their leaders. The reasons for the positive evaluation bias among scholars, in addition to the notion that religion cannot be associated with violence, may be because of a degree of identification and empathy with groups with which direct contact has been established. Field research often leads to genuine warm feelings and friendship between the researcher and his object. There are cases when scholars did establish friendly ties with groups, and then errors become natural, if not completely justified. In other cases, such as that of Aum Shinrikyô, there were no prior contacts, and we can speak of a general evaluation bias.[43]

And when researchers turn to advocacy, it is no surprise when they fail in evaluating data.

Eight

If in the cases of the NRMs described above we could see evidence of a positive evaluation bias, which assumed that religious beliefs could not lead to violence, an opposite bias is also possible. The saying attributed to Voltaire asserts that believing in absurdities will lead to the commission of atrocities. What Voltaire had in mind was clearly all religions, in all their manifestations. Another well-known judgment by Voltaire states that religion is the chief cause of all the sorrows of humanity. 'Everywhere it has only served to drive men to evil, and plunge them in brutal miseries ... it makes of history an immense tableau of human follies.'

Always politically incorrect, Voltaire displays no respect for any religion, of the kind that has become more common since his time. For Voltaire the violent potential, and violent realities, in religion of all varieties, is not an aberration. The destructive potential is so close to the surface that we should be surprised only when it disappears. Of course, the gap between belief and action was much narrower in his lifetime.

Voltaire's age was still one in which religious wars were a reality, and disrespect to religion punishable by death. On 1 July 1766, Francois-Jean Lefebvre, chevalier de la Barre, was burned at the stake, after being beheaded, together with a copy of Voltaire's *Philosophical Dictionary*. His crime: not paying his respects to a religious procession. Voltaire tried to save the young man, aged 19, to no avail. Indeed, since the eighteenth century, as the gap between religious beliefs and the believers' ability to realize them has grown in the West, respect for religion, which carries little cost, has grown. The reigning perception is that religion has become toothless and can cause no damage, but can still bring about benefits. The potential for tragedy and violence in all religions, which has to be taken very seriously, has been noticed, among others by Weston La Barre,[44] who happened to be related to the hapless eighteenth-century victim of religion.

A Voltairian evaluation bias entails not only taking beliefs seriously, and not as abstract or metaphorical claims, but also regarding any religious belief system as potentially dangerous. What is needed to create a balanced a cautious mindset is a Voltairian antidote.

Such a note of caution was sounded originally in 1999:

> Believers are ready to die for their faith, or kill others for its glory
> and for promised heavenly rewards. In the real world faith is tied
> to identity and action, and the lethal struggles which often ensue
> are not over anything metaphorical. In Israel, Palestine, Sri Lanka,
> India, Iran, Afghanistan, and the United States ... [t]aking
> seriously our religious neighbors should be a most practical
> lesson. Those who say they wish to create a Kingdom of Heaven
> on earth may be worth watching closely.[45]

This advice seems just as practical today.

Nine

The three reports published in this volume raise again the issue of the
interaction, if any, between scholars and officials in government
agencies. The perspectives in the two groups are quite different.
Scholars, sitting in the ivory tower, are concerned about theoretical and
abstract questions. Governments are always under pressure, always
anxious to defend against real or imagined threats to the social order.
Scholars, as citizens, may have their own views on keeping or disrupting
existing social arrangements. Ethical questions about collaboration with
governments may seem minute when compared with the gravity of the
risks involved, and the real danger to life and limb clearly in evidence
in these cases.

The pre-2000 reports and the activity they reflect might have
contributed to research by focusing attention and resources on a
marginal phenomenon, which nevertheless arouses our scholarly
curiosity, but is often ignored by non-scholars.

The question of the usefulness of our knowledge is a permanent
challenge for academics who are taunted for being impractical and out
of touch with the 'real world'. Scholars may also be skeptical about the
ability of government agencies to digest abstractions, generalizations, or
just research data. Government officials, on the other hand, have their
doubts about ivory-tower research, seemingly divorced from practical
concerns. Thus, the two camps may have opposite goals, or may be
working in parallel and unrelated universes.

Our attempts at predicting future developments, however feeble and
inadequate, fare no worse than those of economists trying to predict

market conditions and rates of inflation, or intelligence organizations, such as the CIA, which have huge budgets for data collection and still fail miserably in predicting not just specific events, but major historical changes. As has been pointed out often, the CIA failed to predict the building of the Berlin Wall in 1961, and its subsequent disappearance in 1989, and that is only one example. As scholars, we may know a lot more about specific movements or ideologies, but this does not guarantee, as we have seen, better assessments or predictions. It is easy to find cases of failure in assessment and diagnosis, and a few case studies, presented above, decisively demonstrate our woeful inadequacies. In reality we are closer to those in positions of responsibility in our limited ability to forecast. Fortunately, we do not share their responsibilities.

Ten

Can we develop a credible risk assessment system for religious groups? The first and most crucial step is to sort groups into high and low risk, and then decide on risk management policies and their attendant costs. Beyond the basic conceptual issues discussed above, we are faced with one seemingly insurmountable practical problem and that is obtaining reliable intelligence. The scarcity of credible data prevents us from carrying out any serious evaluations. Our failures are no mystery. The simple and correct equation is that only good data can lead to good predictions.

Knowing and predicting NRM behavior starts with reliable information and the truth is, as recent NRM tragedies illustrate so well, that scholars don't really know much about what is going on inside the thousands of religious groups in existence today. For most NRMs, we simply have no solid intelligence. Getting information requires a serious commitment and a considerable investment of resources. If we want intelligence and real-time warnings, we need to invest much more. And we are not sure which groups we are going to invest in. One might claim that in attempting to assess the risk of violence coming from any religious group there is nothing theoretical, but only the direct application of intelligence. The serious errors in the FBI *Project Megiddo*, cited above, prove the need for broader knowledge and evaluation. Raw data need to be interpreted with the help of background information which only scholarly legwork can provide.

Following recent events we may all adopt a catastrophic mindset, assuming that the worst will happen and acting accordingly. Based on bitter experience, it seems reasonable to be hypervigilant and paranoid, but, nevertheless, we are going to be proven wrong often, and be surprised again and again. Our earlier collective optimism meant raising the threshold for perceptions of threat. This threshold will now be lowered. We can only hope that the gap between belief and violent action will most often remain boundless.

NOTES

1. John Maynard Keynes, *Monetary Reform* (New York: Harcourt Brace, 1924), p.88.
2. Ithiel De Sola Pool, 'The International System in the Next Half Century', *Daedalus* 96 (1967), pp.930–35; Herman Kahn and Anthony J. Wiener, 'The Next Thirty-Three Years: A Framework for Speculation', *Daedalus* 96 (1967), pp.705–32.
3. Ithiel De Sola Pool, 'The International System in the Next Half Century' (note 2), p.931.
4. Ibid. This was barely right about De Gaulle, who died in November 1970; but wrong about Mao, who died in 1976.
5. Ibid., p.932.
6. Benjamin Beit-Hallahmi, *The Annotated Dictionary of Modern New Religions* (Danbury, CT: Grolier Publishers, 1993); Benjamin Beit-Hallahmi, *The Illustrated Encyclopedia of Active New Religions* [Revised], (New York: Rosen Publishing, 1998).
7. Benjamin Beit-Hallahmi, *Original Sins: Reflections on the History of Zionism and Israel* (New York: Interlink, 1993).
8. Oswald Spengler, *The Decline of the West* (New York: Knopf, 1926).
9. Benjamin Beit-Hallahmi, *Prolegomena to the Psychological Study of Religion* (Lewisburg, PA: Bucknell University Press, 1992).
10. John Monahan, '"Dangerousness": Violence risk assessment', in Alan E. Kazdin (ed.), *Encyclopedia of Psychology* (New York: Oxford University Press, 2000); Edward P. Mulvey and Charles W. Lidz, 'Conditional Prediction: A Model for Research on Dangerous to Others in a New Era', *International Journal of Law and Psychiatry* 18 (1995), pp.129–43.
11. Edward P. Mulvey and Charles W. Lidz, 'Conditional Prediction: A Model for Research on Dangerous to Others in a New Era' (note 10).
12. John Junginger, 'Command Hallucinations and the Prediction of Dangerousness', *Psychiatric Services* 46 (1995), pp.911–14.
13. Benjamin Beit-Hallahmi,and Michael Argyle, *The Psychology of Religious Behaviour, Belief, and Experience* (London: Routledge, 1997).
14. Benjamin Beit-Hallahmi, 'Religion as Pathology: Exploring a Metaphor', in Halina Grzymala Moszczynska and Benjamin Beit-Hallahmi (eds.), *Religion, Psychopathology, and Coping* (Amsterdam: Rodopi, 1996); Len Oakes, *Prophetic Charisma: The Psychology of Revolutionary Religious Personalities* (Syracuse, NY: Syracuse University Press, 1997).
15. Benjamin Beit-Hallahmi, 'Explaining Religious Utterances by Taking Seriously Super-Naturalist (and Naturalist) Claims', in Giora Hon and Sam Rakover (eds.), *Explanation: Philosophical Essays* (Dordrecht: Kluwer, 2001); Przemyslaw Jablonski *et al.*, 'Metaphor theories and religious language understanding', *Metaphor and Symbol* 13 (1998), pp.287–92.
16. Benjamin Beit-Hallahmi, 'Overcoming the 'Objective' Language of Violence', *Aggressive Behavior* 3 (1977), pp.251–9; Heather A. Wilson, *International Law and the Use of Force by National Liberation Movements* (Oxford: Clarendon Press, 1988).

17. Charles Young Glock, 'On the Study of Religious Commitment', *Religious Education* 57 (1962), pp.S98–S109.
18. Charles Young Glock and Rodney Stark, *Christian Beliefs and Anti-Semitism* (New York: Harper and Row, 1966).
19. Benjamin Beit-Hallahmi and Michael Argyle, *The Psychology of Religious Behaviour, Belief, and Experience* (note 13).
20. Michael Argyle and Benjamin Beit-Hallahmi, *The Social Psychology of Religion* (London: Routledge & Kegan Paul, 1975); Benjamin Beit-Hallahmi and Michael Argyle, *The Psychology of Religious Behaviour, Belief, and Experience* (note 13); Raymond F. Paloutzian, *Invitation to the Psychology of Religion* (Boston: Allyn & Bacon, 1996).
21. Benjamin Beit-Hallahmi, *Prolegomena to the Psychological Study of Religion* (Lewisburg, PA: Bucknell University Press, 1989); Benjamin Beit-Hallahmi, *Despair and Deliverance: Private Salvation in Contemporary Israel* (Albany, NY: SUNY Press, 1992); Raymond F. Paloutzian, *Invitation to the Psychology of Religion* (note 20).
22. Benjamin Beit-Hallahmi, *Prolegomena to the Psychological Study of Religion* (note 9).
23. Leon Festinger *et al.*, *When Prophecy Fails* (Minneapolis, MN: University of Minnesota Press, 1956).
24. Thomas Robbins and Susan J. Palmer (eds.), *Millenium, Messiahs, and Mayhem* (New York: Routledge, 1997).
25. Benjamin Beit-Hallahmi, *The Illustrated Encyclopedia of Active New Religions* (New York: Rosen Publishing, 1993); Benjamin Beit-Hallahmi, *The Annotated Dictionary of Modern New Religions* (Danbury, CT: Grolier Publishers, 1993); Benjamin Beit-Hallahmi, *The Illustrated Encyclopedia of Active New Religions* [Revised], (New York: Rosen Publishing, 1998); Benjamin Beit-Hallahmi, '"O truant muse": Collaborationism and Research Integrity', in Benjamin Zablocki and Thomas Robbins (eds.), *Misunderstanding Cults* (Toronto: University of Toronto Press, 2001).
26. Rob Balch and David Taylor, 'Seekers and Saucers: The Role of the Cultic Milieu in Joining a UFO cult', *American Behavioral Scientist* 10 (1977), pp.839–60; Rob Balch, 'Looking Behind the Scenes in a Religious Cult', *Sociological Analysis* 47 (1980), pp.137–43; Rob Balch, 'Bo and Peep: A Case Study of the Origins of Messianic Leadership', in Roy Wallis (ed.), *Millennialism And Charisma* (Belfast: Queens University Press, 1982).
27. Benjamin Beit-Hallahmi, *The Annotated Dictionary of Modern New Religions* (note 6), p.70; *The Illustrated Encyclopedia of Active New Religions* (note 6), p.36.
28. John R. Hall and Philip Schuyler, 'The Mystical Apocalypse of the Solar Temple', in Thomas Robbins and Susan J. Palmer (eds.), *Millennium, Messiahs, and Mayhem* (New York: Routledge, 1997).
29. Jean-Francois Mayer, 'Les chevaliers de l'apocalypse: L'Ordre de Temple Solaire et ses adeptes', in Francoise Champion and Martine Cohen (eds.), *Sectes et Societe* (Paris: Seuil, 1999).
30. Ibid.
31. Rotem Kowner, *On Ignorance, Respect and Suspicion: Current Japanese Attitudes towards Jews* (Jerusalem: The Vidal Sassoon International Center for the Study of Antisemitism, Hebrew University of Jerusalem, 1997).
32. Mark R. Mullins, 'Aum Shinrikyo as an Apocalyptic Movement', in Thomas Robbins and Susan J. Palmer (eds.), *Millennium, Messiahs, and Mayhem* (note 28), p.321.
33. Ibid., p.320.
34. 'Life Sentence to Aum Member for the Poison Gas Attack', *Reuters News Service*, 27 May 1998.
35. Benjamin Beit-Hallahmi, *The Illustrated Encyclopedia of Active New Religions* (note 6); Mark R. Mullins, 'Aum Shinrikyo as an Apocalyptic Movement' (note 32).
36. 'Life Sentence to Aum Member' (note 34).
37. T. R. Reid, 'US Visitors Boost Cause of Japanese Cult', *The Washington Post* (9 May 1995); Ian Reader, 'Aum Affair Intensifies Japan's Religious Crisis: An Analysis',

Religion Watch (July/August 1995), pp.1–2; Ian Reader, 'Scholarship, Aum Shinrikyo, and Academic Integrity', *Nova Religio* 3 (2000), pp.368–82.

38. James R. Lewis, Personal communication, Oct. 1998.
39. Benjamin Beit-Hallahmi, '"O truant muse"' (note 25).
40. Benjamin Beit-Hallahmi, *The Annotated Dictionary of Modern New Religions* (note 6).
41. Theodor W. Adorno *et al.*, *The Authoritarian Personality* (New York: Harper & Row, 1950); Erich Fromm, *Escape From Freedom* (New York: Rinehart, 1941).
42. Leon Festinger *et al.*, *When Prophecy Fails* (note 23).
43. Howard S. Becker, 'Whose Side Are We On?', *Social Problems* 14 (1967), pp.239–47.
44. Weston La Barre, *The Ghost Dance: The Origins of Religion* (New York: Doubleday, 1970).
45. Benjamin Beit-Hallahmi, 'Explaining Religious Utterances by Taking Seriously Super-Naturalist (and Naturalist) Claims' (note 15), p.226.

WIDER ISSUES IN THE MILLENNIUM DEBATE

Spectres and Shadows: Aum Shinrikyô and the Road to Megiddo

IAN READER

Introduction

Whether in the form of the much hyped Y2K bug, the end-time and disaster scenarios of Hollywood movies, or the popularity of the prophecies of Nostradamus with their apparent predictions of a final cataclysm at the end of the century,[1] 'millennial hysteria', as Charles B. Strozier has termed it,[2] was a prominent element in the general mass culture of the 1990s. Images of cataclysm and expectations that the world was entering an end-time were equally visible in late twentieth-century religious culture, and were especially prominent in the teachings of a number of new religious movements that came to the fore in the last decades of the century in Japan (amongst them Aum Shinrikyô, which will feature prominently in this article),[3] as well as in extreme right-wing Christian movements in North America. Moreover, the idea of the year 2000 along with the end of the calendrical millennium appeared, in the imagination of many such movements, to signify some form of historical watershed holding out the promise of dramatic events such as the collapse of existing civilizations, final confrontations between good and evil, and the onset of a new religious dawn.[4]

Such notions have, of course, been the recurrent fantasy of millennial movements through the ages, and they are not necessarily tied to specific dates or times, a point well recognized in the academic literature on the subject.[5] This did not, however, prevent the coming of the temporal millennium being seen in a dramatic light by the mass media or by various civil and legal authorities around the world as they considered what *might* happen at the millennium and how this event *might* impact on the thinking and behaviour of millennial religious movements. These considerations were certainly a feature of, as well as a motivating factor behind, the various reports produced by law enforcement agencies and intelligence services in North America and elsewhere at this period, that discussed millennial movements and their potential for engaging in violent activities at the millennium. Among such reports were the FBI's *Project Megiddo*,[6] which primarily sought to assess the potential of extreme right-wing religious movements, notably Christian militia groups, in the USA and which framed itself around concerns over domestic terrorism, and the report by the Canadian Security Intelligence Service that sought to delineate commonalities found in millennial movements in general in order, as the report put it, 'to anticipate which groups might pose a physical threat to public safety'.[7]

These reports can clearly be seen as part of a wider precautionary approach taken by governments around the world because of the moral panic generated over the change from 1999 to 2000, especially in the context of the frenzy surrounding the supposed Y2K bug. As such one would naturally expect governments to give some thought to what might possibly transpire at this time, and to ways of guarding against eventualities. Yet it would be wrong to view such reports simply in this manner, as precautionary devices devised to show governmental readiness in the face of any possible situation, for within the reports at hand, and in the context in which they were produced, one can recognize some serious concerns about religious millennialism in the modern day, and about the potential of movements with such orientations to cause trouble.

Such concerns were founded not (as with Y2K) in speculative fears and media-induced hype, but in actual events. The latter part of the twentieth century had, after all, witnessed a number of dramatic and violent episodes centred on millennial religious movements, which included cases of mass suicide, mass terrorism and public confrontations with civil authorities. Among the more dramatic of these were the Waco tragedy of 1993 involving the Branch Davidians, the suicides and murders in the Order of the Solar Temple in Switzerland and Canada in 1994, and the various atrocities, including the nerve gas attack on the Tokyo subway, committed by the Japanese new religion Aum Shinrikyô in 1995. These incidents were not specifically linked in any way, and nor, from any detached academic perspective, could they be seen to represent a cumulative build-up to the millennium. Yet they all concerned millennial religious movements that had set themselves apart from mainstream society and become involved in conflicts with law enforcement organizations. Their very occurrence at this time, and in fairly close succession, helped foster a sense of heightened expectation among millennial movements and civil authorities of further such events.[8]

For security forces, accustomed by their very nature to be on the lookout for potential sources of disorder, events such as these helped give millennial religious movements in general a dangerous veneer and transform them into a threat to public security. This point is amply illustrated by the Canadian Security Intelligence Service report, which flags up 'the challenge of contending with religious movements whose defining characteristic is an adherence to non-traditional spiritual belief systems' as an emerging, but previously overlooked, security issue of the age, and then cites Branch Davidians, the Order of the Solar Temple and Aum Shinrikyô as examples in this respect.

In this context it has been Aum Shinrikyô – the only non-American movement mentioned in *Project Megiddo* – that has cast the longest and most striking shadow and that has most clearly captured the attention of law enforcement agencies.[9] In *Project Megiddo*, for example, Aum is used to exemplify the potential dangers of extremist millennial movements, and is cited as an example of a movement that 'wanted to take action to hasten the end of the world'. The importance of Aum is evident, too, in the Introduction to the Canadian report, which states that:

> Japan's infamous Aum Shinrikyô is a textbook example, where the coupling of apocalyptic beliefs and a charismatic leader fixated on its enemies culminated in an nerve-gas attack intended to cause mass casualties in the hope of precipitating a world war and completing its apocalyptic prophecy.

It is the context of such perceptions, and the evident shadows cast by Aum Shinrikyô, that this article is written. It examines why Aum caused such alarms for intelligence agencies that it came to be portrayed as a 'textbook case' and asks to what extent it could be considered as such, rather than as a rather unique and aberrant case because of the extremity of its actions or because of Aum's specific cultural roots as a Japanese movement, produced in and operating through that society's particular dynamics and circumstances.[10] I shall also examine, through the context of Aum, some premises in the Canadian and FBI reports, and most particularly whether there might be a correlation between particular dates and the onset of millennial mayhem (a view that is prevalent in *Project Megiddo* with its specific focus on the advent of the year 2000), and the assumption (contained in the above citations from *Megiddo* and the Canadian report) that Aum, and consequently perhaps also other millennial movements, commit acts of violence and terrorism with the specific intent of triggering the end of the world.

The Significance of Aum in Law and Security Contexts

It was unsurprising that the Aum case attracted the attention of law enforcement authorities around the world. It was, after all, a highly visible case of violence, with the subway attack giving rise to extensive news coverage showing the mass confusion, hysteria and suffering that was caused as a result of Aum's use of nerve gases on crowded commuter trains. The subsequent police raids on Aum, carried out by legions of police armed with batons, shields and gas masks, heightened the levels of drama in the affair, as did the discovery of Aum's laboratories, the emerging details of its weapons acquisition schemes, and the evidence that emerged of various earlier atrocities committed by the movement.

Indeed, had the story not been real, it might well have passed for the script of an overdone Hollywood movie made to cash in on the millennium, with a plot including a semi-blind, bearded guru (Aum's founder and leader Asahara Shôkô) who believed he was a saviour come to lead the forces of good in a final battle against evil; a cadre of devoted followers who saw themselves as Asahara's warriors in the battle against evil, who were prepared to kill for their cause, and who were willing to perform severe death-defying austerities in order to attain enlightenment; secret laboratories built to manufacture chemical and other weapons that would become part of the movement's grand plan to transform the world; public authorities unable to notice the mayhem being committed by the movement; and a dramatic rush-hour attack using deadly nerve gases on the world's most heavily used subway system, directed at the underground station at the heart of Japan's government district.

Such dramatic events became even more sensationalized through media reporting, which focused on lurid images of 'cults', brainwashing, manipulative gurus and maniacal plans hatched by mad and brilliant scientists involved in a 'doomsday cult' bent on (according to various media versions) world destruction or world domination. The result has been to produce a misrepresentation of what happened in Aum, with the often speculative and hysterical journalistic reporting that arose during the affair becoming recycled and used as source material for subsequent studies and writings on Aum in the context of terrorism and violence.[11]

Beyond the sensational and superficial images produced by the mass media, however, there were a number of serious and distinctive features to the Aum case that made it a natural focus of attention for law enforcement, security and intelligence agencies. One was the manner in which Aum was driven by its religious motivations to commit an act pregnant with symbolic meaning, using nerve gases to strike at the nerve centre of Japanese society.[12] The attack was not, however, just symbolic in nature but was intended to be highly destructive, with its indiscriminate use of poisonous gases in the confined space of the subway intended to cause the maximum amount of casualties. The casualties were high, with close to 4,000 injured, some severely, and 12 dead. They might have been much higher if Aum had the capacity in March 1995 to use pure sarin rather than the impure, diluted form it had available on 20 March 1995. It is clear, too, that if pure sarin had been available to Aum at the time, it would have used it, thereby causing many more deaths and injuries.[13]

Aum displayed no concern about the numbers of people it killed or maimed. Indeed, according to the teachings of its leader Asahara, all those outside the movement were opponents of the 'truth'[14] who not only deserved to die for their sins, but would actually *benefit* spiritually from dying at the hands of Aum's 'true believers'.[15] Asahara had further stated that killing all of humanity (apart from Aum's true believers) would be a wonderful and profound spiritual act.[16] Here, it appeared, was a religious movement that regarded all members of the general public as legitimate victims of its weapons; a movement that, if given the chance, would not hesitate to carry out the most wanton acts of mass destruction and that appeared interested not in making in symbolic terrorist gestures but in causing the maximum possible havoc and in bringing about death on a grand scale. Aum thus appeared to substantiate the argument that religiously motivated terrorism has the capacity to cause far greater upheaval and destruction than secular, politically motivated terrorism, which tends towards more limited, symbolic acts of violence,[17] and to raise fears that other religiously motivated groups might be keen to imitate Aum in such ways.

It was not, however, just Aum's readiness to engage in such religiously motivated indiscriminate terrorism that caused alarms, but the means by which Asahara and his disciples carried out their assault. Aum's espousal of chemical weapons (and the subsequent evidence that it had tried, albeit unsuccessfully, to make biological weapons and to acquire various forms of sophisticated weaponry) was, it was widely considered, the first case in which a non-government or private organization had made use of what has been widely described as the 'poor man's atomic bomb'. As such, there were many, especially in the immediate aftermath of the attack, who were concerned that Aum represented a dangerous new era in the world of terrorism and that, in using chemical weapons on the general public, it had crossed a threshold and had therefore changed the face of terrorism for ever. This was the initial position taken, for example, by Bruce Hoffman when he commented that Aum's use of nerve gases 'marked a significant historical watershed in terrorist tactics and weaponry' and suggested that the subway attack, with its favouring of chemical weapons over the more traditional means of assault of revolutionaries such as bombs and guns, may have changed the face of terrorism for ever.[18] Moreover, the fact that Aum had used such weapons against its own country and against its fellow citizens, was also seen in some quarters as indicative of a new and dangerous departure that conjured up images of other groups carrying out similar acts within their own societies.[19]

This fear of a 'new era' comes through in the aforementioned Canadian Security Intelligence Service report, which states that Aum's manufacture of biological and chemical weapons marked the dawn of a 'New Age'. While the writers of the report felt that in reality there was only a slim chance that any religious group would acquire and use such weapons, they nonetheless felt that 'the Aum case proves that it is within the range of possible action'. Similar perspectives have been expressed by those involved in the FBI's Critical Incident Response Group (CIRG), which has been actively considering issues relating to religiously motivated terrorism in the USA. When I visited the FBI Academy at Quantico, Virginia in March 1998, people involved in the work of this group spoke to me about the impact the Aum affair had made on their thinking. One senior official at the FBI commented to me that they had always expected that chemical and other weapons of mass destruction would be used by a private organisation at some point, and quite possibly by a group with religious orientations (although more probably a movement with Islamic connections[20]). However – and this made the Aum case particularly worrying in their eyes – they had never expected it to come from such a quarter, from Japan, a place normally considered tranquil and lacking in perceived terrorist threats, and from a movement that was unknown to them and off their radar screens.[21]

This raised the spectre that there might be other unknown groups 'out there' planning to commit similar acts of wanton destruction. If Aum could remain unknown to them and yet be capable of assembling laboratories, making chemical weapons and mounting an attack at the very heart of one of the world's greatest metropolises, did this mean that similar things might be going on, unseen, in other places, or that other groups, inspired by Aum's example, might surface and try to follow in its footsteps? In such perspectives Aum could be seen not as a danger that had passed, but as a portent of what might come in future.

In reality, however, the Aum case has not so far proved to be a dramatic threshold crossing event. Hoffman, writing in 2000, has recognised this and effectively withdrawn from his earlier position by stating that the predicted use of chemical weapons in the aftermath of Aum had not materialised and that Aum has so far been 'the exception rather than the rule in providing signposts for future terrorism'.[22] Hoffman's revised position echoes the views of David C. Rapoport who, in 1999, stated firmly that the conclusion made, after the subway attack, that a threshold had been crossed, went 'wildly against the facts'.[23] Rapoport's argument is that bombs and other such conventional weapons of terrorism – used in the main by secular rather than religious terror groups – would continue to cause more casualties than chemical ones, while he also points out that thus far chemical and biological weapons have proved somewhat ineffective when used, whether by state organisations in war situations, or by Aum in its attempted attacks on the Japanese public. As Rapoport notes, Aum was extremely incompetent in its attempts to make and use such weapons, and was only able to get as far as it did because of the inept way in which the Japanese police handled the affair and because its position as a religious organisation offered it some protection against police investigations. In other words, rather than indicating the crossing of a new threshold in terrorism, the Aum case could be used, as Rapoport does, to argue that biological and chemical weapons are less, rather than more, likely to be the choice of terrorists in the future.

My analysis of the Aum affair backs up Rapoport's arguments. The movement proved especially inept in its attempts to harness chemical and biological weapons, and they had few, if any, people capable of actually engaging in a structured programme of weapons manufacture. While the two prime agents in Aum's programme of weapons manufacture, Endô Seiichi and Tsuchiya Masami, both had science degrees, they were first and foremost devout followers of Asahara who had left their studies and work to join Aum, where they spent much of their time in Aum devoted to ascetic religious practices. They were not recruited as scientists, and they did not turn to making weapons until some years after joining the movement. Aum, rather than using trained specialists in its weapons manufacture, relied largely on two dedicated religious practitioners who were inexperienced as scientists and who dwelt in a world of what I have elsewhere called 'imaginative fantasy and technological madness'.[24] Their inexperience and incompetence were rapidly manifest, for they had a virtually unbroken record of causing accidents, inadvertently poisoning their own members, and drawing attention to the movement because of their blunders. They were equally inept in technological terms, and failed to make adequate devices for releasing the gases and other toxins they made.[25]

Aum was also lucky in that, despite the striking trail of clues it left indicating the extent of its illegal activities, it was able to escape close scrutiny because of the particular political and social climate of post-war Japan in which the police, mindful of their terrible pre-war record of oppression, had been consistently reluctant to intervene in the affairs of religious movements (a point to be discussed further later in this article). Aum developed along an increasingly turbulent path between late 1988 (when it first began to manifest signs of violence) and March 1995, when it carried out the subway attack, and yet it was not until this act – carried out nine months after Aum had first used nerve gases to kill seven people in the town of Matsumoto in central Japan and some months after the Japanese media had directly linked Aum with this attack – that the police finally overcame their reluctance to examine the movement.[26]

However, despite Rapoport's arguments about the problematic nature of chemical weapons, and despite the clear indications outlined above that the Aum case was predicated upon particular factors unlikely to be reproduced elsewhere, it is evident that these forms of weapons – and consequently, too, the Aum case – remain extremely potent in the imagination and fears of the authorities and of the public at large. It is evident, from the weight given to Aum in the various reports cited earlier, that law enforcement agencies so far have not drawn the comforting conclusion that religious terrorism using chemical weapons would remain rare and that any groups espousing such means would be incompetent and hence unable to cause serious problems. Rather, they have seen Aum as a warning sign of what *might* occur, and of the potential dangers that could accrue should another religious movement, learning from Aum's mistakes, go about things in a more competent manner – and especially if, as with Aum, security and police forces fail to be vigilant in their activities.

Incompetence is not something that can be depended upon. In Aum's case, this incompetence emanated as much as anything from the fact that the movement was driven by religious impulses and by the distorted imaginings of religious paranoia. The Aum affair may tell us that religious zealots –even those with science degrees – are unlikely to prove particularly competent when they turn their hands to building laboratories and trying to succeed in a variety of diverse areas (it should be emphasised that Aum did not have specialists in chemical weapons, biological weapons or weapons delivery technologies, but had the same small coterie of individuals attempting to deal with all of these at the same time) while they continue to devote major amounts of their attention to asceticism and religious devotionalism. Yet it cannot fully assure us that every other group will be as incompetent or as fuelled by religious priorities that it will make the same mistakes as Aum. Despite the logical arguments that can be made about the ineffectiveness of chemical and biological weapons, especially when handled by non-state organisations, one can never fully evade the fear of what might happen should one group, just once, manage to carry out an attack competently.

The problem is that, while rational argument might tell us that chemical weapon attacks are unlikely to succeed and that terrorists will probably not use such weapons as a result, it cannot extirpate the plain fear and psychological traumas that the mere hint of chemical and biological weapons might bring. These outstrip the fears raised by conventional weapons: the explosion of bombs is something we (at least in the UK, because of the recurrent IRA bombing campaigns of past

decades) have become used to, and blood and overt wounds are, and
have always been, recognisable parts of our understanding. Poisonous
and odourless gases, by contrast, have not been, and that is why they
instil such fear. Everyone I know who was in Tokyo in the weeks after
the subway attack has spoken to me of the immense fear that gripped the
city, and of their own trepidation when riding on the public transport
system, and while being in the subway system, underground. They were
not reassured by the proven incompetence of Aum, or by the arrest of its
leaders, so much as they were gripped by the climate of fear Aum had
created. One lesson of the attack certainly is that, whatever levels of
effectiveness chemical weapons might or might not have, they retain a
singularly potent capacity to cause hysteria, concern and panic among
authorities across the globe.

This became strikingly apparent in the weeks after the atrocities of
11 September 2001. In its aftermath a rational perspective might be that
the people who carried out this attack had attained a peak (in terrorist
terms) that is unlikely to be surpassed. Yet, almost immediately, the
mass media – never slow to raise the spectre that something worse
might be in the pipeline- quickly began to speak of the possibility that
biological and chemical weapons such as sarin might be used next. The
panic that ensued was evident, with mushrooming sales of gas masks
on both sides of the Atlantic. At the same time, there were recurrent and
renewed references to Aum Shinrikyô, both as the first organisation to
use such weapons, and as an indication that there are groups 'out there'
who will use such heinous weapons. I was in Japan on 11 September
and was struck by how quickly the media began to speak of the possible
use of nerve gases by Osama bin Laden's terrorist network, and by the
way in which such reports were accompanied by media footage from
the 20 March 1995 subway attack and by renewed discussion about
Aum's religiously motivated terrorism. By the time I returned, a few
days later, to the UK, the mass media there was also speaking in similar
terms. Rational analysis may inform us that chemical weapons are
unlikely to be the first choice of armoury for terrorists, religious or
otherwise, and that they are more likely than not to prove ineffective,
but it cannot challenge the psychological fears that such weapons
engender in the public perception. Aum, having used chemical
weapons, albeit incompetently, has ensured that, in the public and
media imaginations, the unleashing of such weapons is not a fantasy
but, as the speculations about what the terrorist groups behind the 11

September attacks might do next to top their previous atrocity shows, a believed and feared reality.

A further point to consider is that, despite the general perception that Aum had crossed a threshold, it was not actually the first such case. There had, in fact, already been one previous case in which a religious movement with millennial orientations, the Rajneesh movement based in rural Oregon – led, like Aum, by a charismatic guru who had become paranoid, obsessed with his own (possibly imagined) ill-health – had tried to build laboratories and to develop biological weapons.[27] I have discussed the parallels between the Aum and Rajneesh cases elsewhere but suffice it to note here that both were communal, hierarchic movements with profound world-negating philosophies, that had become embroiled in bitter conflicts with their neighbours and with the civil authorities in the areas where they built their communes. In both cases coercion and violence initially developed inside the movement as a means of enforcing discipline and loyalty among members. Later the violence also became directed outwards, against perceived enemies of the movements. Both Aum and Rajneesh developed extreme millennial visions of a final cataclysm that would decimate humanity, and both were convinced that the end-time was near at hand. Such beliefs infused both movements with a sense of urgency and expectancy. Both likewise became convinced that massive conspiracies existed against them, and both claimed that they were being targeted by the military, complaining about over-flights of their communes by American military aircraft that they asserted were evidence of a conspiracy to attack and destroy their movements.[28]

Like Aum a decade later, the inner elite of the Rajneesh movement developed plans to fight their (imagined) enemies in the conspiracy and to defend their commune against their 'persecutors'. They tried to build a secret laboratory at their commune (named Rajneeshpuram after their guru), and sought to isolate the AIDS virus and to develop other toxins there. They used the poisonous materials they made against perceived local enemies of the movement, including several local officials in Oregon who were subject to poisoning attempts. During this tumultuous period in the life of the movement, fissures developed in the movement's hierarchy, Rajneesh (who claimed later to have been isolated and manipulated by some of his senior disciples) fled the country, and many of his disciples were taken into custody. Later several were charged with a number of crimes, including attempted murder, and some were convicted and sent to prison.

   Doubtless the Rajneesh case did not capture the attention of
intelligence agencies (there is no mention of the movement in either the
Canadian or FBI reports) in the same ways that Aum did because the
Rajneesh movement's violent eruption occurred well before the end of
the millennium, before the development of any form of Y2K induced
'millennial hysteria', because it did not kill anyone, and because the
scale of their criminality was nowhere near as extreme as Aum's.
Moreover the Rajneesh use of poisonous substances occurred in a rather
remote rural part of Oregon, rather than in the media glare of central
Tokyo.

   Yet the case is extremely important since it can in many respects be
seen as an 'earlier Aum', in that the process whereby the Rajneesh
movement went from being a somewhat controversial alternative
religious group centred around a guru-like figure teaching meditation
and other techniques for attaining self-realisation, into becoming an
enclosed, communal group infused with millennial ideas, obsessed with
conspiracies and convinced of the 'need' to acquire weapons to fight its
enemies, displays remarkable similarities to that of Aum. Even its
conspiracy theories looked similar to those of Aum, and played a similar
role in the respective movements, in promoting the belief in each
movement that it 'needed' to arm itself so as to resist such external
threats. In such terms, rather than appearing, in the eyes of law
enforcement agencies, as an aberrant, one-off case, Aum was more
likely to be seen as a further case of escalation along the path of extreme
violence that Rajneesh had previously followed. Indeed, Aum appeared
to have taken the path trod by Rajneesh a stage further, and to a more
lethal level: unlike the Rajneesh movement, Aum did manage to make
chemical weapons, to kill a number of people, to severely disrupt, albeit
temporarily, and instil a sense of fear into one of the world's major
cities. One would be surprised if law enforcement agencies around the
world were not worrying themselves about the 'next Aum' and about
whether it might go beyond Aum in the extremes of its murderous intent
– and be more competent into the bargain. As Robert J. Kisala and Mark
R. Mullins, in their study of Japanese societal responses to Aum, have
commented:

   Aum may be one of the first new religious movements to try and
   achieve its goals with the tools of modern science and technology.
   We may hope that it will be the last, but it would be naïve to ignore

the potential for similar violence and destruction in other marginal apocalyptic movements.[29]

As the public and media responses to the events of 11 September 2001 has shown, the fears surrounding chemical and biological weapons remain very much to the fore. While clinical analysis might well indicate the exceptional nature of the Aum affair and the subway attack, the very fact that Aum – following on from the Rajneesh movement – did make and use chemical weapons, can also be used to suggest that such attacks can no longer be placed beyond the bounds of possibility and that some groups, especially when driven by religious imperatives, might not shirk from using them. At the very least, the use of chemical weapons by Aum in 1995 has added to the post-11 September public paranoia. In a sense, this paranoia is an added indication of why Aum's use of chemical weapons was of such interest to security forces and intelligence agencies, and why it rapidly became seen as a potential 'textbook' study.

There are further reasons why I consider that the Aum affair made a major impression on law enforcement agencies – and why it proved politically useful for them to portray the Aum affair as a textbook example of religious violence. For a start, the ways in which the Japanese authorities handled the case could actually be seen as a textbook case of how *not* to deal with problematic religious organizations. As I have already noted, the Aum affair was characterized by the reluctance of the police to investigate a movement that had been widely suspected of illicit activities and perhaps even murder as far back as autumn 1989, when a lawyer involved in a dispute with Aum disappeared along with his family. Although circumstantial evidence pointed to Aum, the police failed to investigate it fully – an error that effectively allowed the movement to get away with murder. Aum members had, in fact, kidnapped and murdered the lawyer, along with his wife and child, because his opposition and investigations posed a severe threat to the movement. There are many who believe that, had the police intervened and properly investigated matters then, they would have found enough evidence to have Aum's leaders arrested at that point, and that this in turn would have prevented the subsequent atrocities Aum committed between 1989 and 1995.

There were a number of reasons why the police failed to intervene. One has already been alluded to: in the first half of the twentieth century,

and during Japan's turn to fascism from the 1920s onwards, the police
had been used as a tool of the emergent fascist regime, acting either to
coerce religious movements and leaders into compliance with the state's
nationalist and fascist goals or to arrest and imprison those who refused
to comply. The most dramatic case of state intervention in the prewar
period had been centred on Ômotokyô, a millennial movement that
originated in rural Japan the late nineteenth century promising its
followers that a spiritual revolution would transform the world into a
spiritual paradise. By the early 1920s it had developed a mass following
in the major cities, while its then-leader, Deguchi Ônisaburô, had begun
to display airs that implicitly challenged the government and the status
of the Emperor.[30] As a result Ômotokyô was twice severely repressed, in
1921 and again in 1935, its leaders incarcerated and many of its facilities
razed. In the 1930s other religious movements that failed to go along
with the nationalist sentiments of the period, and particularly with the
burgeoning Japanese militarism of the era, were also repressed and their
leaders imprisoned.

In the period prior to the Second World War, then, it is evident that
the state and its police had regarded religious movements (and
especially new religions) as potential sources of dissent and threat to the
emergence of the highly centralized military nationalism centred on the
Emperor. The suppression of new religions such as Ômotokyô, likewise,
can be seen as an intrinsic element in Japan's descent into what is called,
in Japan, the 'dark valley' (*kurodani*) of fascism, militarism and war that
engulfed the country in the 1930s and 1940s. With war defeat,
occupation and the rebuilding of Japan in the postwar period, it is
unsurprising that special care was taken to safeguard religious
movements, so as to guarantee their independence and to guard against
any future eruption of fascism or state control of religion. A consensus
emerged after the war that religions needed protection from the state,
and this was enshrined in the 1946 Constitution, which guaranteed
freedom of religious association and precluded state interference in
religious affairs. Since then the Japanese police have kept their distance
from religious organizations, displaying a reluctance to intervene in
their affairs (even when indications of wrongdoing have surfaced) lest
they be accused of reverting to the religious repression of earlier eras.
Until Aum, there had been very little need for such a consensus to be
ruptured: while a variety of scandals had erupted around various new
religions, these had normally involved money and manipulation of

followers that had been exposed by the mass media (which effectively became the main 'police force' keeping the new religions in check in this period), rather than breaches of security and violence.

Thus, besides being culturally disinclined, because of the shadows still cast by the prewar repression of religions, to examine or intervene in the affairs of religious movements, the Japanese security agencies had become complacent, and had come to assume that new religions in general posed no threat to public order. This point has been well made by Christopher Hughes who argues that, at the time of the Aum affair, the Japanese police and security agencies were simply not looking in the right place for possible sources of trouble. Bound by a rigid Cold War attitude, they had assumed that any terrorist problems in Japan would come from the extreme left (as, indeed, they had in the 1960s and 1970s) and hence they were simply blind to the possibility that a religious group could commit such deeds.[31] Aum, in essence, woke them – and other law enforcement agencies – up to the fact that terror attacks could come from religious groups as well as from extreme leftist movements in Japan and beyond.

With hindsight, it is evident that, besides just 'not looking', as Hughes has put it,[32] the police showed too much caution when evidence of Aum's misdeeds began to appear before them, and they refrained from intervening for fear that they would be accused of religious repression. Such attitudes have rapidly disappeared in post-Aum Japan, where a strong consensus has emerged that religious freedoms need to be balanced with the rights of the forces of law and order to examine and intervene in the activities of religious organizations where necessary in order to protect society and the general public. The postwar consensus on non-intervention in religious affairs had been in part based in the assumption that religious organizations were beneficial institutions conducive to the public good: after Aum, few can unequivocally hold to this notion, and there has been a general consensus that, whilst they can be forces for good, they also might potentially be dangerous and in need of closer surveillance. Going along with this general mood change, the Japanese police have shed their earlier reluctance to become involved in the affairs of religious movements and have become increasingly interventionist whenever public allegations of wrongdoing among new religions have surfaced.[33]

The Aum case thus provided security and law enforcement agencies with an argument for increased police scrutiny of, and intervention in, the affairs of religious movements, at least when they displayed attitudes and orientations that suggested they might espouse radically anti-social agendas, and for placing them under surveillance as potential sources of violence. Such arguments, of course, also helped greatly in the ever-present arguments over the allocation of resources to such agencies.

Aum also provided, for law enforcement agencies, a striking counterweight example to the Waco affair in which federal law enforcement agencies had come under heavy criticism because of their heavy-handed interventionism and mishandling of the raid on and subsequent siege of the Branch Davidian compound. Waco has become a highly charged and symbolic event for a number of different interest groups. For groups on the extreme Christian right (such as those mentioned in *Project Megiddo*), it has become a symbol of the 'evil' perpetrated by the American government and its agents, and an example of needless interference in the rights of religious movements. For many scholars of religions, too, Waco has come to be seen as an example of how external pressures placed on communal, millennial movements may be the prime reason why any such group might implode in violence. The Aum affair, since it involved a movement that turned violent largely because of factors inside the movement, and with little provocation or pressure from outside, seemed to provide a counter-argument to both these points of view, both by suggesting that sometimes government intervention in the activities of religious movements might be necessary and beneficial to the public good, and by demonstrating the idea that alternative and new religions that become violent do so primarily because of external pressures. As the Aum case demonstrated, religious movements can become violent primarily because of internal factors and because of the characteristics and dynamics of the movement itself.[34]

Aum Shinrikyô in Context: Committing Religious Violence in Japan

The above discussion makes it clear that Aum attracted the attention of law enforcement agencies not simply (or even primarily) because it might be a 'textbook case' of the dynamics of violent millennial movements, but for other, political, considerations relating to the post-Waco politics of interpreting new religious movements and to issues of the legitimacy of police intervention in the workings of religious groups. Questions remains, however, about the validity of Aum as a 'textbook example' of how apocalyptic beliefs can lead to violent activities intent on precipitating world war, and about whether the Aum case validates the assumptions made in the Canadian and Megiddo reports about the activities of millennial groups in relation to apocalyptic scenarios. In this context, too, some comments will be made about the ways in which Aum appears to be linked, at least implicitly, to the Christian Identity groups discussed in *Project Megiddo*.

In order to deal with these questions, a few general comments about Aum and its transformation between 1984 and 1995, from a small yoga and meditation group into a murderous religious movement that used chemical weapons on the Japanese public, will be necessary. While it is not my intention to discuss this process at any length since there is growing academic literature on this point, to which I have already made several contributions,[35] it is important to provide a general overview of Aum and its background so that this transformation can be understood and placed in its appropriate context.

Aum Shinrikyô was one of a number of new religious movements that emerged or flourished in Japan in the 1980s. As a product of the social, cultural and religious conditions of late twentieth-century Japan, Aum shared considerable common ground with other of the new religions of the period. Prominent amongst these movements were Agonshû, a Buddhist-oriented new religion that was founded in the 1950s by the charismatic leader Kiriyama Seiyû, but which grew rapidly in the 1980s, and Kôfuku no Kagaku, a movement founded around the same time as Aum, in the mid-1980s, by Ôkawa Ryûhô, a young graduate of Tokyo University who proclaimed himself to be the Eternal Buddha returned to this world. Indeed, Asahara was briefly a member of the former of these movements, while he had a bitter rivalry with the latter in the late 1980s and early 1990s.

The movements of this period had developed against a backdrop of dissatisfaction and alienation of younger people from the heavily rationalist ethic that permeates the demanding Japanese education and work environments. Many younger Japanese were deeply unhappy with the material orientation of society, and were concerned about potential threats to their future wellbeing, whether through nuclear war (an ever-present fear in the one country to have experienced the weapons of the atomic age) or environmental problems. Such fears had produced a potent millennialism in late twentieth-century Japan, which played a part in the prophetic teachings of new religious leaders such as

Kiriyama, Ôkawa and Asahara, all of whom predicted that catastrophe would engulf the world before the end of the century unless there was a fundamental change, and unless the materialism of society was replaced by a more spiritual world view. Each of these leaders, in different ways, emphasized the need for a major spiritual transformation in the world, and each claimed that he had been entrusted with a mission to bring this about.

It was also a major common theme of new religions such as Aum, Kôfuku no Kagaku and Agonshû that they offered their followers a means of salvation from the apparent crisis facing humanity, both in collective and individual terms. Collectively they promised a world transformation in which their followers would play an active role, through engaging in spiritual practices that would help eradicate the evils of the world. Individually, too, they promised that followers could attain salvation and spiritual transcendence through a variety of practices and techniques, ranging from meditation and yoga to esoteric rituals, through which they could acquire psychic powers.[36] In general these promises attracted a young membership, particularly of highly educated followers in the main cities, who had achieved some success and got into prestigious universities, and yet felt disillusioned with the competitive and hierarchic education system and with society in general, and who were searching for new alternatives.

However, although Aum shared a common background with other new religions of its era, it exhibited a number of characteristics that set it apart from them and made it somewhat unique in Japan. Its rejection of the material world and its heavy emphasis on withdrawal from the world, in which ardent members renounced their families and familial names to live as monks and nuns in Aum communes, set it apart. The demand that Aum made of devotees that they renounce their families ran counter to the strong family orientations of Japanese society – orientations that no other new religion had sought to challenge. Equally, Aum's emphasis on severe asceticism (as an intrinsic element in the monastic path followers were required to take) was unique among the new religions, which have normally emphasized practices that are readily accessible by ordinary lay people. Moreover, while, like other new religions, its followers expressed their devotion to a charismatic leader, no other leader of a new religion demanded that their followers display absolute devotion to their guru in the way that Asahara did. And while other new religions had espoused millennial themes and spoke of catastrophes that might arise, they by and large retained an optimistic world view, regarding this world in a positive light. Aum set itself apart from the normative patterns of Japanese religion here by holding on to an essentially world-negating view in which it perceived the world as intrinsically evil. In its millennialism, too, Aum stood apart in the extremity of its views, and in its conceptualization of a physical war that had to be waged against the forces of evil.

In other words, while Aum was a Japanese movement and the product of the Japanese cultural and religious environment of its age, it also stood very much apart from the normative patterns of that environment and can be distinguished as much by its difference as by any similarities it might share with other Japanese movements of its period. In many respects it was these elements of difference – its extreme rejection of the world, its emphasis on harsh physical and ascetic practices and on absolute devotion to its leader, its deliberate secession from the world and rejection of normative social values, and its dark millennial visions of a war between good and evil – that were to prove critical to its turn to violence.

Aum was a world-negating religious movement in that it viewed the present, material world as corrupt, and believed that salvation could only be attained through withdrawal from the world and through the practice of austerities. It was fervently millennialist, believing that a new spiritual order would emerge to overthrow and replace the current materialistic world order, and that this scenario would occur at some point before the end of the twentieth century. Yet initially Asahara was optimistic on this front, believing that his mission of salvation could be accomplished peacefully as long as enough people joined his movement to help bring about the birth of a universal change of consciousness. However, such optimism gave way to increasingly pessimistic views of the future, in which catastrophe, rather than being seen as fearful and threatening, came to be viewed as a welcome means of eradicating the evils of this world and bringing about the spiritual millennium. This transformation occurred because of the movement's failure to recruit as many practitioners as Asahara felt were necessary to bring about a peaceful transition. It was further precipitated by his emphasis on strict asceticism as the way to purify the body and attain spiritual salvation, and by his belief that failing to practise such asceticism would cause the individual to suffer a benighted fate after death. This belief led him to force reluctant followers into greater extremes of asceticism, and to justify such coercion on the

grounds that it would help the practitioner to attain salvation. Such
concepts fostered a belief inside the movement that violence was
legitimate if it hastened salvation.

When an Aum follower died accidentally while undergoing ascetic
practices Asahara felt compelled to cover up the death so as to protect
his movement and mission from police investigation. The death also
required some explanation to make it fit it into Aum's developing
doctrinal structure in ways that made it appear acceptable to those in the
know. This was done by transforming the death into an acceptable event,
in which the follower had been 'assisted' on his path to a better spiritual
realm because he was not capable of making further progress in this one.
In such ways Aum's experiences led to the development of doctrines
that ultimately legitimated violence and death in the furtherance of the
movement's goals.

Because Aum preached that attachments in this world were evil,
many of its devotees severed all links with their families, thereby
provoking conflicts between their families and Aum. Since Aum
regarded anyone who criticized it (such as the parents of followers) as
opponents of the 'truth' it treated them with contempt, just as it did with
those who lived in the vicinity of its communes and who objected to its
activities. All of this led to an increasing atmosphere of hostility and
conflict between Aum and the world at large, which became translated,
in Aum's perception, into a sense of (largely self-induced) persecution.[37]

Aum felt that its message of salvation was being rejected by an
ignorant world. This sense of rejection was intensified after Asahara and
his disciples sought to project their message to a wider audience by
running for election in 1990. It is important to emphasize that Aum was
not a political movement: it established a political party in order to
publicize its religious messages, and its election campaign involved
invoking religious solutions to the world's problems. Such messages
were resoundingly rejected by the electorate at the ballot box, and this
rejection, coming on top of Aum's failures to recruit as widely as it
hoped, came to be seen in Aum as evidence that the world at large had
spurned the offer of truth and salvation, and that it was hence
fundamentally sinful, unworthy of salvation and, therefore, deserving of
death. Aum, and Asahara, reacted to failures – of their proclaimed
mission, of their attempts to attract large numbers of followers – by
shifting the blame on to those outside the movement. Such feelings of
rejection thus became transformed into a burning sense of anger because

of that rejection – and a belief that those who had 'rejected' Aum merited punishment.

Aum's violence thus began inside the movement with the coercion of devotees. It later escalated to include the imprisonment and punishment of dissidents who threatened to leave the movement or (as in the case of the first killing committed by members of the movement) to silence disaffected followers who threatened to alert the police to what was going on inside Aum.[38] The killings eventually spread outside the movement as Aum, in an increasing spiral of paranoia, began to view external opponents as evil forces that sought to destroy Aum's mission of world salvation. The doctrinal legitimation for violence and killing that had formed as a result of internal problems was further developed with arguments that those who opposed Aum were unworthy of salvation and deserved to die because of their refusal to embrace the truth preached by Aum.

As Aum became increasingly introverted and estranged from the world and increasingly inimical towards it, it grew more and more aggressive towards, and paranoid about, the world beyond its confines. Asahara became convinced that he and his movement were surrounded by malevolent enemies who sought to persecute him in order to undermine his mission and prevent the new spiritual dawn from coming. Alienated from the world, in conflict with it and convinced that he and his followers were the victims of persecution, Asahara's visions of an apocalyptic conflict between good and evil moved from a largely symbolic notion of a spiritually oriented future world, to a belief that apocalypse was necessary in order to destroy the forces of evil. As this shift occurred Aum became increasingly convinced that the forces of evil comprised a sinister world conspiracy (similar in many respects to the types of conspiracy theory prevalent in many American Christian militia movements, and involving many of the usual 'conspiracy suspects' such as the US government, the Jews and the Freemasons) that was intent on subjecting and destroying it.

Thus the final confrontation between good and evil became transformed into a war between Aum and the world at large, in which all outside of Aum deserved to die so that the world could be spiritually purified. Initially, in Asahara's earliest prophecies, he had stated that this final war was destined to start in 1999; as the 1990s wore on, and as events in and outside Aum made the movement increasingly beleaguered, the date of the apocalypse moved forward, first to 1997 and then to 1995. Aum began its attempts to acquire weapons with which (in its eyes) to defend itself – and with which it could also wreak vengeance on the world that had spurned it.[39] Attempts to make biological and chemical weapons started in 1990, initially with little success until 1994, when Endô Seiichi and Tsuchiya Masami managed to produce the nerve gas sarin. This was first used by Aum in June 1994 in the Japanese town of Matsumoto, when a group of devotees tried to kill three judges who were about to pass an adverse judgement against Aum in a court case that had grave implications for the movement's future and for Asahara's status as a prophet.[40] Seven people died in this attack. Later, as police investigations indicated that Aum was responsible for this attack, the movement used nerve gases again, in a pre-emptive strike on the Tokyo subway.

On 18 March 1995 Asahara became aware (through a tip-off, probably from the media) that the police were about to raid Aum's commune in connection with its previous activities. The subway attack was hastily planned at this time (with Endô having little time to make and purify sarin) with the direct intention of causing confusion in central Tokyo and thereby stalling the intended police raids.[41] There were clearly other, secondary factors involved as well, particularly a desire to make a symbolic statement of resistance to the police and government and a desire to inflict 'punishment' on the Japanese people, who had rejected Aum. Although in initial analyses of the Aum affair I suggested that the attack was carried out as part of a greater design on Asahara's part to bring about a final catastrophe, subsequent research has indicated that this was not the case.[42] The attack was basically a reactive strike against the authorities because of their planned raids, rather than an act carried out with the specific aim of triggering a wider conflict or of setting in motion a final apocalyptic war, intentions that were at no stage articulated by Asahara when he ordered his followers to carry out the attack.

A Textbook Case?

While Aum was a Japanese movement whose crimes were committed in Japan, and while local factors – most notably the lack of police scrutiny or investigation of Aum when it began committing crimes and the antipathy felt by the young Japanese protagonists in Aum towards Japanese society – played their part in the affair, it would be a mistake to view the Aum affair solely within a Japanese context, or to see Aum as a bizarre and unique product of the Japanese environment that had no parallels or that could not, because of cultural particularities, be replicated elsewhere. To the contrary, as one examines the Aum affair closely it becomes clear that numerous parallels do exist between what went on inside Aum and what transpired in a number of other movements in different parts of the world that have also become embroiled in violence. Indeed, it is easier, from an academic perspective, to consider and locate Aum within the wider category of millennial religious violence, than it is to view it solely as a product of the Japanese cultural environment. This point has already been made when I commented on the similarities between the Rajneesh movement's turn to violence in Oregon and that of Aum in Japan. It is evident also in the above account of Aum's path to violence, in which Aum is discussed as a generic manifestation of a particular type of religious movement (millennial, world-negating, centred on a charismatic leader with a sense of mission and a belief that the world as we know it is coming to an end) rather than considered primarily as a Japanese religious phenomenon.

Similar elements have been present and visible in other movements of the modern age that have come to public attention because of violent episodes. My own extended studies of Aum have drawn attention to a number of similarities and parallels that it shared with other movements including Rajneesh, but also the Order of the Solar Temple and the Peoples Temple.[43] In these movements, as in Aum, one can see evidence of many of the points that the Canadian report describes as commonalities of doctrine and action and that it suggests might be indicators of the potential for violence in a movement. Amongst these are the presence of apocalyptic beliefs, a dualistic world view in which the world is divided into opposing forces of good and evil, and in which the movement concerned represents the forces of good (usually in opposition to the rest of the world, which is evil), a sense that those in the movement are a chosen but persecuted elite who have to defend themselves against their persecutors, and a belief that conflict is necessary in order to enable the group to survive. Coupled with this, the report identifies the importance of a messianic charismatic leader who has control over his disciples and who, in the view of followers, is above normative moral restrictions and is thus able to sanction acts that in other circumstances would appear as wrong. Other elements in the process include withdrawal from the world – as, for example, Aum did by building communes and encouraging members to break all ties with the world beyond the movement. The Canadian report suggests this can lead to increased expectation within the movement that it will become the victim of persecution, and stimulate the feeling that it needs to arm itself in preparation for the final confrontation that is imminent.

In my account of Aum I have drawn attention to many of these traits. Naturally, since the Canadian Security Intelligence Service regarded Aum as a textbook example, it is perhaps unsurprising that Aum's characteristics fit so well with the checklist its report sets out, and one cannot rule out the possibility that Aum has been used by the Canadian authorities as a form of template to categorize potentially violent movements. However, these characteristics are by no means specific only to Aum. In the Peoples Temple, the Rajneesh movement and the Branch Davidians, for example, one similarly finds the presence of apocalyptic beliefs and of charismatic leaders who were driven by a sense of mission. These movements, too, withdrew from the world into compounds or communes where they sought to establish a way of living and a rule that was different from that of mainstream society. They all also believed that the world was entering an imminent end-time and were driven by a dualistic world view, in which they were either a chosen elite threatened by evil persecution emanating from society at large, or were seeking to establish a special paradisal kingdom on earth. Aum shared also with Rajneesh, the Peoples Temple and the Branch Davidians in their Waco compound, a focus on charismatic leadership that exerted a powerful sway over followers, and in which the leader was considered to be beyond or above normative social and moral restraints.

In his comparative study of apocalyptic scenarios in new religious movements, John R. Hall has effectively emphasized the similarities in patterns of development in millennial movements in different contexts, by commenting that there was nothing distinctive about Aum that could not happen elsewhere.[44] Hall especially identifies similarities between Aum, the Peoples Temple at Jonestown and the Branch Davidians at Waco, all of which, he argues, engaged in a 'warring apocalypse' scenario, in which external conflict along with internal millennial dynamics were driving forces in causing these movements to assume confrontational positions vis-à-vis the outside world and to engage in acts of extreme defiance and aggression against the outside world.[45] This did not mean that all these movements would implode or erupt in the same way, or that any movement sharing similar traits would follow similar paths. Hall, for instance, perceives differences between movements fired by a warring apocalypse scenario in which the movement engages at some level in violent resistance to outside forces (evident in the Branch Davidian resistance to the BATF, in the Peoples Temple's attack on the party led by Congressman Ryan, and by Aum's assaults on the Japanese public) and with those that have a mystically charged view of the apocalypse, which leads them, as with the Order of the Solar Temple and Heaven's Gate, to collective suicide and 'transit' to other realms.[46]

The point is that there are enough parallels between Aum and other groups that have been associated with violent upheavals in recent years, to indicate Aum's validity as a possible comparative case study of the dynamics that can occur in millennial movements. Whether it can be used as a 'model', however, especially for movements in the USA that emanate from a rather different system and with some different orientations and attitudes (see below), is a rather different matter, as, indeed, is the question whether any set of characteristics can be seen as predictive of violence. That is a topic that requires more academic attention than has been so far given, although it is an issue unfortunately beyond the scope of this essay. My general sense, however, is that the academic community, which naturally operates from a rather different perspective and set of methodologies than do security services and is concerned with analysing events that *have* happened rather than those that *might*, has so far been highly reluctant to consider that certain forms of patterns or characteristics can be predictive of violence. This is a matter that requires some consideration, given that, as the Canadian report indicates, there appears to be plentiful thought given by intelligence and security agencies to this issue.

Textbook Errors: Aum in the Context of *Project Megiddo*

The preceding discussion has indicated many shared traits and dynamics within the millennial movements that have attained notoriety in recent years. It indicates, too, that, while we need to be mindful of Aum Shinrikyô's particularities in terms of the extremes of its violence and the specifics of Japanese situation, the movement and the path it took have much in common with other groups, to the extent that it has to be included in any comparative discussion of new religions and violence. In the context of the groups discussed in *Project Megiddo*, too, one can discern some striking parallels with Aum, most specifically in the ways in which these groups view the world beyond their own borders.

Like Aum, the movements discussed in *Megiddo* are obsessed with millennial visions of a final confrontation between good and evil, and see anyone in the outside world who does not agree with them as potentially threatening and evil. This world view was a central element in Aum's violence and in its readiness to 'punish' the rest of the world for their apparent sins and complicity with the 'evil conspiracy' that was attacking it. The Christian Identity movements of *Megiddo* appear similarly fixated on such themes and similarly 'threatened' by a vast network of conspiratorial forces beyond their borders. The sinister groupings intent on world domination that form the focus of their particular paranoid visions are much the same, transposed to an American context, as are Aum's. In both contexts the conspiracy provides the 'other' against which such movements ultimately defined themselves, and against which they had to struggle and fight in the final apocalypse. In both cases the democratic government of their own country was a willing and destructive participant in this conspiracy, albeit in each as a pawn or servant of a greater, darker force. Thus Aum viewed the Japanese government and Imperial family as agents of an evil force of world domination led by the US government and assorted conspirators such as the Jews, the Illuminati, and the Freemasons. In the eyes of the American Christian Identity groups the government of the USA was seen as a treacherous organization (and its President as an Antichrist figure) in league with, or acting as the agent for, outside forces (including the UN, the Jews and other such imagined groupings) intent on destroying the freedoms enjoyed by American citizens.[47]

Such conspiracy theories legitimated the drive in these movements towards gathering arms with which to 'defend' themselves against their potential oppressors and to fight the forces of evil. They became central elements in what Mark Juergensmeyer has termed 'the script of cosmic war' that is a common theme in various cases of religious violence he has documented around the globe.[48] This cosmic script of war was an extremely potent force in Aum and it is evident that it is a potent motivating force in the paranoid and conspiracy-obsessed elements within the Christian Identity movement and similar extreme groups in the USA. The parallels between Aum and Christian Identity have also been noted by scholars such as Michael Barkun, who observes that both groups have merged together paramilitary and religious imperatives.[49]

Yet it would be wrong, not just because of their differing social and cultural circumstances, to assume that Aum and Christian Identity are mirror images of each other. The former – with its ultimate implosion and apparent attempt to enact cosmic war on the physical plane – cannot be seen as a blueprint signifying the likely development of right-wing extremist Christian movements in the USA. It is important, in this context, to note a number of cautionary points here, and particularly to comment on some misunderstandings about the Aum case that lead to a distorted picture in the reports cited above, of how millennial movements such as Christian Identity might behave at the millennium.

One striking point of difference between Aum and the Christian Identity movement relates to the fact that Aum (like, I would argue, the other movements that have been mentioned in this article, such as Peoples Temple and the Rajneesh movement) exhibits a far more universalizing attitude to the world than is evidenced in the Christian Identity movement's narrow and bigoted racial exclusivity. Initially, as I noted earlier, Aum held to an optimistic world view in which salvation for all could be accomplished through Aum's spiritual endeavours. Even when it turned away from such views, and assumed a pessimistic and violent millennial stance in which everyone outside Aum was evil, it continued to hold on to some elements of its earlier universalism and to believe in the possibility of universal salvation if only everyone 'woke up' to the truth of its teachings and abandoned the evil ways of the world. Moreover, it never closed ranks or refused to allow anyone to share its vision of the future, no matter what their ethnic origins. Some of its devotees were members of minority groups in Japan, while the movement did not discriminate between the sexes (three of its most highly ranked officials below Asahara were female), attempted to proselytize and recruit followers outside of Japan, and at no stage proclaimed any form of exclusivity that disbarred anyone from entering into its truth. It saw Japan, at least initially, as the place where its mission of world salvation would be located, and Asahara saw the salvation of Japan as part of his mission. Yet there was never a racial exclusivity to this, or a sense that other nations or peoples would either have to become subservient to his own country or that they should be shut out from any future new order that might emerge.

Here there is a clear contrast and difference with the Christian

Identity movement, whose emphasis on white skins, defence of a
particular vision of exclusivity and privilege, and the evident idea that
salvation comes not through belief alone, but through skin colour and
racial circumstance, marks it out as a movement without a universal
vision. Ironically, given the extremes of paranoia that engulfed Aum, it
was, in philosophical terms, never as embattled and entrenched a
movement as Christian Identity. At the same time, because of its belief
that everyone could be saved, Aum developed a particularly virulent
attitude towards everyone in the world at large, because they had
'rejected' the chance to be saved. This in turn helped generate Aum's
extraordinarily violent antipathy to the world at large and made it more
willing to strike out at all beyond its confines, than is immediately
evident in the attitudes of Christian Identity groups.

Another crucial difference, I would suggest, is in the structures of
these movements. Aum was highly centralized and hierarchical, and
focused on the authority of its charismatic leader Asahara. Asahara not
only provided a focus of total authority, but was also the primary guiding
force in Aum's turn to violence. It was because of his orders that Aum
devotees killed and made chemical weapons, and because of his authority
to create new doctrines, that Aum could develop a legitimating
framework for its actions. Moreover, those who committed Aum's acts of
violence were senior disciples whose exalted positions in the movement
had been bestowed on them by Asahara in recognition of their readiness
to accept his absolute authority and because of their dedication to ascetic
practices. Aum's structure thus centred on a dedicated and fanatical elite
who were ready to carry out each and every one of Asahara's orders, and
whose standing in the movement was, in effect, premised on their
readiness to commit themselves to extreme actions. Such attitudes are
clearly illustrated by the case of Nakagawa Tomomasa, a young doctor
who joined Aum. He rose rapidly in the movement because of his
dedication, and within a short while was chosen to take part in an Aum
mission to kill an enemy of the movement. Rather than being horrified at
this order, the young doctor expressed his elation because it showed him
that he had joined the elite, the inner circle of spiritual advanced
practitioners who (in Aum's view) were permitted to kill the unworthy
because of their own spiritual prowess.[50]

By contrast with this hierarchic structure which vested total authority
in a single charismatic leader (a system that encouraged, as we have
seen with Nakagawa, an extremism and readiness to commit acts of

violence), the Christian Identity movement appears fragmented and lacking in the type of centralizing charismatic authority – along with a core of highly dedicated senior disciples – so central to the violence of Aum (and also, one could argue, of the Rajneesh and Peoples Temple movements). The Christian Identity movement, scattered both geographically and structurally in a variety of diverse groups, appears to lack the vital ingredient, as one might put it, of the 'poisonous cocktail' that made Aum so singularly lethal. Whilst one cannot say that only movements with a single, dominant, charismatic leader and the sort of hardened band of close devotees that normally gather around him are liable to turn violent, one can at least suggest that this factor remains one of the more cogent forces in galvanizing religious movements into acts of internalized or externalized violence.

There is perhaps a more important caveat still that needs to be made about the underlying themes in *Project Megiddo* and the Canadian report, at least in their use of Aum Shinrikyô. This concerns the ways in which both reports link specific dates with the notion of millennialism, and the ways in which they assume that millennial movements such as Aum are driven by a belief that they are destined to trigger the final war through their actions and in order to fulfil the prophecies they adhere to. This idea is evident in both *Project Megiddo* which, as I have mentioned before, names Aum as a group that wanted to take action to hasten the end of the world, and the Canadian report, which speaks of Aum's actions having been carried out 'in the hope of precipitating a world war and completing its apocalyptic prophecy'.

The idea that certain types of millennial movement are planning to precipitate the end-times through some dramatic action or other, is certainly extremely expedient for security and law enforcement forces, since it provides further arguments for increased surveillance of potentially 'dangerous' movements. The problem, however, is that such assumptions about dates and apocalyptic triggers are highly problematic: they do not fit the Aum case in any degree and, I would suggest, are rather tenuous in the context of many of the other millennial movements that have been discussed here.

In the eyes of security agencies the date 2000 stood out as a deeply symbolic date tied closely to the apocalyptic visions and millennial rhetoric of many Christian groups of the age. Yet, despite conspiracy theories widespread among extremist Christian groups in the USA that 2000 would be the date at which the 'New World Order' would set in motion its plan to take over the world, one should remember that specific dates have not played an especially noteworthy or striking part in the dynamics of millennialism in historical terms, and that the term 'millennium' itself refers, in the context of millennial religious movements, to the period that occurs after the world has been spiritually transformed (see note 5). Moreover, by no means all millennial movements signify particular dates at which the 'end' will come, and even when they do so (as with Aum) these are not necessarily set in stone. Aum, for example, began by emphasizing 1999 as the date around which world conflict would erupt. It subsequently altered that date as events unfolded inside the movement, and as internal problems coupled with its increasing fractious relationship with the world outside caused the movement to descend into paranoia and violence. As I have argued elsewhere, the date moved forward because of events happening inside Aum, and as the date came closer to hand, and as the movement became increasingly engulfed in violent activities, the focus of the final conflict also changed. Aum's expected apocalypse altered from a possible world war between the USA and Russia (an apocalyptic scenario that Asahara predicted, in 1986, would occur around 1999), to a war that, Asahara stated in 1993, would occur between the USA and Japan in 1997, to a final confrontation between the 'truth' (i.e. Aum) and evil (the rest of the world) that, Asahara stated in January 1995, would start in that very year. Whilst the first date cited had some symbolic value (it was a date widely believed in Japan to signify a period when something might happen)[51] into which Asahara, like many other religious leaders bought, the subsequent shifting of dates – and the shifting of the focus of the final confrontation – revolved around dates with no specific significance or particular temporal resonance. Ultimately 1995 was the year in which confrontation would occur because, by the beginning of that year, Aum had become so beset by conflicts and so riven with paranoia, and had committed so many aggressive acts, that it was unable to keep going without some form of run-in with the authorities.

Aum Shinrikyô's willingness to change the date of the predicted apocalyptic dawn in the light of its internal circumstances shows that its millennialism was not driven by or framed around expectations that something would happen at a particular and rigidly identified date. This is a pattern evident in other movements mentioned in this article, such as the Branch Davidians, the Peoples Temple and the Rajneesh movement, none of which imploded or exploded in a seizure of violence at a time or date that had been identified by their leaders as especially significant. Rather (as my discussion of Aum has indicated) all these movements imploded or exploded because of a process conditioned by internal events in the movement, coupled with some degree of external pressure or confrontation – and with little or no correlation at all to emotionally or symbolically significant dates. 18 November 1978, 19 April 1993 and 20 March 1995 (the dates of, respectively, the Peoples Temple mass suicide, the immolation of the Branch Davidians at Waco, and Aum's subway attack) appear to have had no great symbolic meanings for the movements concerned, and the events that happened on these days did so simply because it was at these times that a particular confluence of events and factors coalesced and came to a head.

If the notion that specific dates may serve as potential triggers to apocalyptic mayhem does not fit with the evidence of the Aum case, there is an even more problematic assumption found in *Project Megiddo* and in the Canadian report. This is the idea that millennial movements, such as Aum, which believe that some form of apocalyptic scenario will unfold, are motivated by the desire to *trigger* that scenario, and that their acts of violence are conducted with that aim in mind. This notion, which was repeated over and over about Aum in Japanese and Western language reporting of Aum, crops up in *Project Megiddo*'s aforementioned comment about Aum's having taken action in order to hasten the end of the world. Indeed, one of the central assumptions in the *Project Megiddo* and Canadian reports is that problematic millennial groups are in control of their destinies in this respect and that they therefore act with directed intent to produce violent confrontations that, they believe, will provoke or trigger the apocalypse.[52]

There is, however, little tangible evidence to sustain such assumptions, at least in the context of Aum. In his numerous sermons and pronouncements Asahara Shôkô warned his followers that the time would come when Aum would have to fight against its enemies, when it would have to defend itself against its 'persecutors', and when it would have to either stand up for the 'truth' or be defeated.[53] Asahara's sermons from the early 1990s onwards (when apocalyptic images begin to dominate his teachings) emphasize defence and resistance, and speak of the necessity of fighting for the truth if Aum is attacked. They also emphasize the necessity of making weapons so as to be ready when the time comes, and in order to defend the truth. However, while emphasizing that Aum's opponents deserve to die, and that Aum is ready to fight and confront the world, Asahara continually uses a rhetoric centred on defensive motifs of fighting against external aggression.

He does not talk about mounting attacks on Aum's enemies so as to precipitate a final war. Rather, an apocalyptic war will occur because of the external conspiratorial forces that are intent on destroying Aum. In his sermons Asahara depicts Aum as under threat and beleaguered, not as an active force about to set in motion the events that will initiate the apocalypse. Indeed, the dramatic attack that brought Aum most directly into a virtual war footing with the authorities in Japan – the subway attack – was carried out, as I have emphasized previously, and as the protagonists have admitted in court, as a reactive measure. Rather than being a proactive deed designed to precipitate the end, it was defensive measure (from Aum's perspective) designed to extricate it from the immediate problem of an imminent police raid.[54]

This is not, I would suggest, a peculiarity of Aum, so much as it is a rather common theme among millennial movements that are enveloped in disasters. The Rajneesh movement's attempts to make weapons – and its attempts on the lives of its 'oppressors' working for law enforcement agencies in Oregon – were based in concepts of resistance to perceived external oppression rather than in ideas of making a first strike that would trigger the end.[55] The idea of triggering the end of the world is not evident in the actions of Jim Jones in Guyana or of the members of the Order of the Solar Temple in Canada and Switzerland. Jones did not tell his followers that in taking the steps they did in Guyana (i.e. in taking cyanide) they would be precipitating the end-time or bringing mass destruction to a world that they no longer felt part of. Rather, they were abandoning this world to its fate, and were going away from it because they had no future in it, and in order to preserve their solidarity and ideals.[56] The members of the Solar Temple or, indeed, of Heaven's Gate, whose collective suicide in 1997 was linked to its millennial orientations,[57] did not announce that their suicides were intended to precipitate the destruction of the world or the onset of an end-time. Rather, both movements, driven by millennial imperatives, had come to believe that their time on earth had run out, and that their missions to save this planet and its people had failed, because no one had listened to their message of truth. As a result, rather than seeking to destroy the world, they abandoned it to its fate and went elsewhere. In the enactment of their dramatic finales, Heaven's Gate and the Order of the Solar Temple, like Aum, were intent on resolving or dealing with their particular predicaments as beleaguered millennial movements, not with setting the fuse that would trigger the end of the world.

Conclusions

As this article has indicated, there are clear reasons why the Aum Shinrikyô affair caught the attention of law enforcement agencies around the world. The drama of the event, the means by which Aum carried out its attack, and the very fact that a movement unknown outside Japan could carry out an atrocity that paralyzed the heart of a major city, raised serious concerns about the future directions and threats of terrorism, particularly of a religiously motivated kind. The Aum case also provided law enforcement agencies with a politically useful counter-example to the Waco affair, of how religious movements might become volatile and dangerous because of their internal nature, and it thus served to bolster the arguments that security and police agencies were able to make about the need for more resources and powers to counter the threat of such groups.

In this context it is worth emphasizing again the points that I made earlier about the extent to which these reports demonstrate misunderstandings of Aum, especially in the context of the idea that Aum sought to trigger the apocalypse. Such misinterpretations of the movement might well have occurred because of flawed analysis, of course, but one also has to consider the extent to which the agendas that have driven the agencies involved in producing such reports might have affected their perceptions. The Canadian report, in essence, indicates this point by arguing that millennial religious movements are a potential new form of public danger that need to be examined by the security forces. In this context Aum (especially when it is misinterpreted in ways that suggest that it was driven by the aim of setting the apocalypse in motion) has fitted in with, and been co-opted to serve the agendas of various law enforcement and intelligence agencies, by providing them with an example which can be used to argue for an extension of their areas of activity, for increased funding and for extended powers of surveillance.

There is clear evidence from Japan that this type of thinking has motivated the actions of that country's intelligence service, the Public Security Intelligence Agency (PSIA). The PSIA was set up at the height of the Korean War in 1952 to monitor and target communist groups in

Japan, and enjoyed a privileged status in funding and other terms during the Cold War era. Since the end of the Cold War and the collapse of communism, however, its position has been undermined by the very absence of the enemy forces and potential threats to security that the agency was established to investigate and defeat. As a result, the PSIA has been put under pressure to show its continued relevance in the post-Cold War era. As Christopher Hughes has shown, the Aum case provided it with an opportunity to do just that, and thus to secure its future. It was the PSIA that sought to initiate Aum's proscription in 1995 under the Anti-Subversives Activities Law – a law passed in 1952, at the time the PSIA was set up, to allow the agency to monitor and suppress potentially dangerous political groups. By attempting to get this law applied to a religious movement, the PSIA was effectively seeking to extend its own remit and to provide itself with a new 'public threat' to counter, replacing the previous spectre of communism with that of 'dangerous' religious movements. The PSIA eventually failed in this quest after a public commission decided that its grounds for using the law in the Aum case were not fully proven. Indeed, its move actually backfired because the political establishment, suspicious of the PSIA's real motives, began to question the very existence of a force set up in, and related to the dynamics of, the Cold War era.[58] Although the PSIA failed in its endeavours, its actions do remind us that such agencies may not always be motivated only by security considerations – a point one should bear in mind in the context of *Project Megiddo* and similar reports.

Yet, even as one questions the underlying political reasons behind such reports and their readings of movements such as Aum, one needs to remember just how potentially serious the implications of Aum's actions were, and to recognize that it did manifest many characteristics and traits that can be seen also in other millennial movements that have also committed acts of violence. It is in such contexts that one can see the relevance of Aum for law enforcement agencies, providing them with a possible 'textbook example' through which they could develop an understanding and a model of volatile religious groups. Aum does, indeed, provide us with one important and suitable frame of reference through which to start considering the patterns of millennial religious violence. However, one must beware both of assuming that just because one millennial movement has many characteristics in common with another, they necessarily share completely common ground, or that one can provide a template model for another. As has been indicated, while Aum and the Christian Identity movement may share some common traits, they also manifest dissimilarities that make Aum a less than reliable model of prediction for the future dynamics of Christian Identity. One certainly also needs to be aware of the extent to which erroneous assumptions (perhaps fuelled by the political motivations of those that make them) about one type of movement might lead to dubious interpretations of others. There are important lessons that should be learned from Aum (notably relating to the process through which religious movements with certain types of structure and world view can veer out of control, and the ways in which they might develop hostile attitudes to the world at large and engage in acts of violence), and in some sense the reports mentioned in this article indicate that at least some law enforcement and security agencies are showing an interest in taking such lessons on board. It is to be hoped that, as their analyses continue, they will be able to draw on these lessons while eschewing the tendency towards modes of analyses that are driven largely by their own self-interest.

NOTES

1. These were especially popular in Japan, where, since translations of Nostradamus's prophecies first appeared in Japanese in 1973, they have had a potent influence on Japanese millennial culture. See Robert Kisala, '1999 and Beyond: The Use of Nostradamus' Prophecies by Japanese Religions', *Japanese Religions* 23/1 (1997), pp.143–57, Ian Reader, *Religious Violence in Contemporary Japan: The Case of Aum Shinrikyô* (Richmond, UK and Honolulu, USA: Curzon Press and University of Hawaii Press, 2000), pp.50–52; Shimada Hiromi *Shinjiyasui kokoro: Wakamono ga shinshin shûkyô ni hashiru riyû* [Minds that find it easy to believe: The reasons why young people follow the 'new' new religions] (Tokyo: PHP Kenkyûjo, 1995), pp.106–7.
2. Charles B. Strozier, 'Introduction', in Charles B. Strozier and Michael Flynn (eds.), *The Year 2000: Essays on the End* (New York: New York University Press, 1997), pp.1–9.
3. Scholars generally date the emergence of the earliest new religious movements (*shin shûkyô*) in Japan from the early nineteenth century, with successive waves of new movements appearing at regular intervals thereafter. Millennial themes have been present in many of these movements, such as Tenrikyô and Ômoto, which emerged in impoverished rural conditions in the nineteenth century, as well as in many religions that emerged in urban late twentieth-century Japan, such as Agonshû, Kôfuku no Kagaku and Aum Shinrikyô. On the millennial themes in the earlier new religions see Emily Groszos Ooms, *Women and Millenarian Protest in Meiji Japan* (Ithaca, NY: Cornell East Asia Series, 1993). On the most recent wave of new religions mentioned here see Shimazono Susumu, *Shinshin shûkyô to shûkyô bûmu* [The 'new' new religions and the religious boom] (Tokyo: Iwanami Booklets No.237, 1992), as well as Shimada 1995 (note 1) and Reader 2000 (note 1), pp.47–52.
4. See, for example, Strozier and Flynn (eds.), 1997 (note 2), which contains numerous essays related to the year 2000 in religious contexts.
5. When I use the terms 'millennial movement' and 'millennialism' in this article and elsewhere, I refer to religious movements that believe in some future and radical change

that will occur – or that is needed – to transform the world, sweeping away the existing order and replacing it with a new spiritual order of peace and harmony that will hold sway on earth. In millennial terms this process of transformation is often seen as brought about by dramatic and even violent events, such as natural disasters, catastrophes and war, and while such disasters are not essential prerequisites of this change, they play a large part in the thinking of many millennial movements, including those mentioned in this article. The term 'millennialism' is associated with the Christian belief that Christ will return to establish a thousand-year (i.e. millennium) period of peace on earth. In this context it is worth noting that the term 'millennium' thus does not refer to a thousand-year period that has elapsed (e.g. the year 1000 or 2000, as thousand-year periods after the birth of Christ) but to the time period that is to come after the dawn of the new era. Although the term millennium is thus especially associated with Christianity, its usage (and the concepts outlined above) have not been limited to the Christian tradition, but have great resonance in other religious traditions too – as, indeed, the Aum case indicates. The term itself is often applied to any religious movements that adheres to an world view along the lines mentioned above, in which the existing order will be swept away and replaced. For further discussions of the concepts associated with the term millennialism (and millenarianism, a term that is virtually interchangeable with millennialism) see Norman Cohn, *The Pursuit of the Millennium* (London: Secker and Warburg, 1957) passim, but esp. pp.xiii–xiv and 1–13, and Catherine Wessinger, 'Introduction: The Interacting Dynamics of Millennial Beliefs, Persecution, and Violence', in Catherine Wessinger (ed.), *Millennialism, Persecution and Violence: Historical Cases* (Syracuse, NY: Syracuse University Press, 2000), pp.3–39, esp. 4–11. Cohn's book provides a detailed account of millennial uprisings in Europe especially in the fifteenth and sixteenth centuries, while Wessinger's outlines various violent episodes involving millennial movements from around the world and from a variety of traditions and eras. Wessinger's examples, which include discussions of nineteenth-century Chinese Buddhist millennial uprisings, medieval Japanese Buddhist millennialism, and seventeenth-century Russian groups, show, as does Cohn's study, that millennialism is not something closely associated with particular dates related to the number 1,000, but with particular types of movement whose prime focus is a belief in the imminent advent of a new era.

6. Federal Bureau of Investigation, 1999 *Project Megiddo* (hereafter referred to as Megiddo), available in HTML format from the Cesnur website (www.cesnur.org/testi/FBI_004.htm) and in PDF from www.fbi.gov.
7. Canadian Security Intelligence Service Report #2000/03 *Doomsday Religious Movements* (hereafter cited in notes as Canadian report) (Report located at www.cesnur.org/testi/canada.htm).
8. The impact of the Waco affair on the thinking of some of those involved in the Christian militias in the USA is well known, and heightened their already rather extreme paranoia that the government is out to get them. Asahara Shôkô, the leader of Aum Shinrikyô, was also influenced by the Waco siege, seeing the destruction of the Branch Davidian compound as having been carried out by the evil world order that he claimed was seeking to destroy Aum. The Waco affair therefore added to his growing expectation of a final confrontation between his movement and society at large. See also Asahara Shôkô, *Vajrayana kôsu. Kyôgaku shisutemu kyôhon* [The Vajrayana course: Teaching manual for (Aum's) doctrinal system] (unpublished Aum text, probably produced in 1994 for ordained members of Aum, and consisting of 57 sermons over the period 1988–94 by Asahara). This text was used as a doctrinal training manual for senior members of the movement. In Reader 2000 (note 1) I have analysed this text extensively to show how Asahara became increasingly paranoid about the world beyond Aum, and how external events (including the Waco siege) were seen by him as evidence for the onset of a catastrophic end-time. The Waco affair, as Jean-Francois Mayer, *Les Mythes du Temple Solaire* [The myths of the Solar temple] (Geneva: Georg, 1996), p.18, has noted, also had an impact on the leaders of the Order of the Solar Temple, who felt

motivated to engineer their 'mass transit' (i.e. collective suicide) in a way that would be more spectacular and attention-grabbing than even the Branch Davidian siege at Waco.

9. I am aware of this from a personal perspective, having received invitations to speak to FBI audiences on occasion and having had various communications from the Critical Incident Analysis Group about Aum – all of which testify to the extraordinary degree of interest this group and the FBI have shown in Aum.

10. As I have commented elsewhere, the most common line in Japan has been to treat the affair as a specific product of the Japanese situation of the time, and to therefore exclude any possibility of placing the movement and affair in any form of comparative context (see Reader 2000 [note 1]), pp.227–8.

11. The Aum affair is a classic example of how hasty journalism can produce all manner of problems and can have negative effects on subsequent study. In the immediate aftermath of the affair, a number of hastily written books appeared, such as D. W. Brackett, *Holy Terror: Armageddon in Tokyo* (New York: Weatherhill, 1996), and David E. Kaplan and Andrew Marshall, *The Cult at the End of the World: The Incredible Story of Aum* (London: Hutchinson, 1996). These relied heavily on Japanese journalistic sources and reports, as well, it would appear, as plentiful media gossip and speculation – much of which turned out to be over-sensationalized and inaccurate. Brackett's book is especially problematic and worthless as a serious 'source' on Aum, while Kaplan and Marshall's work is also deeply flawed. See Richard Gardner (1996 Review article on the Aum affair *Monumenta Niponica* 51/3 (1996), pp.402–5. Sadly, much of the subsequent material published about Aum in terrorist and conflict studies-related areas appears to have used such sources without much questioning, thereby contributing to the continuing process of misrepresentation of what actually occurred in the Aum affair. See, for example, Gavin Cameron, 'Multi-Track Microproliferation: Lessons from Aum Shinrikyo and Al Qaida', *Studies in Conflict and Terrorism* 22 (1999), pp.277–309. See note 1 for more academically valid references to Aum.

12. Kasumigaseki, the station where the five trains on which Aum had released sarin were scheduled to converge, is the station at the centre of Japan's political and government district, and the location of the offices of the National Police Agency: see Reader 2000 (note 1), pp.26–7 for further comments on the symbolic aspects of the attack.

13. There is no evidence to support the supposition that Aum deliberately used diluted sarin to protect its members who were carrying out the attack. Rather, all the evidence to hand indicates that the sarin was weak because Aum made it in a hurry over the weekend of 18–20 March because it knew it was about to be raided by the police. Asahara wanted to carry out the attack on the morning of 20 March (in order to forestall the impending police raids) and ordered his disciples to go ahead even though they had only succeeded in making a dilute batch of sarin at that point. Aum had previously made, and used, sarin in a much more concentrated form (at Matsumoto in central Japan in June 1994) and earlier had been in possession of quantities of pure sarin, which it subsequently got rid of in January 1995 because it feared it was about to be raided by the police and wanted to eradicate all traces of illegal activities.

14. It should be noted that the term 'shinri', which was part of Aum's name, means 'truth', and that Aum used this term in ways that implied Aum Shinrikyô and the truth were synonymous.

15. Aum's doctrinal stance on this matter was based in its conceptualization of the doctrine of *poa* (a term taken originally from Tibetan) that signified the act of performing spiritual services for the spirits of the recently dead so that they could attain a better rebirth. In Aum this doctrine developed into one in which enlightened beings (such as, Aum claimed, Asahara) could intervene in this life to 'assist' people currently living in a spiritually impoverished state to break away from the karmic bonds that tied them to this existence, and to therefore acquire a better rebirth afterwards. For fuller details see Reader 2000 (note 1) esp. pp.18–19, 145–51, 217–18.

16. See Reader 2000 (note 1), esp. pp.193–5.

17. See, for example Bruce Hoffman, *Inside Terrorism* (London: Indigo, 1999), pp.94–5.

Cohn's study of medieval European millennialism (note 5) provides numerous accounts of the ways in which such movements displayed such attitudes and demonstrates how they were prepared to use mass terror and executions to eradicate those who failed to adhere to their tenets (see, e.g., pp.300–301). In Reader 2000 (note 1), p.195 I draw attention to how Aum's sense of mission was driven by similar impulses to that of the medieval millennialists discussed by Cohn, with each believing they had had a righteous mission to kill with impunity.

18. See e.g. Hoffman 1999 (note 17), p.121.
19. This view is expressed by Neal A. Clinehens, a Major in the USAF, in a graduate research report for the Air University Air Command and Staff College. Clinehens is especially worried about the implied potential this showed for a similar group originating in and conducting such acts within the US. See Neal A. Clinehens, *Aum Shinrikyô and Weapons of Mass Destruction: A Case Study* (April 2000: www.au.af.mil /au/database/research/ay2000/acsc/00-040htm).
20. Although the official concerned did not name any names, it was evident that he expected it to be a group such as Osama Bin Laden's al-Qaida group, which, according to Cameron 1999 (note 11) (who also seeks to analyse Aum in this context) has been involved in the microproliferation of weapons of mass destruction and may have made attempts to develop chemical weapons.
21. These concerns were expressed in numerous comments by American officials in the period after the subway attack, and were, again, made to me by FBI officials I met at Quantico in 1998.
22. Bruce Hoffman, 'America and the New Terrorism: An Exchange', *Survival*, Vol.42, No.2 (2000), pp.156–72.
23. David C. Rapoport, 'Terrorism and the Weapons of the Apocalypse', *National Security Studies Quarterly* (Summer 1999), pp.49–67.
24. Reader 2000 (note 1), p.185.
25. Reader 2000 (note 1), especially pp.203–4.
26. On the general background to the affair and the reasons why the police had not intervened before, see Ian Reader, 'Consensus Shattered: Japanese Paradigm Shifts and Moral Panic in the Post-Aum Era', *Nova Religio* 4/2 (2001), pp.225–34.
27. For a detailed account of the Rajneesh movement and its activities in Oregon see James S. Gordon, *The Golden Guru* (Lexington, VA: Stephen Greene Press, 1987).
28. This brief account is a summary of the themes I have set out in Ian Reader, *A Poisonous Cocktail? Aum Shinrikyô's Path to Violence* (Copenhagen: NIAS Books, 1996), pp.101–7. There I discuss the Rajneesh case and show how it manifested some very close parallels to that of Aum Shinrikyô.
29. Robert J. Kisala and Mark R. Mullins, 'Introduction', in Robert J. Kisala and Mark R. Mullins (eds.), *Religion and Social Crisis in Modern Japan: Understanding Japanese Society Through the Aum Affair* (Basingstoke, UK: Palgrave, 2001), pp.1–17.
30. The ideology of the Japanese state of the late nineteenth and early twentieth centuries centred on the elevation of the Emperor to a quasi-divine status as head and symbol of the state and nation. Deguchi implicitly challenged this by donning ceremonial robes and engaging in ritual practices (e.g. riding a white horse, a mount traditionally seen as the mount of the Emperor alone) that were normally reserved for the Emperor and that were connected with his special status. The police suppression of Ômotokyô was carried out ostensibly because of these implicit threats to Imperial status.
31. Christopher Hughes, 'The Reaction of the Police and Security Authorities to Aum Shinrikyô', in Kisala and Mullins (eds.), (note 34), pp.53–69.
32. Hughes 2001 (note 31), p.67.
33. For a fuller discussion of social and political responses to Aum see Reader 2001 (note 26) and Mark R. Mullins, 'The Political and Legal Fallout of the "Aum Affair"', in Kisala and Mullins (eds.), (note 29), pp.71–86.
34. This is the general thesis of Reader 2000 (note 1), esp. pp.28–31.
35. Besides my book (Reader 2000 (note 1)), I have discussed Aum Shinrikyô in a variety

of contexts, including Reader 1996 (note 28) and Ian Reader, 'Imagined Persecution: Aum Shinrikyô, Millennialism and the Legitimation of Violence', in Catherine Wessinger (ed.), (note 5). For further discussions of Aum see also Shimazono Susumu, *Gendai shûkyô no kanôsei: Oumu Shinrikyô to bôryoku* [The potential of contemporary religion: Aum Shinrikyô and violence] (Tokyo, Iwanami Shoten, 1997) and the collection of essays edited by Robert J. Kisala and Mark R. Mullins, 2001 (note 29). The account that follows is based on all these sources although primarily following Reader 2000 (note 1).

36. See Reader 2000 (note 1), pp.47–52 for a general overview of the themes of the new religions of the period. For a fuller discussion of these 'new' new religions see Shimazonon, 1992 (note 3).

37. See Reader, 'Imagined Persecution'. In Wessinger (ed.), 2000 (note 5) for a discussion of how this imagined persecution took hold in Aum.

38. See Reader 2000 (note 1), pp.143–6 for a full discussion of this critical sequence of events and of how Asahara interpreted these events and developed appropriate doctrines to deal with it. It is important to note that Aum's attempts to imprison would-be defectors were based on the belief that if they left the movement they would fall into hell.

39. Aum's first attempt to use such weapons came in the aftermath of its election defeat in 1990, and was intended as a punishment for the Japanese people who had failed to heed its message. See Reader 2000 (note 1), pp. 158–60.

40. See Reader 2000 (note 1), pp.209–11 where I discuss why the judgement was so important to Asahara, and why he therefore felt it necessary to order his followers to kill the judges before they could deliver a verdict that would have undermined his claims to infallible prophecy.

41. The subway station at the centre of the attack was located directly under the main offices of the National Police Agency, and the attack was planned for the height of the rush hour, when many workers at the agency would have been arriving at the station.

42. See Reader 1996 (note 28), pp.91–3, and Reader 2000 (note 1), pp. 217–19, where I alter that earlier assessment.

43. Reader 2000 (note 1), esp. pp.229–49.

44. John R. Hall, with Philip D. Schuyler and Sylvaine Trinh, *Apocalypse Observed: Religious Movements and Violence in North America, Europe and Japan* (New York: Routledge, 2000), p.177.

45. Hall 2000 (note 44), esp. pp.189–201.

46. Ibid.

47. In Reader 2000 (note 1), pp.189–90, I draw attention to the similarities between Aum's paranoid views and those present in American movements.

48. Mark Juergensmeyer, *Terror in the Mind of God: The Global Rise of Religious Violence* (Berkeley and Los Angeles, CA: University of California Press, 2000), p.146.

49. Quoted in Hall 2000 (note 44), p.200.

50. Reader 2000 (note 1), p.150.

51. 1999 was the date that, in the Japanese translations of the prophecies of Nostradamus (which were highly influential among Japanese new religions), some major turning point would occur: on this issue see Kisala 1997 (note 1).

52. It is possible that some of the early academic assessments of Aum, including my own initial – and erroneous – suggestion that Aum's attack was designed to bring forward its perceived millennial agenda (see Reader 1996 (note 28), pp.92–3), might have helped develop this assumption on the part of the authorities. As I have indicated in Reader 2000 (note 1), p.218, further research into Aum's motivations has made me aware that the subway attack was not carried out with such aims in mind, but was far more of a reactive strike because of the impending police raids.

53. These themes extend throughout Asahara's sermons given in Asahara (unpublished text cited in note 8) but especially from 1990 onwards, and are also discussed in Reader 2000 (note 1), pp.187–95.

54. Reader 2000 (note 1), pp.217–19.
55. See Gordon 1987 (note 27) and Reader 1996 (note 28), pp.101–7.
56. For a comprehensive discussion of this matter see Mary McCormick Maaga, *Hearing the Voices of Jonestown* (Syracuse, NY: Syracuse University Press, 1998).
57. On Heaven's Gate see Hall *et al.* 2000 (note 44), esp. pp.151–82.
58. See Hughes 2001 (note 31), pp.57–67, for a full discussion of the political and security issues relating to Aum and the PSIA in Japan.

Apocalypse – Not in Finland. Millenarianism and Expectations on the Eve of the Year 2000

LEENA MALKKI

Purely from the Finnish perspective, it seems silly that someone should write an article on what was expected to happen in Finland at the turn of the millennium in terms of radical religious or political activities. Yes, there was anxiety in the air at the time, but it was mainly due to the possible implications of the Y2K problem with the computers. It was known that there existed some groups who believed in some kind of conspiracy theory or the imminence of doomsday, but for most they seemed very distant, something that could only happen in America – or in Jerusalem for that matter.

Without claiming that Finland is the only or even foremost place where not much was expected to happen at the turn of the millennium in terms of radical actions, it is, however, a good case study to look at as a balance to the concerns and threats perceived in some other countries. Finland exemplifies a country where millenarianism is quite alien to the mainstream culture and radical groups holding millenarian beliefs are practically non-existent.

In this article, the perceptions related to millenarianism and the turn of the millennium in Finland are approached from two different angles. In the first part, a historical look will be taken at the manifestations and role of millenarian themes in Finland. The main focus will be on the religious movements holding millenarian or apocalyptic beliefs. In addition to this, the state of the radical right and the New World Order (NWO) conspiracy theories is briefly discussed, since the latter has been identified as the second driving force of millennial violence (e.g. in the *Project Megiddo*

Report). To put these phenomena into context, readers will be introduced to key traits of the Finnish religious and political scene.

The second part of the article concentrates on the fears and expectations related to the turn of the millennium in Finland. In this part, the focus will be on the expectations and fears of the public at large and the preparations and assumptions of security officials. Public opinion and discussion is analyzed by examining two opinion polls on the fears and expectations related to the approaching year 2000 and newspaper articles published in the last three months of the year 1999. After that, views and preparations of the security officials are discussed, relying mainly on interviews conducted by the author. Along the way, suggestions are made on why millenarian excitement and anti-state political extremism have not found resonance in Finland.

Millenarianism in the Religious and Political Scene in Finland

In the *Project Megiddo* report it is stated that 'religious motivation and the NWO conspiracy theory are the two driving forces behind the potential for millennial violence'. These are the areas which will be examined below to get a view on the situation in Finland with regard to those ideas commonly linked to millenarianism. Before turning to that, however, a brief introduction to the key traits of the Finnish religious scene is necessary.

Religion in Finland

The religious scene in Finland is characterized by the dominance of the Finnish Evangelical Lutheran Church, even though the percentage of the population belonging to it has been slowly declining for decades. At the end of 1999, 85.3 per cent of the population belonged to the Evangelical Lutheran Church, while only 2.1 per cent were members of other registered communities, and 12.6 per cent of the population remained outside registered communities. However, the biggest group among these non-registered communities is the Pentecostal congregations, which have roughly 50,000 members which represent approximately one per cent of the population, making it almost equal in size with the second largest registered community, the Orthodox Church, which has about 55,000 members.[1]

The dominance of the Evangelical Lutheran Church can be understood in the light of its role in the past. In the sixteenth century, the

Lutheran church was declared the state church of Sweden and thus also of Finland, which was at that time part of Sweden. When Finland became an autonomous Grand Duchy of Russia in 1809, the old Swedish laws were retained and thus the Evangelical Lutheran Church maintained its position as the state church. By allowing this, the tsar of Russia hoped to win the loyalty of his new subjects (especially the aristocracy and the clergy). The Lutheran priests were seen as key figures in maintaining order and building loyalty towards the new rulers.

In 1889, the Non-Conformity Act was passed, which meant that other Protestant churches were given an official position. Until that date, everyone had to belong to either the Lutheran or the Orthodox Church. After Finland got its independence in 1917, the state assumed a neutral attitude toward religion. The Constitution of the new republic passed in 1919 and the Law on Freedom of Religion which came into force in 1923, granted the right to found and belong to religious denominations or to remain outside of any religious affiliation. However, freedom of religion did not lead instantly to any massive withdrawal from the Church.

Even though the Evangelical Lutheran Church no longer has the position it used to – especially after the numerous changes that took place in the church–state relationship during the 1990s – it is still not just 'any other church'. To give a few examples, the opening and closing ceremonies of the Parliament still include Evangelical Lutheran church services, religion remains part of the curriculum in the public schools for the members of the church and the state recognizes the marriage solemnized by the church.

However, this is just one side of the story. According to a survey conducted by the Research Institute of the Evangelical Lutheran Church of Finland in 1999,[2] only 8 per cent of the population attend church services at least once a month and some 47 per cent of those interviewed said that they believe in God as taught by Christianity.[3] Beside the strong institutional position of the Evangelical Lutheran Church, two other tendencies must be noted: a strong tradition of secularization and an increasing individualization of religiosity. For many Finns, being a Christian or Lutheran is more a cultural than religious identity, and means primarily that they have been baptized and belong to the Evangelical Lutheran Church.[4] Moreover, the Evangelical Lutheran Church cannot be considered very coherent since it includes various religious streams and movements. Partly as a legacy of nationalist ideas and a response to criticism in the nineteenth century, the church prefers to be seen as a 'folk church'[5] open to every Finn, and has a tolerant and open-minded attitude towards various kinds of views. This can be seen clearly in what has happened with revivalist movements that appeared in the eighteenth and nineteenth centuries (the most crucial of them being Pietism, Laestadianism, Evangelicalism and Supplicationism). While they originally arose as a protest against the official church and secularization, most of them stayed within the church and nowadays, in the Church's view, form an integral and enriching part of parish life.[6]

In the shadow of the Evangelical Lutheran Church there is an increasing number of other religious communities in Finland, ranging from Jehovah's Witnesses, Theosophy and the Salvation Army, which found their way to Finland around the turn of the twentieth century, to more recent phenomena such as Scientology, Wicca, Devil Worship and various kinds of New Age movements. These other religious movements are typically marginal, with few followers. They cannot be considered oppositional in any meaningful sense of the word since they are not directly opposed to the Evangelical Lutheran Church or the state. Instead, it is more apt to describe themselves as alternative religious movements.[7]

Millenarian Religiosity

Millenarian religiosity has always been a relatively marginal phenomenon in Finland. Millenarian thoughts are not among the core elements of Finnish religiosity and culture since they are quite alien to the mainstream Evangelical Lutheranism. This is not to say that we are dealing with a phenomenon which is totally unfamiliar to Finnish culture. With the concise history of Finnish millenarianism and apocalypticism still waiting to be written, I will limit myself to a few examples of Finnish religious movements colored with the belief in the imminence of the end times.[8]

Perhaps the most dramatic case of millenarianism in the area of Finland was that of the Old Believers (also called Raskolniks) in the late seventeenth century. The Old Believers were in fact mainly concentrated in Russia, but they had also spread to the Swedish part of Karelia. They came into conflict with the authorities because they refused to accept the reforms to liturgical texts ordered by the patriarch of Moscow (Nikon). When pursued by the military, thousands of Old Believers committed suicide by locking themselves up in their hiding places in the forest and setting themselves on fire.[9]

Among the revivalist movements that arose in the eighteenth and nineteenth centuries under, e.g., Pietist influences, one can find some apocalyptic and millenarian traits. These movements were mostly quite moderate, but there were also a few more radical groups. As far as the early twentieth century is concerned, the 1920s and 1930s witnessed the high period of Finnish millenarianism. Following the bloody and traumatic civil war in 1918 and the economic hardships of the time, many millenarian movements appeared in Finland and in the Finnish-speaking areas in Sweden. They were characteristically small and local. The Secret Police (established in 1919) followed up religious activities that might endanger the social peace, especially looking at religious persons and movements holding communist or anti-state opinions.[10] Even though most of the movements did not pose any significant danger to internal security, there were some groups which caused problems to authorities. The most notable movements of that time were those formed around Ida Maria Åkerblom, Toivo Korpela, Adam Härkönen and Alma Maria Kartano.

The Åkerblom movement came into existence when a young woman named Ida Maria Åkerblom assumed a role of a preacher and prophet in 1917.[11] Her personality, together with the abovementioned external conditions, attracted a lot of people to the meetings in western Finland, and in the early years, in southern Finland. Åkerblom was believed to communicate direct revelations from God; through her activities God was said to be collecting a group to work on His behalf against the forces of evil. In fulfilling Åkerblom's mission it was thought to be justified to use any means necessary. The main task of the group's members was to win other people for God before the return of Jesus, which they believed was likely to happen soon. Despite many confrontations with the Church, the movement remained loyal to it, for example never questioning the importance of the sacraments.

The heartland of the movement was the area around Kokkola and Teerijärvi in western Finland, where it gained ground in the early 1920s in particular. Rumours about suspicious activities by the movement spread and caused irritation and concern among the local clergy and non-religious people. This resulted in a growing determination to remove the movement from the area. Efforts to do this led to riots and a series of trials where the leaders of the Åkerblom movement were charged first with various incidents of disturbance and later with using false witnesses to rehabilitate the leaders. Åkerblom and her followers were defeated in the trials which, combined with constant persecution and economic difficulties, led the whole group of about 200 people to sell all their belongings and leave for an obscure destination (hinted to be Palestine). The journey stopped, however, at Helsinki where the movement was caught up in a further litigation. When it became clear that even more court cases awaited them in Kokkola, the leaders saw it necessary to eliminate the local governor. The unsuccessful murder attempt led to yet new trials where the leaders were sentenced to long periods of imprisonment in 1927. This did not, contrary to what was expected, lead to the instant dissolution of the movement. In 1932, just before Åkerblom was released from prison, another sleeping preacher appeared and the movement split into two groups. After being released, Åkerblom never managed to assume her role as preacher again. However, the dissolution of her group happened very slowly. This has been explained in part by strict internal control and the fear of new disclosures.

Another revival movement that gave concern for the authorities was the Korpela movement in the Finnish-speaking areas of Sweden. The movement was initially formed around Toivo Korpela, a self-proclaimed Laestadian preacher from central Finland. After being rejected by his own community he travelled to northern Finland to preach in the late 1920s. He found supporters mostly in the Tornio River valley. When Korpela stopped making preaching journeys in the mid-1930s, the movement survived and its content was shaped by its other leading figures. They preached that the new Finnish Old Testament translation brought to use in 1934 was 'the abomination that maketh desolation' predicted in the book of Daniel. It was also told that the last 1,335 days of the world had begun and that there would be an Ark that would take 666 true believers to Palestine, which would appear a year after the two leading figures who had claimed to be the prophets had been taken into heaven. The dogma kept on changing and it was later proclaimed that the Ark would not be an actual vessel, but referred to the spirit of Christ that had been granted to the Korpelians. One of the leading figures began to see himself as the representative of Christ, and thus able to forgive people their sins. He exonerated the Korpelians from sins such as drinking and lewd sexuality. The movement saw its decline in the late 1930s with the Korpela trials, during which 60 Korpelians were given prison sentences on account of immoral behaviour. The leading figures ended up in a mental hospital or prison.[12]

Two other famous movements at that time formed around Adam Härkönen and Alma Maria Kartano. Härkönen was a trance preacher in the years 1919–29. Later, during the Interim Peace between the Winter War of 1939–40 and the Continuation War (1941–44), he preached in March 1941 that there would shortly be a new war and that 9,000 of the soldiers who died during the Winter War were in heaven, while the rest of them were in hell. He also saw several visions of the end times. As result of his activities, a movement carrying his name (in Finnish *härkösläisyys*) emerged in Kainuu in northern Finland. Härkönen attracted thousands of followers. However, the movement began to fade in the late 1940s when Härkönen was revealed to be a false prophet. Nowadays the movement has a couple of hundred members around Kainuu.[13]

Alma Maria Kartano was one of the trance preachers initiated by Härkönen, but they argued and she went her own way. She began to preach actively in the mid-1920s. The central theme of her teachings was the imminence of the end times and the importance of keeping a distance from the 'carefree' world. At its high point, the movement (*kartanolaisuus*) had about 100 members, but many more people gathered at the meetings, which were held in different parts of Finland. The movement attracted a fair amount of attention – curiosity because of its child preachers and, in the 1930s and 1950s, a lot of negative publicity due to court cases over the rough treatment of these child preachers. Nowadays there are few people following the teachings of Kartano and they are integrated into local congregations.[14]

If millenarianism has always been a marginal phenomenon in Finland, after the Second World War it almost ceased to exist. The movements that appeared in the decades prior to the war have lost almost all of their vigour. According to one of the leading scholars of religiosity in Finland, Harri Heino, people are now, with the individualization of religion, concerned mainly about their personal ends in the world, for example, their own or their neighbour's death.[15]

There are still some local groups which hold apocalyptic beliefs, but they are tiny and attract little attention. One of them is a small movement known by the names *Lasarus-veljet* (the Lazarus Brothers) and *Kristus-kirkko* (Christ Church). The movement has its origins in the spiritual revival among the Finns in Israel in 1972. A couple of years later, after returning home, a small group of them began to publish magazines and books, and established their own unregistered church.

There are some 100 members, and the core group lives in a community in Säkylä in south-western Finland. However, their publications reach a considerably larger audience. As for their dogma, they emphasize the importance of conversion and sanctification, and consider the Lutheran and other traditional churches to be secularized and heretical. They believe that the second coming of Christ and the thousand-year kingdom are near and fear that with the End of Days approaching, a bigger and more solid 'world church' will emerge.[16] This group seems to concentrate mostly on preaching and shows no signs of radical action.

Another direction where one might look for millenarian traits in present-day Finland is the Satanist scene. The reason for this is that there was one suicide attempt and one successful suicide around the turn of the millennium by persons known to hold Satanist beliefs. However, it remains unclear if they were related to any kind of millenarian beliefs at all.[17]

Satanists and devil worshippers attracted much attention in Finland during the late 1990s, mostly due to a brutal murder in southern Finland in 1998 and several disturbances of graves. The Satanist scene is quite heterogeneous, ranging from adolescent Satanism to Laveyan Satanists and devil worshippers.[18]

There is no study exploring millenarianism among Finnish Satanists in detail. However, some remarks can be made based on the interviews that Merja Hermonen conducted with the Satanists in Finland during the 1990s. In her interviews it came out that the theme of the end times is perceived as interesting by many Satanists, especially in iconographical terms. However, millenarian thoughts do not characterize the Satanist scene as a whole. Instead, to the extent that millenarian beliefs can be found among the Satanists, it is mostly in the thoughts of single individuals, especially among the Black Metal Satanists and some criminal Satanists who were imprisoned at the time of the interview. Some of those holding millenarian beliefs saw the year 2000 as somehow special in this context, while others did not link their beliefs related to the end times with this particular date. When it comes to Satanists who do not hold any explicit millenarian thoughts, the turn of the millennium did provoke some nervousness because it was felt that one can never be sure what could happen. All in all, the role of millenarian thoughts cannot be considered central to the Finnish Satanist scene.[19]

Around the turn of the millennium, there were few signs of any kind of millenarian excitement in any religious group in the country let alone any group that would fit to the characterization of a cult prone to violence suggested in the *Project Megiddo* report.[20] In this light, the possibility of radical action committed by religious believers at the turn of the millennium was minimal at best.

In the following, the state of the other idea mentioned as a driving force behind the potential for radical millenarian action in *Project Megiddo* – the New World Order conspiracy theory – will be considered.

Millenarianism in Politics

In a newspaper article dealing with the preparations for the possible acts by the doomsday cults in the US and Israel, it was stated that 'In the US it is also possible that people believe that the UN will seize power at the turn of the millennium and take away the civil rights of Americans.'[21] Between the lines one can read that the author of the article considered these kinds of conspiracy theories to be alien to Finnish culture – and the implication is quite correct. While White Power ideology, together with the idea of the Zionist Occupation Government (ZOG), has found its way to Finland,[22] conspiracy theories do not play a notable role in the ideology and action of any group.

There are clearly numerous differences between American and Finnish society and thus to explain adequately why conspiracy theories like the New World Order have found ground in the US but not in Finland is beyond the scope of this article. Instead, the discussion will be limited to bringing to the fore some features of nationalism, the radical right and attitudes towards the state in Finland which may explain in part why fierce opposition towards the power of the state and intermixing religious and political themes are quite foreign to Finnish political culture.

In the 1990s, the most important items on the agenda of the radical right, radical nationalist and racist organizations were relations with Russia, immigrants and membership of the European Union. Many of these organizations hold a critical attitude towards the old relationship with the Soviet Union. The collapse of the Soviet Union aroused many traditional anti-Russian feelings and themes, one of them being the Karelian question, that is, demands for returning the areas in Karelia that were ceded to the Soviet Union in the Peace of Moscow after the Second World War. The question of immigration rose to prominence especially following the arrival of Somali refugees in the early 1990s which, together with increasing immigration from other countries, multiplied the number of foreigners living in Finland. To put this into the context, it must be added that the foreign citizens still represent less than two per cent of the Finnish population. Opposition to membership of the European Union has also been quite common in nationalist circles.[23] Fear of sacrificing Finland's sovereignty, as well as Finnish national identity and culture, is clearly present in the nationalist and rightist discussion, especially in the anti-EU arguments.

The new radical right is an almost negligible phenomenon in Finland. This is somewhat surprising given that the situation in Finland in the 1990s – deep recession combined with an increasing number of foreigners moving to the country – had many characteristics commonly identified as factors helping the radical right movements to gain ground.

A look at the country's history makes the minuscule scale of the new radical right both more understandable and more surprising. The extreme right has not always been a marginal phenomenon. Fascist ideology had a relatively strong foothold in the 1920s and 1930s.[24] In theory, this tradition could give a good and solid ground for new radical right movements. However, things have not turned out that way in Finland. The story of fascist organizations came to an end after the Second World War, when they were forbidden following the peace treaties of Moscow and Paris. This ban was in force until 1991. In the postwar era, the political right has had a very negative connotation. Being labelled right-wing was not desired by any political organization because it implied opposition to President Urho Kekkonen, good relations with the Soviet Union, and the basic interests of the Finnish state. Even with Kekkonen and the Soviet Union gone, the negative attitude towards the extreme right is still largely in place. On the other hand, the 'supply side' of the radical right ideologists has also so far been quite negligible, and no leader comparable to such personalities as Le Pen or Haider has appeared in Finland.[25]

All in all, the radical right scene in Finland is very fragmented and consists mostly of very small local groups.[26] There is no extreme right-wing party that has gained any success worth mentioning, be it in electoral support, number of members or even publicity, even though the Finnish multi-party system provides a proportional vote and strongly personalized electoral campaigns, which make it relatively easy for newcomers to gain parliamentary seats. In fact, some attempts to form a party have stalled due to the difficulty of getting the required 5,000 signatures for party registration.[27] The extra-parliamentary activities of the radical right have been very small-scale, too. The organizations and individuals on the scene have not gained much following or public attention.[28] Some of them have managed to build relations with foreign rightist organizations, which has resulted in an increasing amount of foreign influence.[29]

The ideas and fears of the nationalist and radical right groups have not been linked to any particular idea of conspiracy, nor do they contain any references to apocalyptic beliefs. There is no notable intermingling of millenarian beliefs and political issues, which is hardly surprising given the weak tradition of millenarianism in the country.

The radical right in Finland has not, however, been completely devoid of religious overtones. Mythical belief system colours one group in particular: the Patriotic Right (*Isänmaallinen Oikeisto*, IO) with Väinö Kuisma as its central figure. He first founded the Aryan German Brotherhood (*Arjalainen Germaaniveljeskunta*, AGV) which was inspired by German neo-Nazism. Later Nazi symbols were abandoned and replaced by the symbols of ancient Finnish mythology, and the name was changed to the Patriotic Right. The mythology of the Finnish national epic *Kalevala* plays a central role in Kuisma's ideology. In the rhetoric of the Patriotic Right, history is a great narrative, its sense being the struggle over the perseverance of Finnishness and finding the hidden secret essence of the Finnish people. This is combined with the struggle for the preservation of the white race. The movement is really tiny, having just 50 members, and is unknown to most Finns. It claims to have parliamentary political goals and wants to distance itself from Nazism and the violent and anarchistic skinhead groups.[30]

The activities of the radical right groupings have been relatively harmless. As a whole, the personalities and groups of the new radical right have not been particularly extreme in their actions when compared to other countries, even though they have crossed the limits of legality from time to time. The typical act has, so far, comprised an insult, harassment or campaign involving threatening letters. The targets have been politicians, officials, the media and 'political' enemies.[31] There have also been incidents in which strained relations between immigrants and Finns have produced mostly spontaneous and accidental outbursts of intercommunal violence. Compared to other countries, the level of racist violence in Finland is still low, even though it seems to have increased in recent years.[32]

Besides the fact that radical right ideology and millenarian beliefs are largely rejected by the mainstream, there is also something about Finnish attitudes towards the state that makes fierce opposition against state power and the formation of secular millenarianism, such as that linked to the NWO conspiracy theories, quite unlikely.

As a reason for the relatively positive attitude towards the state, one might point to the fact that Finland is quite a new state. The independence gained in 1917 liberated Finland from the power of Russia and attempts at Russification. Seen in the light of history, the state is thus more likely to be perceived as a guarantor of freedom than as a threat to it. Moreover, as legislation conferring freedom of speech and religion is in place, there are few grounds for alternative political and religious movements to accuse the state of discrimination. Seen from this perspective, the idea that the state would function as an arm of evil forces or as part of some kind of conspiracy seems rather outlandish.

The second thing that might be mentioned in this context is that, to borrow the words of Kyösti Pekonen, the welfare state has so far functioned well enough to 'buy' political tranquillity.[33] Still, even with the privatization of state-owned companies, the role of the state is strong in every sector of society and the welfare state model enjoys wide support among the citizens. Despite the financial problems during the recession of the early 1990s that forced the state into cutbacks in subsidies, the welfare state has so far functioned relatively well and managed to prevent any large-scale displacement. This might also be one of the main reasons for the weakness of millenarian religiosity today.

Beside the fact that the legitimacy of the state is largely unquestioned, there are other factors that would make it difficult and unproductive to form 'militia-type' organizations opposing the state. Even though Finland is a sparsely populated country, the administrative bureaucracy is extensive and systematized so that it is almost impossible to turn one's back completely on society. Conscription creates a further bond between the male population (and female volunteers) and the state.

This is not to say that critics of the political system and the welfare state are non-existent. In fact, according to surveys, attitudes towards party politics are quite negative. Moreover, Finns are relatively uninterested in politics and do not feel that any party is speaking for them. One sign of the diminishing interest in party politics is the voting turnout, which declined from 84 per cent in 1966 to 68 per cent in 1999.

The level is still high when compared to many other countries, but in the context of Finland the decline is truly significant. Some scholars have also talked about growing alienation from party politics, especially among the youth and in the new working-class urban areas. However, this anti-party sentiment has so far manifested as social apathy and apolitical indifference.[34]

One factor that can be viewed both as the reason for and consequence of the relatively modest forms of political protest activity is the attitude towards the police. Respect towards the police in Finland is high. According to the Security Barometer of the Police in 1999, 91 per cent of Finns had an above-average trust in the police. In another study, 55 per cent of the respondents thought that the police had too little power and only four per cent of the interviewed thought that they had too much power. The citizens see the police as impartial, understanding, realistic and professional, and believe they succeed well in the tasks assigned to them.[35] The police have so far not needed to use harsh measures to maintain public order and security, which has in turn helped prevent the polarization of attitudes towards state power.

Following from all of these factors, there are hardly any groups in Finland that openly hold millenarian beliefs. One can quite safely assume that the turn of the millennium did not have any significant religious or political meaning for large majority of Finns. This is not surprising, given that extreme millenarian beliefs are fairly alien to Evangelical Lutheranism, which is one of the key elements of the Finnish culture.

Waiting for the Millennium Party and Bugs – Expecting the Year 2000 in Finland

Despite the weak tradition of millenarianism, the approaching turn of the millennium provoked a fair amount of discussion, anxiety and fears in Finland, just as it did in many other countries. These fears will be approached using three different sources. First, the results of public opinion polls related to the year 2000 will be discussed. After that, the discussion in the newspapers in the last months of 1999 will be analysed and finally, the security officials' views and preparations will be discussed.

The Opinion Polls

The fears and expectations related to the approaching year 2000 were the topic of two (multiple choice) opinion polls conducted by Suomen

Gallup Oy for the Research Institute of the Evangelical Lutheran Church
of Finland. The first opinion poll called 'Vuosi 2000' (Year 2000) was
conducted in May 1997 and the second one, 'Pelot ja uhkakuvat' (Fears
and threat scenarios) in September 1999.[36]

The results of the surveys suggest that on average the Finns were not
very concerned about the turn of the millennium. Moreover, their
anxiety seemed to decline over time. In the 1997 survey, 20 per cent of
those interviewed said that they were somewhat or very nervous, while
in 1999 only 15 per cent gave that answer. Most interviewees did not
believe that fear and mass hysteria would spread widely at the turn of
the millennium. Only some 12 per cent agreed somewhat or totally that
fear and mass hysteria were possible. In a news magazine article, it was
suggested that the peak of millennium excitement was probably in the
winter 1998–99, and thus fell between these two surveys.[37]

It also emerged from the surveys that most Finns did not give any
specific religious meaning to the turn of the millennium, at least in terms
of the return of Jesus or religious revivalist movements. In 1997 for
example, only five per cent and in 1999 only three per cent agreed
somewhat or totally with the argument that Jesus would return to the
earth around the year 2000. About one-tenth (12 per cent in 1997 and
seven per cent in 1999) of those interviewed agreed with the suggestion
that a new revivalist movement would spread around the world at the
turn of the millennium. However, a considerably larger proportion
thought it was possible that religious extremists groups would spread
prophecies of the end times and excite people around the world. This
was asked in the 1999 survey, and 68 per cent of the interviewed found
it at least possible. About the same proportion (69 per cent) found it
possible or probable that there would be great catastrophes around the
world caused by the collapse of information technology systems.

When compared to the other threat scenarios in the surveys, these two
ranked seventh and eighth. The five threat scenarios that were found
possible or even probable by most of the interviewed were the same in
both years. These were a flood of refugees caused by hunger, the collapse
of the Russian economy followed by a flood of refugees to Western
Europe, the use of drugs slipping totally out of the authorities' hands, a
major series of floods and earthquakes, and the death of tens of millions
of persons from diseases similar to AIDS. The proportion of the
respondents who found these threat scenarios possible or even probable
to materialize at the turn of the millennium varied from 70 to 85 per cent.

As can be seen from these surveys, the top fears and threat scenarios were of a very general nature. As it is noted by the Research Institute of the Evangelical Lutheran Church of Finland, these threats and fears would probably have been among the top ones even if the turn of the millennium was not in sight.[38] The respondents were asked to evaluate the statements specifically in the light of the turn of the millennium. How strictly they actually did that can be questioned. Considering that only some 15 to 20 per cent of the respondents said they felt at least somewhat nervous about the turn of the millennium, even though the majority of them found various threat scenarios possible or probable, it seems that the date was not a very significant reason behind the fears.

Since the opinion polls consist of multiple-choice questions, it is possible that there were some fears and threat scenarios that the surveys did not highlight. To obtain more insight on the public discussion and atmosphere, a look will be taken at newspaper articles published in late 1999.

Discussion in the Newspapers

Reading through the main newspaper, two tabloid papers and two weekly papers published between October and December 1999,[39] one notices that the word 'millennium' comes up fairly often. The newspapers featured 117 articles on issues directly related to the turn of the millennium. The most popular topic is how to celebrate the New Year's Eve, as 50 articles deal mainly with this theme. The majority of the articles (77) was published in December and almost half of those (37) in the last week of that month, whereas in October there were only 12 articles on the topic.

Some kind of threat related to the turn of the millennium is discussed in 42 articles. The most common threat scenarios brought out in the articles are Y2K problems with computers and their possible consequences in general and specifically in Finland, the threat posed by millenarian or other kinds of extremists to the US (or that the US authorities were monitoring such groups and individuals), any kind of Y2K problems in Russia, and disturbances in Jerusalem or elsewhere in the Middle East.

The threat taken most seriously was what would happen if Russia had not resolved its Y2K problems properly. Whereas such threats as problems with the supply of energy and water are mentioned, the most critical issue is considered to be what might happen in Russian nuclear power plants.[40] That this threat was taken fairly seriously by the public is shown by the fact that, as the newspapers report, the demand for iodine tablets increased considerably towards the end of the year 1999.[41]

The possibility of action by extremists, and the authorities' actions to prevent them, were discussed in 15 articles. The majority of them (11) were published in December and almost half of the total (7) in the last week of the month. The individual countries that got most attention in this context were the USA and Israel. When discussing the threats faced by the USA, the main focus was usually on the efforts of the authorities to prevent acts by the extremists. In this context, the security measures in Time Square, the arrest of Ahmed Ressam and the search for Abdelmajed Dahoumane, and the cancellation of New Year's celebrations in Seattle, were dealt with. When it came to Israel, attention was drawn to the existence and deportation of groups which were alleged to have planned to act around the turn of the millennium and the measures taken by the authorities to ensure that nothing would happen. Another common theme was the Jerusalem syndrome, a temporary mental disorder (most typical among the pilgrims) under which the person believes himself to be a biblical character.

What is notable is that in these articles dealing with possible disturbance caused by extremists, Finland is mentioned no more than once, and then only to announce that this kind of threat does not exist in Finland. It was reported that, according to the research work by the EU police work group, Europol, and Interpol, that there was no threat of terrorism in Finland (or in many other European countries).[42] No explanation was provided for this, probably because when it comes to Finland, the finding was hardly surprising in any way. All of the other 15 articles that dealt with threats to Finland were related to the Y2K problem. A few critical voices notwithstanding, in almost all of these articles it was confirmed that the preparations had been sufficient and everything should go on without any major problems. This is especially true about the articles describing how the state authorities and different companies had prepared for the year 2000 which were published on the last days of 1999.[43] The citizens were assured that, thanks to good planning and preparation plus extra staff in place on New Year's Eve, everything would go smoothly. When it comes to people's behaviour, the authorities and journalists seem to have been worried primarily about how people would make it to home in one piece after hard celebrations without getting stuck in traffic or lost in the cold winter night.

Security Officials' Point of View and Preparations

What about the security officials? Did they also regard the approaching turn of the millennium as calmly as everyone else? From the perspective of this article the answer is yes and no – officials prepared carefully for New Year's Eve, but for completely different reasons than the threat of radical actions.

The preparations for the turn of the millennium were extensive. As in many other countries, the state and private companies had spent considerable amounts of money to ensure that their systems were Y2K compatible. To give some examples, the rescue services had more people at work on New Year's Eve than ever before, except during major disasters or accidents. Most companies had staff standing by to make sure that there were no problems. Helsinki Energy, for example, had five times more employees at work than normal. The supply of water was ensured by filling water towers to maximum.[44]

Maintaining public order and internal security is the responsibility of the police in Finland. The organization is tripartite, consisting of organs at national, provincial and local level. The police organization is led by the Police Department of the Ministry of the Interior. The Provincial Police Command reports directly to the Supreme Police Command. These organs are responsible for developing and leading the work of the police on their own area of operations. Securing public order and security is the responsibility of the local district police. For this task it receives guidelines from the Supreme and Provincial Police Command, but normally fulfils the task fairly independently at the operational level. In addition to these, there are some national units directly under the Supreme Police Command. These are the National Bureau of Investigation, the Security Police, the National Traffic Police, the Police Technical Centre, the Police School and the Police College of Finland. The Helsinki District Police also report directly to the Supreme Police Command.[45] The police organization ultimately reports to the Minister of the Interior.

From the perspective of internal security and public order, the key organizations in the preparations for the turn of the millennium were the Security Police, the Supreme and Provincial Police Command and the District Police.[46]

As part of its task to monitor and prevent actions that might pose a risk to internal security and international relations, during the years 1998–99 the Security Police investigated the possibility of action that would threaten public security around the turn of the millennium. The investigation focused on the movements that, according to the international experience, might potentially pose a threat. There was no specific incident, report or piece of information that gave an impulse to this investigation. Instead, these kinds of movements are constantly being monitored at some level. The investigation on the risks related to the turn of the millennium was not a major project in the Security Police; the issue was not even mentioned in their annual report for 1999. Instead, the attention of the Security Police was directed mainly to the tasks related to the first EU Chairmanship by Finland (1 July–31 December 1999).

The results of the investigation confirmed the presumption that there were no significant threats caused by the behaviour of some groups or individuals holding beliefs related to the turn of the millennium. The Security Police did not identify any individual or group in Finland as posing a possible threat. When it comes to acts committed by international or foreign groups in Finland, they were, and still are, in general considered to be improbable, and as to the turn of the millennium, this possibility was not specifically discussed within the Security Police. The Security Police were somewhat concerned about the possibility that someone might take advantage of the special occasion and issue a threat directed at information technology systems. However, there were no signs that someone was planning this kind of act. At a more general level, the Security Police had devoted quite a lot of effort to dealing with threats related to the vulnerability of the information system. The Security Police had been concerned with issues like the organized sabotage, destruction, theft or spoiling of information systems. As many of the critical key systems maintained by private companies, the Security Police felt it necessary to expand its guidance and instruction activities in this sphere by, for example, establishing contacts with high-tech companies in the country.[47]

The low probability of radical action around the turn of the millennium was confirmed by the report of the EU police work group discussed in *Helsingin Sanomat* on 24 December 1999. In addition to this, according to Deputy National Police Commissioner Jorma Toivanen, who was interviewed in the same article, Europol and Interpol had no contact with Finland to warn about any specific threat scenarios.[48]

Following from this, the possibility of religiously or politically motivated unrest at the turn of the millennium was not the focal point of the preparations in the police organization. Based on the risk analyses gathered by the Police Department of the Ministry of the Interior, the preparations were directed at risks related to the possible consequences either of the Y2K problem or of the unusual scale of celebrations. To give an example, the Police Department was in contact with the banks to ensure that should there be any problems with the electricity, the security of the banks would be guaranteed. It was also made sure that the police and rescue organizations could operate even if Y2K-related problems occurred.

The Police Department estimated that it should be possible to ensure public order and security without making any exceptional arrangements. Work shifts were planned to ensure that there would be sufficient police officers on duty on New Year's Eve. Should the police forces have needed assistance, there was a mechanism under law to obtain extra manpower and equipment from the defence forces. However, this possibility was not part of the plan – the Police Department had merely checked with the defence forces that everything was working as usual should something come up.

On the local level, the main concern seemed to be the scale of celebrations. For example, in Helsinki it was expected that tens of thousands of people would gather in the city centre to see the fireworks. Planning and preparing for the New Year's Eve in the Southern Police District of Helsinki – comprising the city centre where most of the crucial governmental buildings are located and where most celebrations and demonstrations usually take place – started in July 1999. The police did not expect this particular New Year's Eve to differ from the other ones in quality, only in the scale of celebration. Thus the plan was based on the normal New Year's Eve scheme, but everything was multiplied by three or four. The arrangements were of equal size to those taken around a big state visit, but on the other hand, the readiness of the police was considerably lower than during the Helsinki EU Summit in December 1999.

In practice this meant that there were around 100 policemen around the city centre on the New Year's Eve. Besides the district's own police forces, extra help was obtained from the other police districts of

Helsinki. This is normal practice during special events. There were also some organizations and associations taking part in the arrangements (again as usual on New Year's Eve) and some 60 or 70 stewards assisting during the celebration.

The turn of the millennium went smoothly in Finland. There were almost no Y2K problems at all, which in fact exceeded the expectations of the Ministry of the Interior which had assumed that there would have been at least some difficulties. Moreover, according to the police reports, the celebrations went peacefully and no severe disturbances of public order took place. In the Helsinki city centre about 100,000 persons gathered to see the fireworks. Despite this incredible number of people, everything went almost as on any other New Year's Eve except for the traffic jams.[49]

With regard to actions motivated by millenarian beliefs, there is not much to say. The two suicide cases of Satanists have already been mentioned. It is possible that there were people waiting for doomsday, but none of them did anything that would have made the news or given anyone a reason to file a police report. The Chief Inspector who led the police operation in the Helsinki city centre recalled that he got a couple of announcements about individuals holding some kind of banners and talking about the end of the world. These persons were considered harmless and were left alone, and no written report of these incidents was made.[50]

There are many reasons why everything went so well at the turn of the millennium. In the Y2K matters, the police credit companies and organizations for solving the problems before the year's end. As for the outdoor celebrations, they are actually always relatively modest on New Year's Eve. In addition to this, judging from the newspapers, it seems that by the autumn of 1999 many people were already fed up with the millennium excitement. Many tickets to millennium parties went unsold as many people decided to celebrate the occasion with their family at home.[51] The night of the millennium, anticipated with fear and excitement, turned out to be like any other New Year's Eve. In the end, the turn of the millennium went even more smoothly than expected and there were few signs of anyone waiting for the Apocalypse in Finland.

NOTES

I would like to thank Prof. Jeffrey Kaplan, Prof. Kyösti Pekonen, Dr Tomas Ries and various other scholars and security officials mentioned later in the notes for their assistance and insight.

1. Statistics on the membership of registered communities are provided by Statistics Finland (www.stat.fi/tk/tp/tasku/taskue_vaesto.html). Information on the membership of Pentecostal communities is from Harri Heino, 'Religion and Churches in Finland' (virtual.finland.fi/finfo/english/uskoeng.html). Heino's article is one of the best introductions in English to the Finnish religious scene.
2. The survey is called Gallup Ecclesiastica and it is conducted every fourth year. The results are presented e.g. in Kari Salonen, Kimmo Kääriäinen and Kati Niemelä, *The Church at the Turn of the Millennium. The Evangelical Lutheran Church of Finland from 1996 to 1999* (The Research Institute of the Evangelical Lutheran Church of Finland 2001), pp.17–20. The publication is available on the Internet at www.evl.fi/ kkh/ktk/publication96-99/publ51.pdf.
3. Interestingly enough, the percentage of the interviewees who said that they believe in God as taught by Christianity has risen since 1991 when only 33 per cent gave that answer. One explanation give for this is that the importance of shared communal values increased because of the uncertainty induced by the economic recession (Salonen *et al.* (note 2), pp.17–18).
4. See for example Jouko Sihvo, 'Suomalaisten uskonnollisuus [Finnish religiosity]', in Pertti Suhonen (ed.), *Yleinen mielipide 1997* (Helsinki: Kustannusosakeyhtiö Tammi, 1997), pp.33–53.
5. The concept of the 'folk church' has different meanings. It can be understood to refer to a church which, because a significant majority of people belonging to it, has a special relationship with the state. The folk church can also be seen as an institution providing services, and as such, an analogous institution to the state and the municipalities. In contrast to this functional view referring to the prevailing situation, the folk church has been used to refer to an ideal or theological programme. From this perspective, the folk church can be understood as a missionary concept, for example. For more see Hannu T. Kamppuri, 'The "Folk Church" as an Ecclesiological Concept', in Pirjo Työrinoja (ed.), *The Evangelical Lutheran Church in Finnish Society. Documents of the Evangelical Lutheran Church of Finland* 6 (Helsinki: Church Council for Foreign Affairs, 1994), pp.20–25. While both views have been present in the Finnish discussion, it is the functional view referring to the prevailing situation that seems to be dominant.
6. Salonen *et al.* (note 2), pp.71–4, Heino, 'Religion and Churches in Finland' (note 1).
7. The argument about the alternative rather than oppositional nature of the religious movements was clearly brought up in the conference 'Oppositional Religions in Finland', which took place in Helsinki in 1999. For the papers presented in the conference see Jeffrey Kaplan (ed.), *Beyond the Mainstream: The Emergence of Religious Pluralism in Finland, Estonia, and Russia.* Studia Historica 63 (Helsinki: SKS, 2000).
8. I am greatly indebted to Ilpo Pursiainen for his insights on this topic.
9. Kimmo Katajala, 'Savuna taivasten valtakuntaan. Vanhauskoisten polttoitsemurhat Ruotsin-Karjalassa 1600-luvun lopulla [In smoke to the kingdom of heaven. The self-immolations of Raskolniks in the late seventeenth century in Swedish Karelia]', in Kimmo Katajala (ed.), *Manaajista maalaisaateliin. Tulkintoja toisesta historian, antropologian ja maantieteen välimaastossa. Tietolipas 140* (Helsinki: Suomalaisen Kirjallisuuden Seura, 1995), pp.181–207.
10. Ilpo Pursiainen, 'Salaiset kansiot: Suomalainen millenarismi 1918–1939 Etsivän Keskuspoliisin asiakirjoissa [Secret files: Finnish millenarianism 1918–1939 in the documents of the Secret Police]', in Sulevi Riukulehto (ed.), *Perinnettä vai bisnestä? Kulttuurin paikalliset ulottuvuudet* (Jyväskylä: Atena Kustannus Oy 2001), pp.204–16;

Interview with Ilpo Pursiainen on 18 June 2001.

11. The information on the Åkerblom movement is based on the dissertation of Gustav Björkstrand (Gustav Björkstrand, *Åkerblom-rörelsen. En finlandssvensk profetrörelses uppkomst, utveckling och sönderfall* [Åkerblom movement. The birth, development and dissolution of a Finnish–Swedish prophet movement]. *Meddelanden från stiftelsens för Åbo Akademi Forskningsinstitut, nr 11* (Åbo 1976)). For those interested, there is an English summary available in the end of the book. Almost the same text is published also in Harald Biezais (ed.), *New Religions. Based on Papers Read at the Symposium on New Religions Held at Åbo on the 1st–3rd of September 1974. Scripta Instituti Donneriani Aboensis VII* (Stockholm: Almqvist & Wiksell International, 1975) under title 'Formative Factors of the Maria Åkerblom Movement'.

12. Ilpo Pursiainen, 'Passion and Apocalypticism Under the Midnight Sun: The Apocalyptic Korpela-Movement in North Sweden in the 1930s', in Jeffrey Kaplan (ed.), *Beyond the Mainstream* (note 7), pp.145–56.

13. Ilpo Pursiainen, 'Salaiset kansiot' (note 10), pp. 208–10, 219.

14. Harri Heino, *Mihin Suomi tänään uskoo* [What Finland believes in today] (Porvoo/ Helsinki/Juva: Werner Söderström Osakeyhtiö 1997), pp.170–71; Saara Beckman, *Tiesivätkö he mitä tekivät?* [Did they know what they were doing] (Beckman & Norström AB, 1999).

15. Harri Heino's interview in *Helsingin Sanomat*, Monthly Supplement December 1999, p.67.

16. Heino, *Mihin Suomi tänään uskoo* (note 14), pp.154–7.

17. Interview with Arto Heiska and Teemu Isoaho (the Security Police) on 5 June 2001.

18. Merja Hermonen, 'Aspects of Youth Satanism in Finland', in Jeffrey Kaplan (ed.), *Beyond the Mainstream* (note 7), pp.273–88.

19. Interview with Merja Hermonen on 9 Aug. 2001.

20. *Project Megiddo* report, pp.26–9.

21. *Helsingin Sanomat* (25 Nov. 1999), p.C2.

22. See for example the annual report of the Security Police 1999.

23. Kyösti Pekonen, Pertti Hynynen and Mari Kalliala, 'The New Radical Right Taking Shape in Finland', in Kyösti Pekonen (ed.), *The New Radical Right in Finland* (Helsinki: The Finnish Political Science Association, 1999), pp.38–9.

24. For more about this see Lauri Karvonen, 'From White to Blue-and-Black: Finnish Fascism in the Inter-War Era', *Commentationes Scientiarum Socialium* 36 (Helsinki: The Finnish Society of Sciences and Letters 1988); and Risto Alapuro, 'Mass Support for Fascism in Finland', in Stein Ulgevik Larsen, Bernt Hagtvet and Jan Petter Myklebust (eds.), *Who Were the Fascists. Social Roots of European Fascism* (Universitetsförlaget: Bergen/Oslo/Tromsø 1980), pp.678–86.

25. Mari Kalliala, 'Traditions of the Radical Right in Finnish Political Culture' (pp.75–7); Kyösti Pekonen, 'Introduction to the Essays' (pp.24–5), and Jeffrey Kaplan, 'The Finnish New Radical Right in Comparative Perspective' (pp.209–13), all in Kyösti Pekonen (ed.), *The New Radical Right in Finland* (note 23).

26. The number of studies on the Finnish new radical right is very limited. The most notable effort has been the research project 'Criticism of politics, political detachment and the possibilities of new right-wing populism or radicalism?', which started in 1995. One of the aims of the project was to map out the situation and the ideas of Finnish radical rightwing populist and extremist movements. This is covered in Kyösti Pekonen (ed.), *The New Radical Right in Finland* (note 23), which is an excellent (and so far the only) introduction to the radical right scene in the country.

27. Pekonen *et al.* (note 23), pp. 31–41, 46–51. The most notable of the radical right parties in the 1990s have been The True Finns (*Perussuomalaiset*), The League for a Free Finland (*Vapaan Suomen Liitto*), and The Reform Group (*Remonttiryhmä*). The first one, the True Finns, was earlier known as The Finnish Rural Party (*Suomen Maaseudun Puolue*, SMP), which occasionally got some electoral support in the preceding decades, having even 18 MPs at its high in 1970. Nowadays the party represents just 1.3 per cent

of the electorate.
28. Pekonen *et al.* (note 23), pp.41–6. Extra-parliamentary groups include: the Patriotic National Alliance (*Isänmaallinen Kansallis-Liitto*, IKL) which is an extreme right group with nostalgic orientation, and Great Finland (*Suur-Suomi–yhdistys*), which is known for its strong verbal attacks against Russia and the Somalis in Finland. Perhaps the best-known personality of this scene is Pekka Siitoin. Besides being known as an occultist, he is famous for his overt admiration of Hitler and National Socialism. He got a fair amount of attention (but few followers) in the 1970s and continues his activities on a small scale. For more information on him, see Mari Kalliala, 'Pekka Siitoin – Representative of the Cultic Milieu', in Pekonen (ed.), *The New Radical Right in Finland* (note 23), pp.87–113.
29. The annual report of the Security Police 1996, p.7.
30. Kyösti Pekonen, 'The Patriotic Right as a Myth', Pekonen (note 23), pp.114–36; Jeffrey Kaplan, *Encyclopedia of White Power: A Sourcebook on the Radical Right* (Walnut Hills, CA: AltaMira, 2000), pp.160–62.
31. The annual report of the Security Police 1999, p.10.
32. The first yearly report on racist crimes in Finland compiled by the Ministry of the Interior is from 1997 (for the latest reports see www.intermin.fi). The number of racist crimes reported annually to the police has been about 200–300, with the number of incidents growing each year. However, due to difficulties with the quality of data and changes in the data collection methods, one should be careful about drawing conclusions from these figures. The increase of intercommunal violence was mentioned in the annual report of the Security Police 2000.
33. See for example Kyösti Pekonen, 'The Problem of Political Intolerance in "Decaying" Suburbs: A Finnish Case Study', Paper presented at the Stockholm International Forum Combating Intolerance on 30 Jan. 2001 (http://2001.stockholmforum.se/se/stats/presentpdf/pekonen.pdf).
34. See for example Tuomo Martikainen, 'The Urban Voters: Lost Their Empire?', in Pekonen (note 23), pp.147–58. For information on voting turnout in the 1990s see www.tilastokeskus.fi/tk/he/vaalit/vaalit_en.html.
35. *Poliisin turvallisuusbarometri 1999. Haastattelututkimuksen tuloksia* [Security Barometer of the Police 1999. Results of the interview study] (Sisäasiainministeriö, Poliisiosasto 1999), pp.33–39; EVA, *Mielipiteiden sateenkaari. Raportti suomalaisten asenteista 1999* [The rainbow of opinions. Report on the attitudes of the Finns 1999], www.eva.fi/julkaisut/raportit/asenne99/sisallys.html.
36. The surveys were conducted by a research system called GallupKanava, which is based on a permanent group of interviewees who answer a set of questions every week via computer. The group of interviewees is selected so that it forms a representative sample of the Finnish population. In the 1997 survey, the number of interviewees was 1,422, and in 1999, 1,031. The surveys consist of two sections of multiple choice questions. In the first section, respondents were asked to evaluate the possibility of different kinds of large-scale catastrophes taking place at the turn of the millennium. The alternatives given are 'impossible', 'possible', 'probable' and 'I don't know.' In the second section, respondents were asked if they agreed or disagreed with different kind of arguments about the turn of the millennium. The choices given were 'fully agree', 'partially agree', 'partially disagree', 'totally disagree' and 'I don't know.'
37. *Suomen Kuvalehti* (12 Nov. 1999), p.44.
38. News bulletin of the Research Centre of the Evangelical Lutheran Church 12 Nov. 1999, published on Internet at www.evl.fi/kkh/kt/uutiset/mar99/kthar.htm.
39. The newspapers included in the study are *Helsingin Sanomat* (the leading morning newspaper in Finland by far; despite its name it is practically a national newspaper), *Ilta-Sanomat* (a tabloid paper published by the same company as *Helsingin Sanomat*) and *Iltalehti* (a tabloid paper published by another media group). In addition to these, *Suomen Kuvalehti* (a weekly news magazine) and *Kotimaa* (a weekly newspaper with Christian orientation) were included. The articles included here are those dealing

directly with what would or might happen around the turn of the millennium. Thus, articles using the term 'millennium' in a merely rhetorical sense were not taken into account. Some of these newspapers often divided the articles into several smaller articles under one big heading. In cases where the articles dealt with the same theme, they are counted as one. If the articles are on different topic, they are counted separately.

40. See *Helsingin Sanomat* (4 Nov. 1999), p.C1; *Iltalehti* (14 Dec. 1999), pp.18–19; *Ilta-Sanomat* (13 Dec. 1999), pp.A10–11; *Suomen Kuvalehti* (17 Dec. 1999), p.23.
41. *Helsingin Sanomat* (29 Dec. 1999), p.A10.
42. *Helsingin Sanomat* (24 Dec.1999), p.C2.
43. See for example *Iltalehti* (23 Dec. 1999), p.A41, (30 Dec.1999), p.A3; *Helsingin Sanomat* (29 Dec. 1999), p.A10.
44. *Helsingin Sanomat* (11 Dec. 1999), p.B5; *Iltalehti* (30 Dec. 1999), p.A3.
45. The organizational structure of the Finnish police and the roles and responsibilities are defined in *Poliisilaki* [Police law] 493/1995 and *Asetus poliisin hallinnosta* [Decree on the administration of the police] 158/1996; the organization chart and other information on the topic can be found on the Internet at www.poliisi.fi/english/index.htm and www.intermin.fi.
46. Most documents related to the risk analyses and preparations are still classified and thus have not been used in this study. The following information is based (unless otherwise indicated) on interviews with Chief Superintendent Arto Heiska and Detective Sergeant Teemu Isoaho, the Security Police (5 June 2001), Police Commander Hannu Hannula, the Police Department of the Ministry of the Interior (19 June and 31 July 2001) and Chief Superintendent Jussi-Pekka Lämsä, Helsinki Police District (26 June 2001). I would like to thank them warmly for their contribution. The Provincial Supreme Command's contribution to the preparations is not discussed here since the Helsinki District Police, which is taken as an example of the local level, reports directly to the Supreme Police Command.
47. This aspect of the work of the Security Police is discussed especially in their annual report 1999.
48. *Helsingin Sanomat* (24 Dec.1999), p.C2.
49. *Helsingin Sanomat* (2 Jan. 2000), pp.A5, A8–10; interview with Jussi-Pekka Lämsä on 26 June 2001.
50. Interview with Jussi-Pekka Lämsä on 26 June 2001.
51. See for example *Helsingin Sanomat* (8 Dec. 1999), p.D2, 12 Dec, 1999, p.A9; *Ilta-Sanomat* (17 Dec, 1999), pp.30–31.

Cult and Anticult Totalism: Reciprocal Escalation and Violence

DICK ANTHONY, THOMAS ROBBINS and
STEVEN BARRIE-ANTHONY

Introduction

Millenarian movements have been involved in a number of recent episodes of collective homicidal, or suicidal violence. One result has been an intensification of the stigma which had already been attached to 'cults' and to the menace of cultic 'mind control' or 'brainwashing', which is viewed in some quarters as a linchpin of such groups' violent proclivities.[1] The stigma seems presently to be particularly powerful in Western Europe and in China, where the prosecutorial cult/brainwashing discourse, imported (like many 'cults') from the United States, has become influential. This discourse has been taken up by official public commissions of inquiry and has influenced legislation in France.[2] A variety of heterogeneous and non-violent groups have been assumed in Europe to be similar to the sensationally violent Order of the Solar Temple, which is viewed as the 'quintessential cult'.[3]

Several social scientists have recently argued that while sensational claims about 'brainwashing' in 'cults' are misleading and (to use legal jargon) more prejudicial than probative, nevertheless religio–ideological *totalism*, which is a frequent element in claims about 'mind control', certainly exists and can in certain circumstances and in conjunction with other elements have dysfunctional and polarizing consequences and may sometimes be related to violence and other problems.[4] This article builds on recent discussions by the authors of the psychology of apocalyptic totalism and the issue of violence (see note 4) and also extrapolates the statement of Robert Lifton that 'totalism begets totalism'[5] to develop our view that militant reactions against totalistic sects which are perceived as menacing can acquire a totalistic (and thus a persecutory) quality of their own.

Totalism is a relative rather than an absolute characteristic and such persecution may take the form of over-stereotyping and the tendency to treat a broad range of esoteric groups as equivalent to a tiny minority of notorious and sensationally violent sects. Totalistic anticult ideology treats a bewildering spiritual diversity as polarized between legitimate churches and sinister cults, autonomous and non-autonomous devotees, etc. Anticult activities based upon such dualistic ideology may in turn play a role in triggering the further totalization of a group; a cycle of increasing totalization between both the group and the counter-group response may escalate out of control to the point that it triggers the violent dénouement that was formerly only one of a variety of possible outcomes of the group's development. Thus, a number of factors, including totalistic oppositional provocation, may determine whether and when violence in a totalistic group actually ensues.

Totalism

The totalism concept was originally defined by Lifton's mentor, the psychoanalyst Erik Erikson, who developed it in a seminal article[6] describing the affinity between totalitarian ideologies and the personality makeup of individuals who are predisposed to respond favorably to such ideologies.[7] When people think of 'totalism' they sometimes think of institutional or communal totalism: comprehensive regulation or regimentation of participants' activities in 'total institutions'. In this article, on the other hand, we are concerned with totalism as it was defined by Erikson, and later by Robert Lifton;[8] that is we will focus on totalism as a composite socio-psychological structure or 'milieu', resulting from the interaction between a certain type of individual identity, i.e., individual totalism, on the one hand, and totalistic ideology, on the other.

Lifton applied Erikson's totalism concept to the experiences of 40 interview subjects who had undergone Chinese Thought Reform. He found the concept useful in explaining why only two of these 40 subjects (Father Simon and Miss Darrow) were significantly influenced by thought reform. (These two subjects did not actually convert to communism; at most they had become, in the terminology of the

McCarthyist period, 'fellow travelers' of communism.)

Lifton follows Erikson in viewing the totalism concept as a way of explaining why such totalistic individuals are differentially responsive to totalitarian ideologies. (Lifton refers to such people as having been characterized by 'individual totalism' before they even encountered the thought reform milieu.) Thus, Lifton states that by 'ideological totalism' he means 'to suggest the coming together of an immoderate ideology with equally immoderate character traits – an extremist meeting ground of people and ideas'.[9] In both Erikson's and Lifton's definition of totalism, then, the concept refers to the socio-psychological structure resulting from the interaction between totalistic people and totalistic ideology, rather than simply being a sociological property of totalitarian organizations.

In applying Erikson's totalism concept to the Thought Reform experiences of his subjects, Lifton famously identified eight 'themes' of the totalistic milieu: *Milieu Control*, i.e., monopoly of the spatial and informational environment; *Mystical Manipulation* of powerful symbols; *Demand for Purity*, i.e., the experiential world is sharply polarized between the pure and the impure, the absolutely good and the absolutely evil with respect to ideas, feelings and actions; *The Cult of Confession*, i.e., the obsession with the personal confession of violations of the absolute division between pure and impure ideas, feelings and actions; *The Sacred Science*, i.e., the claim that the ideology provides the ultimate moral vision for the ordering of human existence and that it also expresses airtight logic and absolute 'scientific' precision; *The Loading of the Language*, i.e., totalist ideology is expressed in clichés and verbal formulas which discourage independent thought; *Doctrine Over Person*, i.e., the subordination of individual human experience to doctrinal claims; and *The Dispensing of Existence*, i.e., the totalist milieu draws a sharp distinction between people and non-people, between those true believers who have a right to exist and those with a different world view, who do not. With the notable exception of the sociological property of 'milieu control', these totalist themes pertain primarily to beliefs rather than to patterns of group behavior.

Lifton notes with regard to these eight 'psychological themes' of ideological totalism that:

> Each has a totalistic quality; each depends upon an equally absolute philosophical assumption; and each mobilizes certain

individual emotional tendencies, mostly of a polarizing nature. Psychological theme, philosophical rationale and polarized individual tendencies are interdependent; they require rather than directly cause, each other. In combination they create an atmosphere which may temporarily energize or exhilarate, but which at the same time poses the greatest of human threats.[10]

More recently Lifton has identified totalism as synonymous with 'political and religious fundamentalism' because of fundamentalism's tendency to define the world in absolute, i.e., dualistic, terms. Lifton has stated that

> the quest for absolute or 'totalistic' belief systems ... has produced nothing short of a worldwide epidemic of political and religious fundamentalism – of movements characterized by the literalized embrace of sacred texts containing absolute truth for all persons and a mandate for militant, often violent measures taken against designated enemies of truth or mere unbelievers.[11]

'Fundamentalism', in Lifton's view, 'can create the most extreme expressions of totalism, of the self's immersion in all-or-nothing ideological and behavior patterns'.[12]

The core element of ideological totalism, in our view, is *the radical, absolute division of humanity into dual evaluative categories* such as saved/damned, real persons/false persons, human/subhuman, God's people/'mud people', etc. Elsewhere we have linked ideological totalism with what we have termed *exemplary dualism*, an apocalyptic theme 'in which contemporary sociopolitical or socio-religious forces are viewed as absolute contrast categories in terms not only of moral virtue but also of eschatology and the millennial destiny of humankind'.[13] Exemplary dualism weds dualistic moral absolutism to history and social tension, i.e., 'The great temptation of apocalyptic eschatology is to externalize good and evil in terms of present historical conflicts.'[14] Anthony and Robbins have noted that most of Lifton's eight motifs of ideological totalism 'can be derived from a conception of close-knit, authoritarian movements with intense solidarity and adherence to a distinctly apocalyptic and dualistic worldview'.[15]

In Erikson's and Lifton's usage, the totalism concept is heuristically suggestive but somewhat vague. In this article we attempt to extrapolate their development and application of the totalism concept into a more formal model of totalitarian influence by integrating it with: 1) contemporary research upon millenarian movements; 2) the psychoanalytic concepts of 'splitting' and 'projective identification'; 3) the sociological concept of 'deviance amplification'.

Totalism and Splitting

As we have indicated, Robert Lifton's use of the ideological totalism idea in his thought reform research was an application and extension of the totalism concept originally developed by his mentor Erik Erikson. Lifton found the concept useful in explaining why only two of these 40 subjects were significantly influenced by thought reform. Lifton follows Erikson in viewing the totalistic concept as a way of explaining why such individuals are differentially responsive to totalitarian ideologies.

Erikson viewed totalism as a proclivity or inclination of some persons, 'under certain conditions to undergo ... that sudden total realignment, and, as it were co-alignment which accompanies conversion to the totalitarian conviction that the state may and must have absolute power over the minds as well as the lives and the fortunes of its citizens'.[16]

Erikson saw the total alignments and realignments, which characterize conversion and de-conversion to totalistic ideology, as similar to the affective vicissitudes of early childhood in which a child may suddenly – if only briefly – switch back and forth from total love to total hate of 'primary objects', i.e., mother/father figures. Psychoanalysts see such unstably polarized total responses to parental figures as the origin of the ego-defense of 'splitting', i.e., the tendency to view the world dualistically in terms only of all-bad or all-good categories. (Splitting relates to the trait of 'intolerance of ambiguity', which is characteristic of 'authoritarian' personalities.) 'Splitting' also refers to the dissociative polarization of the self-concept or ego identity into all-bad and all-good components. (Splitting of the object and splitting of the self are viewed as invariably correlated with each other.)[17]

In Erikson's view, individuals who tend to split the world and the self into all-good or all-bad categories are prone to conversion to totalitarian ideologies. According to Erikson, in the psychology of some adults,

   violent loves and hates and sudden conversions and aversions

share with the child's fetishism and fears such factors as the
exclusive focusing of a set of (friendly or unfriendly) affects on a
person or idea; the primitivization of all affects thus focused; and
a utopian (or cataclysmic) expectation of a total gain or a total loss
to come from this focus.[18]

Splitting, which may be normal in a child, is thus viewed as distinctively
conducive to conversions to totalistic ideologies in an adult. Splitting is
fundamental to totalitarian psychology and entails a tendency to divide
all humanity into good and evil, saved and damned, human and
subhuman, etc., and to shift quickly back and forth between these
polarized categories, i.e., a person with a polarized, totalist sense of self
may idealize a person, group or idea today which he vehemently
repudiates and disapproves of tomorrow.

Erikson also uses the term totalism to denote an all-encompassing
belief system which conceptualizes the world in terms of a
comprehensive set of evaluative polarities, with a central duality such as
'Aryan/non-Aryan' or 'capitalist/communist' which renders subordinate
and auxiliary polarities compelling. (Such a division of the world into
polarized all-good and all-bad categories is a more general
manifestation of the concept of splitting discussed above.)

In his later writings Erikson used the term *pseudospeciation* to
denote what we consider a key aspect of totalism: the tendency for
totalists to treat stigmatized categories of persons, identified in terms of
race, class, creed, color, religion, sexual preference, etc., as totally
different, indeed radically inferior, species; in effect subhuman.[19]
Although Lifton does not explicitly use this term in *Chinese Thought
Reform and the Psychology of Totalism*, the pseudo-speciation concept
is convergent with his discussion of ideological totalism, particularly his
notion of the *dispensing of existence*, which implies that non-believers
have no compelling claims or rights, at least when apocalyptic push
comes to shove.[20] Persons who belong to categories stigmatized by
totalist ideologies may be treated as non-persons, even subhuman.

In addition, as we have indicated above, Lifton claimed that Father
Simon and Miss Darrow – the two of his 40 subjects who were
influenced by Chinese Thought Reform – had totalistic personalities
prior to their exposure to the indoctrination process.[21] Thus for both
Lifton and Erikson the core of ideological totalism is an immoderate,
absolutist ideology, particularly attractive to immoderate, volatile and

alienated persons, which *radically divides the world into legitimate and illegitimate species.*

Confrontation, Violence and Projective Identification

Totalistic movements are not necessarily violent, but elements of the psychology of totalism may place a premium on *confrontation* with perceived exemplars of evil. The role of *contrast symbols* is psychologically vital. An elect group is specified whose members are encouraged to define their collective and personal identities in terms of absolute contrasts with radically devalued, hostile categories of outsiders. The group envisions itself as an enclave of truth, purity and virtue in a corrupt, evil and doomed world, and it may anticipate or even welcome the world's hostility.

Ideological totalism/exemplary dualism, then, presents to adherents an idealized system of exemplary leaders and values contrasted with its radically devalued opposite. Followers with polarized self-constructs or 'divided selves' can identify with heroic leaders and the ideals they embody, while they themselves can hope to become new, heroic exemplars of such ideals. At the same time rejected feelings of weakness, failure, lack of worth, sinfulness, shame and guilt, which were once part of dissociated or split-off self-images, can now be projected onto designated outsiders viewed as innate inferiors or vile 'enemies' – *contrast symbols* perceived as alien to the idealized community of believers. Through the dynamics of 'projective identification' converts actually become somewhat psychologically dependent upon the human scapegoats or personified contrast symbols who symbolize evil.

The psychoanalytic/object relations concept of *projective identification* refers to a psychological defense mechanism which is associated with splitting. Splitting and projective identification are viewed as 'primitive' ego defenses which complement each other in a flawed attempt to support self-esteem and a coherent sense of self.

> The primitive defense of 'splitting', of seeing oneself and others as all good, and dumping the all-bad object [and dissociated bad component of the self] externally onto another person, can be viewed as the forerunner of the more mature defense of repression...
>
> The second primitive defense is 'projective identification' which is a forerunner of the more mature defense of projection... with

projection being solely an intrapsychic defense, and projective identification both an intrapsychic and interpersonal defense mechanism. *One individual evacuates a good or bad, self or object image externally onto another person, who then serves as a container for this projection. However, the other is induced through verbal and non-verbal communication into thinking, feeling, or behavior in accordance with this projection.* Thus there is an attempt to transplant one's internal split image into another and to manipulate the other to collude with it. The other's evoked response is then reinternalized through identification, thereby serving as a negative feedback loop, so that objective reality reinforces the projector's internal world of images. (emphasis ours)[22]

Simple projection, then, describes a one-person activity, whereas projective identification involves an interactive, two-person activity. In simple projection a person avoids the person upon whom he/she has projected unconscious motives, so that the targeted person is not directly affected by this intrapsychic maneuver. In projective identification, on the other hand, a person projects split-off, unconscious motives (sexuality, aggression) or self-attributions (inferiority, evil) onto another and also manipulates him or her in such a way that they come to identify with the projected motives or attributions as their own. The targeted person then acts out the projected motives or personal characteristics in relation to the person doing the projecting, with the result that the original projections come to constitute *a self-fulfilling prophecy.*

For instance, person X is hostile towards person Y and projects this emotion onto Y so that X comes to feel that Y is actually hostile towards him. X then begins to treat Y as an enemy which in turn leads Y to resent X and to defensively treat X as an enemy, thus apparently confirming the accuracy of X's original projection.

The *paranoid-schizoid* stage of development is the childhood stage at which splitting and projective identification are the primary defense mechanisms. Those who continue to be fixated at this stage are viewed by psychoanalysts as suffering from 'personality disorders', i.e., as having polarized selves which are split between unrealistically positive and unrealistically negative self-concepts. Such polarized selves alternate in relation to the fluctuation of external circumstances, with even minor fluctuations tending to trigger a shift from a grandiose to a very negative sense of self.

Such people are prone to projecting in turn each side of this split sense of self onto others, and to interacting with them in such a way that such alternately positive and negative projections are confirmed by the behavior of the others towards them. When they idealize the other person it tends to produce positive attitudes towards themselves, but when minor disappointments lead them to demonize the other person, it tends to trigger negative attitudes and disruptions in relationships. Because such unstable splitting and projective identification tends to result in unstable personal relationships and vocational histories, then those prone to such tendencies are continuously searching for some more stable solution to their unhappy lives.

One solution to such paradoxes of identity, which Erikson referred to as 'identity confusion', may be to convert to totalistic religious or political movements in which: 1) the negative self images of members are split off and projected onto the mainstream world; 2) the grandiosely positive self images of members are affirmed and stabilized by membership in a group viewed as embodying the solution to the world's evil nature; 3) the group through projective identification interacts with the outside world in a manner which tends to confirm such projections and identifications of the dualistically split selves of the members; 4) totalistic ideology, often of an apocalyptic or millenarian type, rationalizes both the projective identification of the negative self images with the outside world and also the projective identification of positive self images with the group.

The resulting confrontations with the evil outside world may become essential for valorizing the system and reinforcing participants' heroic identities. A sense of taking dynamic action against the forces of evil and their human embodiments may become necessary to maintain devotees' sense of wholeness and to preserve the rigid boundaries of the totalist self.

Our explanatory account of splitting and projective identification as the socio-psychological mechanism underlying the volatility of totalistic confrontations is consistent with the observations – at a more global level of description – of Lifton and other students of the dynamics of millenarian development. For instance, Lifton maintains that fundamentalist totalism is 'always on the edge of violence, because it ever mobilizes for an absolute confrontation with designated evil, thereby justifying any action taken to eliminate evil'.[23]

Charisma, Projective Identification and Instability

Totalist movements generally have charismatic leaders – 'heroic' exemplars of the movement's ideals. Charismatic leadership is viewed by some social scientists as inherently volatile by virtue of both the absence of institutionalized *restraints* on the leader's arbitrariness and the absence of institutionalized *supports for* the leader's authority. In the absence of institutionalized support for his authority, a charismatic leader may attempt to maintain his position by aggressively curbing dissent, expelling rivals and provoking confrontations ('crisis mongering') to dramatically demonstrate his indispensability.[24]

Another factor encouraging charismatic volatility may be the tendency for the leaders of totalistic groups to be afflicted by personality disorders, and the unstable polarized selves, splitting and projective identification referred to above. According to some clinicians, charismatic prophets and gurus leading deviant sects often exhibit 'narcissistic' personality syndromes and tend to perceive the movement and its participants as *extensions of themselves*, which may lower inhibitions against risking their followers' lives.[25]

Followers, on the other hand, may narcissistically project their aims and aspirations onto the charismatic leader such that they may sometimes mislead themselves as to the (perhaps shifting) nature of his leadership and goals and the direction in which he is taking the group. Some messianic leaders of totalist groups have grandiose identities which lead them to equate the fate of humankind with their personal aggrandizement and thus to demonize any internal or external opposition.[26]

It is likely, then, that at least the more extremely totalist–dualist movements tend to recruit persons with dissociated aggressive tendencies. The dualistic, pseudo-speciating movement provides a setting in which such tendencies may be enhanced and, more importantly, *channeled* and directed toward the movement's ideological scapegoats and contrast symbols. Actual violence and other modes of aggressive acting-out may also come to the fore. According to the author of a study of a racist Christian Identity group, members engage in self-idealization and project weakness and deviance onto devalued outsiders. 'To perceive oneself as pure, impure feelings and impulses must be projected on to a world where they become embodied in others.'[27] The charismatic racist leader can thus 'empower' alienated, rebellious or ambivalent recruits by legitimating their pent-up hostility and directing it to scapegoated contrast symbols. 'As a transitional object, the cult leader helps members express hostile impulses ... When the leader initiates an antisocial act ... members become free to act in a guiltless and violent way.'[28]

However, the solutions to identity problems provided by totalistic movements are often unstable. In part such identity solutions are unstable because the 'projective identifications' (which bond followers to the leader and also create a type of psychological dependency of the group on its devalued contrast symbols) are prone to *sudden reversal*. Beloved leaders and comrades can almost instantly become excoriated betrayers.[29] Exalted ideals must be embodied precariously in flawed and fallible leaders. The sacrifices which participants make in a highly disciplined, authoritarian sect feed into a build-up of latent resentment which may quickly erupt under certain conditions and induce apostasy.

According to Catherine Wessinger, various developments including disconfirmed prophecies, failure to achieve grandiose goals, traumatic high-level defections, internal conflicts, diminishing charisma of the leader, and lack of movement growth, can enhance a group's volatility and thus the probability of a violent response to external threat.[30] According to Lifton similar vicissitudes and traumas can undermine the internalized psychological support system of 'functional megalomania' which reinforces the grandiose self-concept of a messianic totalist leader such as Shôkô Asahara of Aum Shinrikyô, with the result that the psychological reinforcement system disintegrates under stress and becomes transformed into rampant and volatile paranoia.[31]

Notwithstanding these dynamics, violent confrontations *arise only with respect to a small minority of totalist/dualist movements*. The urge to palpably confront evil may not always be overwhelming, and, moreover, there are other, more manageable and routinized ways of confronting evil's human objectifications. These include: *proselytization* (which may produce a validating sense of 'winning over the enemy'); *aggressive prayer* (e.g., Pentecostal 'prayer warrior' mystiques); political *action*; or even just 'waiting for the end', when the sense of an imminent cataclysmic finale produces a thrill of expectation and validation of heroic movement-based identities.

Unfortunately, such milder forms of the confrontation with evil may sometimes become less effective. For instance, proselytization may for various reasons be curtailed (e.g., the movement retreats to an isolated wilderness enclave) or may appear to be losing its efficacy (the same may be said for political activism).[32] Confrontation may sometimes actually be sought by the opponents of totalist movements, e.g., as occurred in different ways at Jonestown, Ruby Ridge and Waco.[33] The features often associated with totalist movements including messianic charismatic leaders, authoritarian regimes, strong internal pressures for conformity, social encapsulation and isolation of participants, rigid puritanism (or occasionally wild antinomianism), nasty scapegoating of certain social groups and categories, utopiate or apocalyptic visions, and absolutistic condemnation of the status quo, will generally ensure that there is no dearth of vehement opposition to such groups.

Such opposition may sometimes be confrontational (and may even come to possess a somewhat totalistic quality) and persecutory. Totalist groups make handy scapegoats and thus may sometimes be victimized. Occasionally rival totalist movements will furiously fight it out, sometimes literally as with Nazi storm troopers and communist cadres battling on the streets of the Weimar Republic. More recent examples include communists vs. clansmen in North Carolina and neo-Nazis vs. their strident European opponents.

In our view, anticult totalism may be one factor that tends to initiate such cycles of escalating reciprocal totalism: a point we shall return to later.

The Breakdown of 'Normal' Totalism

In the view of Erik Erikson, totalism presents a risk of violence or dangerous extremism, but it is not necessarily pathological relative to the individual totalist's emotional condition. Totalism can address 'split self' and 'negative identity' patterns by allowing a convert to identify with heroic virtues and externalize devalued personal attributes, thereby resolving identity confusion and imparting a sense of wholeness, personal integrity and authenticity.[34] Thus totalism, particularly in its milder forms, is often therapeutic. In this connection, involvement in a 'charismatic group' not infrequently produces relief from symptoms of neurotic distress,[35] and can, particularly if involvement is temporary, assist a young person in transcending a traumatic disruption of adolescent or post-adolescent development and in negotiating the transition to adulthood.[36] The shrill articulation of strident dualistic values can actually provide an empowering transition to an adult sense of efficacy and self-confidence on the part of some withdrawn and inarticulate young persons.[37]

To some degree totalism and dualistic moral absolutism are built into our culture and can be seen in various themes and orientations which are not necessarily combined with institutional-communal totalism.[38] Various dualistic orientations including racism, sexism, homophobia, anti-communism, and even anti-cultism, have totalistic overtones.

The spread of multiculturalism as a social ethos has been associated with an aggressive attack against traditional quasi-totalistic, dehumanizing orientations such as racism, sexism, homophobia, etc. It is arguable that the strident contemporary reaction against deplorable traditional prejudices may itself take on a somewhat totalistic quality. The relentlessly conformist quality of social campaigns against traditional invidious dualisms such as sexism, racism or homophobia may occasionally actually work in favor of targeted totalisms which may benefit from an 'individualist' reaction against conformist 'political correctness'.[39] In any case the breakdown of 'normal totalism' and dualistic norms against women, minorities, and some sexual preferences, can at least contribute to a transitional milieu of anomie or perceived moral ambiguity in which new totalist movements can emerge,[40] as well as strident anti-totalist campaigns.[41]

As archetypal enclaves of intolerant totalistic thinking, authoritarian 'cults' have become prime targets of the attack on received dualistic moral absolutism and traditional totalistic pseudospeciation. The attack on cults is thus partly related to strident multiculturalist ideology and contemporary 'intolerance of intolerance'.[42]

'Totalism Begets Totalism'

Lifton first articulated the principle that totalism begets totalism in the section of his book on Chinese Thought Reform where he discussed the reciprocal escalation of totalistic themes in the conflicts between communism and American anti-communism (especially McCarthyism). He later expressed this same principle in commenting on the extremist tactics employed by the anticult movement against controversial new religions, in particular coercive deprogramming.[43] We shall extrapolate and generalize this principle.

First of all, totalism is a somewhat imprecise and not clearly bounded concept. It is not always employed very precisely even by

Lifton, who popularized the term/concept which had originated in Erikson's seminal article. The totalism concept thus lends itself to over-generalization and to use as an ideological weapon against minority movements and heterodox ideologies. An influential legal manifesto drew on Lifton's work to condemn 'religious totalism' and justify coercive deprogramming as a legitimate therapeutic intervention when it transpired under guardianship or conservatorship orders issued by courts and not under vigilante auspices.[44]

Professor Richard Delgado's treatise, *Religious Totalism*, which became the theoretical spearhead of legal measures and litigation tactics in the 1980s aimed at combating the alleged use of 'mind control' in religious sects, emphasized the pernicious use of deception by totalistic cults to lure recruits. Delgado treated deception as a functional equivalent of the raw physical coercion by which inmates are placed in POW camps. However, Delgado's analytical model entailed a wild generalization to 'cults' *per se* of one notorious instance of unequivocal deception.[45]

Religious Totalism became the legal linchpin of a genre which employs the Cold War 'brainwashing' mystique and the analogy between cults and communist POW camps to mobilize support for 'anti-cult' measures which critics such as the writers of this article believe jeopardize religious liberty and human rights.[46] Although currently less influential in the United States than it was in the 1980s, this genre is presently influential in Western Europe and China, and may possibly be revived in the United States under the impact of recent incidents of extreme violence involving millennialist groups.

Discourse alleging religio-ideological totalism is thus frequently subject to distortions and over-generalization, particularly when it evolves into Cassandra rhetoric about sinister brainwashing. In brainwashing formulations the concept of 'totalism' becomes entirely divorced from its 'Eriksonian' origins as the individual predisposition of some persons with fragmented identities to convert to highly authoritarian movements and ideologies. Instead 'brainwashing' is often conceived as a kind of *omnipotent psychotechnology* which destroys autonomy. The brainwashing concept expresses a duality between 'cult slaves',[47] who have lost their free will and thus their essential humanity, and free, autonomous citizens who are not enmeshed in evil cults.[48] When this distinction is absolutized, a kind of totalistic pseudospeciation emerges, i.e., by radically dividing humanity into those who have and those who do not have free will, cult/brainwashing theory represents a form of totalistic pseudospeciation and religious intolerance which may be particularly adapted to a multicultural milieu.[49]

In our view, then, cult/brainwashing discourse amounts to a form of dehumanizing pseudospeciation in that it radically divides humanity into those who are fully human, have free will and deserve to be granted the freedom to believe in and practice their religion on the one hand, and those who are not fully human – enslaved robots who do not deserve or are incapable of exercising religious liberty – on the other.[50]

It is worth noting that the totalistic absolutism of cult/brainwashing discourse inheres not only in the distinction between brainwashed and non-brainwashed persons – cult slaves vs. real persons – but also in the absolute distinction between the brainwashing techniques of 'destructive cults' and the legitimate, non-mind controlling patterns of influence found in non-stigmatized spiritual groups. According to Philip Jenkins, when anticult writers in the 1980s 'described the sinister methods used to induce and maintain personality change [in cults], they were often describing practices like repetitive chant and movement, which are commonly used in religious systems, including large sections of Eastern Orthodox Christianity and even American Protestant revivalism'.[51] As two psychiatrists have noted, ritual sequences in non-stigmatized black Baptist and black Pentecostal churches are just as plausible candidates for having powerful, manipulative psycho-active effects as are somewhat similar rituals in allegedly coercive 'cults'.[52]

Finally, anti-cult totalism manifests in connection with extreme over-generalization and stereotyping, e.g., the present tendency in continental Western Europe (especially France) to see the sensationally violent Solar Temple movement as the 'quintessential cult' and thereby to see small, close-knit, esoteric spiritual movements as inherently suspect and requiring stringent controls.[53] It is worth noting that even the Branch Davidians at Waco, who shot federal agents and may have 'suicidally' started a fire, are pointedly excluded by Robert Lifton from his rogues' gallery of highly dangerous groups willing to 'force the end' by precipitating an apocalyptic scenario through sensational symbolic violence.[54] In addition, movements much less violent than the Branch Davidians have been stigmatized as potential 'Jonestowns' and threatened with persecution.

In our view, then, crusaders against cults share a dualistic proclivity to see all such movements as more or less *interchangeable* malefactors in whom extreme violence is an inherent, fundamental property rather than a situated contingency. The error is not in the description of some movements as totalistic – such allegations may in some cases be accurate – but rather in the totalizing tendency to oversimplify spiritual diversity by the use of polarizing either/or categorizations and dualistic visions from which any ambiguity has been excluded.[55] In this area the totalist visions of cults – of apocalyptic prophets, gurus, and preachers – have their counterparts in the anathemas of their zealous antagonists.[56]

Deviance Amplification, Escalating Cycles of Totalistic Confrontation and Violence

As we have seen, stigmatizing a movement on the basis of a vague evocation of its internal milieu as constituting mind control can itself be a form of totalistic pseudospeciation. Moreover, under the principle that totalism begets totalism, stigmatization could lead a targeted group to enhance its internal totalism and apocalyptic paranoia. Given the principles of projective identification that we have discussed above, at times this can even lead to violence. This is all the more likely to the extent that such totalistic persecution is enforced through concrete activities that effectively limit the group's freedom of religious belief and conduct.

As we have seen, Lifton regards at least some anticult activities such as coercive deprogramming as themselves manifestations of totalism. Besides coercive deprogramming, which in the US at least has declined since the 1970s and early 1980s, there are various other measures which arguably prevent 'cultists' from practicing their religion – a privilege restricted to putatively autonomous and non-brainwashed 'free' citizens. These measures include lawsuits seeking damages against religious movements for various alleged harms (e.g., intentional or negligent infliction of emotional distress) which are primarily defined in terms of alleged cultic brainwashing. Large damage awards in this area definitely have implications for destroying (e.g., bankrupting) certain minority religious organizations.[57]

Other legal actions seek custody of the children of devotees when a parent claims that an ex-spouse involved in a devalued sect is by virtue of brainwashing insufficiently mentally competent (i.e., human enough) to be allowed to raise his or her children or even to be granted extensive non-custodial visitation rights. Members of devalued sects often lose custody of their children (and sometimes substantial visitation rights) if their apostate ex-spouses contest custody. Finally, new legislation passed in France makes it possible for the state to actually disband religious organizations which are convicted of a single instance of alleged mind control. Religious belief of which the state disapproves is criminalized.[58]

Given the ambiguity and lack of scientific meaning of brainwashing allegations, it is important to realize that these several means of suppressing alleged cultic brainwashing through legal action boil down to the use of state power as a way of suppressing the world views and shared lifestyles of certain religions or political movements. As we discussed above, Erikson defined totalistic ideology first of all as 'the totalitarian conviction that the state may and must have absolute power over the minds as well as the lives and the fortunes of its citizens'.[59] By Erikson's definition it would seem, then, that these various types of state action, designed to reduce or eliminate allegedly totalistic belief and conduct, are themselves intrinsically totalistic. If totalism begets totalism, through projective identification or other means, such totalistic state action is more likely to create or at least enhance totalism than it is to eliminate or reduce it. Such totalistic consequences may include the incitement of violence within social movements that otherwise would not have occurred.

The use of state power to suppress religious or political belief and conduct by these several means is arguably itself, implicitly at least, a type of violence; if these groups were to refuse to cooperate with such state-imposed legal action, they would be compelled to submit to it by physical force. Targeted groups may come to feel that their only defense against such forceful suppression of their world views would be defensive violence directed against either the state or themselves. (Arguably both types of defensive violence occurred at Jonestown, where the Peoples Temple responded to the congressional investigation of its activities by murdering Representative Leo Ryan and members of his party, as well by carrying out both murders and suicides with respect to its own members.)

Brainwashing ideology arguably has influenced state action which is even more overtly totalistic, such as that which has occurred in the US at Waco and in China against the Falun Gong. In these situations the connection of such totalistic attributions to escalating reciprocal violence seems self-evident.

Brainwashing ideology also has colored American and Canadian governmental reports on the potential for violence in millenarian religious and political movements. Predictions of millenarian violence in such reports may potentially constitute the sort of self-fulfilling prophecies we are discussing here.

The FBI *Project Megiddo* report relies substantially on the work of Margaret Singer, the most influential American theorist of this genre,[60] and its descriptions of the ominous internal totalitarianism of cults incline somewhat in the direction of inflammatory demonology. While the Canadian report on 'Doomsday Religious Movements' is less perfervid, Jenkins has criticized the related stereotypical notion of 'doomsday cults'. According to Jenkins the doomsday cult concept comes:

> close to making millenarian expectations *ipso facto* a token of cult-like behavior and even a warning symptom of likely mass suicide ... There are few limits to the force that can be levied against any group once it has been designated a doomsday cult, a self-fulfilling title if there ever was one. Invoking the specter of mass suicide almost ensures that mass deaths will ensue.[61]

This self-fulfilling prophecy of allegedly being a doomsday cult may actually have affected the escalation of the Waco confrontation into its violent dénouement. Federal agents had been influenced in their aggressive response to the Dravidians' refusal to admit them by anticult conceptions of a fanatic, suicidal, mind-controlling cult.[62]

It has been argued that the eruptions of violence and other antisocial behavior in apocalyptic movements occur in part because the movements become 'deformed' or 'destabilized' by virtue of aggressive harassment that they receive from opponents including 'anti-cult' activists, recriminating apostates, sensationalist media, 'concerned relatives' of devotees and state officials.[63] Spiraling sequences of 'deviance amplification' may ensue whereby the mutual antipathy and suspicion between deviant groups and the votaries of a governmental crackdown reinforce each other, gradually escalating out of control until a catastrophic dénouement unfolds.

In the words of the Canadian report:

> Sanctions applied by authorities are often interpreted by a movement as hostile to its existence, which reinforces their

apocalyptic beliefs and leads to further withdrawal, mobilization and deviant actions, and which in turn elicits heavier sanctions by authorities. This unleashes a spiral of amplification, as each action amplifies each reaction, and the use of violence is facilitated as the group believes this will ultimately actualize its doomsday scenario.[64]

The Canadian report concludes that 'three factors (apocalyptic beliefs, charismatic leadership and [provocative] actions by authorities), whether inherent to the dynamics of a Doomsday Religious Movement or in response to the actions that it engages in, translates into a predisposition toward violent behavior'.

James Richardson has discussed the convergence of 'deviance amplification' and 'conflict/interaction' perspectives in his analysis of cycles of escalating violence between new religions and their anticult antagonists in a wide range of empirical situations. His article is probably the most even-handed, theoretically sophisticated, and empirically detailed application of the deviance-amplification/conflict-interactionist perspective to new religions presently available. He states:

> Obviously, if a group's beliefs justify violence, then it is more prone to occur if external entities also expect violence and act on its inevitability. Thus an interactional spiral toward violence can develop as the two entities interact with each other either directly (such as through face to face negotiations) or indirectly (through media coverage or intermediaries such as informants or others). Thus the interactionist perspective is akin to Roy Wallis' provocative concept of the amplification of deviance developed out of his study of Scientology. What can develop through interactions based on shared views of the other's propensity for violence is an amplification of violent expectations, which in turn can lead to violence itself.[65]

It should be realized that such processes of 'deviance amplification' or 'conflict interaction' observed by sociologists may be the sociological manifestations of the clinical and socio-psychological processes of splitting, projective identification and totalism begetting totalism which we have described. There may be considerable scientific and practical value in integrating these sociological, social-psychological and psychological levels of description rather than in viewing them as competing explanations or independent processes.

Conclusion: Internal vs. External Causes of Violence

The relative salience of 'endogenous' (internal or intrinsic) and
'exogenous' (external or extrinsic, i.e., persecutory) factors in outbreaks
of violence involving deviant sects has been recently described by
scholars.[66] In this connection the FBI *Project Megiddo* report
distinguishes between 'defensive violence' and 'offensive violence'
perpetrated by 'cults'.[67] According to the FBI report, defensive violence,
epitomized by the Branch Davidians at Waco, 'is utilized by cults to
defend a compound or enclave that was created specifically to eliminate
most contact with the dominant culture'. In contrast, some 'cults with an
apocalyptic agenda … appear ready to *initiate* rather than *anticipate*
violent confrontations to bring about the Armageddon or fulfill
"prophecy" [and] present unique challenges to law enforcement
officials.' Somewhat similarly Robert Lifton sees certain groups such as
Aum Shinrikyô and the 'Manson Family' prepared to 'force the end' in
the sense of precipitating through sensational violence an anticipated
apocalyptic scenario.[68]

From the point of view we have developed in this article, the
distinction between endogenous and exogenous causes of violence in
religious or political movements may represent an artificial dichotomy.
In both Erikson's and Lifton's treatment of it, totalism vs. non-totalism
is a relative rather than an absolute distinction. All social groups are
totalistic to one degree or another, and thus, all religious or political
movements have both: 1) an endogenous potential for violent acting out
in relation to contrast groups onto which they project their disowned
negative qualities; 2) a tendency to increase their own totalism and
potential for violence as a response to totalistic persecution by outside
groups.

As we discussed above, in its original psychoanalytic usage
projective identification refers to an interaction between two people,
each reacting to the other, i.e. one who is doing the projecting and
another who is identifying with the motives or self-attributions that are
being projected. So described, projective identification has both
endogenous and exogenous dimensions, which can vary independently,
but which are never entirely separate from each other.

The endogenous variable in projective identification, that is the
tendency to project disowned attributes and motives, may vary
substantially from person to person, but is never entirely absent from

any person's defensive functioning. Similarly, the exogenous variable, the tendency to identify with and to act out other people's projections, also varies from person to person, but is never entirely absent from anyone's makeup.

In this article we have suggested that the projective identification concept may be generalized from a description of the interaction between individuals to a description of the interaction between groups. So extended it may help to explain Lifton's principle that totalism begets totalism, as well as the sociological process of deviance amplification. Assuming such to be the case, an accurate explanation of any specific occurrence of group violence must include assessment of both the degree of endogenous causation and the degree of exogenous causation. Some groups may be so highly totalistic that they are very vulnerable to the triggering effect (i.e., prone to identifying with and acting out) even very modest degrees of totalistic projection from the outside world. This may have occurred at Waco or Jonestown.

Other groups may be relatively non-totalistic, and thus highly resistant to identifying with unflattering projections from the outside. That is, they can resist identifying with even relatively extreme attributions of evil or pseudo-speciation and can continue to interact in a moderate manner even when they are being treated as the enemy to a relatively extreme degree. Nevertheless, given the interactive model we are proposing, even such a relatively non-totalistic group could be driven to become more totalistic, or even to some form of totalistic violence, given sufficient totalistic persecution from the outside.

In either case, it is highly inadvisable to use the power of the state to attempt to restrict totalistic belief.

NOTES

1. On 'cults' and the controversies surrounding them, see Benjamin Zablocki and Thomas Robbins (eds.), *Misunderstanding Cults: Searching for Objectivity in a Controversial Field* (Toronto: Toronto University, 2001) and Lorne Dawson, *Comprehending Cults: The Sociology of New Religious Movements* (Oxford: Oxford University Press, 1998).
2. James Richardson and Massimo Introvigne, ' "Brainwashing" Theories in European Parliamentary and Administrative Reports on Sects and Cults', *Journal for the Scientific Study of Religion* 40/2 (Summer 2001); Thomas Robbins, 'Combating "Cults" and "Brainwashing" in the United States and Western Europe', *Journal for the Scientific Study of Religion* 40/2 (Summer 2001).
3. Jean Francois Mayer, 'The Vain Hopes of the Tabachnik Trial', *La Liberté* (30 April 2001). Distributed by *The Family*. See also note 2.
4. Dick Anthony and Thomas Robbins, 'Religious Totalism, Violence and Exemplary Dualism', *Terrorism and Political Violence* 7/3 (1995), pp.1–30, Reprinted in Michael

Barkun (ed.), *Millennialism and Violence* (London: Frank Cass, 1996); Dick Anthony and Thomas Robbins, 'Religious Totalism, Exemplary Dualism and the Waco Tragedy', in Thomas Robbins and Susan Palmer (eds.), *Millennium, Messiahs, and Mayhem* (New York: Routledge, 1997), pp.261–84; Thomas Robbins, 'The Sources of Volatility in Religious Movements', forthcoming in David Bromley and J. Gordon Melton (eds.), *New Religions, Cults and Violence in Contemporary Society* (Cambridge: Cambridge University Press, in Press); Steven Barrie-Anthony and Dick Anthony, 'Be Careful in the Pursuit of Monsters: Anticult Brainwashing Theory as a Totalistic Ideology', in preparation; Dawson (note 1).

5. Robert Lifton, 'Cults, Religious Totalism and Civil Liberties', in Robert Lifton (ed.), *The Future of Immortality and Other Essays for a Nuclear Age* (New York: Basic Books, 1987), p.219.

6. Erik Erikson, 'Wholeness and Totality – A Psychiatric Contribution', in Carl F. Friederich (ed.), *Totalitarianism* (Cambridge, MA: Harvard University Press, 1954), pp.156–71. For a fuller discussion of Erikson's concept of totalism than will be provided here, see note 4, Anthony and Robbins, 'Religious Totalism, Violence and Exemplary Dualism'. See also below.

7. Erikson's totalism theory is a member of the general class of 'totalitarian influence' theories which describe the affinity between totalitarian ideologies and the personality makeup of individuals. The best known example of such a totalitarian influence theory is that of the 'authoritarian personality'. See Theodor W. Adorno, Else Frenkel-Brunswick, Daniel Sanford and R. Nevitt Sanford, *The Authoritarian Personality* (Boston: Norton, 1950). For a detailed discussion of the relation of Erikson's theory to other members of this class, see Dick Anthony, *Brainwashing and Totalitarian Influence: An Exploration of Admissibility Criteria for Testimony in Brainwashing Trials* (Ann Arbor, MI: UMI Dissertation Services, 1996).

8. Robert Lifton, *Chinese Thought Reform and the Psychology of Totalism* (New York: Norton, 1961), pp.419–38 (ch. 22).

9. Lifton (note 8), p.419.

10. Ibid., p.420.

11. Robert Lifton, 'Preface to the 1989 Edition' of *Chinese Thought Reform and the Psychology of Totalism* (Chapel Hill, NC: UNCU, 1989), p.vii.

12. Robert Lifton, *The Protean Self: Human Resilience in an Age of Fragmentation* (New York: Basic Books, 1993), p.16l. See also Charles Strozier, *Apocalypse: On the Psychology of Fundamentalism in America* (Boston: Beacon, 1984), pp.153–66.

13. Anthony and Robbins 'Religious Totalism, Exemplary Dualism and the Waco Tragedy' (note 4), p.419. The Report on *Doomsday Religious Movements* of the Canadian Security Intelligence Service notes that within the dualistic world views of some movements 'The world is fractured into two opposing camps of Good and Evil, which confers a profound significance on small social political conflicts as evidence of this great cosmic struggle, and which could precipitate a violent response'.

14. Bernard McGinn, *Antichrist: Two Thousand Years of Human Fascination with Evil* (San Francisco: Harper, 1994), p.32.

15. Anthony and Robbins 'Religious Totalism, Exemplary Dualism and the Waco Tragedy' (note 4), p.274.

16. Erikson (note 6), p.159.

17. For a discussion of the concept of 'splitting' as used in contemporary psychodynamic psychology see Manfield, *Split Self/Split Object: Understanding and Treating Borderline, Narcissistic and Schizoid Disorders* (London and Northvale, NJ: Aronson, 1992). For a discussion of intolerance of ambiguity as characteristic of authoritarian personalities see Adorno *et al.*, note 7. See also Else Frenkel-Brunswick, 'Intolerance of Ambiguity as an Emotional and Perceptual Personality Variable', *Journal of Personality* (1949), pp.xviii.

18. Erikson (note 6), p.160.

19. Erikson's use of the 'pseudospeciation' term is discussed extensively in L. Friedman,

Identity's Architect: A Biography of Erik H. Erikson (New York: Scribners, 1999), pp.54–5, 187, 352, 442–3.

20. Lifton (note 8), pp.433–5.

21. For a fuller discussion of the theme of individual predispositions to totalistic conversion in Lifton's early work, see Dick Anthony and Thomas Robbins, 'Brainwashing and Totalitarian Influence', in Howard Friedman (Editor in Chief), *Encyclopedia of Mental Health* (San Diego: Harcourt, Brace, Jovonovich, 1998). Reprinted from the *Encyclopedia of Human Behavior* (Academic Press, 1984). See also Anthony and Robbins 'Religious Totalism, Violence and Exemplary Dualism' (note 4).

22. S. Slipp, *The Technique and Practice of Object Relations Family Therapy* (Northvale, NJ and London: Jason Aronson, 1991), pp.86–7. Slipp reports extensive research on the roles of splitting and projective identification in causing dysfunctional family dynamics and related personality disorders. For other discussions of the interaction of splitting and projective identification as primitive defense mechanisms see T. Ogden, *The Primitive Edge of Experience* (Northvale, NJ and London: Jason Aronson, 1989), pp.19–30. See also S. Akhtar, *Broken Structures: Severe Personality Disorders and Their Treatment* (Northvale, NJ and London: Jason Aronson, 1992), pp.92–4.

23. Lifton (note 12), p.202.

24. See Roy Wallis and Steven Bruce, 'Sex, Violence and Religion', in Roy Wallis and Steven Bruce (eds.), *Sociological Theory, Religion, and Collective Action* (Belfast, UK: Queens University, 1987), pp.115–27. See also Frederick Bird, 'Charisma and Leadership in New Religious Movements', *Religion and the Social Order* 3A (1993), pp.75–92.

25. Len Oakes, *Prophetic Charisma: The Psychology of Revolutionary Personalities* (Syracuse, NY: Syracuse University, 1997). See Also Anthony Storrs, *Feet of Clay: Saints, Sinners, and Gurus* (New York: Free Press, 1996); and Robert Lifton, *Destroying the World to Save It: Aum Shinrikyo, Apocalyptic Violence and the New Global Terrorism* (New York: Henry Holt, 1999).

26. Interestingly the FBI's *Project Megiddo* report strongly plays up the importance of charismatic leaders and somewhat plays down ideology. 'The potential for violence on behalf of members (sic) of biblically-driven cults is determined almost exclusively by the whims of the cult leader … Cult members generally act to serve and please their leader rather than accomplish ideological objectives … The cult leader's prophecies, preachings, orders and objectives are subject to indiscriminate change.' This viewpoint has some cogency, but it is certainly overstated. It may be recalled that during the 1993 Waco siege an FBI official in a commanding field position reportedly referred to David Koresh's insistence on preaching to the agents as 'bible babble'. But charismatic prophets can be prisoners of ideological perspectives, and the latter can influence their and their followers' actions. On the other hand prophets such as David Koresh can have sudden revelations which can alter doctrine. According to the *Project Megiddo* report the premium should be on 'examination of the cult leader, his position of power over his followers, and an awareness of the responding behavior and activity of the cult', which is more important than attention to formal beliefs and group goals. However, the Canadian report on *Doomsday Religious Movements* notes that in a crisis intervention, 'negotiators dealing with the movement must understand its belief structure, as ignorance of the minor differences between the beliefs of respective groups can have drastic outcomes'.

27. Thomas Young, 'Cult Violence and the Identity Movement', *The Cultic Studies Journal* 7/2 (1990), pp.150–57.

28. Young (note 27), p.157. The author drew on an earlier important theoretical paper by Fred Wright and Phyllis Wright, 'The Charismatic Leader and the Violent Surrogate Family', *Annals of the New York Academy of Science* 347 (1980), pp.226–76. As a 'transitional' object and parental surrogate the totalist charismatic leader helps (sometimes troubled or alienated) young persons manage their hostilities. This can be therapeutic and/or dangerous depending upon the world view and aggressiveness of the

leader. A former German neo-Nazi leader remembers that he and his colleagues 'spent a lot of time indoctrinating beginners – not necessarily to make them more violent but to take the violence that was already in them and channel it in a politically useful manner'. Ingo Hasselbach and Tom Reiss, 'How Nazis Are Made', *The New Yorker* (8 Jan. 1996), pp.36–57.

29. This point is explored in more detail in Anthony and Robbins 'Religious Totalism, Violence and Exemplary Dualism' (note 4).

30. Catherine Wessinger, *How the Millennium Comes Violently* (New York: Seven Bridges Press, 2000). The Canadian *Doomsday Religious Movement* report highlights the 'early warning sign' of an apocalyptic movement being discomfited by the emergence of 'a humiliating circumstance running counter to their supposed glorious salvation before the onslaught of the apocalypse', as particularly seen in the Solar Temple violence. Volatility can be enhanced 'should a group be humiliated to the extent that either its leader or apocalyptic scenarios appears discredited'. The psychological dependency of devotees and leaders on their contrast symbols gives authorities unappreciated leverage 'over doomsday movements; which depend upon them to fulfill their apocalyptic scenarios. Failure to comprehend this symbolic role often results in actions that trigger violence.' See also Anthony and Robbins, 'Religious Totalism, Violence and Exemplary Dualism', and Anthony and Robbins, 'Religious Totalism, Exemplary Dualism and the Waco Tragedy' (note 4).

31. Lifton (note 25), pp.169–78.

32. Some reports concerning the violent Aum Shinrikyô sect in Japan have noted the decline of the movement's growth rate and the failure of the leader's political ambitions prior to the onset of major acts of collective violence. See Catherine Wessinger, *How the Millennium Comes Violently* (New York: Seven Bridges Press, 2000), pp.120–57. See also Ian Reader, *A Poisonous Cocktail: Aum Shinrikyo's Path to Violence* (Copenhagen: Nordic Institute of Asian Studies Book, 1996). Psychiatrist Marc Galanter has developed a social systems model of 'cults' or 'charismatic groups' in which curtailment of proselytization leads to a redirection of energy from goal attainment to internal control and surveillance with the result that negative feedback is suppressed and the group becomes increasingly defensive and sensitive to the threat of external intrusion and violation of the group's boundary. Marc Galanter, *Cults: Faith, Healing, and Coercion* (New York: Oxford University Press, 1989, 1999).

33. *Doomsday Religious Movements* warns against 'Hasty action' by authorities which 'can trigger violence on the part of the [millennialist] group by forcing it to act out its "endtimes" scenario, especially when its grandiose apocalyptic scenario appears discredited under humiliating circumstances.' A similar point has been made by two of the authors; see Anthony and Robbins: 'Religious Totalism, Violence and Exemplary Dualism' (note 4); and Anthony and Robbins 'Religious Totalism, Exemplary Dualism, and the Waco Tragedy'. (note 4).

34. Erikson (note 6). See also Anthony and Robbins 'Religious Totalism, Violence and Exemplary Dualism' (note 4).

35. Research by psychiatrist Marc Galanter has pointed to a 'relief effect' whereby significant mitigation of neurotic distress symptoms is experienced by recruits to totalistic movements such as the Unification Church. Galanter's research also indicates that approximately 30 per cent of such recruits have experienced serious distress shortly prior to joining the group. Recognizing that the powerful psychological forces for identity transformation which are mobilized by close-knit 'charismatic groups' can also have dangerous (e.g., violent) and pathological consequences, Galanter develops comparisons between cults and therapeutic support groups. See Galanter (note 32).

36. Saul V. Levine, *Radical Departures: Desperate Detours to Growing Up* (London: Harcourt, Brace, Jovanovich, 1984); see also Saul V. Levine 'Radical Departures', *Psychology Today* 18/8 (August 1984), pp.20–29.

37. Thomas Robbins, Dick Anthony, Thomas Curtis and Madalyn Doucas, 'The Last Civil Religion: The Unification Church of Reverend Sun Myung Moon', *Sociological*

Analysis 37/12 (1976), pp.111–23. There is a tradeoff here, e.g., we wouldn't applaud the creation of self-confident Nazis. On the other hand a student of one of the authors, who joined the Unification Church as a college undergraduate, developed journalistic and organizational skills working in the movement's divisions, and after leaving the Church became an executive in an important media enterprise.

38. Dr Lifton treats 'nuclearism' as a pathological mode of ideological totalism which was influential in the late-twentieth century 'Cold War' United States. Robert Lifton, *The Future of Immortality and Other Essays for a Nuclear Age* (New York: Basic Books, 1989).

39. This appears to be an implication of an interesting recent Canadian movie *White Lies*. A college student played by the young actress Sara Polley innocently questions a dictum of a liberal instructor, who stigmatizes her in class as a possible racist. Reacting against the unfair implication and the stifling milieu of political correctness, the student increasingly associates with seemingly iconoclastic, anti-conformist young persons who are really vicious 'White Power' racists. She is drawn into a violent neo-Nazi group from which she eventually defects.

40. A recent analysis of the worldwide surge of 'religious terrorism' identifies as a significant factor a reaction of young, pious males against sexual liberation and the related equality of women. Mark Jurgensmeyer, *Terror in the Mind of God: The Global Rise of Violence* (Berkeley, CA: University of California Press, 2000), pp.195–207.

41. Some sociologists have suggested that the surge of agitation against cults in Western Europe, although greatly intensified by the trauma of the Solar Temple murder-suicides, is also related to anxieties over national and cultural integration in a period of shifting ethno-demographic patterns, foreign in-migration, and the growth of Islam. Many religious movements which are viewed as problematic are also seen as 'alien' imports and 'religious multinationals' and thus make convenient scapegoats in a xenophobic or at least particularistic reaction against cultural globalization. See James Beckford, '"Cult" Controversies in Three European Countries', *Journal of Oriental Studies* 8 (1998), pp.174–84; Beckford, 'Religious Movements and Globalization', in Robin Cohen and Shirin Rai (eds.), *Global Social Movements* (London: Athlone Press, 2000), pp.166–83; Thomas Robbins, 'Alternative Religions, The State and The Globe', *Nova Religio* 4/2 (2001), pp.172–186; and Robbins (note 2).

42. This may be why, notwithstanding the significant phenomenon of (primarily evangelical) Christian anticultism or 'countercultism', the attack on cults so often seems to come from the left. For example, repressive legislation against minority religions accused of 'mental manipulation' was recently introduced in the French National Assembly by the Socialists. The legislation was passed although the mental manipulation term was removed. Other language in the final law arguably produces the same effect of criminalizing minority religious beliefs.

43. In *Chinese Thought Reform and the Psychology of Totalism* Lifton states:

> Such political inquisitions occur – as in thought reform – when ideological totalists set up their own theocratic search for heresy. One example of this variety of totalism in recent American history would be McCarthyism, a bizarre blend of political religion and extreme opportunism … And among those most actively engaged in the McCarthyist movement were many former Communists turned anti-Communist – all of which again seems to confirm (at varying levels of politics and individual emotion) THE PRINCIPLE THAT TOTALISM BREEDS TOTALISM.' Lifton (note 8), pp.457–8 (emphasis ours).

In a later publication he applies this principle to the tensions between the anticult movement and new religions. Lifton states 'Totalism begets totalism – and there can be notable totalism in so-called deprogramming. What is called deprogramming includes a continuum from intense dialogue on the one hand to physical coercion and kidnapping on the other … I am against coercion at either end of the cult process.' Lifton (note 5), p.219

A somewhat similar point has been made more fervently by Lee Coleman: 'New

Religions and "Deprogramming": Who's Brainwashing Whom?', in Thomas Robbins, William Shepherd and James McBride (eds.), *Cults, Culture and the Law* (Chico, CA: Scholars Press, 1985), pp.71–80. The tendency for totalistic attacks on movements to strengthen the internal totalism of targeted groups is illustrated by the effect of the fear of coercive deprogramming in the 1970s and early 1980s in increasing the suspicion felt by devotees toward outsiders. See Eileen Barker, *The Making of a Moonie: Choice or Brainwashing* (New York: Blackwell, 1984), p.64.

44. Richard Delgado, 'Religious Totalism: Gentle and Ungentle Persuasion Under the First Amendment', *So. California Law Review* 51 (1977), pp.1–99. Professor Delgado later backed off support of court ordered coercive deprogramming and shifted his focus to litigation by ex-members against the groups alleged to have psychologically imprisoned them. On the history of legal 'cult wars' in the United States, see Dick Anthony and Thomas Robbins, 'Negligence, Coercion and the Protection of Religious Belief', *Journal of Church and State* 37 (1995), pp.509–36.

45. The Unification Church indoctrination center in Booneville, N. California, was notorious for 'luring' targeted recruits without first informing them under whose auspices the camp was being run. Delgado seems to have extrapolated this operation into a general model of cult recruitment and conversion.

46. Dick Anthony and Thomas Robbins, 'Law, Social Science and the "Brainwashing" Amendment to the First Amendment', *Behavioral Science and the Law* 10/1 (Winter 1992), pp.1–30. For the senior author's recent strong critique of 'brainwashing' models with particular emphasis on legal testimony – which has been influential in continental Western Europe, where the climate seems currently more repressive than in the USA – see Dick Anthony, 'Pseudoscience and Minority Religions: An Evaluation of the Brainwashing Theories of Jean-Marie Abgrall', *Social Science Research* 12/4 (Dec. 1999), pp.421–56. For a variety of viewpoints on cult/brainwashing issues, see contributions by Dick Anthony, Lorne Dawson, Stephen Kent and Benjamin Zablocki in Benjamin Zablocki and Thomas Robbins (eds.), *Misunderstanding Cults: Searching for Objectivity in a Controversial Field* (note 1).

47. Congressman Richard Ottinger, 'Cults and Their Slaves', *Congressional Record* (1980), E3578–3579. Cong. Ottinger proposed a National Conservatorship law through which parents could forcibly remove adult children from totalist movements.

48. Barrie-Anthony and Anthony (note 4). See also Eileen Barker's discussion of dehumanization in 'the construction of "otherness"' in cult conflicts'. Eileen Barker, 'Watching for Violence: A Comparative Analysis of Five Cult-Watching Groups', in David Bromley and Gordon Melton (eds.), *New Religions, Cults and Violence in Contemporary Society* (Cambridge: Cambridge University Press, 2002).

49. In a pluralistic society with a multicultural ethos it is difficult to degrade persons by reference to either their innate characteristics such as race or their religious beliefs. However the issue of personal autonomy/heteronomy provides a basis for stigmatization and control. Non-autonomous persons can be held subject to special controls, and rights and freedoms can be viewed as presupposing autonomy. On the focus upon autonomy as the key value motif in modern society see Richard Sennett, *Autonomy* (New York: Random House, 1981). See also James Beckford, *Cult Controversies* (London: Tavistock, 1985).

50. Richard Delgado refers to cultists as 'cheerful robots' who aren't aware of their actual enslavement and degradation. Richard Delgado, 'Religious Totalism as Slavery', *New York Review of Law and Social Change* 4/1 (1979–80), pp.51–68. The models of brainwashing employed by crusaders against 'cults' have been related by Dick Anthony and Thomas Robbins to the early anti-communist rhetoric of Edward Hunter, a CIA publicist, who referred to Maoist brainwashing as creating 'robots' and 'puppets'. See Edward Hunter, *Brainwashing In Red China* (New York: Vanguard, 1951) and *Brainwashing: From Pavlov to Powers* (New York: The Bookmaster, 1961). Anthony and Robbins have contrasted this 'robot' brainwashing model with the 'totalitarian influence' models exemplified by Robert Lifton and Edgar Schein. See also Anthony

and Robbins (note 21).

51. Philip Jenkins, *Mystics and Messiahs: Cults and New Religions in American History* (New York: Oxford University Press, 2000), p.197.

52. John Young and Ezra Griffith, 'A Critical Evaluation of Coercive Persuasion as Used in the Assessment of Cults', *Behavioral Science and the Law* 10/1 (1992), pp.89–101.

53. See note 3.

54. Lifton (note 25), pp.329–30.

55. Thomas Robbins, 'Balance and Fairness Toward Alternative Religions', in Benjamin Zablocki and Thomas Robbins (eds.), *Misunderstanding Cults: Searching For Objectivity In A Controversial Field* (note 1).

56. Anthony and Robbins suggest that at the Waco siege 'federal agents were also thinking and acting in a dualistic and apocalyptic mode such that extreme inflexibility and machiavellian subtlety [were] attributed to a stressed sect leader, who was actually vacillating and confused'. Anthony and Robbins 'Religious Totalism, Exemplary Dualism and the Waco Tragedy' (note 4), p.282. In his theoretical treatise on the rhetoric of apocalypticism, Stephen O'Leary comments that at Waco, 'In the end the government's agents were probably motivated by the same sense of ending that governs the logic of apocalyptic drama: the need to control the script by seizing the initiative and seeking some form of narrative closure.' Stephen O'Leary, *Arguing the Apocalypse* (New York: Oxford University Press, 1994), p.228. Movement totalism and anti-movement totalism interact explosively and, reinforcing each other, contribute through deviance amplification to a catastrophe such as the tragedy at Waco.

57. Anti-cult activists and 'experts' often testify to alleged cultic brainwashing on behalf of ex-devotee plaintiffs in civil suits against the movements which have allegedly enslaved them. See Anthony and Robbins (note 44). Other 'experts' testify for the defense upon the alleged scientific flaws of the cultic brainwashing theory upon which the legal action is based. (Dick Anthony is the scholar who has most often performed this role.)

58. Richardson and Introvigne (note 2). See also 'French Senate Passes Anti-Sect Law With Amendments', Human Rights Without Frontiers News Brief, see www.hrwf.net (5/17/01). The new legislation criminalizes mind control or the use of techniques that 'aim at altering the capacity or judgment' to create a 'state of subjection' (physical or psychological). Offenders can be imprisoned for five years and heavily fined. Religious organizations can be dissolved. For detailed coverage of recent (late 1990s through 2000) legal and church-state vicissitudes involving alternative religions or 'cults', see: James Richardson (ed.), 'Justice and New Religious Movements', special issue of *Social Justice Research* 12/4 (Dec. 1999); Pauline Coté (ed.), *Frontier Religions in Public Space* (Ottawa: Oxford University Press, 2001); 'Symposium: New Religions in Their Political, Legal and Religious Contexts Around the World', *Nova Religio* 4/2 (Spring 2001).

59. See note 6.

60. The section of the *Project Megiddo* report on 'Apocalyptic Cults' has three citations to a work co-authored by Dr Margaret Singer, a psychologist and an influential theorist of cult/brainwashing dynamics, Margaret Singer and Janja Lalich, *Cults in Our Midst: The Hidden Menace in Our Everyday Lives* (San Francisco: Jossey-Bass, 1995). Another cited work emphasizes how the isolation of members in a totalistic cult undermines the capacity for critical thought. Kevin Gilmartin, 'The Lethal Triad: Understanding the Nature of Isolated Extremist Groups', accessed at www.leo.gov/tlib/leb1996/sept96/text (sic). In partial contrast the editors of the Canadian report on *Doomsday Religious Movements* appear to have been less influenced by clinicians and 'cult experts' and more open to the somewhat different views of sociologists of religion and students of millenarian movements. However, this is not an absolute contrast, and the Canadian report and the 'cult' section of the *Project Megiddo* report manifest some conceptual and analytical overlay, particularly involving nuances of apocalyptic beliefs.

61. Jenkins (note 51), p.222.

62. Hall *et al.* argue that anti-cult activists and officials influenced by them conceptualized

the problem posed by the Branch Davidians in terms of a mass suicide stereotype arising from the prior Jonestown catastrophe and were therefore led to take forceful actions which helped provoke the holocaust they feared, i.e., the 'dynamic entry' which federal agents planned at Waco was intended to transpire so rapidly as to forestall the emergence of mass suicide during a lengthy siege. Mass suicide and the threat of 'another Jonestown' became a 'narrative of law enforcement' which ultimately helped create the Waco debacle. John Hall, Philip Schuyler and Salvaine Trinh, *Apocalypse Observed: Religious Movements and Violence in N. America, Europe and Japan* (New York: Routledge, 2000), pp.44–67.

63. Hall (note 62). See also James Richardson, 'Minority Religions and the Context of Violence: A Conflict/Interactionist Perspective', *Terrorism and Political Violence* 13/1 (Spring 2001), pp.103–33.

64. What is being described here is what sociologists have termed the *deviance amplification* process which entails a model of spiraling escalation between a deviant religious or cultural minority and alarmed public authorities. Both parties become enmeshed in mutual interpretive feedback loops which mediate concurrent increases in both sectarian alienation and official control. Neither party may thus be exclusively responsible for a culminating violent catastrophe. Although initially developed by British experts in crime and deviance, the classic application to cult/state conflicts is Roy Wallis' discussion of conflicts involving the Scientology movement in the United Kingdom and Australia. See Roy Wallis, *The Road to Total Freedom: A Sociological Analysis of Scientology* (New York: Columbia University, 1977). A much more recent application has been made to Christian Identity paramilitarists; see Michael Barkun, 'Millenarians and Violence: The Case of the Christian Identity Movement', in Thomas Robbins and Susan Palmer (eds.), *Millennialism, Messiahs, and Mayhem* (New York: Routledge 1997), pp.247–60. Thomas Robbins has made a somewhat cryptic application to huge, incendiary mass suicides in early modern Russia among the Old Believers. Thomas Robbins, 'Apocalypse, Persecution and Self-Immolation', in Catherine Wessinger (ed.), *Millennialism, Persecution and Violence* (Syracuse, NY: Syracuse University Press, 2000), pp.205–19. See also Thomas Robbins, 'Religious Mass Suicide Before Jonestown: The Russian Old Believers', *Sociological Analysis* 41/1 (1986), pp.1–20. Finally, see Barker (note 48). The Canadian report includes *Millennium, Messiahs, and Mayhem* (note 4) in its bibliography and may have been influenced by the contribution by Michael Barkun dealing with deviance amplification and Christian Identity and the Anthony–Robbins chapter on exemplary dualism and Waco.

65. James Richardson, 'Minority Religions and The Context of Violence: A Conflict/Interactionist Perspective', *Terrorism and Political Violence* 13/1 (Spring 2001), pp.103–33. Richardson cites and discusses the conflict interaction perspective on violence by Sandra Ball-Rokeach, 'Normative and Deviant Violence from a Conflict Perspective', *Social Problems* 28/1 (1980), pp.45–62. In the note attached to the passage we've quoted in our text, Richardson cites the 'fine discussion of such interactions' in Michael Barkun, 'Millennial Violence in Contemporary America', in Catherine Wessinger, *Millennialism, Persecution, & Violence; Historical Cases* (Syracuse, NY: Syracuse University Press, 2000), pp.352–63; and Barkun (note 64), pp.247–60.

66. As noted above, the most complete and even-handed analysis of endogenous vs. exogenous factors in violence involving new religions is Richardson's article (note 65). For recent discussions of a debate concerning the relative salience of such factors, see Thomas Robbins, ' "Quo Vadis": The Scientific Study of New Religious Movements', *Journal for the Scientific Study of Religion* 39/4 (Dece. 2000), pp.515–23; and Robbins, 'Sources of Volatility in Religious Movements' (note 4). In fact the relative weight of internal or external inputs to millennialist mayhem appears to differ markedly from fiasco to fiasco, as does the role of the state. Action by the state was probably hasty and provocative toward the defensive Davidians at Waco in 1993, but tardy and belated in Japan with respect to the escalating criminality of Aum Shinrikyô in 1995, i.e., less

aggressive officials might have saved lives in Texas while more aggressive officials might have saved lives in Japan. Thomas Robbins, 'Religious Movements and Violence', *Nova Religio* 1/1 (1997), pp.13–29. This contrast is related to the emergence of partly competing 'post-Waco' and 'post-Aum' modes of scholarly reaction and recrimination. This has been noted by Ian Reader, ' "Scholarship," Aum Shinrikyo and Academic Integrity', *Nova Religio* 3/2 (2000), pp.368–82.

67. In this connection *Project Megiddo* cites the work of Jeffrey Kaplan, who distinguished between *defensive, revolutionary* (offensive) and *rhetorical* violence in the Christian Identity subculture (rhetorical violence predominated). See Jeffrey Kaplan, *Radical Religion in America: Millenarian Movements from the Far Right to the Children of Noah* (Syracuse, NY: Syracuse University Press, 1997).

68. Lifton (note 25), pp.59–88, 270–340. Charles Manson's 'Family' actually 'committed at least ten murders and probably many more as part of a project that was meant to destroy the "bourgeois" world and bring about Armageddon' (p 274). Lifton also compares homicidal Aum Shinrikyô and the suicidal Heaven's Gate group (pp.306–27) and appears to interpret the ideology of the latter group as a dualist–totalist world view in which 'Luciferians' or demonic space aliens/fallen angels/world conspirators represent the exemplars of ultimate evil (p.314). The Peoples Temple is also discussed in terms of a lethal apocalyptic totalism led by an unhinged prophet (pp.281–302). However, the Branch Davidians, 'an armed but not violent small apocalyptic religious sect', are treated as primarily victims of the FBI's 'tragically ill-advised assault after a long siege in Waco, Texas in 1993' (p.329). They are exempted from the rogues' gallery of violent movements which aim to 'force the End'.

THE MEDIEVAL CONTEXT

11

What Happens when Jesus Doesn't Come: Jewish and Christian Relations in Apocalyptic Time

RICHARD LANDES

The First Massacres of Jews in Northern Europe

France, winter, AD 1010. The news arrives that the Muslim Caliph al-Hakim has destroyed the Holy Sepulcher in Jerusalem. The news astonishes and dismays. The pope circulates an encyclical calling for an armed force to go to Jerusalem. Rumors spread rapidly alleging that the Jews provoked the action, sending secret messages to the caliph urging him to destroy this central shrine of Christianity. In a number of places – Limoges, Normandy, Mainz, even, according to one chronicler, all of Christendom – the Jews are given an ultimatum: convert or die. Their refusal brings on the first case of massacres of Jews in Western Europe. It stands as harbinger of worse times to come in the course of a long and painful millennium for the Jews in Europe, from the crusading slaughters at the end of the eleventh century to the Nazi genocide of the mid-twentieth century.

Why the Latin Christians? Why, specifically, the Western Franks? The question focuses our attention on a particularly revealing irony: the worst violence apparently came precisely where Jews and Christians showed the most signs of cultural cooperation and creativity – what is today France and western Germany. This area between two of the flashpoints of anti-Jewish violence, Limoges (1010) and Mainz (1012), marks the very birthplace of both Ashkenazic Jewry and 'modern' Latin Christendom. Arguably these two cultures, among the most vigorous expressions of Judaism and Christianity in the millennia-long history of both those religions, were co-emerging together, marking the origins of modernity.

Nor was the violence foreseeable on the basis of past experience. Previously Latin Christianity in Europe had not seen violence between Jews and Christians exceed the norms of rival societies in cultures of judicial 'self-help' (i.e., vendetta and revenge). Why did this explosion of sacred violence spring up suddenly at this time, creating a permanent feature of modernity – violent anti-Judaism? What relationship between modernizing trends and Jewish–Christian relations might the modern social analyst discern from a better understanding of this event?

Before answering these questions, let me warn the reader. The following reconstruction and analysis of 1010 represents a mixture of a very close study of the sources,[1] and of conjectures that many professional historians consider imprudent. In particular I differ from most medievalists who think that apocalyptic beliefs at this time were few and insignificant.[2] On the contrary, basing myself on a body of strong but inconclusive evidence, I use as a working hypothesis the principle that 1000 represented the long-awaited date at which Christians believed that Christ would return and resolve the terrible problem of why the evil flourished and the just suffered. The traces of evidence for the belief are strongest in England, Germany and France;[3] and I find it much more revealing to understand the welter of unusual events of the day like this outburst of anti-Jewish violence, as the product of people acting in apocalyptic time. This widespread public belief in the approaching 'End of Days' reached a first climax at the approach of the year 1000 and then, after that passed, perhaps more intensely, at the millennium of the Passion in 1033. Hence I look for and use the insights of social observers working on contemporary groups who operate in apocalyptic time to try and understand the events of those days.

More cautious historians use a working hypothesis that holds that people neither knew nor cared about the date; that evidence of apocalyptic beliefs is too inconclusive to permit sweeping characterizations about widespread beliefs.[4] This reluctance to conjecture – even as a working hypothesis[5] – reflects a more general feeling that one cannot read so distant a past in terms of the present. I think that current developments not only shed important light on this past, but that, properly understood, this past sheds important light on our present. In particular, the insights of scholars working on the social dimensions of current apocalyptic dynamics can help illuminate developments at the millennial cusp of 1000 in ways that medievalists cannot, with their traditional techniques, detect.[6] Moreover, armed with such insights about this past, we can then return and draw some important lessons about the year 2000.

The Two Strains of Millennialism in Christianity and their Manifestations Around 1000

The study of Christian millennialism (the coming ideal world) reveals that it has two major millennial visions – egalitarian and hierarchical – and two major apocalyptic (transitional) scenarios – transformative and catastrophic. The transformative apocalypse most often leads to an egalitarian millennium, as in the vision of Micah (4: 1–4)/Isaiah (2:1–3). Here the 'end of days' anticipates a dramatic, mass 'turning' to the ways of God all over the world, and culminates with the nations turning their 'swords into plowshares and spears into pruning hooks'; that is, the disarmament of the aristocracy. The millennial kingdom it anticipates involves a new socio-political paradigm: one where peace, fellowship, justice and abundance reign. 'And each shall sit under his vine or his fig tree, undisturbed' (Micah 4:3) – the end of aristocracy, the fellowship of honest labor. This brand of millennialism tends to emphasize an activist moral eschatology – you are saved by, and the messianic age comes through, moral excellence. Modern Christian theologians have called this activist kind of expectation *post-millennialism* – i.e., Jesus comes *after* the millennium has been established by divinely inspired (moral) humans.

The cataclysmic apocalyptic strain believes that before this millennial realm of peace, this 'thousand-year kingdom', can come, the evil that so pervades this world must be utterly destroyed, and that only after cosmic devastation would the 'millennial kingdom' come about. This, theologians (misleadingly) call *pre-millennialism* – i.e. Jesus comes *before* the millennium (but really *after* catastrophic destruction on a cosmic scale), and fashions the millennial kingdom himself. This latter apocalyptic scenario encourages visions of worldwide conspiracies led by the ultimate cosmic villain, the Antichrist, who only meets defeat at the hands of an angelic host in apocalyptic wars where blood flows in rivers. This brand of millennialism emphasizes passive, credal eschatologies – only God's chosen remnant will be saved because they believed in him, while the end time brings on warfare against the identifiable enemies of the Lord, the infidels. It also tends to couple with visions of a millennial kingdom ruled over by an all-powerful conqueror, a supremely harmonious hierarchical court modeled on that of heaven.

Generally, the only time we can actually observe millennial *behavior* (as opposed to beliefs)[7] is when believers become apocalyptic. Then they openly espouse their views and become (hyper)active. This periodic *'apocalyptic* time', unlike the normal and normative time that precedes and follows it, is highly dynamic, indeed volatile. In such moments of intensity, various millennial beliefs and apocalyptic expectations mingle, shift and mutate, producing a kind of apocalyptic jazz to sustain the powerful sense of imminence that propels these believers forward. Apocalyptic millennialists shift rapidly from passive to active modes, from pacific to belligerent and back again. And of course, in the still-rarer cases where millennial movements gain power and begin to 'inaugurate' the millennium, they shift from egalitarian to hierarchical and (less often) back again.

Most clerics in normal time (i.e., the time of writing and documentation) preferred a catastrophic version of Christ's return and a celestial kingdom – a theology first hammered out by Augustine and formally taught in Latin Christian schools from the fifth to the eleventh centuries. The 'end of time' and Christ's return would occur at an unknowable moment in the future,[8] and would bring with it the apocalyptic catastrophes of the Antichrist, at last released from his pit at the end of the 1,000 years. Believers in this scenario differed on what would happen after this cataclysmic convulsion. According to Augustine and most well-trained clerics, this final defeat of Antichrist would take place *after* the completion of the ecclesiastical millennium (i.e., there was no genuinely peaceful millennium on earth), and would inaugurate the Last Judgment, sending the good to heaven and the bad to hell. Others embraced the more subversive expectation that Antichrist's defeat would bring the advent *here on earth* of the millennial kingdom.

At the core of all the current apocalyptic expectations in the early Middle Ages (500–1050), millennial or not, stood the Antichrist, whose advent would set in motion the final events.[9] Despite having virtually no place in the New Testament, the Antichrist had a lurid mythical role in Christianity, elaborated from the cosmic villains of Revelation (12–18) conflated with those of Daniel (7–12), the most important apocalyptic texts in the Christian canon. Early Christians looked to persecuting

Roman emperors (Nero, perhaps, first) as their earliest candidates for Antichrist. But within less than two centuries, the apocalyptic scenario had shifted, and the Antichrist had become a Jew, born of the tribe of Dan, a pseudo-messiah who would convert everyone to Judaism. Both strains of Antichrist speculation continued to hold sway, although the clerical leadership, especially after the 'conversion' of Rome to Christianity and therefore the approval of imperial power, preferred the Jewish Antichrist.

The fantastic elaboration of the tradition seems to have played well in both clerical and lay circles. Among dissidents, the identification of the Antichrist as current figure served to spark apocalyptic expectations of the 'End'. Among clerics in normal time, it seems largely to have played an *anti*-apocalyptic role, seeking to discourage anyone from *wanting* to live in the time of the final events. Given the Antichrist's power, most believers would do better to die before his arrival and sleep till Judgment Day than to endure the Antichrist's trials and temptations, (almost surely) falling prey to his damning seductions. Linking these terrifying accounts to a passage in one of Paul's letters (II Thess. 2:3), which spoke of the existence of an 'obstacle' to the Antichrist's advent, theologians argued that the continuation of the Roman Empire (and, after the fifth century, its successor kingdoms), kept the Antichrist at bay.

In the meantime, as the clerical Augustinians insisted, before the unknowable end, the faithful must live with this gray, even somber universe. The humble Christian must, therefore, tolerate evil whether it comes from unjust rulers and ruthless people who abuse their power, or infidels, i.e., heretics, Jews and scoffers. Especially, Christians must tolerate the rulers who, by assuring order by any means no matter how unjust, hold back the horrifying final offensive of the Antichrist. This non-apocalyptic stance served the temporal concerns of the post-Constantinian church well. Until the final events, the church had a valid excuse for supporting rulers who obviously did not live up to even the minimal standards of Christian ethics, much less 'turn the other cheek'. Thus the (pre-millennial) cataclysmic tradition operated as a counterpoint to the (post-millennial) transformative one. Those not so eager to see the advent of the millennium with its reversal of power relations between the powerful and the weak, tended to emphasize the terrors of the Antichrist's coming. Those longing for the millennium preferred to believe that the worst had already happened and the next great event would see the inauguration of a great and just kingdom.

While we can document the clerical Antichrist tradition in some detail, we have more trouble following the egalitarian ('post-millennial') strain, the one anticipating the creation of the millennial kingdom through a great transformation of the hearts of people. We might call it either the Jubilaic strain of millennialism, or the commoner's millennium. It foresees a great moment of liberation, of social egalitarianism, of sharing – the millennium where the swords of the rapacious aristocracy are beaten into the tools of honest labor. This belief views the catastrophes at the onset of the Apocalypse as calls to repentance, calls to live *as if* the millennial kingdom of peace and fellowship had already come, calls to greet the bridegroom in joy. Although such beliefs are quite evident in the origins of Christianity – Jesus' career and the 'sermon on the Mount' are classics of such millennial ethics – their disconcerting anti-authoritarianism and increasingly anti-Roman vituperation rapidly made them unwelcome in the Church. Churchmen accommodating themselves to the repeated failure of prophecy to predict Jesus' return, and to the demands of living in the Roman Empire, found it advisable to expel these ideas as foolish and dangerous ravings.

By Augustine's day (early fifth century), therefore, millennialism – the expectation that God's rewards at the end of days would be in *this world* and that mankind might play a role in its advent (transformative apocalyptic and egalitarian (post-)millennialism) – had been banned from formal Christian theology. In the period from Augustine's day until that of the *Pax Dei* (late tenth century), when documents describe an openly millennial movement – i.e., the product of this banned theology – they depict dangerous popular movements that need to be suppressed. Ironically these churchmen seem moved by the same conservative and aristocratic impulses that had driven the Romans to eliminate Jesus and many other Jewish millennialists in the first century. As a result of this hostility, we can only find traces of the existence of popular millennialism in the documentation of the clerical elite. On the other hand, those traces that do survive indicate a vigorous and perduring presence of millennial hope and recurring enthusiasm among the populace throughout the first Christian millennium.

Christian Apocalyptic Expectations Around the Turn of the First Millennium

At the end of the tenth century in Western Europe, for a wide variety of reasons, but especially because of the eschatological significance of the year 1000, it seems as if virtually every Christian tradition reached apocalyptic intensity – both the hierarchical and cataclysmic (pre-millennial) of the clerics and the egalitarian and transformative (post-millennial) of the populace. The very breadth and intensity of this apocalyptic expectation produced an extraordinary and unprecedented array of popular millennial behavior.[10] Some of this activity took traditional, if greatly intensified forms – pilgrimage, public penitential processions, and missionary drives to convert non-believers; radical religious behavior that in some cases provoked accusations of heresy from more conservative churchmen. But the period also saw one of the most exceptional expressions of millennialism ever – the first recorded case of a mass religious peace movement, known to contemporaries as the 'Peace of God'. A wave of peace assemblies of thousands of participants swept through parts of southern France in the 990s, especially through Aquitaine and Burgundy. This represents the first recorded case of a popular, transformative millennial movement that received the approval and encouragement of the elite. And it occurred precisely in the Frankish kingdom, the place where we get the most detailed reports of the anti-Jewish outbreaks of 1010.

The peace assemblies first occurred in response to local or regional catastrophes – famines, plagues, outbreaks of the 'holy fire' (psychedelic ergot poisoning), political disorders provoked by the appearance of a new class of dominators, the castellans and their mounted warriors. The high aristocracy, threatened by this newly powerful class of lesser aristocrats, brought together large numbers of relics in open fields – an unprecedented move – that attracted huge assemblies of people of all classes and ages, of both sexes, many of whom were direct victims of these takeovers by protection rackets. Here, in a revivalist atmosphere filled with miracles and music and dancing, encouraged especially by the monks of the new reforming houses such as Cluny, we find the warriors of the society compelled to take oaths before the religiously aroused populace. With these oaths, the weapons bearers – the *potentes* – renounced the right to use violence against unarmed people, protecting peasants, priests, pilgrims, women, travelers. In the most extreme cases, they may even have engaged in emotionally charged sessions of mutual forgiveness and renounced the right to 'self-help' justice (i.e., vendetta).[11]

We might call this an anti-terrorist oath; and we can readily identify places in today's world (Middle East, Africa, Southern Asia, the Balkans) where such an oath would be as welcome to the inhabitants of the land as it apparently was to the inhabitants of Gaul and France at the time. And some of the more candid accounts of the behavior of the Frankish aristocracy in the post-Carolingian era suggest that they unabashedly slaughtered commoners with the temerity to act autonomously. When we realize the enormous difficulty of extracting an anti-terrorist oath, even in an age where international pressure opposes those who massacre the unarmed, one must wonder how it came about at a time where 'military might' always made political 'right'.[12] After all, the moments in world history when elites have voluntarily renounced privileges, and especially the right to use violence, are extremely rare. Normally only a powerful monarch could hope to rein in the domineering tendencies of warrior aristocracies.[13] With France 'ruled' by one of its weakest kings, the second of a new and still questionably legitimate dynasty, one can imagine only with difficulty what drove these warriors to take such public oaths.[14] It surely did not come easily.

Jules Michelet has offered the only serious explanation when he spoke of terrors and catastrophes of the day:

> These excessive miseries broke their hearts and brought out a measure of pity. They sheathed their swords, trembling themselves before the sword of the Lord ... they gathered voluntarily before the bishops, agreeing to respect the churches, no longer to plague the highways with their robberies. It was called the *Peace of God*.[15]

In other words, the warriors who took the oath genuinely feared the Day of Judgment, and the peace movement, in its initial stages, was a product of apocalyptic fears (warriors, *potentes*) and millennial hopes (commoners, *impotentes*).

This may strike the modern reader as rather silly. After all we have spent the last thousand years of our high culture weaning ourselves from such powerful yet consistently erroneous beliefs, and who would seem less likely to take Christian pacifism seriously than a warrior elite? But we must remember that the clerical elite of this culture believed in and taught an eschatological universe in which *at some point* God's judgment would become manifest, and warriors are notoriously superstitious.[16] In the early fifth century the bishop of Constantinople, John Chrysostom, described the (temporary) reaction of the powerful to an apocalyptic earthquake in the following manner:

> Did you see how fragile and broken is the human race: when the earthquake happened, I wonder: Where now is rapine? where cheating? where unjust rule? where luxury? where dominion? where oppression? where the ravagers of the powerless? where the proud arrogance of the rich? Where the rule of princes, where the threats, where the intimidated?[17]

They did not have a scientific theory that debunked such beliefs; nor did their historiography emphasize how often in the past such beliefs had failed humiliatingly. On the contrary, their historiography told them that the final age was at hand, perhaps precisely in the year 1000; and their eschatology, however cautious it might be about the timing of the End under normal circumstances, tended to become torridly apocalyptic at times of major crisis. These apocalyptic episodes were especially strong when they corresponded with 'big dates', of which the end of the millennium was the most widespread and closely watched.[18]

Certainly clergy often used the threat of the terrible punishments of Judgment Day as a means to rein in the violence of the laity.[19] At the approach of the millennial year, with the middling aristocracy in an uncontrolled battle for dominion at the local level, they would find such apocalyptic rhetoric at once desperately needed and particularly powerful. And one can imagine no better site for the deployment of such 'chastizing' apocalyptic rhetoric[20] than the peace assemblies, where the presence of the wonder-working saints and vast throngs of enthusiastic believers brought enormous psychological weight to bear on these warriors. Elites rarely permit large, unstructured gatherings of commoners; still more rarely do they encourage them in situations which amplify their collective strength and give them a voice in public affairs.[21] Only retrospective vision (which historians have in abundance) could trivialize such exceptional behavior.

In corresponding fashion, the commoners who attended these assemblies read them as the fulfillment of the millennial prophecies. Speaking of a particularly powerful early peace council, one monk noted that at last 'swords were beaten into plowshares and spears into pruning hooks'.[22] And the belief apparently went beyond the (unwonted) exaggeration of an enthusiastic monk. A still more candid source tells us that the populace saw the wave of peace assemblies that came at the advent of the millennium of the Passion (1033), as a covenant, the dawn of the new age, the final establishment of God's peace on earth.

> At the sight of these miracles, all those assembled raised their palms skyward and shouted 'Peace! Peace! Peace!' This was the sign of their marriage to God in a perpetual covenant. It was understood that after five years all should repeat this wonderful celebration in order to confirm the peace. In that same year there was such a plentiful abundance of corn and wine and other foods that the like could not be hoped for in the following years. All food was cheap except meat and rare spices: truly it was like the great Mosaic jubilee of ancient times. For the following three years food was no less plentiful.[23]

At their height then, in the decade before the millennium of the Incarnation (1000), and again in the decade approaching the millennium of the Passion (1033), peace assemblies could sustain for years at a time a concrete, society-wide sense of having entered a new age. And, in a development filled with importance for Jewish–Christian relations, for the first time in history an entire Christian people – lay as well as clergy, commoners as well as elite – felt themselves to be the new Israel. The millennial *Pax Dei* of 1033 may have played a similar role for the *Francia* of the day that the covenant on Sinai played for the children of Israel.

And yet, the Peace movement has only received serious attention from a handful of scholars. Most medieval historians, encountering its bizarre expectations that voluntary oaths would in fact lead the aristocracy to lay aside their weapons and their accustomed belligerence in dealing with commoners, have dismissed it as a *curiosum*, a predictable failure. In their work, it appears as a footnote to more substantive efforts to assure the peace that came later – the communes and the king's peace.[24] But students of millennialism know well how often such outlandish and unrealistic hopes produce significant results. In studies of apocalyptic believers, the first rule states: 'wrong does not mean inconsequential'. It is precisely in terms of the Peace as a society-wide millennial movement which, for over a generation (990s through the 1030s) had enormous credibility at all levels of the culture, that I wish to examine the issue of Christian–Jewish relations in 1009.

The Peace, the Jews, and the New Chosen People at the Turn of the Millennium

Although we have little or no direct evidence to confirm such a conclusion, it seems reasonable to conjecture that this movement had a significant impact on Christian relations with the Jews of the regions where it occurred. Jews were, in those days, weapons bearers, and any social contract that involved traders and travel would obviously influence, if not include, the Jews. Our sources do not inform us of this connection directly, although the broader, indirect evidence suggests exceptional cultural contact – economic, social, intellectual – between Jews and Christians during the next centuries.[25] Jews were probably not present at the relic-filled assemblies (unless summoned), but the pact, often administered after the councils to those not there, would obviously suit the Jews. Were they involved? We have indirect evidence including a conciliar decree: *On not kissing Jews.* The kiss involved here, I suspect, was the *kiss of peace*, the sealing of a compact of peace.[26]

Nor was the link between Jews and Christians merely pragmatic. This Jubilaic Christian tradition corresponds closely to that of the Jewish millennial tradition, and historically speaking, some millennial Christians, as they become more apocalyptic, tend to become more philo-Judaic, adopting Jewish beliefs and practices and enthusiastically seeking out Jewish contacts. Indeed, from the patristic period on, millennialism was often denounced as 'Judaizing' by clerics who liked neither Jews nor millennialism, and the ecclesiastical shift from portraying the Antichrist as a tyrannous ruler to a messianic Jew aimed at neutralizing precisely this tendency. Thus, with an outbreak of transformative egalitarian millennialism on the scale of the Peace movement, we can imagine a fairly enthusiastic encounter between Christians who believed they were putting war behind them and Jews who thought that they were finally dealing with gentiles who respected justice and peace. For these 'post-millennial' Christians, giving Jews the kiss of peace was part of living in the millennial kingdom.

The Peace may indeed mark the beginning of 'post-millennial' trends within Christianity. It certainly marks the first time on any significant scale that the elite encouraged Jubilaic millennial behavior rather than repressing it. And it constitutes a sea-change to a more activist vision of humanity's role in bringing on the millennium, the beginning of a trend towards the 'post-millennialism' that has increasingly marked the last ten centuries.[27] Such Jubilaic millennial activity uniting elites and commoners stimulated popular activity at all levels. This was quite understandable. These people believed that they lived in that great generation that brings on the millennium through its own 'turning' to 'walk in the ways of the Lord'. And part of what made that empowerment work was the willingness of at least some of the elites to accept and encourage, and cooperate with, these popular initiatives. These were times of abundance, but also times of abundant change.

The Peace movement obviously had its enemies, of which the first was time. Since God had demonstrated over the previous 3,000 years an infuriating reluctance to show up according to the prophetic promises and apocalyptic calculations of humans, we inhabitants of Y2K know – although they surely could not – that Y1K was not the millennium, not the Last Judgment, Apocalypse *not* now. Writing with the hindsight of a decade (*c*.1044–45), Rodulfus Glaber admitted the failure of the councils that had peaked at the millennium of the Passion. (Augustine predicted it. Man is fallen and cannot live justly; the millennium cannot happen in this world.) With rare candor for a monastic historian, Glaber names the culprits: the aristocracy, lay and clerical, who, like dogs returning to their vomit, reneged on their oaths and returned to their plundering ways. The middling people followed, and the covenant was broken.[28] Little remained of the enthusiastic resolve that had, at the edge of Apocalypse, led the warriors to circumscribe their violence.

Put another way, the passage of time strengthened the enemies of the Peace movement. These enemies were primarily the aristocrats who resented their own humiliating concessions to the commoners, especially when the expected Doomsday did not occur. Such rulers had their allies within the Church, among that 'old-boy' network that normally handed out the episcopal benefits to the next younger son in line. For these men, millennialism was a menace, the peace a disastrous loss of arbitrary power, and the changes it brought marked the onset of an intolerable subjugation to civil society.[29] For a brief but powerful moment, however, they seemed helpless to stem a popular tide that swept bishops and counts, archbishops and dukes and even King Robert along, so that they sponsored assemblies that no aristocrat should ever contemplate. In a matter of years, though, the apocalyptic fever passed and with it the millennial wave of popular Peace assemblies. The aristocracy now sat firmly in the saddle, perhaps even more solidly since, as part of the peace deal, peasants had disarmed and accepted the 'rulership' of their oath-taking lords – the establishment of the seigneurial system.

But things were never the same. There were new and effective actors on the scene now, above all the commoners, but also their allies and inciters among the elite. The eleventh and twelfth centuries see the extraordinary emergence of aristocrats, both clerical and lay, willing to work with the commoners, urging their enthusiastic participation in church reforms, allowing them to clear forest land, to establish autonomous communities (rural and urban communes), to use the roads unmolested, willing to invest in new technology like water mills and irrigation projects. And of course, all these advances for civil society and its accompanying prosperity meant the Jews, whose social cohesion had long worked by these principles, became ever more influential. Wherever the peace 'worked', even momentarily, social and economic change quickened.

This process was not without its growing pains, however. The struggle had been joined between the forces pushing for civil society – substitution of discourse and law for violence, equal rights before the law – and those fighting to preserve the aristocratic privileges of violent domination and honor. It is in this context that we should return to the issue of 1010.

Apocalyptic Scapegoating and Holy Violence: France, 1010

We are in a period of great difficulty. Obviously the Last Judgment had not occurred in 1000, and neither had the Peace succeeded. The wave of assemblies in the decade before 1000 had subsided. By messianic standards, it had failed. Oath-taking had retreated to aristocratic circles. Worse, widespread famines marked the middle of the decade (1003–5); and then in 1006 a nova, visible around the world, filled the sky. A new round of apocalyptic expectations ensued. Al-Hakim began his self-deification (for a Muslim, even for a Shiite, that was a bit much), while Latin Christians apparently went over to a more catastrophic 'pre-millennialism'. One of them, no less a figure than the Emperor's chaplain, converted to Judaism and fled to Spain, provoking outrage and fear among the Christians he left behind.

Thus, when news arrived that al-Hakim had taken Jerusalem, it provoked an apocalyptic crisis to rival that of 1000. All could agree. This event marked the public triumph of the Antichrist. Whatever earlier candidate one might have believed in (the illegitimate Capetian king, Bishop Ascelin who had betrayed the last Carolingian, the local castellan), al-Hakim trumped them all. No need for allegorical interpretation here: he had taken the holy city. He had trampled the Temple (a bit of a fudge, but Glaber calls the Holy Sepulcher the Temple). He had set himself up as God and demanded that all bow down to him. And he was circumcised and demanded circumcision (surprisingly, the Antichrist was not a Jew, but a Muslim). Daniel, Revelation, all the apocalyptic lore of the ages had reached its promised climax. These were now officially the three and a half years before the apocalyptic judgment. The same intensity of open, public expectation of the end that had animated the Peace was now responsible for another wave.

But this time, Christians suffered from a desperate sense of impotence. The Antichrist raged in Jerusalem and Europe could not respond. At the height of the apocalyptic crisis in Limoges, where various natural and celestial disturbances had further intensified the fears, the monk Ademar of Chabannes left his sleeping mat in the middle of a tempestuous night and looked up at the heavens. There he saw not the apocalyptic vision of Christ returning on the clouds in power and glory, but Christ still crucified on a cosmic cross planted in the heavens, weeping rivers of tears, the color of fire and blood. One cannot imagine a more powerful symbol of disappointed horror and catastrophic foreboding.

But this time, the apocalyptic crisis did not lead to peace assemblies as it had in the 990s. We do not hear of either the penitential processions or the relic assemblies that led from catastrophes to Jubilaic rejoicing. One can imagine why. The peace assemblies had failed, and the dangerous consequences of 'jumping the gun' had become apparent. Radical religious ideas were spreading among the populace, whose aggressive behavior on pilgrimage, at shrines, in public discourse, became ever more radical. There were even some who, citing Psalm 115 ('Idols of the Gentiles…'), refused to bow down before the crucifix and before the relics of the saints.[30] Equally worrisome, the prospering Jews, who would bow down neither to men nor statues and who lived independently by their own laws, encouraged these millennial

Christians in their effrontery.

The lack of peace councils was almost surely not because of any lack of popular interest. Popular leaders might argue that the advent of the Antichrist required clerics to repeat the moral apocalyptic choice they had made at the approach of 1000 and abandon their support of the current ruling elite. The time had come for the meek to inherit the earth, for another, more glorious round of peace assemblies that, this time, not only pruned back the warrior class, but did away with them.

But apparently the clerical opponents of this popular Jubilaic millennialism returned in strength. And their argument took an aggressive cataclysmic apocalyptic (pre-millennial) turn. Yes, they agreed, the time had come for final choices, but those choices were not moral but credal. The people who must choose sides were not the Christian aristocrats, lay and clerical, but the infidels, Jews and heretics. And in order to shift attention from issues of social justice to issues of credal warfare, the elites produced a shocking accusation. The Jews had, through a runaway serf disguised as pilgrim, sent secret messages to al-Hakim instructing him to destroy the Holy Sepulcher. This treacherous people who had betrayed Jesus 1,000 years ago had now betrayed the millennial generation. The king of France cooperated: he had the serf executed; he may even have instructed his dukes, after the manner of Ahasuerus, emperor of the Persians (Book of Esther), to wipe out any Jew who would not convert.

The apocalyptic reasoning here seems relatively clear: the peace had failed and the millennium had not arrived, not because of any moral failings on the part of the nobles (let no one say such a thing!), but because of the credal failure of the Jews to convert. And now that the final battle was engaged, the Jews, with their false peace and treacherous scheming, had openly sided with the Antichrist – they were his principal minions, his instigators. The painful apocalyptic choice fell on the Jews, who must at the end of time either convert or die in the battle of Armageddon by the side of the defeated Antichrist.

Such a reading offered a perfect myth of apocalyptic scapegoating for an unhappy and disoriented time. The clergy could, thereby, enlist the lay aristocracy, unhappy with the restrictions that the peace had placed on its freewheeling use of violence, in a sacred battle. The clergy, of late so optimistic about the peace, could return to a more authoritarian mother Church by debating these Jews publicly, giving them one last chance to convert before loosing the violence of the warriors upon them.

And the populace could find solace in the knowledge that they, unlike the Jews, would be spared both the temporal sword and the credal judgment of God. Here we find all the elements of the future demonizing of the Jews which would so mark the next millennium of European history – accusations of an international Jewish conspiracy to destroy Christendom at the end of time, slaughter of a defenseless apocalyptic enemy. Scapegoating offered violent rage as a solution to apocalyptic anxiety and disappointment. And once the fever had passed, it left the initiating elite more firmly in control of the political scene. Indeed, in a little more than a decade, the Church would turn to executing religious dissidents for the first time.[31]

The swing vote here was the reforming monastic party, the liberals of the day; the figures who, only a decade earlier, had enthusiastically supported the Peace assemblies. But now, their two most prominent historians, Rodulfus Glaber and Ademar of Chabannes, both strong supporters of the Peace of God, independently report the accusations as true, and view the slaughter of the Jews with heartfelt approval. Here we have some rapid apocalyptic improvisation, where two parts of the clergy – conservatives and radicals, lately at millennial odds, come together to fight off an even more radical threat.

The power of this ecclesiastical *re*-alliance was that, when the millennial forces within the clergy turned to apocalyptic scapegoating, they carried immense weight among the larger populace, whose favor they had gained in their more populist early phase. Thus, while this is hardly the first time the clerical voices had denounced Jews – in a sense the early Middle Ages contains a litany of complaints from clergy that the laity frequented the Jews too much – this is the first time that the calumnies fell on receptive ears. Popular antisemitism was born in the crucible of apocalyptic fear *and* disappointment.

Such an analysis, drawn in part from the sources, in part from modern case studies of millennial violence,[32] holds interesting implications for the study of millennial violence, especially millennial terrorism.

- First, because apocalyptic believers consider themselves to be taking part in the final and ultimate conflict, normal considerations, including future consequences do not carry weight. Apocalyptic time, with its sense of urgency and threat, conflates means and ends, making unthinkable violence acceptable under certain conditions.

This holds especially true for cataclysmic, conspiracist visions.

- Second, because apocalyptic believers tend towards a megalomaniac sense that they stand at the center of the cosmic battle, whatever they do takes on cosmic significance. Hence, no matter how small a percentage of Jews were affected by these massacres, for the Christians involved it was a global event (Glaber speaks of a universal drive to exterminate the Jews). By acting locally, one could trigger cosmic events.

- Third, authoritarian impotence seems to foster this kind of violence: the authors, both in thought and deed, of these attacks felt helpless to resist the Muslim assault in the East, and threatened in their dominion by popular Christianity (Peace movement, apostolic 'heresies') at home. By designating an apocalyptic scapegoat and making it into the cosmic villain, they could transform their sense of being assaulted into an occasion to rally an assault.

- Fourth, the authors of this attack on the Jews offered this sacred violence as a discharge for the anxiety of those who expect imminently to stand before God in judgment. In so doing, they projected the sense of sin from self to the dehumanized, apocalyptic 'other', shifting from moral to credal eschatology and reasserting the dominion of the violence that underlay their dominion.

The Two Faces of Jewish–Christian Relations in Apocalyptic Dynamics

What did all this mean for Jewish–Christian relations at the time and in succeeding generations? We might say that it was the best of times and the worst of times. Ashkenazic Jewry flourished over the next century, becoming a major locus of scholarly activity, transforming Europe from a backwater of Jewish life to an international center of Jewish culture – from Rabbenu Gershom of Mainz to Rashi of Troyes and his schools. And the same thing happened among Christians. Europe, and especially France, went from a culture constantly invaded, incapable of production (its major export had previously been primary products, including human beings), scarcely able to maintain clerical literacy, to a center of cultural and economic activity that would transform first Europe, and then the world. And yet, despite (or perhaps because of) this often mutually creative activity, some of the most virulent religious propaganda of hatred of the Jews first becomes widespread in the period, initially exploding in the violence of 1010. In transformative and moral millennial space, the Jews and the Christians, both now chosen people of the One God, may have been able to share the privilege. But in cataclysmic and credal apocalyptic time, sharing gave way to rivalry: only one could be *the* chosen people.

And those newly chosen Christians, who either watched the Jews served up as an apocalyptic holocaust, or joined in the destruction of the Lord's enemies, thinking that they would thereby be spared, were wrong. Twelve years later the king burned over a dozen heretics, again in Orleans – the first such executions in Latin Christendom. With this, Robert and the churchmen who instigated it declared war on popular heresy and opened the path to a widespread and long-term violence that seems to have taken up where the attacks on the Jews had left off. One report accuses the Frankish warrior class of such rage that they would kill peasants just because they were pale (i.e., they had been fasting). In the later 1030s, some of the peace assemblies took to creating militias of all people over 15 – commoners and aristocrats – to fight against the peace-breakers. They were wiped out by a mounted, armed and armored warrior elite.[33]

These slaughters of the 'enemies' of Christendom – Jews, heretics, uppity commoners – were the beginnings of a redirection of the violence of the warriors. Although the peace may have failed to bring the millennial age, it had made the daily recourse to violence by the aristocracy problematic. If one wanted a jolly good slaughter, one had better go outside Christendom. As the Peace of God oath at Narbonne in 1055 put it: 'to kill a Christian is to shed the blood of Christ'. Credal enemies became legitimate targets. And so we find Frankish warriors everywhere on the borders of Christendom – the Reconquista of Spain, the Norman invasion of England, the *Drang nach Osten* of the Slavic frontier – lustily fighting the enemies of the faith and importing a new generation of free peasants from the West.[34] For these people, the meaning of the enduring crucifixion was not a call to humility, but a call to vengeance. In classic tribal fashion, they viewed the humiliation of their Lord as a shame that demanded revenge. If the Jews crucified him, the deicides deserved to die.

When, in 1096, the new waves of apocalyptic expectation swept through Europe and the pope again called for crusade, an immense response of both commoners and warriors arose to the cry 'God wants it!' and set off with violent enthusiasm. They ended up paving the way, from Europe to Jerusalem, with the blood of their enemies – men, women, children, Jew, Muslim and Christian. The crusades of 1095–1100 (popular and knightly) crystallized an active apocalyptic tradition within Christianity that would reappear repeatedly over the course of the next millennium, paroxysms of exterminationist violence driven by a belief that the final battle had begun, and the Jews were major agents of the Antichrist.[35] The advent of modern times and sensibilities, despite its apparently 'secularizing' elements, had no impact on dampening either the apocalyptic or the antisemitic elements of medieval Christianity; rather they reappeared in secular forms that, in some cases, proved more virulent than their religious predecessors.[36] Nine centuries later, *mutatis mutandis*, this tradition produced the most colossal act of technological millennial violence ever witnessed, the Holocaust. Men raised as Christians, believing that Hitler was their messiah (Führer), sought to exterminate the Jews and enslave all mankind on their path to the millennial kingdom (*tausendjähriger Reich*).[37]

The events of the eleventh century suggest a pattern that historians can observe at other times in Christian–Jewish relations. The onset of apocalyptic time brings on a wave of enthusiasm among Christians which, among other things, leads them to seek out Jews in fellowship. Partly they do so in order to convert the Jews at the end of time; partly they discover in Jewish religiosity something more closely akin to their own millennial tendencies than the ecclesiastical religiosity that brands them 'Judaizers'. But with the failure of the apocalyptic moment, in the bitter and dangerous disappointment that follows, the temptation of apocalyptic scapegoating becomes enormous. Far easier than admitting error, Christians can blame the Jews: had they only converted, *then* Jesus would have come.[38] Hell hath no fury like an apocalyptic lover scorned.

The End of the Second Christian Millennium: Philo-Judaic Ascent

Let us return to the year 2000. We now face similar dynamics, but in a different configuration. We are now in the single most enduring and intense wave of philo-Judaism in the history of Christianity and possibly of the history of Judaism. Never before have Jews at all levels of society had the freedom, the respect, and the access to channels of expression and power that we now do. Whence such extraordinary behavior? Three major causes present themselves.

1) *The workings of civil society:* Jews and women regularly benefit from the workings of civil society, or the substitution of discourse for violence in dispute settlement. Professional meritocracies based on learning obviously favor groups with such a developed tradition of mental learning. The steadily more consistent application of the egalitarian rules of civil society to Jews has gone on in fits and starts since the advent of constitutional democracies in the late eighteenth century. Nor has this been merely a practical advantage Jews have taken advantage of: Jews permeate academia and have generated paradigmatic shifts (Freud, Einstein, Kuhn).

2) *The impact of the Holocaust:* Once the news spread of what the Germans had done, a revulsion against the culture of antisemitism occurred, especially among those most committed to civil society. Such circles made any public antisemitism taboo, and considered the *Protocols of the Elders of Zion* a vile forgery. Jews were given a voice in public culture, and they have taken advantage of the opportunity. Some Christians have seriously rethought their relationship to Jews and Judaism, most often with a burst of admiration for Judaism and a warm desire to dialogue with Jews.[39]

3) *The Christian apocalyptic wave of the last 50 years:* With the creation of the state of Israel in 1948, a broad population of Christians in America saw this as the single greatest event in the fulfillment of the apocalyptic scenario. They believed firmly that they lived in the final generation of mankind. This belief has strengthened over the past 50 years, spectacularly affirmed by the reunification of Jerusalem in 1967, and spreading along with Rapture ideology from the early 1970s. And in addition to this push from history came the pull of the approaching year 2000.

This apocalyptic component of our day's philo-Judaism constitutes the wild card. We don't know how strong it is, how widespread, and we don't know how to interpret its favorable attitude towards the Jews. We can, however, safely say that it constitutes the most sustained and unusually philo-Judaic apocalyptic manifestation in the history of Christianity.[40] If indeed there had been a philo-Judaic element to the peace movement of 1000, it triggered a broad and violent abreaction within a couple of decades. The clerics of 1000 believed in a Jewish Antichrist, and that meant that *any* Jewish messianic activity – *aliyah*, for example – could trigger violent abreactions. In this sense, the *Protocols of the Elders of Zion* represents just such a Christian abreaction to Jewish messianism.

But today, on the contrary, Christian Zionists greet the Jewish messianic desire to rebuild the Temple with immense fervor and excitement. Christian farmers want to raise the red heifer needed for Temple sacrifice; Christian archeologists want to find the ashes of the last one; Christian prospectors want to find a huge oil deposit that will make it all possible. And, with Jewish messianic believers like Gershon Solomon riding high on the immense enthusiasm of Christian well-wishers, we have the first recorded time that a genuinely and halachically Jewish messianic movement has found so much inspiration in Christian millennialism and vice versa.[41]

All of this may seem somewhat quaint; an anthropologist's field day in the midst of the modern world. But there are tens of millions of highly motivated people involved, and they have achieved considerable political prominence. Right now, Christian Zionists are the political mainstay of Zionism. Their money and unstinting support has been welcomed not only by Likud and other Zionist 'hawks', but also by the liberal Jewish organizations to whom they have offered their assistance. Everyone knew about the apocalyptic program that lay behind these kind offers. But most were satisfied with the clever response: 'When Jesus comes, we'll deal with it.' In the meantime, there was real political and financial clout to be gotten from cooperation with these friends.

Islam and Apocalyptic Scapegoating

There is a second, even wilder card at play: the Arab–Israeli conflict. The basic apocalyptic rule that had Christians so violently hostile to Jewish messianism now holds special meaning for Muslims: one person's messiah is another's Antichrist. Thus Zionism, which holds so prominent and positive a place in some Christian and Jewish millennial thought, has become the incarnation of evil for most of Islamic apocalyptic thought and for its more secular variant, Arab nationalism. From a millennial perspective, Islam, especially Islamism, represents the most thoroughly cataclysmic of the apocalyptic traditions now active,[42] overwhelmingly credal (hence the easy legitimacy of terror), with highly authoritarian millennial politics.[43]

Israel, on the other hand, represents for the most part a successful commoners' millennial movement (socialist Zionism) in the midst of authoritarian regimes.[44] These latter, in their efforts to eliminate Israel, follow the standard pattern of such dominating elites from the ancient world to the present. Their lack of success so far has only intensified the fury of their apocalyptic rhetoric and behavior, most notably in the 'logic' of suicide terrorism. In other words, one of the major differences between the turn of 1000 and the turn of 2000 is that, unlike the peace militias crushed in the later 1030s, the primarily egalitarian millennialism of Zionism has been able to defend itself against the assault of the Islamic authoritarian elites who do not hesitate to use the apocalyptic rhetoric of total warfare.[45]

The approach of 2000, with its growing Christian–Jewish rapprochement, drew the attention of Muslims, especially those engaged in the struggle with Zionism. These figures, often not the formal religious elite, but nonetheless publishers of extremely successful books, viewed this alliance of Christian and Jewish Zionists as a sign of the coming *Dajjal* (Muslim equivalent of the Antichrist), as a sign of imminent and total war. For them the enthusiasm of Christians for the year 2000 made it an apocalyptic year for them as well, one that portended terrible events against which Islam had to guard vigorously.[46]

The outbreak of the 'al-Aqsa' intifada in October 2000 may turn out to be one of the most important developments of that 'millennial' year. The apocalyptic dimensions of the struggle against Zionism have long been noted, although perhaps rarely taken seriously.[47] But when one examines the nature of Islamic rhetoric, especially that surrounding the suicide bomber-martyrs, one finds that apocalyptic themes play a central role.[48] Do we have here the same scapegoating apocalypticism, the same sacred violence that marked Latin Christianity at the turn of the last millennium?

The Millennial Dangers: While the Messiah Tarries

The problem is not when the messiah comes – when *that* happens we will be reduced to asking if it's the first or second visit. Rather, the problem arises when Jesus, or the *Mahdi*, or the ingathering of the exiles in the full Promised Land does *not* come. How long can an apocalyptic wave continue? What will be the timing and dynamics of disappointment? Does all this Christian apocalyptic philo-Judaism of the upswing imply a coming wave of equally intense anti-Judaism in the wake of (inevitable) disappointment? Is there a way out of the cataclysmic and scapegoating anti-Judaism of Islamic anti-Zionism?

At the crux of all these issues for Christians lies the most delicate and explosive of all – conversion. Among the most decisive elements in determining which way a Christian millennial movement will 'land' from their disappointed expectations, from 'apocalyptic time' into 'normal time', the importance of converting the Jews stands out. The more vital that element, the more bitter, disappointed and rejected the millennial Christian feels in the aftermath.[49] Ironically, therefore, those who 'love' Jews most beforehand are most at risk of hating them afterwards.[50]

There are, of course, other apocalyptic attitudes among Christians towards the Jews; attitudes that closely resemble those of Muslim cataclysmic apocalyptic thinking. For these Christians and their more secular sympathizers, modernity is a plot by the Jews to destroy Christianity and enslave mankind.[51] These people cultivate a conspiracist world view in which they are beset on all sides by the forces of evil: forces about which they teach a self-protective and self-righteousness hatred. This culture of conspiracy covers a wide range of people, some just enthusiastic watchers of the *X-Files*, others the avid readers of books such as the *Illuminati* and *The Protocols of the Elders of Zion*, or the still more committed stockpilers of survivalist gear and weapons, militias, revilers of the US government, the ZOG (Zionist Occupied Government). How big a community is this committed fringe world?[52] Small, unquestionably, by both numbers and influence in the West, although the vigor of authoritarian conspiracism among Third World intelligentsia holds a far more central role. But the Christian far right, no matter how small in number, lives on the borders of apocalyptic time; active, imbued with a sense of the imminent surfacing of the conspiracy, the apocalyptic sense that the day for the cosmic battle is about to begin. As long as things go well their views are not likely to spread; should things turn bad, they wait in the wings with their cataclysmic prophecies.[53]

In the meantime, we need to note that some of the most philo-Judaic Christians at the moment are not that far distant from the culture of world conspiracy, militia and hate groups. Indeed from the perspective of apocalyptic logic, the most philo-Judaic Christians are only a slight and often adjusted detail of the apocalyptic scenario apart from each other. The pre-tribulation Rapture (i.e., God takes the saved off the planet before the seven-year terrors that climax with the Antichrist's reign) of the vast majority of pro-Zionist Christian fundamentalists could conceivably shift to a mid-tribulation Rapture (God takes them off just before the victory of Antichrist midway through the period of chaos and suffering). This might open the door to teachings of a few apocalyptic preachers who entertain darker scenarios of antisemitism, conspiracy theories, and the belief that ethnic mixing and godless modernity threaten their way of life.

The eschatological link is direct: the dictatorial 'one world government' that every member of this world view believes is imminent is, in Christian apocalyptic mythology, the Beast, the dictator who will bring it on, the Antichrist, and the conspiracy is a Jewish one. We even have clear evidence for this link in the rather 'mainstream' figure of Jerry Falwell, a man with a large audience in the pre-millennial Christian community who claimed in the waning months of the last millennium that the Antichrist was an adult male Jew.[54] Similarly, in ways he may not be aware, Pat Robertson, in his *New World Order*, has restated the basic theme of the *Protocols* – modernity is a trick to enslave mankind. For an audience in the philo-Judaic period of the post-Holocaust, however, the identity of the evil force behind the cabal is not explicitly Jewish, but rather capitalists and secularists. Can the Jews, who are not explicitly identified as the plotters in the new scenarios, rely upon such exegetical restraint permanently?

Right now Jerry Falwell, Pat Robertson and their fellow pre-millennial dispensationalist believers abjure any connection to this world of antisemitism, and point to their love of Zion as their guarantee. And many are not only sincere, but honest. How many, however, are only sincere? Five years from now, the Rapture not come, the Middle East engaged in endemic conflict and the politics of compromise rather than millennial temple-building, their hopes for sweeping Jewish conversions crushed, how many Christians, leaders and followers will find the lure of conspiracy and apocalyptic enmity difficult to resist?[55] How many will turn to those who can recharge their apocalyptic energies through scapegoating, some turning on the faithless Jews who refuse to convert, others anointing Islam with the Antichrist's role? Certainly the cultural ground for either such move has been prepared.[56] And how many others, not enraged but nonetheless angry and hurt, will allow these people a public voice they should never have?

Seffi Rachlevsky, in a book that so enraged the observant Jewish community in Israel that they missed some of his most important points, has argued that the millennial enthusiasts – religious Zionists, Christian Rapture believers – view their apocalyptic 'allies' – secular Zionists, Jews – as their 'messiah's donkey', a (disposable) vehicle for their anticipated redemption.[57] Certainly significant numbers of apocalyptic millennialists out there, Christian and Jew, conceive of their relations with the 'apocalyptic other' in such ways, even if some of them don't yet know it. Indeed many would express horror at the thought that upon realizing that their vehicle has not arrived at the messianic age, indeed refuses to take them there, that they might turn to beating, even killing the incompetent beast. Admittedly, American millennialism has a long and worthy history of very limited violence, and a strong preference for passive recalculations of the future date over the suicidal embrace of present apocalyptic warfare. But every generation meets new challenges, and ours may be in for one of global proportions.

The last thousand years of Jewish–Christian relations have been both poisoned and stimulated by the Christian need to convert Jews (and, one might add, their fear of being converted by them).[58] The Holocaust was only the most recent wave of millennial fervor around a catastrophic and violent apocalyptic scenario, one in which fear of an international conspiracy headed by Jews led to an orgy of sacred violence aimed at wiping them out. This is the terrible pattern we see with such unusual clarity take hold in the apocalyptic wake of 1000, in the massacres of 1010. And each succeeding wave derived from a particular response to apocalyptic disappointment: the disappointed believers channeled their immense frustration into sacred rage, into a credal war. The need to convert produced the initial warmth *and* the sense of rejection. Post-apocalyptic rage finds an ideal solution in an activist authoritarian millennialism – 'God did *not* come because he wants *us* to prepare His way, *us* to convert the Jews, to free Jerusalem, to eliminate the heretics'. A love intended to ravish, once spurned, repeatedly became rape. The statues of the synagogue, with her broken staff and downcast eyes, depicted this victim, the Jew in medieval (i.e., politically dominant) Christendom. At the heart of religious violence in European history – inquisitorial, crusading, civil – lies the need to convert the other, the need to turn all mankind into oneself.

It is reasonable for Jews to look askance at this Christian ardor. Like a wife whose husband regularly gets amorous when he starts drinking and, drunk and rebuffed, turns to wife-beating, Jews must feel immensely suspicious when their Christian colleagues assure them that the millennial brew they are drinking and the amorous intentions they are expressing are not like earlier ones. This time, they assure the Jews, it really will be different. But can a millennium of repetitious compulsion change in only one generation, even the generation after the Holocaust?

Of course, it is also reasonable for a modern American Jew or Israeli to think that this time it really is different, that even if Christians want to Jew-beat, the restraints of civil society will prevent them from so doing. Certainly Lester Furrow's attempt to trigger an explosion of violence by attacking a Jewish daycare center came to naught: Los Angeles in 1999 was not the Rhineland in 1096 or 1939. But can we safely ignore this vestigial remnant (or leave it to the workings of our police forces), or is it the tip of a more persistent iceberg that, in one way or another, involves, engages, and appeals to people around the world, certainly Muslims, indeed even some Jews? Certainly his thinking coincides with that of cataclysmic apocalyptic hopefuls everywhere: the social world is like a huge earthquake faultline under enormous pressure, and if only 'we' can set off an explosion in the right place, it will trigger the cosmic one. Take the Temple Mount, for example.

The answer, ultimately, depends on us, all of us: Christians, Jews, Muslims, atheists, agnostics, members of civil society, members of other communities and civilizations that want to become players in the emerging global civilization of this new millennium. It is up to us to stabilize this unusually warm moment in Jewish–Christian relations, rather than let it slip, perhaps disastrously, from our hands. If we can do that, if we can effect a fundamental sea-change in Jewish–Christian relations from the patterns that have dominated for at least 1,000, probably 2,000 years, then perhaps we will, in some way, have redeemed the catastrophe of the Holocaust. Who knows? Maybe therein lies a way out of the cataclysmic apocalyptic relations between Jews and Muslims, between modernity and the Arab world, between an arrogant and 'missionary' secular West and the wisdom of other cultures.

NOTES

1. I have analysed the sources related to this incident in 'The Massacres of 1010: On the Origins of Popular Anti-Jewish Violence in Western Europe', in Jeremy Cohen (ed.), *From Witness to Witchcraft: Jews and Judaism in Medieval Christian Thought* (Wolfenbüttel: Wolfenbüttler Mittelalterlichen-Studien, 1996), pp.79–112; for my handling of a large dossier of manuscripts from the period, see my *Relics, Apocalypse, and the Deceits of History: Ademar of Chabannes, 989–1033* (Cambridge, MA: Harvard University Press, 1995).
2. Sylvain Gouguenheim, *Les fausses terreurs de l'an mille: Crises eschatologiques ou approfondissement de la foi?* (Paris: Picard, 1999); Bernard McGinn, *Antichrist: Two Thousand Years of Fascination with Evil* (San Francisco: Harper, 1994), pp.99–100; for a discussion of the methodological problems facing the historian trying to trace millennial beliefs and apocalyptic activity, see R. Landes, 'Owls, Roosters, and Apocalyptic Time: A Historical Method for Reading a Refractory Documentation', *Union Seminary Quarterly Review* 49 (1996), pp.165–85.
3. R. Landes, 'The Historiographical Fear of an Apocalyptic Year 1000: Augustinian History Medieval and Modern', *Speculum* 75 (2000), pp.97–145.
4. 'Because Anno Domini dating (setting the annual calendar from the birth of Christ) was still relatively new in AD 1000, historians doubt the year had much apocalyptic significance for medieval men and women. A Burgundian monk named Raoul Glaber spoke a few years later of "numerous signs and prodigies that had occurred before, after, and around the year 1000" and more around 1033 (the millennium of Christ's death and resurrection) but that's about the only evidence for first-millennium fever.' E. Randolf Daniel, 'Looking for the Last Emperor', *Christian History*, Winter 1999. Readers could not imagine from such remarks that AD dating dominated all the historical and liturgical (Easter Table) dating and much of the diplomatic (charter) dating in England, France and Germany from the middle of the eighth century. Nor would they know from such statements that Glaber's entire history is structured around these two dates (see R. Landes, 'Rodulfus Glaber and the Dawn of the New Millennium: Eschatology, Historiography and the Year 1000', *Revue Mabillon* n.s 7 (=68) [1996], pp.1–21); nor that a dozen other texts explicitly privilege the years 1000 or 1033 – an awareness and attention that no other date had ever received.
5. Hence, as in the above-cited case, their reluctance to even mention the dissenting position with which they do not agree.
6. It is noteworthy that few scholars of early or medieval Christianity cite (or even implicitly use) the anthropological literature on millennialism.
7. Millennial beliefs are sometimes recorded in prophetic visionary literature and in its exegesis, and in this form tend to be studied by theologians and intellectual historians; millennial behavior is recorded in historical narratives, and is largely studied by social and religious historians. Much of the dialogue of the deaf that often characterizes (the lack of) millennial studies derives from social historians' lack of interest in religion in general and theological commentary in particular on the one hand, and, on the other,

intellectual historians' unfamiliarity with and lack of interest in the thoughts and activities of 'illiterate' commoners.

8. Augustine, who formulated this theology in the early fifth century, insisted that, despite the obvious implications of the text and exegesis, the '1,000 years' (Rev. 20:7) should not be read literally to refer to a thousand-year period; see Fredriksen, 'Tyconius and Augustine on the Apocalypse', in R. K. Emmerson and B. McGinn (eds.), *The Apocalypse in the Middle Ages* (Ithaca, NY: Cornell University Press, 1992), pp.20–37.

9. Daniel Verhelst, 'La préhistoire des conceptions d'Adson concernant l'Antichrist', *Recherches de théologie ancienne et médiévale* 40 (1973).

10. For a discussion of both the historical evidence and the various analyses of that evidence – many of which dismiss the apocalyptic year 1000 as a later historiographical invention – see Landes, 'The Fear of an Apocalyptic Year 1000' (note 3). This wave of apocalyptic expectation may have escaped the attention of most historians partly for the reasons mentioned above (note 7).

11. We do not have too much detailed evidence for how this happened around 1000, but we do have some detailed accounts of just such sessions during the 'Great Allelulia' of 1233 (see Augustine Thompson, *Revival Preachers and Politics in Thirteenth-Century Italy: The Great Devotion of 1233* (Oxford: Clarendon Press, 1992).

12. Medievalists, well aware of the overwhelming role of force in establishing order back then, tend to assume the oath made no serious concessions and (somewhat paradoxically) that it was rapidly abandoned.

13. Even Charlemagne barely did so, and his descendents failed miserably. See Heinrich Fichtenau, *The Carolingian Empire* (New York: Harper, 1964), pp.144–76.

14. The one place where the strength of the regional ruler, the duke of Normandy, clearly played a key role in forcing the assemblies merely illustrates the problem: the warriors do not willingly make these kinds of oaths, and therefore why would they do so? See J. F. Lemarignier, 'Paix et réforme monastique en Flandre et en Normandie autour de l'année 1023', in *Droit privé et institutions régionales. Etudes historiques offerts à Jean Yver* (Paris: Presses Universitaires, 1976), pp.443–68.

15. Jules Michelet, *Histoire de la France* (Vol. 1, livre 4, Ch. 1); ed. Claude Mettra as *Le Moyen Age* (Paris: Hachette, 1981), p.231.

16. We have a report that in 968 the emperor's troops fled a battle because an eclipse of the sun triggered an apocalyptic panic (*Gesta episcoporum leodensium*, edited in the *Monumenta Germaniae Historica, Scriptores* IX, p.202).

17. John Chrysostom, Homily 7 on *Acts, Patrologia Graeca* (60, col. 66); see discussion in Alan Cameron, 'Earthquake 400', *Chiron* 17 (1987), pp.343–60.

18. This is certainly the case in the better-documented thirteenth century (e.g., 1250 and 1260). Rather than argue, as do most historians, that this kind of chronologically enervated apocalyptic millennialism dates from the later twelfth century, I would contend that it had never really subsided, despite periods of relative (documentary) quiescence, since the very origins of Christianity. It is particularly visible in the anti-apocalyptic chronological tradition of the 'sabbatical millennium'. See Richard Landes, 'Lest the Millennium Be Fulfilled: Apocalyptic Expectations and the Pattern of Western Chronography, 100–800 CE', in W. D. F. Verbeke, D. Verhelst and A. Welkenhysen (eds.), *The Use and Abuse of Eschatology in the Middle Ages* (Medievalia Lovaniensia ser. 1, studia XV; Louvain, 1988), pp.137–211.

19. John Chrysostom urged the faithful to consider every earthquake (there were several during his tenure as bishop of Constantinople, 389–405) as the onset of Judgment Day, and repent of their sins (see *Patrologia Graeca*, 67, cols. 1026–44).

20. See Stephen O'Leary's analysis of the role of apocalyptic 'rhetoric' as one of the great motivators of any cultural repertoire, *Arguing the Apocalypse: A Theory of Millennial Rhetoric* (New York: Oxford University Press, 1994).

21. John Hall, *Powers and Liberties: The Causes and Consequences of the Rise of the West* (Penguin: London, 1985), pp.29–33; Crone, *Pre-Industrial Societies* (Oxford: Blackwell, 1989), pp.71–4.

22. Ademar of Chabannes, Sermon 3; *Patrologia Latina*, 141 col. 118.
23. Radulfus Glaber, *Five Books of the Histories* (IV.5.16), (Clarendon Press: Oxford, 1989), pp.194–5.
24. Georges Duby and some of those working in his school have given the peace a central prominence in the transformations of the year 1000: Duby, *The Three Orders: Feudal Society Imagined* (Chicago: University of Chicago Press, 1981) Part I, ch. 2, Part III, ch. 2; Pierre Bonnassie, *Les sociétés de l'an mil: Un monde entre deux âges* (De Boeck: Brussels, 2001), pp.215–354; Christian Lauranson-Rosaz, 'Peace from the Mountains: The Auvergnat Origins of the Peace of God', in Thomas Head and Richard Landes (eds.), *The Peace of God: Social Violence and Religious Response in France Around the Year 1000* (Ithaca, NY: Cornell University Press, 1992). The school that denies any significant change to the period around 1000 predictably reduces the peace to its most banal and inconsequential dimensions (Barthelemy, *L'an Mil et la paix de Dieu* (Paris: Fayard, 1999), pp.261–3; Sylvain Gouguenheim, *Les fausses terreurs de l'an mil* (Paris: Picard, 1999), pp.177–84).
25. Indeed, a thirteenth-century commentary in France overturns a Talmudic conclusion that one should recite a prayer for surviving danger (*gomel*) when one travels from one city to another – an exceptional testament to the relative safety of such travel in France in the High Middle Ages (commentary of Rabbenu Asher, end of thirteenth century, Berachot 9, Halacha 3). The only other case of such an abandonment of the custom came in the 1960s when travel from the US to Israel was no longer considered a reason to say this prayer.
26. Ademar uses the expression '*iustitia et pax osculatae sunt*' [justice and peace were kissed] (Paris: BN Lat. 2460, fol. 64v).
27. Landes, 'While God Tarried: Modernity as Frankenstein's Millennium', *Deolog* 4 (1997), pp.6–9, 22–7, 41, 45.
28. Glaber, (note 23), IV.5.17, pp.196–7.
29. See Nietzsche's description of the 'blond beast' injected with the poison of 'bad conscience' in *Genealogy of Morals*, Essay 2, tr. Walter Kaufmann, *On the Genealogy of Morals and Ecce Homo* (New York: Vintage, 1967), pp.57–96.
30. R. Landes, 'The Birth of Popular Heresy: A Millennial Phenomenon', *Journal of Religious History* 24 (2000), pp.26–43.
31. Ibid.
32. See the collection edited by Catherine Wessinger, *Millennialism, Persecution, and Violence* (Syracuse, NY: Syracuse University Press, 2000).
33. See Thomas Head, 'The Judgment of God: Andrew of Fleury's Account of the Peace League of Bourges', in Head and Landes (eds.), *The Peace of God*, pp.219–38.
34. See Robert Bartlett, *The Making of Europe* (Princeton, NJ: Princeton University Press, 1994).
35. See, in particular, Andrew Gow, *The Red Jew: Antisemitism in an Apocalyptic Age* (Leiden: Brill Academic Press, 1995) and Norman Cohn, *Pursuit of the Millennium* (London: Oxford University Press, 1990), especially the cases of the 'Shepherd's Crusade' and the Drummer of Nickelshausen. The explicitly apocalyptic *Protocols of the Elders of Zion* (see introduction to the 'editor', Russian mystic Sergei Nilus) replicates this pattern of thought in great detail.
36. On the secularization of millennialism, see Arthur Mendel, *Vision and Violence* (Ann Arbor, MI: University of Michigan Press, 1994, 2000); Eugen Weber, *Apocalypses* (Cambridge, MA: Harvard University Press, 1999); review of Weber with discussion of Jewish–Christian relations, R. Landes, 'The Fruitful Error: Reconsidering Millennial Enthusiasm', *Journal of Interdisciplinary History* 32/1 (2001), pp.89–98.
37. It is something of a self-evident observation for millennial scholars that the Nazis and the communists were millennial movements (a point first made by F. Voigt, *Render unto Caesar* (1934); rearticulated by Cohn, *Pursuit*; and a number of books and articles have been published on the subject: James Rhodes, *The Hitler Movement: A Modern Millenarian Revolution* (Stanford, CA: Stanford University Press, 1980); Arthur

Mendel, *Vision and Violence* (note 36), pp.195–222; Robert Ellwood, 'Nazism as a Millennial Movement', in C. Wessinger (ed.), *Millennialism, Persecution and Violence: Historical Cases* (note 32), pp.241–60. See also Eric Zeusse, *Why the Holocaust Happened: Its Religious Causes and Scholarly Cover* (Lincoln NE: SuperiorBooks.com, 2000). Historians trained in conventional historiographical schools have tended to shy away from the issue, partly because they have a minimal sense of millennialism and its dynamics, so that they think of millennialism as religious and Nazism as secular – a kind of Aristotelian positivism (discrete entity *a* excludes *non-a*) that unfortunately still dominates much of modern historiography (see Peter Novick, *That Noble Dream: The 'Objectivity Question' and the American Historical Profession* [Chicago: University of Chicago Press, 1988]). In addition, since millennialism represents the 'missing link' to certain forms of Christianity, many scholars prefer not to open that can of worms.

38. The classic case here of such disappointment is Luther, whose initially positive attitude towards the Jews was based on the premise that they had justifiably rejected the corrupted form of Christianity offered them by the Catholic Church, but would now convert when introduced to 'true Christianity'. His disappointment produced an anti-Jewish rhetoric that surpassed all but the most virulently antisemitic Christian thinkers (e.g., John Chrysostom). See Heiko Oberman, *The Roots of Anti-Semitism in the Age of Renaissance and Reformation* (Philadelphia, PA: Fortress Press, 1984); Gow, *Red Jew* (note 35). A more recent case of such a dynamic concerns the British Israelites who, until the establishment of Israel, had been philo-Judaic; disappointed in their expectations of participating in the creation of the millennial kingdom with the Zionists, they produced the Christian Identity Movement, one of the most virulently racist and antisemitic Christian movements currently active, with strong Neo-Nazi tendencies; see Barkun, *Religion and the Racist Right* (Chapel Hill, NC: University of North Carolina Press, 1994), pp.97–9, 128, 132–6; see especially the case of C. F. Parker, *A Short History of Esau-Edom in Jewry* (London: Covenant Publishing, 1949).

39. For a recent manifestation of such an impulse, see James Carroll, *Constantine's Sword: The Church and the Jews* (New York: Houghton Mifflin, 2001).

40. Contemporary philo-judaism is most visible in the United States, but significant currents exist in Western European countries like England (e.g., the public prominence of Jonathan Sacks, the Chief Rabbi), France (e.g., the reception of the work of Emmanuel Levinas) and Germany (e.g., the reception of Goldhagen's *Hitler's Willing Executioners*).

41. Gershom Gorenberg, *The End of Days: Fundamentalism and the Struggle for the Temple Mount* (New York: Free Press, 2000).

42. On 'Islamism', an auto-designation by militant and fundamentalist proponents of a politically active Islam in the modern period, see Muhammed Tózí, 'The State: Muslim Perspectives and Islamist Objectives', *TransState Islam*, Spring 1997; Bassam Tibi, *The Challenge of Fundamentalism: The Politics of Islam and the New World Disorder* (Berkeley, CA: University of California Press, 1998); Khalid Duran, *The Children of Abraham: An Introduction to Islam for Jews* (Hoboken, NJ: Ktav Publishing, 2001), pp.51–69. On the nature of current Islamic apocalyptic publications, see David Cook, 'Modern Muslim Apocalyptic Literature: Part I: Sunni Arabic Material', *The Hour Shall Not Arrive until … Studies in Muslim Apocalyptic Literature* (Darwin Press, forthcoming) and 'Islam and the Year 2000', *Middle East Quarterly* 5/2 (1998), www.meforum.org/meq/june98/muslim.htm.

43. For an example of the authoritarian politics of Islamic messianism, see the fate of the Iranian revolution (originally 'demotic'). Also note the enormous place of conspiracy thinking in the Islamic world; see Dan Pipes, *The Hidden Hand: Middle East Fears of Conspiracy* (New York: Palgrave, 1998).

44. I use the term 'egalitarian' with reference to Zionism because of the primordial and radical role that egalitarianism played in many of the secular aspects of the movement (the Kibbutzim being the most prominent example of not only legal but material egalitarianism). This is not to say that there are not cataclysmic and authoritarian

elements in some forms of Zionist messianism, especially among some of the more irredentist forms of religious Zionism like Gush Emunim and Kach: see Aviezer Ravitsky, *Messianism, Zionism, and Jewish Religious Radicalism* (Chicago: Chicago University Press, 1998); Ehud Sprinzak, *Brother against Brother: Violence and Extremism in Israeli Politics from* Altalena *to the Rabin Assassination* (New York: Free Press, 1999); and Sefi Rachlevsky, *Hamoro shel Meshiach* [Messiah's Donkey, Hebrew] (Tel Aviv: Yediot Aharonot, 1998). But these have remained minoritarian and the object of widespread public disapproval so far. Given that the threat of outside attack has historically turned the most egalitarian millennialism into militant hierarchies with totalitarian tendencies – the Anabaptists at Münster (1533–35); the French revolutionary 'Terror' of 1793–94, the Soviet 'Dictatorship of the Proletariat' of 1918–89); Khoumeini's Iran (1979–) – the fact that over the past 50 years, Zionism has not turned into a dictatorship illustrates the profundity of the egalitarian element (see Mendel, *Vision and Violence* (note 36)). The fate of socialism in the Arab world, where the Ba'ath party became the platform from which Hafez al Assad and Saddam Hussein built their dictatorships, illustrates the ephemeral quality of egalitarian ideals in authoritarian political cultures.

45. The apocalyptic nature of the Islamic and Arab Nationalist assault on Israel has not received as much attention as it deserves, partly because in the former case, most formal Islamic 'theology' is explicitly anti-apocalyptic (as is all Catholic and most Protestant) and in the latter, although secular ideologues will use apocalyptic rhetoric, they will not make the case explicitly. The common use of apocalyptic tropes from the Crusades, especially the one about the Gharqad tree and the extermination of the Jews, however, illustrates the pervasiveness of a rhetoric that need not articulate an explicit system. See note 46.

46. Note that the *Dajal* has not historically played the same political role in Islam that the Antichrist has played in Christianity, but that very recently, as a result of the influence of political events (Shiite revolution in Iran, conflict with Zionism) and of the absorption of Christian apocalyptic themes and styles into Islam, it has begun to resemble the Christian Antichrist. David Cook, 'Islam and the Year 2000' (note 42); Bernard McGinn, *Antichrist* (note 54), pp.111–13; Gershom Gorenberg, *The End of Days* (note 41), pp.185–99; Paul Steinberg and Anne-Marie Oliver, (www.mille.org/people/steinbergoliver.html).

47. This is particularly noticeable in the fascination of Arab anti-Zionism for the infamous European antisemitic forgery, *The Protocols of the Elders of Zion*. Given the wide range of exterminationist movements this forgery has inspired (Nazism, Stalinism, Nasser's pan-Arabism), it constitutes one of the most powerful cataclysmic apocalyptic texts of the anti-modern movement.

48. Anne Marie Oliver and Paul Steinberg, 'Information and Revolutionary Ritual in Intifada Graffiti', in Akiba A. Cohen and Gadi Wolfsfeld (eds.), *Framing the Intifada: People and Media* (Norwood, NJ: Ablex Pub. Corp., 1993).

49. See above on Luther, note 38.

50. Brenda Brasher, 'When Your Friend is Your Enemy: American Christian Fundamentalists and Israel at the New Millennium', in Martha F. Lee (ed.), *Millennial Visions: Essays on Twentieth-Century Millenarianism* (Westport, CT: Greenwood Publishing Group, 2000).

51. See the work of Chip Berlet and Matthew N. Lyons, *Right-Wing Populism in America: Too Close for Comfort* (New York: Guilford Publications, 2000). The American rightwing militia movement has both a Christian religious current and a secular one; both share the same world view towards modern liberal society and the pervasiveness of the Jewish influence.

52. I do not consider the enthusiasts of popular culture conspiracism (shows like *X-Files*, movies like *Clear and Present Danger* and *Enemy of the State*) to be part of the fringe. They represent, however, a population receptive to such thinking, and a path that dedicated conspiracists hope to travel to more mainstream success under certain circumstances.

53. Hence the enthusiasm of apocalyptic survivalists for the predicted catastrophes of Y2K (e.g., Gary North, www.garynorth.com/).

54. See Andrew Gow, 'The Myth of the Jewish Antichrist: Falwell Stumbles Badly', www.mille.org/scholarship/papers/gow.falwell.html. Most of the controversy concerned the Jewish identity of the Antichrist, despite the longstanding prominence of that aspect of Christian apocalyptic thought. Bernard McGinn, *Antichrist: Two Thousand Years of Fascination with Evil* (San Francisco: HarperCollins, 1994). The really important element was 'adult' – i.e., the imminence of his 'rule'.

55. See Hal Lindsey's recent effort to warn pre-millennialists of the dangers of fascism and antisemitism that can derive from a shift to a more active 'post-millennial' eschatology.

56. Samuel Huntington, *The Clash of Civilizations and the Remaking of the World Order* (New York: Simon & Schuster, 1996).

57. Seffi Rachalevsky, *Hamoro shel Mashiach* (Yediot Aharonot: Tel Aviv, 1996).

58. See Yaakov Ariel, *Evangelizing the Chosen People: Missions to the Jews in America, 1880–2000* (Chapel Hill, NC: University of North Carolina Press, 2000).

12

Medieval Apocalypticism, Millennialism and Violence

E. RANDOLPH DANIEL

Did a majority of people in Western Europe await midnight on 31 December 999 with bated breath, convinced that either Jesus would return in glory during that night or that the millennium envisioned in Apocalypse (Revelation) 20:1–6 would begin before dawn? As the end of the year 999 approached, did such expectations lead them to join millennialist sects that turned to violence in order to help bring in the millennium? Can studies on medieval apocalypticism and millennialism cast useful light on possible relationships between religious expectations and violence at the beginning of the third millennium?

This article will survey apocalyptic currents during the Middle Ages in order to shed light on links between apocalypticism and violence in the medieval and modern worlds. Apocalypticism is usually defined as the expectation of the imminent end of history, but recent research has shown that reformist apocalyptics such as Abbot Joachim of Fiore (died 1202 CE) expected a thoroughgoing reform of the existing church and world, rather than the second coming of Christ.[1] Millenarian sects, according to Norman Cohn, defined salvation as collective, terrestrial, imminent, total, and miraculous.[2] The reformists were gradualists who expected the existing world to be significantly improved, while the millennialists were revolutionaries who looked for the total overthrow of the present world and its replacement by a completely new one. Reformists might revolt in order to compel the authorities to carry out reforms, but they accepted the continuation of the present world. Millennialists wanted the utter and complete collapse of the existing institutions, so that new ones might emerge from the cleared soil.

The nineteenth century was 'the Christian era':

> For Christianity, the evangelization of the whole world seemed
> within reach ... It is easy enough to understand why Christian
> millenarianism should have offered itself as (an) universal
> interpretative historical framework for this unheard-of advance,
> and for the optimistic faith in progress of the people captured by it
> ... In this kingdom, immeasurable progress in every respect is still
> to be had – everything in it is perfectible; but there are no
> fundamental, revolutionary changes any more. The final
> revolution took place with the seizure of technological and
> political power over the whole world. Now everything is simply a
> matter of evolution and proper development.[3]

Moltmann's modern Christian millenarianism resembles reformist
apocalypticism and contrasts sharply with Norman Cohn's
millennialism. Optimistic Christians of the nineteenth century saw
themselves on the road to universal triumph by means of missions that
were closely linked to the imperial conquests of the British, French,
German and other empires and the increasing global dominance of
Western technology and trade. These millenarians wanted to enhance
their world, not end it. Their technological triumph was not truly
revolutionary but evolutionary. Cohn's millennialists desired the
diametrical opposite. Both meanings of millennialism are significant
for understanding apocalypticism and violence in the contemporary
world.

Medieval messianism was usually presented in the form of the last
world emperor, a Roman ruler who would defeat all the enemies of
Christendom, spread Christianity throughout the world, and at the end
of his reign go to Jerusalem and surrender his crown, which would be
the signal for the advent of the Antichrist. Adso gave the notion wide
currency in the middle of the tenth century, although he stipulated
that the last world emperor was to be a Frankish king.[4] The Tiburtine
Sibyl, the Pseudo-Methodius, and Adso all specified that the reign of
the last world emperor would end with the immediate arrival of the
Antichrist. Hence last world emperor prophecies appear to be clearly
apocalyptic, but in fact it is difficult to be certain whether the texts
were actually understood in that way or whether readers focused on the
charisma of the ruler and dismissed the apocalyptic ending by
interpreting it figuratively.

Intellectual history alone, however, cannot adequately answer the questions raised in *Millennial Violence: Past, Present and Future*. Any study of the impact of apocalyptic concepts on human actions demands a grasp of the social and economic structures as well as the mental ones. Because the social and economic structures are part of overall historical periods and cannot really be grasped without that periodization, this article will first sketch the early and high Middle Ages.

Forty years ago, the notion prevailed that there was one 'Middle Age' that stretched from the end of the Roman world – whenever that happened – to the beginning of the early modern world, roughly from the Germanic 'invasions' of the late fourth and fifth centuries CE to the end of the fifteenth century. Outside the ranks of medieval historians, that notion is still widely accepted. Today, however, a majority of medieval historians are convinced that the most profound changes took place between the time of Charlemagne and that of Dante, not between Constantine and Charlemagne or between Dante and Louis XIV. The world of *Beowulf* is so totally different from the world of Thomas Aquinas and Dante that it is impossible to keep them within a single historical period.

Beowulf, whether it was written down in the eighth or the tenth centuries, belonged to a heroic age when bards sang unwritten sagas about heroes to the kings and their warriors. Public rituals, not written documents, were used to record and preserve most transactions. Some literacy existed among the nobility and the clergy, but most surviving manuscripts were the product of monastic scriptoria. Monks were virtually the only ones who insisted on charters as written records of the publicly enacted transfers by which the monasteries were given land. A number of the best-known manuscripts, such as the gospel book of Kells, were really precious treasures to be displayed rather than read. By comparison to the period after 1100, many fewer manuscripts were copied and even fewer are preserved.

Everyone except the outlaw was bound by personal ties to kin, to lord, and perhaps to residents of the same village or manor. All others were strangers and it did not matter whether the stranger was a Christian, a Muslim or a Jew. The clergy perhaps cared about one's religion, or at least some did, but the laity apparently did not. Hence anti-Judaism was confined to a few clerics and Latin Christians were only slightly aware even of the existence of Islam.[5]

Localism prevailed everywhere. The marriage of a woman to a distant king or lord provided a personal connection between

geographically distant places, but even in these cases the outlook was
confined to matters having to do with the kinsperson. Merchants and
pilgrims carried stories, especially sensational ones, from place to place.
Nevertheless, for virtually everyone, the areas beyond their own village
were unknown and alien. As in *Beowulf*, monsters could be imagined to
live not far from the lord's hall.

We focus geographically on the north of Europe, an area that had
never been more than superficially Romanized and where cities had
always been few and small even during the glory days of the Roman
Empire. Most people were either lords or peasants and not townspeople.
The lords included both the upper clergy and the monks, while local
priests were probably peasants. Peasants comprised at least 90 per cent
of the population.

How Christian were these lords and peasants? Carlo Ginzburg and
George Huppert have argued that even in the sixteenth century, the
beliefs of most ordinary Christians bore little resemblance to the
orthodox theology that was taught to and propounded by theologians in
the universities. John Van Enghen has tried to argue more positively for
'popular Christianity'. In fact, before about 1100, we do not really
know what most of the people, i.e. the peasants, thought. Their religion
may have been only slightly 'baptized' paganism. We also have little
knowledge about parish churches. Was there even a network of parish
churches throughout the west such that everyone could have gone to
mass readily? Many monks believed that only monks could be saved
and, if the monks were from noble families, would they have been
concerned at all with the salvation of the peasantry?[6]

Oral epics have survived only if they were later written down and
public rituals involving sales, etc., died with the memories of those who
witnessed them. The sources up to the end of the tenth century are,
therefore, extremely scanty, and most of them survive in versions from
the late eleventh or the twelfth centuries, and, accordingly, their
interpretation is often controversial, not least because of possible later
interpolations or alterations.[7] Qualitative questions can be answered
with some accuracy, but questions of quantity usually receive nothing
more than guesses. Many of the key issues having to do with the year
1000 are more quantitative than qualitative, most especially the popular
prevalence of millennialism at the end of the first millennium. Most
statements on these issues can, therefore, only be treated as
sophisticated guesses.

Richard W. Southern characterized the transition from the early medieval to the high medieval eras as a shift from an epic to a romance outlook:

> The change of emphasis from localism to universality, the emergence of systematic thought, the rise of logic – to these we may add a change which in a certain sense comprehends them all: the change from epic to romance. The contrast … is a reflection of a more general change of attitude … Briefly, we find less talk of life as an exercise in endurance, and of death in a hopeless cause; and we hear more of life as a seeking and a journeying. Men begin or order their experience more consciously in accordance with a plan: they think of themselves less as stationary objects of attack by spiritual foes, and more as pilgrims and seekers…[8]

Beowulf was an oral folk-epic before an anonymous scribe wrote it down. Dante's *Divine Comedy* is the work of a highly literate poet who imagined his own pilgrimage from the dark wood of sin through hell and purgatory to paradise, and in so doing sought to 'order [his] experience more consciously' and deliberately. *Beowulf*'s world was heroic, dominated by male warriors who simply acted, never stopping to ask themselves why they were attacking monsters. By contrast, women held key places in the romance world. Beatrice was Dante's guide to paradise and the reason why Virgil was sent to guide Dante through hell and purgatory. Benedict's chapter on humility in the *Regula*, written in the late fifth or early sixth century, mentioned 12 rungs on the ladder of life, but 'these rungs really turn out to be varying manifestations of a fundamental attitude – the sense of living in the presence of God'.[9] In the twelfth century, Anselm of Canterbury and Bernard of Clairvaux transformed this ladder into an internal, logically ordered, psychological progression from egotism to true *caritas*, the desire to do God's will always without any wish to obtain something in return. Loyalty gave way to love and an external shame culture to an internal guilt one.

Broadening horizons manifested themselves in the Crusades as well as in the translations from Arabic to Latin in Spain that brought scholars at Paris in contact with the works of Aristotle, Ptolemy, Averroes, Avicenna and Maimonides. At Paris, Oxford and Bologna the universities provided *loci* where scholars commented on these texts, debated their meaning, formulated systematic questions, and ultimately sought to order all of this knowledge into rationally planned *summe*. The attraction of logic was its universality, i.e., its ability to prove that certain propositions were true everywhere, to everyone, always, as well as its ability to discern truth from opinion and to slot all knowledge into a unified synthesis.

Nothing is more indicative of this change than the shift from a world of unwritten custom where county and shire courts relied on *boni homines* – presumably mature and trusted persons from the community, to say what the custom of that community or kin group was – to a world where the laws were written and where those wishing to sue in the courts had to retain attorneys who had graduated from the law faculties, because only these attorneys had the specialized knowledge of the law and its procedures without which one might lose one's suit on procedural grounds alone. By the thirteenth century, custom was being 'systematized' in written collections, and this process was redefining and codifying the multifarious relationships between lords and lords, and lords and peasants, according to written prescriptions.[10]

Oral communication gave way to written documents, and literacy both in Latin and in the vernacular became more common at least among the nobles, the clergy and especially the townspeople. Charters multiplied by the thousand while notarial registers enable historians to study the emerging towns. Chronicles and histories become numerous and massive. By the fourteenth century some more or less accurate quantitative results are possible.

The social and economic changes were sweeping. The population increased at least 300 per cent between the tenth and early fourteenth centuries. Farmers enlarged their existing fields, cleared new fields and migrated to new villages that were being systematically established by ambitious lords. This internal frontier was matched by an external one. In 1000 most of northern Europe east of the Elbe and Saale rivers was populated by people who spoke Slavic languages. Between about 1120 and 1300 German lords conquered and colonized what became the duchies of Brandenburg and of Prussia and until recently comprised the German Democratic Republic. Other German-speaking colonists migrated eastward from Bavaria, founding Austria. Slavic and Magyar lords settled villages of German-speakers in Poland, Bohemia and Hungary. The Iberian Reconquest which began in the eleventh century and culminated in the 1240s was a similar history of conquest and colonization by the Christian kingdoms of the Muslim-ruled al-Andalus.[11]

New inhabitants changed the character of the old towns and numerous new towns sprang up, especially in northern Europe where the woolen cloth industry drove the formation and growth of Flanders. By 1300 Flanders, the Rhineland, southern France, Lombardy and Tuscany had significant urban minorities among their populations. Across eastern Europe, numerous towns were founded and were usually settled by German-speakers. Townspeople waged a lengthy campaign to win basic urban privileges, especially legal freedom from their lords. The maxim *Stadtluft macht frei* (town air makes one free) came to apply all across Europe after a century of struggle that was sometimes violent, especially in the cities where the bishops were the lords. An example of such communal violence took place at Laon in France in 1112 during which Bishop Gaudry was slain.[12] The impact of the towns was enormous because townspeople promoted change and innovation as well as literacy. The coming of the orders of friars, the Franciscans and the Dominicans, testified to the growing need to preach and minister to the towns' inhabitants. The numerous representative assemblies that emerged in the late thirteenth century testified eloquently to the growing political weight that town patricians and their money could exert.

Sometime in the late ninth or early tenth century, Christian of Stavelot, commenting on Matthew 24:14, where Jesus had prophesied that the gospel of the kingdom had to be preached to all the nations and then the end could come, said that the conversion of the Khazars to Judaism and of Khan Boris of the Bulgars to Christianity (856) were hints that the gospel had indeed reached all the nations, a comment that clearly delineated Christian's notion of the limits of the world to the east because the Khazars were living along the Volga and the Bulgars in modern Bulgaria. By contrast the widening mental horizons and the establishment of the Mongol hordes from Russia to China opened up Asia to many Latin Christians, not just to Marco Polo.[13] John of Monte Corvino, OFM, wrote from Beijing about his successes and the need for more friars to come and help him.[14] Roger Bacon, OFM, made geographical knowledge of Asia one of his key requirements if the Latin Christians were going to battle peoples such as the Mongols.[15]

The role of the 'feudal revolution' in the onset of the high Middle Ages is still being debated. This 'revolution' was centered in France between about 980 and 1030. The combination of Viking attacks and the decline of the Carolingian kings – who were replaced from 911 in Germany by Conrad I and from 987 in France by the Capetians – meant that the counts and the public courts lost their authority. Castle holders, using retinues of armed soldiers, seized control over the lands and people who lived within range of their castles, defying the old authorities, and effectively taking what had been public rights into their own private hands. The term *bannum* summed up these public rights and, therefore, the new seigneurs have been described as banal lords and the obligations they imposed as *banalités*. The counts and the churchmen whose lands, rights and positions were being usurped fought back by promoting relics, public assemblies and the 'Peace of God'.[16]

Pope Leo IX (1049–54) launched the campaign which is usually identified with Gregory VII (1073–85) and known as the Gregorian reform. Bishops, whose positions were prized by local families because of the wealth and power they could wield, dominated the church, and episcopal posts were regularly bought and sold. The guardian of the shrine of St Peter was the pope, whom other Latin bishops consulted when it suited them and otherwise ignored.[17] Gregory VII, like the late Martin Luther King, was a prophet with a dream, in this case a vision of a church totally purified and rightly ordered from top to bottom. According to Gregory's notion of a just order, the lowest cleric outranked the highest layperson and, therefore, a layperson ought never to preside over a cleric. Lay investiture of clerics and the trial of cases involving clergy in lay courts were the primary battlegrounds. Moreover, sacral kings blurred the line between clergy and laity and the line had to be drawn more sharply. The reformers created a privileged clerical order stimulating the laity to create their own rationale for kingship, to become anti-clerical and to search for ways to salvation that bypassed the clergy and the sacraments.

Above all, lay investiture was sanctioned by longstanding custom. Gregory insisted that justice took precedence over custom. Gregory was, accordingly, a genuine ideologue. The papal reformers precipitated the first ideological conflict which in turn produced a sizable amount of propaganda on both sides.

Within the clergy Gregory and his successors claimed *plenitudo potestatis*, the fullness of power, which meant that bishops and the other clergy derived their rights from the popes and had to obey papal edicts. By 1150 the reformers had created a papal monarchy which had rapidly surpassed the lay monarchies in the sophistication of its governing, juridical and financial machinery.[18]

Apocalypticism is rooted ultimately in the exodus paradigm of deliverance from bondage, a journey through the wilderness, and the arrival in the promised land.[19] The prophets, especially Isaiah and his continuators, responded to the Assyrian deportation of the Israelites and the Babylonian exile of the peoples of Judah by predicting another exodus. The book of Daniel, composed about the time of the Maccabean revolt against Antiochus Epiphanes (167–164 BCE), presented fully matured apocalypticism. The struggle was no longer between Israel, Judah and their neighbors and rivals in the near east, but a cosmic struggle between God and Satan. The key forces were not human armies but archangels fighting demons. The dead who had taken God's side would rise.

Apocalypticism flourished between the Maccabean victory and Jesus' ministry, if the Dead Sea scrolls and the pseudo-epigraphic texts are any indication. The synoptic gospels presented Jesus as an apocalyptic prophet who predicted the imminent coming of the Son of Man in glory.[20] Paul believed that when he completed his ministry by going to Spain from Rome, he, the restrainer, would be removed, and the man doomed to perdition would appear and herald the *parousia*.[21]

John of Patmos wrote the Apocalypse late in the first century CE. After several series of sevens that continue to fascinate interpreters, John predicted the fall of Rome, depicted as a whore riding on a beast. Then, Satan would be chained in an abyss, Jesus would come and he and the martyrs would reign on earth for 1,000 years, at the end of which Satan would be set free, the final struggle would ensue, Jesus would come again, preside at the last judgment, and, finally, a new heaven and a new earth would surround a new Jerusalem.[22]

2 Peter 3:8 reassured Christians, disturbed because Jesus had not already returned, that with the Lord a day was like 1,000 years. This became the notion that history would last 7,000 years, divided into seven 'weeks' of 1,000 years each. The last of these would be millennial, like the Sabbath of creation week. Lactantius argued that the seventh world week would begin about 500 CE.[23]

The conversion of the emperor Constantine to Christianity and the emperor Theodosius' decision to make Christianity the official religion of the empire had profound effects on Christian apocalypticism. Eusebius of Caesarea argued that Jesus had come during the reign of the emperor Augustus because God intended to use the Roman Empire to achieve the kingdom of God on earth. Hence Eusebius anticipated modern political millennialism. Eusebius naturally redated the end of the sixth world week to *c*. 800 CE, a date safely in the future.

Augustine, bishop of Hippo, went far beyond Eusebius. Following the lead of the Donatist theologian, Tyconius, Augustine argued that the Apocalypse should be interpreted as an allegory of the struggle between God and Satan for the individual soul. God created human beings in order that the predestined elect might replace the fallen angels in heaven. History must last, therefore, until the birth and salvation of the last of these chosen persons. The 1,000 years of Apocalypse (Revelation) 20 was an indefinite period of time that began at the birth or, alternatively, the death of Jesus and would last until the end of history. Augustine divided history into seven ages (*aetates*). The first five ages preceded Jesus' birth, the first two of ten generations each, the final three of 14 each. This was a neat way of doing away with the world week because of course generations in the Hebrew scriptures varied in length of years. The sixth and the seventh *aetates* began with Jesus and would run concurrently until the second coming. The sixth represented the turmoil and suffering of the elect who were living on earth, while the seventh referred to the rest of their souls that were already in heaven.

Augustine thus individualized apocalypticism and combined it with an individual reform process that each predestined person ought to pursue. Augustine had been a Manichean and then had become a neo-Platonist, a philosophical allegiance which underlay his Christianity. Asceticism, the desire to purify oneself from the contamination of this worldliness, suffused Augustine's thought.[24]

The eighth-century Anglo-Saxon historian the Venerable Bede (*c*. 673–735) dated the birth of Jesus to the year 3952 *anno mundi*, thus postponing the end of the sixth world week to 2048 CE or AD, a date that is still in the future. Moreover, Bede took up the notion of an obscure monk, Dionysus Exiguus, who in the late fifth or early sixth centuries was responsible for counting the years from the birth of Jesus (or alternatively the death) rather than from the creation.[25] Bede was also a key figure in historicizing the first four of the seals of Apocalypse 6:1–8:5 as the times of the apostles, of the martyrs, of the doctors and of the monks.[26] Bede's 'World Chronicle', entitled 'The Six Ages of this World', uses *anno mundi* chronology down to the year 4680 (728 CE) and then adds chapters on the duration of the sixth age, opinions about the coming of Jesus, and the life of the Antichrist. Bede first cited Matthew 24:36: 'But about that day and hour no one knows, not even the angels in heaven, not even the son; only the father', a text that was to be used repeatedly to rebuke attempts to calculate the time of the end. Bede admitted that some people speculated that the world would last 6,000 years and that then there would be 'a seventh age after the resurrection, in this same life (but) immortal, and in the midst of pleasures and great happiness'. Bede described such notions as 'heretical and frivolous'. Nothing in the text indicates whether Bede was talking about Lactantius and other earlier Christian thinkers or about some of his contemporaries.[27] Two signs will indicate the coming of the last judgment: first the conversion of the Jewish people to Christianity, and second the coming of the Antichrist, which will be preceded by the arrival of the two witnesses, Enoch and Elijah. After the annihilation of the Antichrist, there will be an indefinite period before the second coming itself.[28]

Robert Lerner has called this period between the death of the Antichrist and the second coming 'the refreshment of the saints' and traced it to Jerome who, commenting on Daniel 12:11–3, explained the discrepancy between 1335 days and 1290 days (a total of 45 days) as a period when the elect will be allowed to rest (or be tested) after their sufferings at the hands of the Antichrist. Lerner has traced the development of this notion into an indefinite period of time with some millennial characteristics during the ninth through the twelfth centuries.[29]

Reformist apocalypticism grew out of papal reform. Gregory VII saw the struggle against the emperor Henry IV and other opponents as apocalyptic. Bernard of Clairvaux (1090–1153), told Pope Eugenius III (1145–53) that he had been made 'Vicar of Christ' not in order to enrich the wealthy, whose attorneys were constantly besieging him, nor to usurp the temporal duties of the emperor by commanding troops, but to complete the reform of the church.[30] Gerhoch of Reichersberg (1092/93–1169) urged Pope Hadrian IV (1154–59) to implement the reforms that Bernard had advocated to Eugenius.[31] Hildegard of Bingen (1098–1179) had addressed her *Sciuias* to Eugenius, the basic thinking of which was Augustinian.[32] The schism with Pope Alexander III (1159–81) shocked both Gerhoch and Hildegard. Gerhoch reluctantly concluded that although Alexander was the legitimate pope, he was Antichrist on the seat of Peter because he would not clear himself of charges that simony was involved in his election. Hence, Gerhoch still believed that Jesus would cleanse the church but he did not know how or by whom it would be done. Hildegard predicted that the lay princes would despoil the clergy of their temporal possessions and inaugurate an era that would be almost millennial, combining earthly prosperity with peace. Non-Christians would attack and eventually be defeated, the emperor would lose his authority almost entirely and the pope would be reduced to bishop of Rome before the end of history finally came.[33]

Abbot Joachim of Fiore (c.1135–1202), a Calabrian, gave up a promising career at the Norman court in Palermo to become a monk. He was Abbot of Corazzo when he began writing in the 1180s. Robert Lerner has labeled Joachim a millennialist and equated the abbot's third *status* of the Holy Spirit with the post-Antichrist 'refreshment of the saints' discussed above. I have argued that Joachim was a reformist apocalyptic, a disciple of Augustine of Hippo, whose third *status* had already begun with Bernard of Clairvaux, who believed that twin persecutions – perhaps by Muslims and heretics – would cleanse the church, and that two future orders (one of preachers and one of contemplatives) would help a future pope to lead Christendom into a holier, purer and more spiritual era long before the eventual end of history would come.[34]

The reformists were supporters of the Gregorian ideology which dreamed that the church would be thoroughly reformed by means of an apocalyptic crisis. Defenders of the kings and emperors, inspired by the imperial tradition of a sacral ruler, exalted various rulers as messianic leaders who would lead Christendom to universal victory and peace. Among those who were suggested as messiahs were the emperor Henry IV, Louis VI of France and the emperor Frederick Barbarossa.[35]

Apocalypticism changed decisively during the thirteenth century. The trend was toward shorter, usually pseudonymous texts that merged papalist with imperialist and reformist with millennialist programs in increasingly detailed, eclectic scenarios. One catalyst was the conflict between the emperor Frederick II (reigned 1215–50) and the papacy, a struggle that became truly apocalyptic in the 1240s and that echoed in prophetic texts well into the fourteenth century. The other catalyst was the coming of the two orders of mendicant friars, the Order of Friars Minor, founded by Francis of Assisi, and the Order of Preaching Friars, founded by Dominic.

The papal reformists were not forgotten. Abbot Joachim's *Liber de concordia noui ac ueteris testamenti* was copied and studied both at Paris and in Florence and his *Liber figurarum* possibly influenced Dante.[36] Gebeno of Eberbach chose the most important texts from

Hildegard's works and combined them in his *Pentachronon*, in which form they circulated widely.[37]

Innovative reformist thinking did not entirely disappear either. An anonymous German monk authored a fascinating work in 1237–38 that utilized the letters of the Latin alphabet to characterize the centuries from the founding of Rome in 752 BCE to the end of history. Under the letter 'x', 1248–1348 CE, the church would be thoroughly reformed and during 'y', 1348–1448, the Jews would convert, as well as many other non-Christians. History would end about 1598.[38]

The pseudo-Joachim, *Super hieremiam*, a commentary on Jeremiah that Joachim himself may have begun, but that was glossed and enlarged at least twice before 1248, was a key text in the transformation of apocalypticism. The final version was extremely hostile to Frederick II, but critical of the papacy, and predicted the coming of the two orders of friars.[39]

Gerard of Borgo San Donnino, OFM, published his *Liber introductorius* in 1254 or 1255, which included an introduction and editions with glosses of some of Abbot Joachim's writings. According to its opponents Gerard argued that in 1260 the present status of the church would end, both the clergy and the sacraments would be abolished, and a new church of the 'barefoot' would begin. This 'millenarian' interpretation of Joachim set off a storm of protest among the theologians at Paris, who used Gerard to attack the mendicant orders. Meanwhile other friars minor, most notably John of Parma, who headed the order between 1245 and 1257 and the chronicler Salimbene, became 'Joachites'.[40]

Peter Olivi, OFM (died 1298) studied Joachim's writings carefully and in his *Lectura super apocalypsim* created a powerful and influential synthesis of Franciscanism and Joachitism. Ubertino da Casale in turn incorporated Olivi's thinking into his massive *Arbor uitae*. Olivi attracted a cult following among both the friars and the laity in Provence and Catalonia, until John XXII ordered it repressed.[41]

Johannes de Rupescissa or Jean de Roquetaillade, a Franciscan friar (*c*.1310 to *c*.1366) wrote numerous works in which he synthesized Franciscans, Joachimism, French messianic kings and reforming popes. According to Robert Lerner he was the only medieval thinker who predicted a literal millennium of 1,000 years that should have begun about 1370. His *Vade mecum in tribulatione* circulated widely both in the original Latin and in vernacular translations.[42]

Augustinian friars and the Jesuits both sought to use Joachim's and Joachimist texts as predictions of their coming and role within the church, just as supporters of the Franciscans and Dominicans had done earlier. French prophecies of a second Charlemagne and German predictions of a third Frederick combined Joachimism with the earlier tradition about the last world emperor. A widely copied series of prophecies predicted a series of reforming popes.[43] Humanists linked Joachimism with Renaissance notions of a new age.[44]

The diffusion of 'Joachimism' among mainstream clerics and laity has been further documented by studies of individual prophecies. Robert Lerner's study of the Tripoli prophecy demonstrated that it was circulated and copied primarily among clerics.[45] Studies of the English and the continental manuscripts of the 'Columbinus prophecy', a Joachimist text, showed the same type of audience.[46]

Marjorie Reeves suggested the study of prophetic anthologies, manuscripts into which a collection of apocalyptic texts and prophecies were copied, because such anthologies showed who was reading prophecies, what they were reading, and to a limited extent how they reacted to the texts.[47] Henry of Kirkstede, who was librarian at Bury St Edmund, an old Benedictine house, compiled *Corpus Christi College Cambridge 404* in the middle of the fourteenth century. Henry added a brief treatise of his own entitled 'De antichristo et fine mundi', which indicated that he was struck by how the texts he had collected offered different and even contradictory interpretations of the events of his century.[48] Luke of s. Gemignano, who had copied prophetic texts from the middle of the fifteenth century onward, was in Florence when Friar Savonarola was preaching about his apocalyptic visions for the future of Florence.[49] Reformist apocalypticism, messianism and millennialism were available at least among the literate who could afford manuscripts and were being popularly preached by the late fifteenth century in a center of humanist learning like Florence.

The spread of 'Joachimism' continued steadily into the middle of the seventeenth century.[50] From its high medieval roots, apocalypticism became a key driving force among the mainstream clergy and laity through the middle of the seventeenth century at the least.

Norman Cohn traced a series of 'millenial' sects and movements from the eleventh into the sixteenth century. Cohn characterized the adherents of such sects as *pauperes*; those who had been uprooted and found themselves alienated from the communities in which they were then living.[51] The sociology and the millennialism of some of these movements remain under debate, for example the crusade movements headed by Peter the Hermit and Count Emich of Leisingen. Others are clearly seen as millenial.[52] John Ball, whom Froissart blamed for the 1381 peasant revolt in England, was probably a millennialist, but the peasants' demands were for the abolition of villeinage and for higher wages, which indicate that the peasants were rebels, not revolutionaries, and were driven by reformist concerns as well as by 'rising hopes', i.e., the dearth of laborers after the Black Death that created economic trends favorable to the peasants.[53] Robert Lerner argued that the 'Free spirits' were mystics, but not peaceful anarchists as Cohn had contended.[54] The Tabards or Picards, perhaps the most extreme group among the Hussites, were certainly millennialists.[55] Thomas Münzer was a 'Joachimist' and religious reform certainly was a significant factor in the German peasants' revolt of 1525, but once again, the peasants were rebels, not millenarian revolutionaries.[56] The Anabaptist leaders at Münster, Jan Mathijs and Jan of Leiden, were certainly millennialists who briefly established a revolutionary regime in the city.[57]

In summary, before 1000 CE, Augustinian thinking loomed large in a world where the monks dominated Christian thinking and writing, although there is evidence that notion of the world week and the coming of the millennium after the year 5999 *anno mundi* continued to attract some attention. The 'refreshment of the saints' was 'millennial', but it was confined to books written and read by learned monks. The papal reform stimulated both reformist and imperial apocalypticism. 'Joachimism' became widespread in mainstream thinking from the middle of the thirteenth century onward and here and there truly millennial or revolutionary sects appeared in the fourteenth, fifteenth and sixteenth centuries. The evidence strongly suggests that apocalypticism was a monastic and clerical phenomenon before 1000, but that it had been much more widely diffused by 1500, by which time one can accurately speak of 'popular apocalypticism' and 'popular millennialism'.

What then about millennial expectations focused on the year 1000 CE? Richard Landes argues that there was intense popular expectation that culminated with the coming of the year 1000, and that played out in various phenomena, heretical sects and anti-Jewish pogroms.[58] The evidence is scarce and ambiguous. Rodulfus Glaber observed that many

events worthy of comment occurred about the year 1000. Abbon of
Fleury's *Apologeticus* mentioned a sermon that had been preached at
Paris in his youth that had argued that the Antichrist would come about
the year 1000. Archbishop Wulfstan of York's three homilies include
one on the time of Antichrist and another on the Antichrist himself, and
Adso composed his treatise on the Antichrist about 954.[59]

These texts show that apocalyptic expectation existed in the tenth
century and that Glaber, as well as the anonymous preacher at Paris, saw
some apocalyptic significance in the year 1000 CE; but was there a
widespread 'popular' expectation that erupted in heretical movements
and anti-Jewish pogroms?

This notion rests on two doubtful assumptions. The first is that there
was a dichotomy between literate elite thinking and the 'popular'
mindset. Peter Brown called this into question with regard to the use and
veneration of relics in late antiquity, arguing the collection and display
of relics for veneration reflected the beliefs and wishes of Bishop
Ambrose, for example, not a concession to 'the people'.[60] Ninety per
cent of the population in 1000 were peasants and we do not know
anything about their understanding of Christianity, as was pointed out
above. The warrior world was primarily an oral culture as reflected in
Beowulf, where the Christian gloss was superficial at best. A few
laypersons such as Einhard were literate, but most of the writing was
done by monks and, as has been already pointed out, the monks were
overwhelmingly influenced by Augustine and Bede. In my opinion, the
social and cultural structures of the tenth century world make it
extremely difficult to assume that there was a 'people' who were
strongly imbued with millennialism.[61]

The notion that the church had condemned and deliberately
repressed millennialism is an anachronism when it is applied before
1200. After all, the millennium had obvious scriptural proof: Apoc.
(Revelation) 20:1–6. To my knowledge, there never has been an official
condemnation, either before or since 1000. Augustine and Bede were
prominent thinkers, but they were not popes. Moreover, the popes
before the papal reformers were not monarchs ruling a centralized
church, but instead were guardians of the shrine of Peter. Local bishops
ruled their dioceses independently of a central ecclesiastical power. The
high Middle Ages brought an openness that only slowly gave way to
increasing rigidity and repression. The notion that there was only one
church, that it had existed from the beginning, that in all essentials it was

one and unchanging, and that anyone who disagreed with that was a heretic, began to appear in the thirteenth century, gained strength in the fourteenth and fifteenth centuries, but really came into its own during the religious wars and the confessionalism of the period from the 1540s to the 1640s. To read this kind of 'fortress mentality' back into the period before 1000 is to commit an anachronism.

Augustine and Bede had individualized apocalypticism and had tried to supplant the world week with its notion of a seventh millennial period by a scheme of seven *aetates* that discarded chronological reckoning in favor of the individual pursuit of salvation. For Augustine and Bede, the 'millennium' or seventh age was the rest of the souls of the elect with Christ in heaven after death. The 'refreshment of the saints' had an earthly millennial component, but it was only an idea. *Anno domini* dating was in origin anti-millennial, and it is not clear why those who looked for an *anno mundi* millennium would suddenly adopt AD dating as millennial. Most dating was done by regnal years and indictions rather than by either AM or AD chronologies.[62] I do not think, therefore, that more than a handful of churchmen knew about the year 1000 or cared about it.

The Romans were extreme traditionalists for whom piety was to carry on the tradition, for whom anything new was automatically bad, and for whom change could only be from bad to worse. Millennialism, even when it only implied change for the better, was un-Roman. However, the last decades of the tenth century were also the first decades of the high Middle Ages, so that if there were 'millennial' movements, they had more to do with beginnings of the new 'romance' thinking and the 'feudal revolution' than with any repressed 'popular millennialism'.[63]

What then about the *Megiddo Report* and the end of the second millennium? First of all, the survey of high medieval and early modern apocalypticism has shown that reformists might sometimes encourage violence, that revolts might have apocalyptic origins, and that truly millennial, revolutionary sects did occur. The peasant revolts in England and Germany were due both to religious ferment and to economic conditions, particular the rising expectations created by the Black Death, the dearth of laborers, and the relative abundance of land. Religious expectation helped motivate the peasants but neither 1381 nor 1525 had millennial connotations as years. Most Hussites were reformists, as were the leaders of the magisterial reformations, but revolutionary Tabards were part of the Hussite revolt and millenarians took over reformed Münster.

Research is badly needed to bridge the gap between the late seventeenth century and the nineteenth century in order to prove or disprove the notion that modern apocalypticism was a continuation or a resumption of high medieval and early modern patterns.[64] Marxism, anarchism and fascism certainly had millennialist and revolutionary elements, but political millennialism was also widespread.[65]

I have argued that there was no popular millennial expectation in 999 CE. I am an active Christian and I never perceived any widespread popular expectation in the last months of 1999, much less in December 2000, either among the Christians whom I know or among my other friends. When 1 January 2000 came quietly and the computers did not all crash, my own thinking was that most of the alarm had been nothing but media hype, and I suspect this thinking was widely shared. Mainstream Christian churches have been reluctant to acknowledge apocalypticism, much less millennialism, although they were strongly rooted in political millennialism. Rarely does a minister preach from the Apocalypse, and the book's interpretation has been left to those denominations or sects that have made it the focus of their thinking.

Is there, then, no real link between apocalypticism, millennialism and terrorism? Yes, there is and the real danger of focusing on 31 December 999 or 31 December 1999 is that after those 'fateful dates' passed, we relaxed and assumed that religion is not a factor in terrorism.

According to the *Megiddo Report*, 'religious motivation and the NWO conspiracy theory are the two driving forces behind the potential for millennial violence'. The report saw religious forces behind the racial holy war violence committed by Buford O. Furrow, Jr., and also behind the New World Order conspiracy theory. Racial tensions have not abated in the United States, and the evidence suggests that white supremacists remain as much a threat now as they were in 1999. Tensions also remain high among the black underclass. Certainly NWO thinking continues, and the election of a Republican conservative, G. W. Bush, probably did not reassure the hardcore believers and make them any less likely to engage in violence.

The most widely publicized terrorist act in the USA until 2001 was the bombing of the Federal Building in Oklahoma City on 19 April 1995, an act to which Timothy McVeigh confessed. McVeigh had a copy of *The Turner Diaries* in his possession when he was arrested. This book was written by William Pierce, the leader of the white supremacist National Alliance. It outlined both a takeover of the federal government and a race war. McVeigh apparently, however, was primarily motivated by the desire to avenge those who had died during the FBI's final assault on the Branch Dravidian compound at Waco in April 1993, and he probably was also acting against what he perceived as a government that he thought was out to destroy him and his beliefs.

Was the bombing in Oklahoma City a classical anarchist act, an attempt to bring down the existing governing structure and perhaps the social and economic structures as well? No evidence exists to link McVeigh to such an anarchist conspiracy. Violent anarchists are the contemporary parallel to the Tabards and Münsterites, but such groups have been European, not American. Nevertheless, in so far as both religious sects and NWO conspiracy groups are anarchists, the potential for violence continues.

On 29 May 2001, four Muslims were convicted of global conspiracy in the bombing of the US embassies in Nairobi, Kenya, and Dar es Salaam, Tanzania on 7 August 1998. According to a recent article in the *New Yorker*, former FBI Director Louis Freeh is still pursuing the bombers who destroyed the Khobar Towers in Saudi Arabia on June 25, 1996, as well as the attackers of the USS Cole in October 2000, in particular investigating whether officials in the Iranian government were involved.[66] Shiite Islam has also had a messianic component and this has been a significant factor in Iranian policy since the expulsion of the Shah alongside the desire of fervent Muslims to abolish the 'Western-type' state and recreate an Islamic regime.

Religious conflict is nowhere more complicated and potentially explosive than in the case of the old city of Jerusalem. Lawrence Wright, writing in *The New Yorker*, described how a cattleman from Mississippi, Clyde Lott, read Numbers 19:1, 'Tell the Israelites to bring you a red cow without blemish or defect' to carry out a purification rite, and concluded that such a red heifer had to be found in Israel so that the temple could be rebuilt and the Jewish messiah come who, of course, to Lott would be the Antichrist. In Rabbi Chaim Richman, who belonged to the Temple Institute, a group dedicated to rebuilding the temple, Lott found a willing partner. Lott and Richman began an effort to export cattle to Israel in order that such a pure red heifer might eventually be born there.[67] This is a case where two apocalyptic scenarios, one Christian and one Jewish, coincide and, because rebuilding the temple is

294 MILLENNIAL VIOLENCE

involved, the potential exists for explosive consequences. Religious
revivals are going on among Jews, Christians and Muslims, and these
reinforce apocalyptic currents widely present in our world. The potential
for violence did not end or diminish on 1 January 2000.

NOTES

1. E. Randolph Daniel, 'A New Understanding of Joachim: The Concords, the Exile, and
the Exodus', in Roberto Rusconi (ed.), *Gioacchino da fiore tra Bernardo di Clairvaux
e Innocenzo III* (Rome: Viella, 2001), pp.209–22, at 219; Daniel, 'Reformist
Apocalypticism and the Friars Minor', in Michael F. Cusato, OFM, and F. Edward
Coughlin, OFM (eds.), *That Others May Know and Love: Essays in Honor of Zachary
Hayes, OFM* (St Bonaventure, NY: The Franciscan Institute, 1997), pp.237–53;
Kathryn Kerby-Fulton, *Reformist Apocalypticism and 'Piers Plowman'* (Cambridge:
Cambridge University Press, 1990), pp.4–9, first developed the concept of reformist
apocalypticism.
2. Norman Cohn, *The Pursuit of the Millennium*, revised and expanded edition (New York:
Oxford University Press, 1970), p.15 (unnumbered).
3. Jürgen Moltmann, *The Coming of God: Eschatology Today* (Minneapolis, MN: Fortress
Press, 1996), p.3. Moltmann's book is probably the best overall study of apocalypticism
available today.
4. The sources of the last world emperor notion are the Tiburtine Sibyl and Pseudo-
Methodius. For the texts in translation see Bernard McGinn, *Visions of the End*,
Columbia Records of Civilization, no. xcvi, (New York: Columbia University Press,
1998), pp.43–50, 70–76. For Adso, see Bernard McGinn, *Apocalyptic Spirituality* (New
York: Paulist Press, 1979), pp.81–96, which includes the translated text.
5. See Richard W. Southern, *Western Views of Islam in the Middle Ages* (Cambridge, MA:
Harvard University Press, 1962), pp.1–33. On the Jews see for example Bernard
Bachrach, *Early Medieval Jewish Policy* (Minneapolis, MN: University of Minnesota
Press, 1977).
6. Carlo Ginzburg, *The Cheese and the Worms* (Harmondsworth, Middlesex: Penguin
Books, 1982); George Huppert, *After the Black Death: A Social History of Early
Modern Europe* (Bloomington, IN: Indiana University Press, 1998), pp.134–48; and
John Van Engen, 'The Christian Middle Ages as an Historiographical Problem',
American Historical Review 91(1986), pp.519–52.
7. See for example Patrick J. Geary, Richard Landes, Amy G. Remensnyder, Timothy
Reuter and Barbara H. Rosenwein (coordinator) 'Qui a peur de l'an mil? Un débat
électronique aux approches de l'an 2000', in Monique Bourin and Barbara H.
Rosenwein (eds.), *Médiévales 37: L'an mil en 2000* (Saint-Denis: Presses universitaires
de Vincennes-Paris VIII Autumn 1999), pp.15–55, especially the discussion concerning
a charter from St Victor of Marseilles, the date and interpretation of which are here very
much in dispute (pp.20–28).
8. Richard W. Southern, *The Making of the Middle Ages* (New Haven, CT: Yale University
Press, 1953), pp.221–2. Marc Bloch, *Feudal Society*, Part II, (Chicago: University of
Chicago Press, 1964), pp.59–120 is equally fundamental to an understanding of the two
eras and the shift from one to the other. Charles Homer Haskins, *The Renaissance of the
Twelfth Century* (Cambridge, MA: Harvard University Press, 1927) surveyed the
twelfth century through a Burckhardtian paradigm of the Italian renaissance.
9. Southern, *Making* (note 8), p.24. Benedict's God was a harsh, aristocratic deity who
insisted on totally crushing the proud. Hence Roman aristocrats, to whose ranks
Benedict belonged, had to be ground down and abased like slaves in order to satisfy
God. God, in other words, was like 'Big Brother' in George Orwell's *1984*.

10. See Susan Reynolds, *Fiefs and Vassals: The Medieval Evidence Re-Interpreted* (Oxford: Oxford University Press 1994), pp.1–16; James A. Brundage, *Medieval Canon Law* (London and New York: Longman, 1995), pp.59–69.

11. Robert L. Reynolds, 'The Mediterranean Frontiers, 1000–1400', in Walker D. Wyman and Clifton B. Kroeber (eds.), *The Frontier in Perspective* (Madison: University of Wisconsin Press, 1965), pp.21–34; Robert Bartlett, *The Making of Europe: Conquest, Colonization and Cultural Change 950–1350* (Princeton, NJ: Princeton University Press, 1993).

12. The Laon commune and its revolt were described in the third book of Guibert of Nogent's *A Monk's Confession: The Memoirs of Guibert of Nogent* (University Park, PA: Penn State University Press, 1996), pp.121–81.

13. Christianus Druthmar, *Expositio in Matthaeum euangelistam*, in J. Migne (ed.), Patrologia latina (PL) vol. 106, (Paris: J.-Migne editores 1864), col. 1,456.

14. Christopher Dawson, *Mission to Asia* (New York and Evanston, IL: Harper and Row 1966), pp.224–31, contains translations of the letters. The letters are dated 1305 and 1306.

15. E. Randolph Daniel, *The Franciscan Concept of Mission in the High Middle Ages* (Lexington, KY: University Press of Kentucky 1975; reprinted St Bonaventure: The Franciscan Institute, 1992), pp.55–66.

16. The 'feudal revolution' goes back to Marc Bloch's *Feudal Society* (note 8). Important studies include Georges Duby, *La société aux xie et xiie siècles dans la région mâconnaise* (Paris: A. Colin, 1953); Duby, *The Three Orders: Feudal Society Imagined* (Chicago: University of Chicago Press, 1980); Jean-Pierre Poly and Eric Bournazel, *The Feudal Transformation: 900–1200* (New York and London: Holmes & Meier, 1991); Guy Bois, *The Transformation of the Year 1000: the Village of Lournand From Antiquity to Feudalism* (Manchester: University of Manchester Press, 1992). Bois' study showed that the collapse of public order and the public courts put the lesser landowners at the mercy of the new seigneurs. Cf. the charter from St Victor and the discussion cited above in note 7. On the 'feudal revolution' and the Peace of God movement, see Richard Landes, *Relics, Apocalypse, and the Deceits of History: Ademar of Chabannes, 989–1034* (Cambridge, MA: Harvard University Press, 1995) and Thomas Head and Richard Landes (eds.), *The Peace of God: Social Violence and Religious Response in France Around the Year 1000* (Ithaca, NY: Cornell University Press, 1992).

17. Southern, *Making* (note 8), pp.118–39.

18. On the papal reform see Gerd Tellenbach, *Church, State and Christian Society at the Time of the Investiture Contest* (New York and Evanston, IL: Harper and Row, 1970; orig. pub. London: Basil Blackwell and Mott 1959); Colin Morris, *The Papal Monarchy: The Western Church from 1050 to 1250* (Oxford: Oxford University Press, 1989); I. S. Robinson, *The Papacy 1073–1198: Continuity and Innovation* (Cambridge: Cambridge University Press, 1990); H. E. J. Cowdrey, *Pope Gregory VII 1073–1085* (Oxford: Oxford University Press, 1998); Caroline Walker Bynum, *Jesus as Mother: Studies in the Spirituality of the High Middle Ages* (Los Angeles and Berkeley: University of California Press, 1982), pp.9–21, has one of the best short treatments of the consequences of the reforms. Richard W. Southern, *Western Society and the Church in the Middle Ages*, The Pelican History of the Church 2 (Harmondsworth, Middlesex: Penguin Books, 1970) remains one the best assessments of the outcome of the reforms.

19. Michael Walzer, *Exodus and Revolution* (New York: Basic Books, 1985).

20. Most portraits of the 'historical Jesus' do their best to explain away this apocalypticism, although recent studies have begun to accept it. See for example Bart D. Ehrman, *Jesus: Apocalyptic Prophet of the New Millennium* (Oxford: Oxford University Press, 1999).

21. Johannes Munck, *Paul and the Salvation of Mankind* (Richmond, VA: John Knox Press, 1959); Munck, *Christ and Israel* (Philadelphia: Fortress Press, 1967). This interpretation of Paul is controversial. The primary texts are 1 Thessalonians 4:13–5:11, Romans 9–11, 1 Corinthians 7.

22. For surveys of apocalypticism see Bernard McGinn, *Antichrist: Two Thousand Years of*

the Human Fascination With Evil (New York: HarperSanFrancisco, 1994); McGinn
(ed.), *The Encyclopedia of Apocalypticism* (3 vols.) (New York: Continuum, 1998);
Richard Emmerson and Bernard McGinn (eds.), *The Apocalypse in the Middle Ages*
(Ithaca, NY: Cornell University Press, 1992); Christopher Kleinhenz and Fannie J.
LeMoine (eds.), *Fearful Hope: Approaching the New Millennium* (Madison, WI: The
University of Wisconsin Press, 1999); Caroline Walker Bynum and Paul Freedman
(eds.), *Last Things: Death and the Apocalypse in the Middle Ages* (Philadephia:
University of Pennsylvania Press, 2000).

23. On the world week and *anno mundi* dating see Richard Landes, 'Lest the Millennium be
    Fulfilled: Apocalyptic Expectations and the Pattern of Western Chronography 100–800
    CE', in Werner Verbeke, Daniel Verhelst and Andries Welkenhuysen (eds.), *The Use
    and Abuse of Eschatology in the Middle Ages* (Mediaevalia lovaniensis, series 1, studia
    15; Leuvan: Leuvan University Press, 1988), pp.137–211. For Lactantius see McGinn,
    Apocalyptic Spirituality (note 4), pp.17–80.

24. On the notion of reform see Gerhart B. Ladner, *The Idea of Reform* (New York and
    Evanston, IL: Harper and Row, 1967), pp.153–283. The best life remains Peter Brown,
    Augustine of Hippo (Los Angeles and Berkeley: University of California Press, 1969).

25. Bede, *Bede: The Reckoning of Time* (trans., with introduction, notes and commentary by
    Faith Wallis; Liverpool: The Liverpool University Press, 1999), pp.126, 195.

26. On the seven seals, see Douglas W. Lumsden, *And Then The End Will Come: Early
    Latin Christian Interpretations of the Opening of the Seven Seals* (New York and
    London: Garland Publishing, 2001).

27. Bede, *Reckoning*, pp.239–40.

28. Ibid., pp.241–3.

29. Robert Lerner, 'Refreshment of the Saints: The Time After Antichrist as a Station for
    Earthly Progress in Medieval Thought', *Traditio* 32 (1976), pp.97–144.

30. Bernard of Clairvaux, *Five Books on Consideration: Advice to a Pope* (Cistercian
    fathers series, no. 37), (Kalamazoo, MI: Cistercian Publications, 1976).

31. Gerhoch of Reichersberg, 'Letter to Pope Hadrian About the Novelties of the Day', in
    Nikolaus Haring (ed.), Studies and texts 24 (Toronto: Pontifical Institute of Medieval
    Studies, 1974).

32. Hildegard of Bingen, *Sciuias* (New York: Paulist Press, 1990). See especially book
    three, visions 9–11, pp.451–511.

33. E. Randolph Daniel, 'Reformist Apocalypticism', pp.242–5; Kerby-Fulton, *Reformist
    Apocalypticism*, pp.45–56.

34. Robert Lerner, *The Feast of Saint Abraham: Medieval Millenarians and the Jews*
    (Philadephia: University of Pennsylvania Press, 2001) is the most recent exposition of
    Lerner's views on Joachim. For a review of his earlier articles see E. Randolph Daniel,
    'Joachim of Fiore: New Editions and Studies', *cristianesimo nella storia* 21 (2000),
    pp.673–83. For my interpretation see Daniel, *A New Understanding*, 'Reformist
    Apocalypticism', pp.245–8, 'Exodus and Exile: Joachim of Fiore's Apocalyptic
    Scenario', in Bynum and Freedman, *Last Things* (note 22), pp.124–39.

35. Daniel, 'Reformist Apocalypticism', pp.250–51.

36. For the *Liber de concordia* see Abbot Joachim of Fiore, *Liber de concordia noui ac
    ueteris testamenti: Books 1–4* (ed. E. Randolph Daniel, Transactions of the American
    Philosophical Society, vol.73, pt.8) (Philadelphia: American Philosophical Society
    1983), pp.xliii–lix; E. Randolph Daniel, 'The Manuscripts of the *Liber de concordia* and
    Early Joachimism', in Antonio Crocco (ed.), *L'eta' dello spirito e la fine dei tempi in
    Gioacchino da fiore e nel gioachimismo medievale* (2 vols.) (S. Giovanni in fiore:
    Centro internazionale di studi gioachimiti 1986), vol.2, pp.357–65. For the *Liber
    figurarum* see Marjorie Reeves and Beatrice Hirsch-Reich, *The* Figurae *of Joachim of
    Fiore* (Oxford: Clarendon Press, 1972). For the possible influence on Dante see
    pp.317–29.

37. Kerby-Fulton, *Reformist Apocalypticism* (note 1), pp.28–31.

38. Daniel, 'Reformist Apocalypticism', pp.248–9.

39. Robert Moynihan, 'The Development of the "pseudo-Joachim" Commentary *Super hieremiam*: New Manuscript Evidence', *Mélanges de l'École française de Rome, moyen âge–temps moderne* 98 (1986), pp.109–42.

40. On Joachimism see Marjorie Reeves, *The Influence of Prophecy in the Later Middle Ages: A study in Joachimism* (Oxford: Clarendon Press, 1969; reprinted Notre Dame, IN: University of Notre Dame Press, 1993); Reeves, *Joachim of Fiore and the Prophetic Future*, (London: SPCK 1976; reprinted Stroud, England: Sutton Publishing, 1999). *Joachim of Fiore* devoted more space to Joachim himself than did *The Influence*, was shorter than its predecessor, and was intended for a less specialized readership. A number of Prof. Reeves' important articles have been collected in Marjorie Reeves, *The Prophetic Sense of History in Medieval and Renaissance Europe* (Aldershot: Ashgate variorum, 1999).

41. On Olivi see David Burr, *Olivi's Peaceable Kingdom* (Philadephia: University of Pennsylvania Press, 1993). On the cult of Olivi and on Ubertino see Daniel, *Franciscan Concept* (note 15), pp.86–90.

42. Johannes de Rupescissa, *Liber secretorum euentuum*, ed. Christine Morerod-Fattebert (Spicilegium friburgense, 36; Fribourg Suisse: Éditions universitaires fribourg suisse 1994). For the *Vade mecum* see Daniel, *Franciscan Concept* (note 15), pp.95–7.

43. Martha H. Fleming (ed.), *The Late Medieval Pope Prophecies: The Genus Nequam Group* (Tempe, AZ: Arizona Center for Medieval and Renaissance Studies, 1999).

44. Reeves, *Joachim of Fiore* (note 40), pp.83–115.

45. Robert Lerner, *The Powers of Prophecy* (Los Angeles and Berkeley: University of California Press, 1983).

46. 'The Columbinus Prophecy, as it stands in most English manuscripts, is composed of three distinct sections. The first of these, which originally stood on its own, was written by a Joachimist some time after 1260, who was concerned to update the timetable for the end of the sixth seal and the beginning of the seventh. The second section was added after 1291 by a writer more concerned with politics than with apocalyptic patterns: he began with the fall of Acre in 1291 and the papal call for a crusade, then proceeded to contemporary conflicts in Europe, especially those in which the king of France was embroiled, which in his opinion prevented the realization of papal plans. The third section prophesied the election in 1312 of an emperor in the line of Frederick II, and predicted dire events to befall the papacy and the clergy. Because the third section returned to the anti-Hohenstaufen theme of the first part, the prophecy gives an impression of textual unity, but it is unlikely that one person wrote all three sections. Rather what we now have is a patchwork of prophecies, the first of which was written as much as a generation before the second and the third.' E. Randolph Daniel and Kathryn Kerby-Fulton, 'English Joachimism, 1300–1500: The *Columbinus Prophecy*', in *Il profetismo gioachimita tra quattrocento e cinquecento*, Gian Luca Potestà (ed.), (Genoa: Marietti, 1991), pp.313–50, which studied the English manuscripts. See also Elizabeth A. R. Brown and Robert Lerner, 'On the Origins and Import of the Columbinus Prophecy', *Traditio* 45 (1989–90), pp.219–56.

47. Reeves, *Influence of Prophecy* (note 40), appendix C, pp.536–542.

48. The text is found on fol. 65r. See Reeves, *Influence of Prophecy* (note 40), p.541; Daniel and Kerby-Fulton, *Columbinus* (note 46), p.324; Lerner, *Powers of Prophecy* (note 45), pp.93–101.

49. Reeves, *Influence of Prophecy* (note 40), p.252, no.5 and 434. Luke's notebooks are now in Florence, Biblioteca nazionale centrale, Magl. classe VII, codice 1081, and Magl. classe XXV, codice 344. An English translation of Girolamo Savonarola's 'The Compendium of Revelations' can be found in McGinn, *Apocalyptic Spirituality* (note 4), pp.183–275.

50. Reeves, *Joachim of Fiore* (note 40), pp.157–65; Christopher Hill, *Antichrist in Seventeenth-Century England* (London: Verso, 1990). Michael Walzer, *The Revolution of the Saints* (Cambridge, MA: Harvard University Press, 1965) argued that English puritans were among the first formulators of a revolutionary ideology.

51. Norman Cohn, *Europe's Inner Demons* (Chicago: University of Chicago Press, 1993), p.xi: 'the chiliastic fantasies portrayed in *The Pursuit of the Millennium* flourished amongst the marginal elements in society – free-lance intellectuals and semi-intellectuals, landless, rootless peasants, the poorest, most desperate elements in the urban population...'.

52. Cohn, *Pursuit* (note 2); Gary Dickson, *Religious Enthusiasm in the Medieval West* (Aldershot: Ashgate, 2000) collects a number of articles about such movements by a historian from the University of Edinburgh.

53. R. H. Hilton and T. H. Aston (eds.), *The English Rising of 1381* (Cambridge: Cambridge University Press, 1984); R. B. Dobson, *The Peasants' Revolt of 1381* (London: MacMillan Press, 1983). The first offers interpretative articles, the second sources. Christopher Dyer, 'A Redistribution of Incomes in Fifteenth-Century England?', in R. H. Hilton (ed.), *Peasants, Knights and Heretics* (Cambridge: Cambridge University Press, 1981), pp.192–215; and Dyer, *Standards of Living in the Later Middle Ages*, (Cambridge: Cambridge University Press, 1989) are careful studies of the economic trends. R. H. Hilton, *Class Conflict and the Crisis of Feudalism* (London: Verso, 1990) offers a Western Marxist interpretation. For a succinct interpretation balancing religious and economic factors see M. M. Postan, *The Medieval Economy and Society* (Harmondsworth, Middlesex: Penguin Books, 1975), pp.171–3.

54. Cohn, *Pursuit* (note 2), pp.148–86; Robert Lerner, *The Heresy of the Free Spirit in the Later Middle Ages* (Los Angeles and Berkeley: University of California Press, 1972; reprinted Notre Dame, IN: University of Notre Dame Press, n.d.).

55. Cohn, *Pursuit* (note 2), pp.205–14; Howard Kaminsky, 'Chiliasm and the Hussite Revolution', in Sylvia L. Thrupp (ed.), *Change In Medieval Society* (New York: Appleton-Century Crofts, 1964), pp.249–78; Kaminsky, *A History of the Hussite Revolution* (Los Angeles and Berkeley: University of California Press, 1967), pp.310–60.

56. Reeves, *Joachim of Fiore* (note 40), pp.141–2; Cohn, *Pursuit* (note 2), pp.234–51; Peter Blickle, *The Revolution of 1525* (Baltimore, MD: Johns Hopkins University Press, 1985).

57. Cohn, *Pursuit* (note 2), pp.252–80; H. C. Erik Midelfort, 'Madness and the Millennium at Münster, 1534–1535', in Kleinhenz and LeMoine, *Fearful Hope* (note 22), pp.115–34.

58. Richard Landes, 'The Fear of an Apocalyptic Year 1000: Augustinian Historiography, Medieval and Modern', *Speculum* 75 (2000), pp.97–145; Landes, 'The Massacres of 1010: On the Origins of Popular Anti-Jewish Violence in Western Europe', in Jeremy Cohen (ed.), *From Witness to Witchcraft: Jews and Judaism in Medieval Christian Thought* (Wolfenbütteler Mittelalter-Studien, bd. 11; Wolfenbüttel: Herzog August Bibliothek, 1997), pp.79–112. Also see note 22.

59. Rodulphus Glaber, *Historiarum libri quinque* in *Opera*, ed. Neithard Bulst, trans. John France and Paul Reynolds (Oxford: Clarendon Press, 1989), pp.2–3. Geary *et al.* 'Qui a peur' (note 7), pp.29–30, has the Latin text and a French translation of the passage from Abbon. Zacharias Thundy, *Millenium: Apocalypse and Antichrist*, (Notre Dame, IN: Cross Cultural Publications, 1998), pp.231–9, has translations of Wulfstan's sermons. For Adso, see McGinn, *Apocalyptic Spirituality* (note 4), pp.81–96. In addition to the judgments expressed by the various participants in 'Qui a peur', see Henri Focillon, *The Year 1000* (New York and Evanston, IL: Harper and Row, 1971).

60. Peter Brown, *The Cult of the Saints* (Chicago: University of Chicago Press, 1981), pp.12–18; Daniel Boyarin, *Dying for God: Martyrdom and the Making of Christianity and Judaism* (Stanford, CA: Stanford University Press, 1999), p.43.

61. Ibid., pp.6–7, 18–21.

62. Dean Ware, 'Medieval Chronology: Theory and Practice', in James M. Powell (ed.), *Medieval Studies: An Introduction* (Syracuse, NY: Syracuse University Press, 1992), pp.252–77.

63. The question of heresy needs more development than I can give here. Overall see Jeffrey Burton Russell, *Dissent and Reform in The Early Middle Ages* (Los Angeles and

Berkeley: University of California Press, 1965). The topic of apocalypticism, millenialism, and anti-Judaism is far too complex to treat here.

64. For modern use of medieval apocalypticism see Moltmann, *Coming of God* (note 3); Marjorie Reeves and Warwick Gould, *Joachim of Fiore and the Myth of the Eternal Evangel in the Nineteenth Century* (Oxford: Clarendon Press, 1987); Reeves, *Joachim of Fiore* (note 40), pp.166–79.

65. James H. Moorhead, *World Without End: Mainstream American Protestant Visions of the Last Things, 1880–1925* (Bloomington, IN: Indiana University Press, 1999) treats a critical period in American thinking. Ehrman, *Jesus* (note 20), pp.3–14, discusses Edgar Whisenant and Hal Lindsay.

66. Elsa Walsh, 'Louis Freeh's Last Case', *The New Yorker*, 14 May 2001, pp.68–79. M. Hossein Nosrat, press secretary to the Permanent Mission to the UN from Iran, disavows any Iranian involvement in a letter printed in *The New Yorker*, 4 June 2001, p.6.

67. Lawrence Wright, 'Forcing the End: Why do a Pentecostal Cattle Breeder From Mississippi and an Orthodox Rabbi From Jerusalem Believe That a Red Heifer can Change the World?', *The New Yorker*, 20 July 1998, pp.42–53.

Abstracts

Project Megiddo, the FBI and the Academic Community
MICHAEL BARKUN

After the Branch Davidian standoff in 1993, the Federal Bureau of Investigation began to systematically make contacts with religion scholars. On the FBI side, most of these links were established by the Critical Incident Response Group (CIRG), a crisis management unit formed after Waco. On the academic side, the contacts were facilitated by the American Academy of Religion (AAR). While the value of these relationships was demonstrated during the Freemen standoff in Montana in 1996, it is too early to assess their overall influence. Due to organizational compartmentalization, the CIRG–AAR contacts took place separately from the drafting of the pre-2000 'Project Megiddo' report.

Questioning the Frame: The Canadian, Israeli and US Reports
EUGENE GALLAGHER

To varying degrees Canadian, Israeli and US reports on the possibility of millennial violence misconstrue the nature of millennialism. Their focus on the year 2000 places too much emphasis on the common calendar and not enough on the internal logic of millennial thought. They rely on a static image of 'cults' as being controlled by very powerful leaders whose 'whims' are eagerly carried out by followers, and dismiss the significance of interaction between groups and their opponents. Also, their focus on Jerusalem misses the capacity of millennial thought to transform any obscure location into the site of a final apocalypse.

Ten Comments on Watching Closely the Gaps Between Beliefs and Actions
BENJAMIN BEIT-HALLAHMI

Can we develop a credible risk assessment system for new religious movements? We are challenged by the complexity of interactions between beliefs, individual members, leadership and the surrounding environment. In addition, our ability to predict the actions of specific groups is severely hampered by a strong apologetic bias on the part of most NRM researchers. Beyond the problem of bias, we are faced with one practical problem and that is obtaining reliable intelligence. The truth is that scholars do not really know much about what is going on inside the thousands of religious groups in existence today.

Spectres and Shadows: Aum Shinrikyô and the Road to Megiddo
IAN READER

This article examines intelligence agency reports, such as the FBI's *Project Megiddo*, that focus on millennial religious movements and the year 2000. It does so in the context of the Japanese millennial religion Aum Shinrikyô, whose use of chemical weapons was cited in the reports as a significant watershed in the history of terrorism. Showing why the reports used Aum in this way as a 'textbook case' of millennial violence, it analyses the Aum affair in comparative millennial contexts and shows how and why its violence occurred. In so doing it shows how Project Megiddo and other reports err in many of their claims, such as the possible parallels between Aum and Christian Identity movements, the notion that Aum was trying to precipitate a final war, and the assumption that specific dates such as 2000 serve as triggers for millennial violence.

Apocalypse – Not in Finland. Millenarianism and Expectations on the Eve of the Year 2000
LEENA MALKKI

This article describes the role of millenarian beliefs in Finland. The first part focuses on religious millenarian movements and the state of the new radical right, backed up with information on Finnish religious and political scene in more general level. The second part describes how the possibility of radical religiously or politically motivated acts was perceived at the turn of the millennium and what kind of preparations were made to ensure public order and internal security. The overall conclusion is that the threat of radical actions committed by persons holding millenarian beliefs was perceived to be minimal. This view is supported by the academic research on ideologies and groups that have been viewed as possible threat elsewhere.

Cult and Anticult Totalism: Reciprocal Escalation and Violence
DICK ANTHONY, THOMAS ROBBINS and
STEVEN BARRIE-ANTHONY

Religio-ideological totalism entails an absolute division of humanity into dual categories such as saved/damned, human/subhuman, godly/demonic, etc. Totalistic 'cults' are not necessarily violent, but the psychology of totalism does feature an impulse to validate an absolute worldview by confronting demonized exemplars of evil as contrast symbols. Such confrontations can become violent under certain circumstances, which may include totalistic persecution by the anticult movement. As Robert Lifton has noted, 'Totalism begets Totalism', and anticult confrontations of totalistic movements may themselves take a totalistic and hence persecutory form. Lifton specifies the totalism begets totalism principle somewhat cryptically, and does not articulate either its theoretical or its practical implications in any detail: a defect which we attempt to remedy in this article. We discuss research which documents a cycle of increasing totalization of both the group and the counter-group response, which may escalate out of control to the point that it triggers a violent dénouement. We also develop a model of the interactively totalistic nature of both cult and anticult ideologies and activities which highlights both the psychological concept of projective identification and the sociological concepts of deviance amplification and conflict/interaction. In our discussion of this model we describe projective identification and these sociological concepts as complementary rather than competitive explanations, at different levels of description, of the 'totalism begets totalism' principle. We discuss this model in relation to a variety of research studies on millenarian religious and political movements, including two very different North American governmental reports which were apprehensive of millennial violence in 2000.

What Happens when Jesus Doesn't Come: Jewish and Christian Relations in Apocalyptic Time
RICHARD LANDES

Anti-Jewish violence in the last ten centuries follows a millennial pattern that moves from 1) apocalyptic optimism in which Christians, anticipating the *voluntary* conversion of the Jews before the advent of the millennial kingdom, engage in a period of mutually beneficial relations that contribute to economic development and social change but also generate 'anti-modern' reactions; to 2) the (inevitable) disappointment in the failure of the millennium; to 3) apocalyptic scapegoating in which the Jews, blamed for the failure because they refused to convert, become the object of demonizing from the elite and violence from the populace. This article compares and contrasts the situation at the turn of the first and the second Christian millennium (Y1K and Y2K), considering the exceptionally long period of philo-Judaism among Westerners in the period after the Holocaust, and speculating on various Christian, Muslim and secular dynamics that might produce another round of anti-Judaism and anti-Semitism in the aftermath of 2000.

Medieval Apocalypticism, Millennialism and Violence
E. RANDOLPH DANIEL

Evidence for widespread millennial expectation connected to the advent of the year 1000 is scarce. By contrast massive evidence is accumulating to show that apocalyptic and millennial expectations were becoming increasingly widespread after 1200 CE. Scholars are agreed that there were some millennial, that is, revolutionary movements after 1300. Both religious and economic factors played a role in these.

Biographical Notes

Dick Anthony is a research psychologist who has supervised a number of research programs on the psychological and social concomitants of membership in new religious movements. These programs were funded by, among others, the National Institute of Mental Health, the National Institute on Drug Abuse, the National Endowment for the Humanities, and the Ford, Rockefeller and San Francisco Foundations. He has published the results of this research widely, and recent publications have focused upon the issue of new religions and violence. He often serves as an expert witness and consulting expert in legal cases involving new religions.

Michael Barkun is Professor of Political Science in the Maxwell School at Syracuse University. His books include *Religion and the Racist Right* (1997), *Crucible of the Millennium* (1986), and *Disaster and the Millennium* (1974). He edits the Religion and Politics series for the Syracuse University Press. He has just completed a book manuscript on the spread of New World Order conspiracy theories.

Steven Barrie-Anthony has authored or co-authored a number of professional publications on religion and also several articles in the *Los Angeles Times* and the *Los Angeles Times Sunday Magazine*. He is a student at Occidental College in Los Angeles.

Benjamin Beit-Hallahmi received his Ph.D. in clinical psychology from Michigan State University in 1970. Since then he has held clinical, research and teaching positions in the USA, Europe and Israel. He is the author, co-author, editor or co-editor of 17 books and monographs on the psychology of religion, social identity and personality development. In addition, he has a special interest in questions of ethics and ideology in psychological research and practice. In 1993 he was the recipient of the William James Award for his contributions to the psychology of religion.

E. Randolph Daniel is Professor Emeritus of the Department of History of the University of Kentucky. A native Virginian, he earned his Ph.D.

from the University of Virginia in 1966, and became a member of the Department at Kentucky in the fall of that year. Earlier he had received degrees from Davidson College, Union Theological Seminary in Virginia, and a Th.M. from Harvard University. His primary research specialty is the history of apocalypticism and prophecy in medieval Europe, especially Abbot Joachim of Fiore [died 1202]. His edition of the first four books of Joachim's *Liber de concordia noui ac ueteris testamenti* was published by the American Philosophical Society in 1983. His most recent article on Joachim was published in the proceedings of the Congress held in 1999 at S. Giovanni in Fiore in Calabria, Italy, and printed by Viella in Rome. His other focus is on the early history of the Order of Friars Minor or Franciscan Order. Daniel's *The Franciscan Concept of Mission in the High Middle Ages*, originally published in 1975, is now available from the Franciscan Institute at St. Bonaventure. He is currently working with Prof. David Burr on a translation of Angelo Clareno's *Liber chronicarum siue tribulationum ordinis minorum*, a history by a leading Spiritual of the controversies within the Order of Friars Minor.

Eugene V. Gallagher is the Rosemary Park Professor of Religious Studies at Connecticut College. He is the co-author of *Why Waco? Cults and the Battle for Religious Freedom in America* and several essays on new religious movements.

Jeffrey Kaplan is the author of *Encyclopedia of White Power: A Sourcebook on the Radical Racist Right* (2000); *Radical Religion in America: Millenarian Movements From the Far Right to the Children of Noah* (1997); *The Emergence of an Euro-American Radical Right* [Co-authored with Leonard Weinberg] (1998); *Beyond The Mainstream: The Emergence of Religious Pluralism In Finland, Estonia And Russia* (2000); and is co-editing with Bron Taylor *Encyclopedia of Religion and Nature* (forthcoming 2003). He has in addition edited several anthologies as well as a number of articles in such journals as *Terrorism and Political Violence*, *Nova Religio* and *Christian Century*. He is currently Assistant Professor of Religion at the University of Wisconsin Oshkosh.

Richard Landes is a medieval historian specializing in the social and religious history of France in the central Middle Ages. He is also the director of the Center for Millennial Studies at Boston University. He is the author of *Relics, Apocalypse and the Deceits of History*, and the *Encyclopedia of Millennial Movements*. Landes is preparing a two-volume study of millennial movements in the West, the first entitled *While God Tarried: Millennialism from Jesus to the Peace of God: 33–1033*, the second, *'No King but God': The Commoner's Bible and the Origins of Civil Society in the West*.

Leena Malkki is a graduate of the University of Helsinki (Finland). She previously studied Moluccan radicalism in the Netherlands and is currently working on her Ph.D. on radical political movements in Europe at the University of Helsinki Department of Political Science.

David C. Rapoport, the co-editor of *TPV*, has written, edited or co-edited six books. The latest is *The Democratic Experience and Political Violence*, with Leonard Weinberg. He is currently editing a multi-volume edition of *New York Times* reports on terrorism since the 1880s. He is the founding Director of the Center for the Study of Religion, UCLA.

Ian Reader is Professor of Religious Studies at Lancaster University, England. His main field of study is on Japanese religions in the modern day, and he previously held academic positions in Scotland, Hawaii, Japan and Denmark. Among his recent books are *Religious Violence in Contemporary Japan: The Case of Aum Shinrikyo* (2000) and *Practically Religious: Worldly Benefits and the Common Religion of Japan* (co-authored with George J. Tanabe, 1998).

Thomas Robbins is an independent scholar (Ph.D., University of North Carolina, 1973) living in Rochester, Minnesota. He is the author of *Cults, Converts and Charisma* (1988) and co-editor of *In Gods We Trust* (1981, 1990) as well as *Millennium, Messiahs, and Mayhem* (1997) and *Misunderstanding Cults* (2001). He has authored numerous articles and essays.

Index

Voltaire 139
Waco (1993) 2–5, 34, 43, 47, 57, 69, 97,
  98–9, 101, 133, 148, 162, 227, 230, 231
Wagner-Pacifici, Robi 115
Wallis, Roy 229
Waqf guards 66
war 165
  'war games' 81
Washington, Robert 100
weapons of mass destruction 16
Webster, Michael 101
Wessinger, Catherine 3, 4, 5, 101, 102,
  113, 114, 224
west 131
  western 16, 110, 132, 276
West, Louis 6
Western (wailing) Wall 48, 121
Western calendar 124
White Power ideology 195
white supremacists 12, 32, 40–2, 44
  see also National Alliance, American
  Nazi Party, National Socialist White
  People's Party

Wicca 165
Wickstrom, James 35
Wiener, Anthony J. 124
Wiley, Stephen 104
Wilson, John 37
women 223, 249, 277
World Church of Creator 41
World Congress 39

X-Files 265

Y2K 9, 10, 29–31, 34–6, 43, 125, 147, 148,
  187, 201, 203, 206
Yahweh Ben Yahweh 44–5
  Nation of Yahweh 133
Yeshua, return of 34

Zablocki, Benjamin 8
Zionism 264
  anti-Zionism 265
  socialist Zionism 264
Zionist Occupation Government 4, 195,
  265

Books of Related Interest

The Psychology of Terrorism

John Horgan and **Max Taylor**,
both at University College, Cork

What are terrorists really like? Why would someone make a decision to join a terrorist organization? What is life like inside such movements and what is it that encourages people to eventually leave? John Horgan and Max Taylor provide the answers to these and many other pressing questions rarely answered with such clarity.

Often controversial, the author's assessment of today's behavioural research on terrorism calls for a fundamental rethinking of what the psychology of terrorism should ultimately entail. The authors argue that psychological research on terrorist behaviour needs to pursue previously unexplored avenues and in doing so, they describe how research on extremist movements can be conducted.

256 pages 2002
0 7146 5262 8
0 7146 8239 X

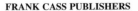

FRANK CASS PUBLISHERS
Crown House, 47 Chase Side, Southgate, London N14 5BP
Tel: +44 (0)20 8920 2100 Fax: +44 (0)20 8447 8548 E-mail: info@frankcass.com
NORTH AMERICA
5824 NE Hassalo Street, Portland, OR 97213 3644, USA
Tel: 800 944 6190 Fax: 503 280 8832 E-mail: cass@isbs.com
Website: www.frankcass.com

Science, War and Terrorism
From Laboratory to Open Conflict

Jacques Richardson

In *Science, War and Terrorism* Jacques Richardson describes the application of research to the evolution of weapons, including some of the most lethal.

Have we allowed science to become 'an extension of war by other means'? Today's military-industrial complex depends on creative research to conceive novel and more efficient weapons. Modern arms result from streamlined co-operation between laboratory investigators, designers, manufacturers and client governments. The killing power of the best equipped fighters depends, therefore, on scientific information.

Funding of scientific research is also considered. Scientific research around the world has been funded, as much as 60 per cent, by military establishments. Finally the author asks whether governments can, would or should continue to be so generous with the research community in years to come.

300 pages 2002
0 7146 5312 8 cloth
0 7146 8269 1 paper

FRANK CASS PUBLISHERS
Crown House, 47 Chase Side, Southgate, London N14 5BP
Tel: +44 (0)20 8920 2100 Fax: +44 (0)20 8447 8548 E-mail: info@frankcass.com
NORTH AMERICA
5824 NE Hassalo Street, Portland, OR 97213 3644, USA
Tel: 800 944 6190 Fax: 503 280 8832 E-mail: cass@isbs.com
Website: www.frankcass.com

Globalisation and the Future of Terrorism

Patterns and Predictions

Brynjar Lia and **Annika S Hansen**,
both at Norwegian Defence Research Establishment, Norway

The authors identify a gap in current literature on the future of terrorism and for the first time, address the effects of globalisation and theories on the cause of terrorism. The study dissects the varied and complex globalisation processes by outlining some twenty propositions on the future global security order and their possible impact on future patterns of terrorism.

It explores the security dynamics of demographic changes, the growth of legal and illegal transnational migration, the continued rise in economic inequalities within states, the marketisation and individualisation of labour, the global expansion of corporations, and the globalisation of transnational organised crime.

128 pages 2002
0 7146 5261 X cloth
0 7146 8238 1 paper

FRANK CASS PUBLISHERS
Crown House, 47 Chase Side, Southgate, London N14 5BP
Tel: +44 (0)20 8920 2100 Fax: +44 (0)20 8447 8548 E-mail: info@frankcass.com
NORTH AMERICA
5824 NE Hassalo Street, Portland, OR 97213 3644, USA
Tel: 800 944 6190 Fax: 503 280 8832 E-mail: cass@isbs.com
Website: www.frankcass.com

Terrorism Versus Democracy

The Liberal State Response

Paul Wilkinson, *University of St Andrews*

> *'No one understands terrorism better than Paul Wilkinson ... If policy makers read this book they will understand the problems better. If terrorists read it they will come to understand themselves a little better'*
>
> **Professor Michael Clarke,**
> **Centre for Defence Studies, King's College, London**

This major work examines both the new terrorist networks and those that have been around for decades. The author also provides us with some much needed criteria for distinguishing between terrorists and freedom fighters, and an explanation of the uses of terrorism as a political, social, criminal and religious weapon. Wilkinson also links the use of terrorism to a wider repertoire of struggle.

272 pages 2000, repr. 2001
0 7146 5139 7 cloth
0 7146 8165 2 paper

FRANK CASS PUBLISHERS
Crown House, 47 Chase Side, Southgate, London N14 5BP
Tel: +44 (0)20 8920 2100 Fax: +44 (0)20 8447 8548 E-mail: info@frankcass.com
NORTH AMERICA
5824 NE Hassalo Street, Portland, OR 97213 3644, USA
Tel: 800 944 6190 Fax: 503 280 8832 E-mail: cass@isbs.com
Website: www.frankcass.com